Problems in Epistemology and Metaphysics

Online resources to accompany this book are available at: www.bloomsbury.com/problems-in-epistemology-and-metaphysics Please type the URL into your web browser and follow the instructions to access the Companion Website. If you experience any problems, please contact Bloomsbury at: companionwebsites@bloomsbury.com

ALSO AVAILABLE FROM BLOOMSBURY

An Ethical Guidebook to the Zombie Apocalypse, by Bryan Hall

Debating Christian Religious Epistemology, edited by John M. DePoe and Tyler Dalton McNabb

Epistemology: The Key Thinkers, edited by Stephen Hetherington

Explaining Evil, edited by W. Paul Franks

Problems in Value Theory, edited by Steven B. Cowan

Philosophy of Language: The Key Thinkers, edited by Barry Lee

Problems in Epistemology and Metaphysics

An Introduction to Contemporary Debates

**EDITED BY
STEVEN B. COWAN**

BLOOMSBURY ACADEMIC
LONDON • NEW YORK • OXFORD • NEW DELHI • SYDNEY

BLOOMSBURY ACADEMIC
Bloomsbury Publishing Plc
50 Bedford Square, London, WC1B 3DP, UK
1385 Broadway, New York, NY 10018, USA

BLOOMSBURY, BLOOMSBURY ACADEMIC and the Diana logo are trademarks of Bloomsbury Publishing Plc

First published in Great Britain 2020

Copyright © Steven B. Cowan and Contributors, 2020

Steven B. Cowan has asserted his right under the Copyright, Designs and Patents Act, 1988, to be identified as Editor of this work.

For legal purposes the Acknowledgments on p. xiv constitute an extension of this copyright page.

Cover design: Louise Dugdale
Cover image: © Busà Photography / Getty Images

All rights reserved. No part of this publication may be reproduced or transmitted in any form or by any means, electronic or mechanical, including photocopying, recording, or any information storage or retrieval system, without prior permission in writing from the publishers.

Bloomsbury Publishing Plc does not have any control over, or responsibility for, any third-party websites referred to or in this book. All internet addresses given in this book were correct at the time of going to press. The author and publisher regret any inconvenience caused if addresses have changed or sites have ceased to exist, but can accept no responsibility for any such changes.

A catalogue record for this book is available from the British Library.

A catalog record for this book is available from the Library of Congress.

ISBN: HB: 978-1-3500-1605-7
PB: 978-1-3500-1606-4
ePDF: 978-1-3500-1607-1
eBook: 978-1-3500-1609-5

Typeset by Deanta Global Publishing Services, Chennai, India

To find out more about our authors and books visit www.bloomsbury.com and sign up for our newsletters.

Contents

List of Contributors viii
Acknowledgments xiv

Introduction *Steven B. Cowan* 1

PART ONE Problems in Epistemology

Introduction to Part One *Steven B. Cowan* 17

1 Can We Have Knowledge? 26

We Can Know *Michael Huemer* 26
We Can't Know *Markus Lammenranta* 38

Responses 52
Lammenranta's Response to Huemer 52
Huemer's Response to Lammenranta 56

2 How Are Beliefs Justified? 61

Beliefs Can Be Justified by Experience *Daniel Howard-Snyder* 61
Beliefs Are Justified by Coherence *Kevin McCain and Ted Poston* 72

Responses 86
McCain's and Poston's Response to Howard-Snyder 86
Howard-Snyder's Response to McCain and Poston 90

3 Must the Grounds of Knowledge Be Accessible to the Knower? 95

The Grounds of Knowledge Must Be Accessible *Ali Hasan* 95
The Grounds of Knowledge Need Not Be Accessible *Stephen Hetherington* 107

Responses 119
Hetherington's Response to Hasan 119
Hasan's Response to Hetherington 123

4 Do Religious Beliefs Require Evidence? 127

Religious Beliefs Require Evidence *Trent Dougherty* 127
Religious Beliefs Do Not Require Evidence *Thomas D. Senor* 139

Responses 150
Senor's Response to Dougherty 150
Dougherty's Response to Senor 154

5 Can Science Discover the Truth about Reality? 158

Science Discovers the Truth about Reality *Stathis Psillos* 158
Science Does Not Discover the Truth about Reality *Darrell P. Rowbottom* 170

Responses 181
Rowbottom's Response to Psillos 181
Psillos's Response to Rowbottom 185

6 Are Scientific Explanations Limited to Natural Causes? 190

Scientific Explanations Are Limited to Natural Causes *Robert C. Bishop* 190
Scientific Explanations Are Not Limited to Natural Causes
Bruce L. Gordon 202

Responses 221
Gordon's Response to Bishop 221
Bishop's Response to Gordon 227

Essay Suggestions 233
For Further Reading 235

PART TWO Problems in Metaphysics

Introduction to Part Two *Steven B. Cowan* 239

7 Are There Universals? 247

There Are Universals *Paul M. Gould* 247
There Are No Universals *Guido Imaguire* 259

Responses 273
Imaguire's Response to Gould 273
Gould's Response to Imaguire 276

8 What Is the Mind? 282

  The Mind Is Material *Andrew Melnyk* 282
  The Mind Is Immaterial *Charles Taliaferro* 293

  Responses 307
  Taliaferro's Response to Melnyk 307
  Melnyk's Response to Taliaferro 311

9 Is Free Will Compatible with Determinism? 316

  Freedom Is Not Compatible with Determinism *Christopher Evan Franklin* 316
  Freedom Is Compatible with Determinism *Steven B. Cowan* 327

  Responses 341
  Cowan's Response to Franklin 341
  Franklin's Response to Cowan 345

10 Does God Exist? 350

  God Exists *Joshua Rasmussen* 350
  God Does Not Exist *Bruce Russell* 363

  Responses 374
  Russell's Response to Rasmussen 374
  Rasmussen's Response to Russell 379

Essay Suggestions 385
For Further Reading 386

Index 389

Contributors

Robert Bishop (Ph.D., University of Texas at Austin) is Associate Professor of Physics and Philosophy and the John and Madeleine McIntyre Endowed Professor of Philosophy and History of Science at Wheaton College. His research involves history and philosophy of science, philosophy of physics, philosophy of social science, philosophy of mind and psychology, and metaphysics. He is particularly interested in chaos and complex systems and their philosophical implications. He has written *The Philosophy of the Social Sciences* (Continuum, 2007), co-edited *Between Chance and Choice: Interdisciplinary Perspectives on Determinism* (Imprint Academic, 2002), and coauthored *Understanding Scientific Theories of Origins: Cosmology, Geology, and Biology in Christian Perspective* (InterVarsity, 2018).

Steven B. Cowan (Ph.D., University of Arkansas) is Professor of Philosophy and Religion and Director of the Philosophy and Religion Program at Lincoln Memorial University. He specializes in the philosophy of religion and the metaphysics of free will, topics on which he has published numerous articles in academic journals and popular magazines. He has authored or edited several books including (with James Spiegel) *Idealism and Christian Philosophy* (Bloomsbury, 2016) and *The Love of Wisdom: A Christian Introduction to Philosophy* (B&H, 2009).

Trent Dougherty (Ph.D., University of Rochester) is Associate Professor in the Philosophy Department and a fellow of the Honors College at Baylor University. He publishes regularly in epistemology, philosophy of religion, and philosophy of language. He is the author of *The Problem of Animal Pain: A Theodicy for All Creatures Great and Small* (Palgrave Macmillan, 2014). He is editor of *Evidentialism and Its Discontents* (Oxford, 2011), the coeditor (with Justin McBrayer) of *Skeptical Theism: New Essays* (Oxford, 2014), and coeditor (with Jerry Walls) of *The Plantinga Project* (Oxford University Press, 2018). He is also author of numerous essays, reviews, and reference works in his areas, including the *Stanford Encyclopedia of Philosophy*, the *Routledge Encyclopedia of Philosophy,* and *Oxford Bibliographies.*

Christopher Evan Franklin (Ph.D., University of California-Riverside) is Associate Professor of Philosophy at Grove City College. He works at the intersection of ethics and metaphysics, on problems of agency, free will, and moral responsibility. He is author of *A Minimal Libertarianism: Free Will and the Promise of Reduction* (Oxford University Press, 2018) and numerous articles that have appeared in *Australasian Journal of Philosophy*, *Mind*, *Pacific Philosophical Quarterly*, and *Philosophical Studies*, among other venues.

Bruce L. Gordon (Ph.D., Northwestern University) is Associate Professor of the History and Philosophy of Science and a scholar-in-residence at Houston Baptist University. He is also a Senior Fellow at the Center for Science and Culture at Discovery Institute. His research focuses on foundational and interpretive issues in quantum physics, relativity, cosmology, and biology, with connections to intelligent design theory, philosophical theology, and questions of the relationship between Christianity and science. He is the author of numerous journal articles and book chapters and the coeditor of two books, *The Nature of Nature: Examining the Role of Naturalism in Science* (ISI Books, 2011) and *Biological Information: New Perspectives* (World Scientific, 2013).

Paul M. Gould (Ph.D., Purdue University) teaches philosophy and apologetics in the College of Graduate and Professional Studies at Oklahoma Baptist University. He is the author of *Cultural Apologetics* (Zondervan, 2018), editor of *Beyond the Control of God? Six Views on the Problem of God and Abstract Objects* (Bloomsbury, 2014), and coauthor and (with Jamie Dew) of *Philosophy: A Christian Introduction* (Baker, 2019), and coeditor (with William Lane Craig) of *The Two Tasks of the Christian Scholar: Redeeming the Soul, Redeeming the Mind* (Crossway, 2007); (with Richard Davis) of *Loving God with Your Mind: Essays in Honor of J. P. Moreland* (Moody, 2014); (with Corey Miller) of *Is Faith in God Reasonable? Debates in Philosophy, Science, and Rhetoric and Christianity* (Routledge, 2014); and (with Richard Davis) of *Four Views on Christianity and Philosophy* (Zondervan, 2016). He is the founder and president of the Two Tasks Institute.

Ali Hasan (Ph.D., University of Washington) is Associate Professor of Philosophy at the University of Iowa. He works primarily in epistemology, philosophy of perception, and ethics. He has written several journal articles, reviews, and reference works, in such places as *Philosophical Studies*, *Notre Dame Philosophical Reviews*, and the *Stanford Encyclopedia of Philosophy*. He is also author of *A Critical Introduction to the Epistemology of Perception* (Bloomsbury, 2017).

Stephen Hetherington (Ph.D., University of Pittsburgh) is Professor of Philosophy at the University of New South Wales, in Sydney. He has written several books on epistemology, including *Epistemology's Paradox* (Rowman & Littlefield, 1992), *Good Knowledge, Bad Knowledge* (Oxford University Press, 2001),

Self-Knowledge (Broadview, 2007), *How to Know* (Wiley-Blackwell, 2011), and *Knowledge and the Gettier Problem* (Cambridge University Press, 2016). His edited books include *Epistemology Futures* (Oxford University Press, 2006), *Epistemology: The Key Thinkers* (Continuum, 2012), and *What Makes a Philosopher Great?* (Routledge, 2017). He is the general editor of the four-volume *The Philosophy of Knowledge: A History* (Bloomsbury, 2018).

Daniel Howard-Snyder (Ph.D., Syracuse University) is Professor of Philosophy at Western Washington University. He has authored over seventy articles, chapters, entries, and critical reviews in epistemology, philosophy of religion, and moral psychology, and he has edited or co-edited *The Evidential Argument from Evil* (Indiana 1996), *Faith, Freedom, and Rationality* (Rowman & Littlefield 1996), *Divine Hiddenness* (Cambridge 2001), *The Blackwell Companion to the Problem of Evil* (Wiley-Blackwell 2013), and *Approaches to Faith* (Springer 2017). He has coauthored *The Power of Logic* (McGraw-Hill 2013, 5th edition). His current research focuses on intellectual humility and the nature, value, and rationality of faith.

Michael Huemer (Ph.D., Rutgers University) is Professor of Philosophy at the University of Colorado at Boulder. He is the author of more than 70 academic articles in ethics, epistemology, political philosophy, and metaphysics, as well as six brilliant and fascinating books that everyone should buy, including *Ethical Intuitionism* (2005), *The Problem of Political Authority* (2013), and most recently, *Dialogues on Ethical Vegetarianism* (2019).

Guido Imaguire (Ph.D., Ludwig-Maximilians University, Munich) is Professor of Philosophy and Logic at the Federal University of Rio de Janeiro. He specializes in the philosophy of mathematics, philosophy of language, and metaphysics, topics on which he has published numerous articles in academic jornals. He has authored or edited several books including *Russell's Frühphilosophie*, *On Denoting (1905-2005)* (with B. Linsky), *Possible Worlds* (with D. Jacquette) and *Handbook of Mereology* (with H. Burkhard, J. Seibt, and S. Gerogiorgakis).

Markus Lammenranta (Ph.D., University of Helsinki) is University Lecturer and Docent in Theoretical Philosophy at the University of Helsinki. His research interests include naturalistic and social epistemology, skepticism, and theories of justification. His publications include "Reliabilism and Circularity," *Philosophy and Phenomenological Research* 61 (1996); "Is Descartes's Reasoning Viciously Circular?" *British Journal for the History of Philosophy* 14 (2006); "The Pyrrhonian Problematic," in J. Greco (ed.), *The Oxford Handbook of Skepticism* (Oxford, 2008); "Disagreement, Skepticism, and the Dialectical Conception of Justification," *International Journal for the Study of Skepticism*

1 (2011); and "Neo-Pyrrhonism," in D. Machuca & B. Reed (eds.), *Skepticism: From Antiquity to the Present* (Bloomsbury, 2018).

Kevin McCain (Ph.D., University of Rochester) is Assistant Professor of Philosophy at the University of Alabama at Birmingham. He is the author of two books: *Evidentialism and Epistemic Justification* (Routledge) and *The Nature of Scientific Knowledge: An Explanatory Approach* (Springer). He is the coeditor (with Ted Poston) of *Best Explanations: New Essays on Inference to the Best Explanation* (Oxford University Press) and *The Mystery of Skepticism: New Explorations* (Brill).

Andrew Melnyk (D.Phil., Oxford University) is a professor of philosophy at the University of Missouri, where he has taught since 1991. In much of his work he has tried to formulate and argue for a comprehensive thesis of physicalism, but he is interested in all aspects of the philosophy of mind and in many aspects of the philosophy of science. His work has appeared in the *Journal of Philosophy*, *Noûs*, *Philosophy and Phenomenological Research*, *Mind*, and the *Australasian Journal of Philosophy*, among others. His book, *A Physicalist Manifesto: Thoroughly Modern Materialism*, was published by Cambridge University Press in 2003.

Ted Poston (Ph.D. University of Missouri) is Director, McCollough Institute for Pre-Medical Education, and Professor of Philosophy at the University of Alabama. He is the author of *Reason & Explanation: A Defense of Explanatory Coherentism* (Palgrave Macmillan). He has published many articles in epistemology on explanatory coherentism, foundationalism, and practical knowledge. He, along with Kevin McCain, edited *Inference to the Best Explanation* (Oxford University Press).

Stathis Psillos (Ph.D., King's College London) is Professor of Philosophy of Science and Metaphysics at the University of Athens, Greece, and a member of the Rotman Institute of Philosophy at the University of Western Ontario (where he held the Rotman Canada Research Chair in Philosophy of Science between 2013 and 2015). He is the author or editor of seven books and of more than 120 papers and reviews in learned journals and edited collections, mainly on scientific realism, causation, explanation, and the history of philosophy of science. He is member of the Academy of Europe, of the International Academy of Philosophy of Science. He is a former president of the European Philosophy of Science Association (EPSA) and former editor of *Metascience* (2009–2014).

Joshua Rasmussen (Ph.D., Azusa Pacific University) is Associate Professor of Philosophy at Azusa Pacific University. Rasmussen's research focuses on topics related to the foundation of reality, including basic categories, grounding, and necessary existence. He is author of *Defending the Correspondence Theory of Truth* (Cambridge University Press, 2014) and coauthor (with A. Pruss) of *Necessary Existence* (Oxford University Press, 2018). He is founder of www.necessarybeing.com and the Worldview Design YouTube channel.

Darrell P. Rowbottom (D.Litt., Ph.D., Durham University) is Professor and Head of Philosophy at Lingnan University, Hong Kong. He studied physics as an undergraduate (at Bristol), and history and philosophy of science (at the LSE) and philosophy (at Durham) thereafter. He subsequently held posts at several universities in the UK, including Bristol, Edinburgh, and Oxford. His current research focuses on general issues in the philosophy of science (e.g., scientific method, scientific realism, and scientific progress) and the philosophy of probability (e.g., intersubjective probability and measurement paradoxes). He also has interests in epistemology, metaphysics, and the philosophy of education. His textbook, *Probability*, recently appeared with Polity Press. He has also recently completed a research monograph, *The Instrument of Science* (Routledge), which articulates and defends a new form of instrumentalism about science.

Bruce Russell (Ph.D., University of California-Davis) is Professor of Philosophy at Wayne State University. He writes on issues in epistemology and meta-ethics and is especially interested in questions about *a priori* justification and inference to the best explanation. He is the author of the entry on *a priori* justification and knowledge in the *Stanford Encyclopedia of Philosophy*. He applies his views in epistemology to questions in philosophy of religion, especially to the problem of evil and in criticisms of the epistemological views of many of the leading theistic philosophers. Russell has written essays on the philosophical limits of film, on Tarantino's films, and in defense of moral intuitionism, which appear in *Does Anything Really Matter?: Essays on Parfit on Objectivity* (2017), an anthology on Derek Parfit's *On What Matters*, edited by Peter Singer.

Thomas D. Senor (Ph.D., Arizona) is Professor of Philosophy at the University of Arkansas, where he previously served as Department Chair for seventeen years. He was also Visiting Professor of Philosophy at Georgetown University and the Alvin Plantinga Fellow at the University of Notre Dame. He works in philosophy of religion and epistemology. Senor is the editor of *The Rationality of Belief and the Plurality of Faith* (Cornell University Press, 1995) and the author of numerous articles in epistemology and philosophy of religion.

Charles Taliaferro (Ph.D., Brown University) is Professor of Philosophy and Chair of the Department of Philosophy at St. Olaf College. He is the author, coauthor or editor of over twenty books, including *The Image in Mind* (Continuum) and *Turning Images in Philosophy, Science, and Religion* (Oxford University Press) both with Jil Evans, and *Contemporary Philosophical Theology* (Routledge) with Chad Meister. He is the Editor-in-Chief of *Open Theology*. His first book was *Consciousness and the Mind of God* (Cambridge University Press).

Acknowledgments

I wish to express my appreciation to the staff at Bloomsbury Publishing for allowing me to undertake the project of editing this series, and especially Colleen Coalter, Helen Saunders, and Becky Holland for all of their advice and support through the many months it has taken to bring the project to completion. Many thanks also to the contributors to this work; without them it would not exist. And, as always, I am grateful to my lovely wife, Ronda, and my precocious son, Oliver, for their love and patience while I wrapped up work on the manuscript. I am truly blessed to have a family like them.

Introduction

Steven B. Cowan

The unexamined life is not worth living.
—SOCRATES

All men by nature desire knowledge.
—ARISTOTLE

At the beginning of every introduction to philosophy course, I tell my students two things. First, I tell them that the study of philosophy is the most practical course of study they will take in college. Second, I tell them that *not* engaging in some philosophical study at some point in their lives can be dangerous. These statements are likely to strike you the same way they strike my students at first. Maybe you are thinking: "Isn't philosophy about a lot of impractical, abstract ideas far removed from daily life? How can it be practical? And how can not doing philosophy be dangerous? I'm doing fine so far!"

My response to this reaction is this: studying philosophy is practical because the kinds of questions and issues that philosophers address can have a big impact on how you choose to live. And not studying philosophy is dangerous because, whether you realize it or not, you are bombarded with philosophical ideas every day, some of which, if you accept them, may lead you astray. Let me explain.

What Philosophy Is All About

Philosophers study the most fundamental questions that people can ask. Sometimes these are called the "Big Questions." Here are a few examples:

- What is ultimately real?—Matter? Spirit? Both?
- Why is there something rather than nothing?

- Does God exist?
- Is there life after death?—If so, how? What's it like?
- What are human beings?—Collections of atoms? Do we have a soul?
- Do we have free will or is everything we do determined?
- How do we know things?—What are the sources of human knowledge?
- *Can* we know anything?
- Is morality just a matter of cultural preferences?
- How do we discover what is morally right and wrong?
- Where does civil government get its authority?

These are just some of the questions that philosophers ask and seek to answer. Many of these questions are abstract; they are not the stuff of daily life. Nonetheless, the answers one gives to such questions have important practical implications. *Ideas have consequences*. For example, if you believe that matter (i.e., atoms, molecules, physical energy) is ultimately what is real, then you won't believe that God exists, and you probably won't believe in life after death. That's bound to affect some of your lifestyle choices. Also, if you believe that people do not have free will, that will influence what you believe about things like criminal punishment, raising your children, and the assessment of your own behavior. The point here is that *what you believe matters*. It matters for how you live. And some of what you believe is *philosophical*. Look back at the above list of philosophical questions. Don't you already have beliefs about some or all of those things? Of course, you do. Do you think it might be good to be right about such beliefs if you can? If you agree, then you already see the importance of studying philosophy.

This leads me to the danger of not studying philosophy. You already have some philosophical beliefs, as we have seen. But where did you get them? Most likely, you did not get them from the formal study of philosophy. Many of them you no doubt inherited from your parents. Perhaps you acquired them from your church or from peers at school. But where did *they* get them, and are they the right ones? As we have noted, philosophers deal with questions and ideas that can be very abstract and removed from everyday life. This is why many people think that philosophy is just an "ivory tower" activity. And in many ways it is. The trouble is that philosophical ideas that begin in the ivory tower never stay there. Philosophers usually enter the ivory tower trying to answer a question or solve a problem. And when they think they have the answer, they tell other people about it. And so philosophical ideas always make their way down from the ivory tower to the "person on the street."

INTRODUCTION 3

    I mentioned some of the potential sources for how you got your philosophical beliefs. Let me mention another. Possibly the most significant way that philosophical ideas are communicated to the wider culture is through *the arts*. This includes the fine arts—paintings, sculpture, classical music—but especially the popular arts: pop music, novels, films, and so on. Whenever you read a novel or watch a movie, you are being taught some philosophical idea, whether you realize it or not. If you don't realize it, you can be led to believe that idea without any critical reflection. This can be dangerous since it may turn out that the idea being taught is false (and keeping in mind, of course, that what you believe matters).

    By way of example, let's briefly discuss three movies starring the acclaimed actor, Tom Hanks. All three movies are about the meaning of life, and they all convey different messages about it. The first is the comedy *Joe vs. the Volcano* in which Hanks plays a man named Joe who works at a meaningless job under dreary conditions, working with very unlikable people. He wonders whether his life has any significance. While on a sea voyage, however, Joe has a profound religious experience that convinces him that, despite its difficulties, life is meaningful because it is a gift from God who helps to make sense of it all. The second is the movie *Castaway*. In this film, Hanks portrays a man who is stranded on a deserted island for four years. What keeps him clinging to life is the hope of being reunited with his fiancé. When he is finally rescued, though, he finds that his fiancé presumed he had died and had married another man. Through these tragic events, Hanks's character learns that the meaning of life is an arbitrary subjective choice that each person makes for himself or himself. The third movie is *Forrest Gump* in which Hanks plays a man with a mental disability who, through a series of fortuitous events, manages unexpectedly to go to college, survive the Vietnam War, become a millionaire, and eventually win the heart of his childhood sweetheart. Near the end of the movie, Forrest remarks, "I don't know if we each have a destiny, or if we're all just floatin' around accidental like on a breeze. But I think maybe it's both." The message seems to be that life is a paradoxical mixture of chance and fate (though perhaps with an emphasis on chance as symbolized by the feather floating in the wind at both the beginning and the end of the film). These three perspectives on the meaning of life cannot all be true, and the point here is that studying philosophy can, first, help you discern what a movie (or novel or song) is trying to convince you to believe, and, second, enable you to evaluate the merits of that perspective.

    All of this is why the ancient Greek philosopher, Socrates (c. 470–399 BC), said that "the unexamined life is not worth living." Whatever else may be required for a worthwhile life, surely it involves knowing *what you believe and why*—and thus knowing why you have chosen to live the way you live for the things you choose to live for. This, by the way, is the ultimate goal of philosophy. The word "philosophy" comes from two Greek words: *philo* (love) and *sophia* (wisdom). So, etymologically and ideally, philosophy is "the love of wisdom." The lover of wisdom—the philosopher—seeks to follow the admonition of Socrates to examine his life with the ultimate goal of *wise living*.

The Approach of This Series

I noted that philosophers seek to answer the "Big Questions" such as "What is real?" or "How do we know?" It is the nature of these questions to be *difficult*. This is evident in the fact that philosophers have been discussing many of the same questions for centuries. And the fact that philosophers often *disagree* on the right answers underscores their difficulty as well. You might say that these tough questions present us with puzzles or mysteries to solve not unlike the questions that scientists pursue in their work. So, another way to characterize philosophy is that it seeks to *solve problems*—problems related to answering the Big Questions. Call these *philosophical problems*. There are many such problems, as many and more as there are Big Questions. Sometimes these problems are so well known and so specific that they have special names, for example, the Gettier Problem, the Mind-Body Problem, the Problem of the One over the Many, and so on.

It's because philosophy involves solving philosophical problems that the two volumes in this series are entitled *Problems in Epistemology and Metaphysics* and *Problems in Value Theory*. They are designed to introduce students to some of the most important and interesting philosophical problems and the ways in which philosophers have attempted to solve them. The problems addressed in the two volumes come from three major areas of philosophy: (1) *epistemology*, which deals with questions related to knowledge, (2) *metaphysics*, which deals with problems having to do with the nature of reality, and (3) *value theory*, a broad area that covers problems related to ethics, aesthetics, and political philosophy. The current volume is devoted to addressing problems in epistemology and metaphysics, while the other addresses problems in value theory.

Each chapter in each volume contains a "point-counterpoint" debate, two major essays by contemporary philosophers arguing for different answers to the philosophical question posed in the chapter. After each set of point-counterpoint essays, the authors also offer critical responses to their philosophical opponent's essay.

The advantages of this approach are twofold. First, it allows students *to explore different perspectives on philosophical problems with those who hold the actual views in question*. Rather than have all sides of a debate presented and evaluated by a single author (who no doubt has his or her own biases), the point-counterpoint format allows the student to read the arguments for skepticism presented by an actual skeptic, the arguments for God's existence defended by a theist, the arguments for consequentialism defended by a consequentialist, and so on. Learning about a particular viewpoint on any topic from the "horse's mouth," so to speak, is almost always preferable to the alternative. Second, the approach of this series lets the student *see how philosophy is actually done today*. Students can observe firsthand how professional philosophers in the field today make a case for a solution to a philosophical problem and interact with each other to advance philosophical discussion.

A word of warning, though. The point-counterpoint format of this book necessitates that only two sides of each philosophical topic are represented. The reader should not get the impression from this that there are or have been only two possible solutions to a philosophical problem. In many cases, there are *several* options that philosophers have explored and debated. Covering all the options in a book in which philosophers debate and respond to each other would, however, be too long and too complicated for an introductory text. So I have chosen the two perspectives on each topic that seem to me to allow the beginning philosophy student the best exposure to the major aspects of the problem under discussion.

To aid both students and instructors, I have also included in the book some pedagogical features. First, at the beginning of each chapter, I have provided a list of "Study Questions." These questions are designed primarily to facilitate reading comprehension, to help the reader follow the author's train of thought and understand the major points and arguments presented. They can also be used by instructors to enable students' classroom preparation. Second, at the end of every chapter are "Questions for Reflection." These questions require students to critically evaluate what they have read in the chapter and to explore additional related issues. These questions can be utilized to facilitate classroom discussions or provide small group exercises. They could also be used for writing assignments.

At the end of each part of the book, I have included a third pedagogical aid in the form of "Essay Suggestions." These are potential topics for philosophy papers. I have included at least one suggestion related directly or indirectly to each philosophical problem discussed in the book. Also at the end of each part of the book, I have provided a list "For Further Reading." Each list is comprised of books that will allow the student to expand his or her knowledge of the areas of philosophy and the specific problems addressed in the book.

Online Resources

Bloomsbury Publishers provides some additional online resources for students and instructors to accompany the two volumes of *Problems in Epistemology and Metaphysics* and *Problems in Value Theory*. First, there is a set of *historical essays*. The plan and format of this series focuses on contemporary debates in philosophy. Though most of the contributors do provide some historical background to the problems they discuss, no doubt many instructors would like their students to have the opportunity to explore this background in more depth. The online historical essays are organized into sections that parallel the eighteen chapters in the two volumes of this series.

Second, we have provided online an appendix on *How to Write a Philosophy Paper*. Instructors who assign students to write essays or term papers on philosophical topics should direct their students to read this appendix for helpful guidance for completing their assignment.

The Philosopher's Toolkit

Every profession has its tools. Carpenters have hammers, saws, and blueprints. Scientists have microscopes, test tubes, and double-blind experiments. Philosophers are no different. There are three major "tools" they use to solve philosophical problems.

Arguments

A great deal of philosophical work involves the construction, defense, and evaluation of arguments utilizing the principles of logic.[1] An *argument* is a group of statements some of which provide reasons or grounds for accepting one of the others. The statements given as reasons are called the *premises*, and the statement they provide reasons for is called the *conclusion*.

Arguments come in two major types: deductive and inductive. A *deductive* argument is one which purports that the premises provide conclusive grounds for accepting the conclusion. In a good deductive argument, it is impossible for the premises to be true and the conclusion false. Consider the following arguments:

> All men are mortal.
> Socrates is a man.
> Therefore, Socrates is mortal.

If an NFL football team makes a touchdown, they get six points.
My favorite NFL football team made a touchdown.
Therefore, my favorite NFL team got six points.

You can see that if the first two statements in each of these arguments (the premises) are true, then the last statements (the conclusions) also have to be true. Deductive arguments like these are said to be *valid*. This means that an argument has the right kind of form or structure so that the premises, if true, guarantee the truth of the conclusion. Here are the forms of these arguments:

All M are P
All S are M
Therefore, all S are P

If P, then Q
P
Therefore, Q

Any argument that matches these forms is valid because such arguments transfer truth from the premises to the conclusion. This doesn't mean that the conclusion or the premises of a valid deductive argument *are*, in fact, true. An argument can be valid even if every statement in the argument is false as in this example:

All dogs are collies.
All collies are police dogs.
Therefore, all dogs are police dogs.

Every statement here is obviously false. Yet, *if* the premises were true (just pretend), then the conclusion would be true, too. So validity has to do with the form of an argument, not with the truth or falsity of any of its statements. However, when an argument is valid *and* it has true premises, then the argument is said to be *sound*. A good deductive argument is both valid and sound.

Care must be taken in evaluating deductive arguments, however, because they can also be *invalid*. An invalid argument fails to have the appropriate form to transfer truth from the premises to the conclusion. With an invalid argument, the conclusion does not follow logically from its premises. Consider these argument forms:

All P are M
All S are M
Therefore, all S are P

If P, then Q
Q
Therefore, P

Any argument that follows these patterns is invalid. To see why, consider the following arguments that match these forms:

> All cats are animals.
> All dogs are animals.
> Therefore, all dogs are cats.

> If George Washington was assassinated, then he is dead.
> George Washington is dead.
> Therefore, George Washington was assassinated.

In both of these arguments, the premises are true, but the conclusions are false. Clearly, the conclusions do not follow from their premises. Since valid arguments preserve truth from the premises to the conclusion, any arguments that have these patterns must be invalid. There are many more valid and invalid forms of argument, but these will suffice to show you what it means to have a good (or bad) deductive argument.

An *inductive* argument is an argument in which the premises, if true, provide *some* support for accepting the conclusion. In a very good inductive argument, the truth of the premises can make the conclusion highly probable. But, unlike deductive arguments, even good inductive arguments do not guarantee the truth of the conclusion. Here is a simple example:

> Most Republicans are pro-life.
> Jim is a Republican.
> So, it's likely that Jim is pro-life.

Supposing that the premises of this argument are true, they certainly provide some grounds for believing the conclusion, perhaps strong grounds. Nevertheless, the conclusion could be false since Jim might be among the small percentage of Republicans who are pro-choice. There are many different kinds of inductive arguments: statistical syllogisms like the one above, arguments from analogy, generalizations, causal inferences, arguments to the best explanation, and more. Regardless of type, when the premises of an inductive argument are true, and the probabilistic connection between premises and conclusion is strong, the argument is said to be *cogent*.

The reader of this book will encounter many arguments of several types within its pages, both deductive and inductive. It will be your job to evaluate these arguments to decide whether they are valid, strong, sound, and cogent.

Definitions

Another tool in the philosopher's toolkit is *definitions*. Sometimes a philosophical problem can be illuminated or even resolved by getting clear on the meaning of a key term (or terms) in the debate. Famously, the eighteenth-century philosopher, David Hume (1711–1776), believed that the age-old debate over whether or not free will is compatible with determinism could be resolved simply be giving clear definitions of "free will" and "determinism." (Most subsequent philosophers have disagreed with Hume on this.) On other occasions, a philosophical problem itself *just is* the matter of finding a correct definition, as is the debate over the meaning of "knowledge" (see Chapters 1 and 3 of Volume 1). Further, a premise in an argument may take the form of a definition, so that an adequate evaluation of the argument requires considering the adequacy of the definition.

There are many different kinds of definitions but not all are relevant to doing philosophy. For example, a *lexical definition* is the kind you find in a dictionary. Lexical definitions merely list the ways that a term is commonly used in a given language. What philosophers are primarily concerned with, however, are *descriptive* or *analytic definitions*. An analytic definition sets out the necessary and/or sufficient conditions that something has to meet in order to be that kind of thing. A simple example involving geometrical shapes will help you see what I mean. Consider this definition of a square:

A geometrical figure is a *square* if and only if

(i) it has four straight sides,

(ii) its sides are of equal length, and

(iii) it has four right angles.

Using the expression "if and only if" (sometimes abbreviated "iff") indicates that this definition is an attempt to set forth both the necessary and sufficient conditions for a figure's counting as a square. This means that anything that meets the three conditions is a square, and anything that doesn't meet all three conditions is not a square. That is, meeting all those conditions is *sufficient* for being a square, and meeting each condition is *necessary* for being a square.

The "square" example is fairly straightforward. When you are trying to define more complex concepts, however, coming up with the correct set of necessary and sufficient conditions can be difficult (as you will see in several chapters of this book). So, philosophers have devised ways to evaluate the adequacy of definitions. The most important way is to design, if possible, a *counterexample* to the definition. This involves doing one (or both) of two things: (1) identifying something that *doesn't* meet one or more of the conditions but clearly is an example of the kind of thing being defined (thus showing that one or more of the conditions is not necessary); or (2) identifying something that meets all the conditions but clearly *is not* an example of the kind of thing being defined (thus showing that the conditions are not sufficient). Suppose, for example, that you were presented with this definition:

A geometrical figure is a *square* if and only if

(i) it has four straight sides, and

(ii) it has four right angles.

This definition fails to provide a sufficient condition for being a square. A (non-square) rectangle would meet these conditions and is a counterexample of the second kind. Now consider this definition:

A geometrical figure is a *rectangle* if and only if

(i)   it has four straight sides,

(ii) its sides are of equal length, and

(iii) it has four right angles.

While a square (a kind of rectangle) meets all these conditions, there are many rectangles that fail to satisfy condition (ii), thus providing a counterexample of the first kind.

Even though philosophers often seek to provide analytic definitions that state both necessary and sufficient conditions, often they will attempt to give incomplete definitions that state only necessary conditions or sufficient conditions but not both. Here are two examples:

A geometrical figure is a *rectangle* if it is a square.

A geometrical figure is a *square* only if it has four sides.

The first of these examples provides a sufficient condition for being a rectangle. Being a square is *enough* to count as a rectangle (though other shapes can be rectangles too). The second example provides a necessary condition for being a square. Whatever else something has to have, nothing counts as a square *unless* it has four sides. In order to know whether an analytic definition states a necessary condition, a sufficient condition, or both, pay careful attention to the connectives that are used: "if," "only if," or "if and only if." The following table will help you keep it straight:

An analytic definition states...	...if it uses the connective...
a sufficient condition	if
a necessary condition	only if
necessary and sufficient conditions	if and only if

The reader will come across several discussions of definitions throughout this book. Be prepared to use the "counterexample method" to determine the adequacy of these definitions.

Thought Experiments

When constructing or evaluating an argument, one of the things that must be considered is whether or not the premises of the argument are true. Truth, of course, is a necessary condition for even a valid argument to be *sound* (as mentioned earlier). But what determines if a premise is true? Often philosophers will offer additional arguments in support of the premises of an argument. And in some cases, the premises of these additional arguments will be defended with still more arguments. Eventually, however, one comes to a point where there are no additional arguments to give. At this point, a philosopher will typically appeal to what is called *rational intuition*. He or she will claim, that is, that a particular premise or statement is intuitively true, or known by intuition. Sometimes the same thing is meant by saying that a statement is "self-evident." Before you balk at this notion, you should realize that you, the reader, have used rational intuition as a source of knowledge more than once while reading this introduction. How did you know, for example, that the first deductive argument I presented above (the one with "Socrates is mortal" as its conclusion) is valid? You could just "see" it, right? How do you know simple mathematical truths like "$3 - 4 = -1$"? Answer: rational intuition. So philosophers sometimes justify the premises of arguments by appealing to intuition.

But what if philosophers don't share the same intuitions? Or what if a philosopher presents a claim that he can't defend by argument and that he thinks may prove controversial? This is where the third item in the philosopher's toolkit comes in. Philosophers seek to justify (or sometimes criticize) appeals to intuition by using *thought experiments*. A thought experiment is a hypothetical scenario or case study in which intuitions are tested. They very frequently take a narrative form. The basic idea is to imagine the implications or consequences of the story and determine what, if any, intuitions are supported by the story.

Consider the following thought experiment offered by Judith Jarvis Thomson to justify abortion:

> But now let me ask you to imagine this. You wake up in the morning and find yourself back to back in bed with an unconscious violinist. A famous unconscious violinist. He has been found to have a fatal kidney ailment, and the Society of Music Lovers has canvassed all the available medical records and found that you alone have the right blood type to help. They have therefore kidnapped you, and last night the violinist's circulatory system was plugged into yours, so that your kidneys can be used to extract poisons from his blood as well as your own. The director of the hospital now tells you, "Look, we're sorry the Society of Music Lovers did this to you—we would never have permitted it if we had known. But still, they did it, and the violinist is now plugged into you. To unplug you would be to kill him. But never mind, it's only for nine months. By then he will have recovered from his ailment, and can safely be unplugged from you."[2]

Thomson grants, for the sake of argument, that an unborn human fetus has a right to life. No matter, Thomson argues. In this thought experiment, it is clear that you are not obligated to remain plugged up to the violinist. You are perfectly within your rights to unplug and walk away even though the violinist will die. Applied to the case of abortion, the thought experiment seems to support the conclusion that it is morally permissible for a woman with an unwanted pregnancy to "unplug" from her fetus by having an abortion.

Of course, like arguments and definitions, thought experiments can be criticized. A couple of ways to undermine a thought experiment are (1) to show that the thought experiment doesn't really support the intuition or conclusion its author claims it does, but rather *some other* conclusion; and (2) to show that the thought experiment is based on faulty assumptions. Thomson's violinist scenario may be criticized on both fronts. First, it has been argued that the thought experiment, at best, supports abortion only in cases of pregnancies resulting from rape. After all, the person in the thought experiment was kidnapped and hooked up to the violinist against her will. Second, we may question whether the thought experiment is really analogous to typical cases of pregnancy. In the normal pregnancy, a woman does not have to be bedridden for nine months. Moreover, abortion does not involve merely "walking away" from the fetus as in the violinist case, but it involves actively killing the fetus.

Many of the chapters in this book make use of thought experiments. Some of them can be quite clever and imaginative, and they all are designed to drive your intuitions in a certain direction. You will have to think hard and use your own imagination to decide if you are being driven in the right direction.

Notes

1. *Logic* is a branch of philosophy to which many books and college courses are devoted. One commonly used textbook of logic is Patrick J. Hurley, *A Concise Introduction to Logic*, 12th ed. (Stamford, CT: Cengage Learning, 2015).
2. Judith Jarvis Thomson, "A Defense of Abortion," *Philosophy & Public Affairs* 1, no. 1 (Fall 1971): 47–66.

PART ONE

Problems in Epistemology

Introduction to Part One

Steven B. Cowan

Epistemology is that branch of philosophy concerned with the nature, scope, and justification of knowledge. The question, "What do we know and how do we know it?" is a simple way of expressing what epistemology deals with. Have you ever wondered about how much of what you believe you actually know?

Human beings have many beliefs about many things. We have belief about our immediate surroundings ("There is a desk in front of me"). We have beliefs about certain states of affairs in the world ("Mars is the fourth planet in the solar system"). We have beliefs about the past ("Thomas Jefferson wrote the *Declaration of Independence*") and the future ("It will rain this weekend"). We have scientific beliefs ("Water freezes at 32°(F) at sea level"), political beliefs ("Democracy is the worst form of government—except for all the others"), moral beliefs ("Lying is generally wrong"), religious beliefs ("God exists and He cares about me"), and aesthetic beliefs ("The *Mona Lisa* is a beautiful painting"). We have lots of beliefs about lots of things. But how much of what we believe counts as *knowledge*?

All of us at some time or another have had the experience of finding out that something we believed was false. Perhaps you discovered that some belief you had about the past was mistaken, or some scientific belief was not quite right. Maybe you found out that someone you thought was a trusted friend was really an enemy. In such cases, there was some statement or proposition that you believed to be true and maybe even considered an item of knowledge, say, "*Santa Claus will bring me presents this Christmas.*" And yet you found out that the statement is false. Certainly a false belief cannot count as knowledge.

So when can we claim to know something? What is it that transforms a mere belief into knowledge? Going as far back as Plato (427–347 BC), knowledge has been defined as *justified true belief*. Call this the "tripartite analysis of knowledge" or the *JTB Account* of knowledge. It may be stated this way (where *S* stands for some person and *p* stands for a proposition):

S knows *p* if and only if

(i) *S* believes *p*,

(ii) *p* is true, and

(iii) *S* is justified in believing *p*.

In some of the chapters that follow, the question will arise as to whether or not the JTB Account adequately captures what it means to know something. But even if it does, the problem of explaining when a person knows is difficult. Most of the difficulty surrounds condition (iii), the *justification* condition. What is required for a belief to be justified? Take the *Peanuts* character Linus's belief that the Great Pumpkin will make an appearance every Halloween. We might take this as a paradigm case of an *un*justified belief. Why? Well, it might be a matter of evidence. That is, Linus's belief is unjustified because he has no evidence for it. But what kind of evidence and how much of it would be required to justify his belief?

These are the kinds of questions that occupy epistemologists. In this part of the book, we will consider six epistemological problems: the problem of skepticism, the structure of justification, the internalism/externalism debate, the question of whether or not religious beliefs require evidence, the question of what science can tell us about reality, and the problem of the scope of scientific explanations.

Skepticism

The first question in the field of epistemology is the question of whether or not we have any knowledge at all. As noted above, we have lots of beliefs about many things. And we often think that we *know* some of these things. But *do* we?

Skepticism is the view that we have no knowledge. There are different varieties of skepticism, though. *Pyrrhonian skepticism* denies that we have any knowledge whatsoever. According to Sextus Empiricus (AD second century?) and Pyrrho of Elis (360–270 BC) who inspired him, for any proposition that we might believe, there is an equally plausible proposition that asserts the opposite. So, when confronted with any knowledge claim, the appropriate response is to suspend judgment—to neither affirm nor deny the proposition in question.

Less radical, but no less serious, is *Cartesian skepticism*. This form of skepticism is primarily concerned about our alleged knowledge of the external world. Most of us believe that there are things that exist "outside" of or independent of our minds such as the computer keyboard that I'm typing on just now, or the tree outside my window. Rene Descartes (1596–1650), however, shows that for any claim that we perceive some "external world" object, there are alternative explanations for what we think we perceive. Perhaps I'm actually asleep right now and the tree I seem to perceive is actually part of a dream. Or maybe I am trapped in some kind of computer-generated virtual reality like the character Neo in the movie *The Matrix*. If either of these scenarios were the case, then the "tree" is just in my mind. A Cartesian skeptic claims that I cannot rule out these skeptical hypotheses. Therefore, none of my beliefs about the external world can be justified.

Chapter 1 takes on the problem of skepticism. Michael Huemer (University of Colorado-Boulder) begins the debate, arguing that we can, in fact, have knowledge in direct response to both Pyrrhonian and Cartesian skepticism. Huemer contends that the skeptic sets the standard for knowledge too high, and that the burden of proof actually lies with the skeptic rather than with the one who claims to know.

Cartesian skepticism is given a robust defense by Markus Lammenranta (University of Helsinki). He argues that we have no justification for rejecting the skeptical hypotheses (e.g., that I am dreaming right now) in favor of the realist or non-skeptical hypothesis. Most attempts to rebut skepticism assume the truth of *fallibism* (the view that knowledge does not require certainty), but Lammenranta argues that fallibilism is false, and even if it were true, there are strong skeptical arguments that are consistent with fallibilism.

The Structure of Justification: Foundationalism versus Coherentism

As noted earlier, a difficult epistemological problem is knowing under what conditions our beliefs are justified. An important aspect of that problem has to do with the *structure of justification*. At least some of the things we believe depend upon other things we believe. For example, suppose I believe I hear a rustling sound coming from outside my office window. *Based* on that belief, I *infer* that the leaves on the nearby tree are rustling, and from that belief I infer that the wind is blowing. Suppose also that I notice that it's sunny outside, so I *don't* believe that the wind is blowing due to an incoming storm. Recalling that it's late September, say, I come to believe that the best explanation for the wind's blowing is that autumn has arrived.

As this illustration shows, our beliefs are related in complex ways. Some beliefs are inferred logically or probabilistically from other beliefs. Some beliefs are explained by others. The way a person's beliefs are related via these (and other) kinds of connections is called a *noetic structure*. A person's noetic structure is his or her entire set of beliefs together with the logical and explanatory relations among those beliefs.

The philosophical problem addressed in Chapter 2 is the problem of understanding how a person's noetic structure should ideally be arranged so that his or her beliefs are justified. In the history of philosophy there have been two major theories for understanding the structure of justification. The first is called *foundationalism*. According to foundationalism, the ideal (or justification-conferring) noetic structure is hierarchical or "tree-like" with beliefs at the foundation or "roots" that are immune (or at least resistant) to doubt. Other beliefs are then "built-up" from these foundational beliefs and are justified in virtue of ultimately being based on or traceable back to (through logical and explanatory connections) those foundational beliefs.

To make this work, the foundationalist distinguishes two kinds of beliefs: basic beliefs and nonbasic beliefs. *Nonbasic beliefs* are beliefs that are based on (i.e., justified by) other beliefs—such as, in the example given earlier, my belief that the wind is blowing. *Basic beliefs* are beliefs that a person has that are not based on or derived from other beliefs. The foundationalist might cite my belief that I hear a rustling sound as a basic belief. When a basic belief is justified it is called a *properly basic belief*. How are basic beliefs justified if not by other beliefs? Most contemporary foundationalists would say that basic beliefs are justified by some kind of experience. So, the foundationalist claims that beliefs are justified if they are either properly basic beliefs or based on properly basic beliefs.

The second theory for understanding the structure of justification is *coherentism*. For the coherentist, the ideal noetic structure is "web-like." Every belief in the "web" depends for its justification on every other belief. The coherentist holds that there are no basic beliefs—that is, all beliefs are justified by other beliefs. So, for the coherentist, beliefs are justified if they cohere with all the other beliefs in a person's noetic structure. What does it mean for a belief to cohere with other beliefs? Minimally it means that the beliefs are logically consistent, but most coherentists today would add that the beliefs must be related by various inferential and explanatory relations and that at least some of the beliefs in the system must be derived from experience.

In Chapter 2, Daniel Howard-Snyder (Western Washington University) defends a modest version of foundationalism called *Experiential Foundationalism*. He argues that there are basic beliefs and that they are justified by ordinary experiences like seeing, hearing, remembering, and how things seem on introspection. Among other things, Howard-Snyder contends that foundationalism is the best solution to the so-called regress problem: consider a proposition p and let's suppose that p is justified by q. Well, what justifies q? Let's say r. Surely, we can't keep going like this forever if we want to say that p is actually justified. The foundationalist can stop the regress of justification if, say, r is a basic belief justified by experience.

Kevin McCain (University of Alabama-Birmingham) and Ted Poston (University of Alabama) argue for a version of coherentism in which coherence is understood in terms of explanatory relations among beliefs. They offer some case studies that seem to support the idea that it is such coherence of our beliefs, and not basic beliefs, that provides justification to our noetic structures. McCain and Poston reject all the traditional solutions to the regress problem, including foundationalism. Coherentism, they argue, avoids the problem altogether by claiming that justification is holistic rather than linear.

Internalism versus Externalism

Another crucial aspect of the justification of belief and its role in acquiring knowledge is the debate over internalism and externalism. Suppose your roommate is having trouble finding his calculator. He asks, "Have you seen my calculator?" And you reply, "It's under your bed." Rather than looking, your roommate asks, "How do you know it's under my bed?" Annoyed, you answer, "Because I remember seeing it there last night!"

In this scenario, what makes your knowledge claim legitimate? In virtue of what is it appropriate to attribute knowledge to you of the location of your roommate's calculator? Well, one obvious answer lies in your response to your roommate's "How do you know?" question. You recall or remember seeing it under the bed. Your ability to access your memory and remember seeing the calculator there justifies your belief that the calculator is under the bed. *Internalism* is the view that justification and/or knowledge depend upon our having "internal access" to the grounds of our knowledge. Such internal access can take many forms (remembering, seeing, an argument, an experiment, testimony, etc.), but the key idea is that the grounds of knowledge are somehow accessible to the knower.

Externalism is the view that justification and/or knowledge depend upon "external" factors that make the belief in question likely to be true. Whether the knower has access to the grounds of his or her knowledge is irrelevant. The externalist might answer your roommate's question by saying that the reason you know your belief is true is because it was produced in you by a reliable belief-forming mechanism—in this case your memory faculty. Now the fact that you can "access" your memory is certainly a plus, but whether you can access it or not is beside the point, what matters is how the belief was produced.

Internalism is explained and defended in Chapter 3 by Ali Hasan (University of Iowa). Hasan uses several thought experiments to argue that internalism satisfies our deepest intuitions about justification and knowledge. He also appeals to thought experiments to show that externalism is neither necessary nor sufficient for justification.

Stephen Hetherington (University of New South Wales) argues that typical versions of internalism face a dilemma: either it commits would-be knowers to an endless quest for accessible evidence or it requires that knowers satisfy only an externalist requirement for justification. He also maintains that a modified form of internalism called "active-internalism" actually motivates a form of externalism.

Religious Beliefs and Evidence

Most people in the world are followers of some religion—Christianity, Judaism, Islam, Hinduism, Buddhism, and many others. These people have religious beliefs. Many of them believe in the existence of an omnipotent, omniscient, and omnibenevolent God to whom human beings owe worship and obedience. Others believe that all that truly exists is One all-pervasive impersonal "force" called Brahman or the Tao, and that *I am* that One. Common also among most religions is a belief in some kind or afterlife that involves resurrection or reincarnation and, ultimately, life in a future paradise. Of course, this barely scratches the surface of what we call religious belief.

No doubt most religious believers think that their religious beliefs are epistemically justified. Many think that they have religious *knowledge*. But do they? In the past, the idea that religious believers had religious knowledge (or at least justified beliefs) would have been fairly uncontroversial. For example, in the Middle Ages, some religious beliefs were supported by rigorous philosophical arguments, such as arguments for the existence of God. Beginning with the eighteenth-century Enlightenment, however, these theistic arguments came into disrepute. And by the time we get to the middle of the twentieth century, most philosophers held that religious beliefs were unjustified if not positively irrational. Dominating the thinking of these philosophers was a view called *evidentialism* which asserts that religious beliefs, if they are to be justified, must be based on sufficient evidence. The problem, though, was that it seemed to most philosophers that there is little evidence for religious beliefs.

Evidentialism received a powerful challenge in the 1980s, however, through the work of Alvin Plantinga, Nicholas Wolterstorff, and others.[1] Plantinga in particular argued that evidentialism suffered from several defects not least of which is that it is self-defeating (that is, it contradicts itself in that its central thesis fails to meet its own standard of justified belief). Plantinga argued, moreover, that belief in God can be properly basic, which means that belief in God can be justified even apart from any arguments for God's existence.

Chapter 4 addresses the viability of evidentialism with regard to religious beliefs. Trent Dougherty (Baylor University) takes up the mantle of defending evidentialism, though a more moderate version than found in earlier advocates. Dougherty understands evidence in terms of a view he calls *Reasons Commonsensism*: *if it seems to you that P, then you thereby have a reason to believe that P, in proportion to the strength of the seeming*. Accordingly, a religious belief can be justified for a person if it seems to that person that the religious belief is true. Obviously, in Dougherty's version of evidentialism, many religious beliefs will be justified.

Opposing evidentialism, Thomas Senor (University of Arkansas) argues that religious beliefs need not be based on either of the two fundamental kinds of evidence—experiential evidence (seeing, hearing, feeling, etc.) or the evidence provided by other beliefs (via argumentation or inference). Using data from cognitive science, Senor shows that we have many justified beliefs, even nonreligious ones, which do not meet the requirements of evidentialism. These beliefs are justified in virtue of being produced by reliable cognitive processes. So it's possible that religious beliefs are produced in us by reliable cognitive processes that God has built into us to produce these beliefs. If so, such beliefs would be justified apart from evidence.

Scientific Realism versus Nonrealism

The last two chapters in Part One deal with issues in the *philosophy of science*. This is a subdiscipline within philosophy that addresses philosophical questions and problems that arise within the context of the natural sciences. Because science is commonly purported to be a source of knowledge (some would claim *the* source of knowledge), and because some of the questions listed here overlap with the concerns of epistemology, it is appropriate that we include discussion of some issues in the philosophy of science in Part One of this book.

Chapter 5 asks the question, "Can science discover the truth about reality?" To many readers this may sound like a dumb question—"*of course*, science discovers the truth about reality!" However, this is one of the most controversial questions in the philosophy of science. Consider the old Ptolemaic, or *geocentric*, view of the solar system which claimed that the earth was stationary and all the heavenly bodies revolved around the earth. For over a thousand years this view held sway in philosophical and scientific circles until it was eventually replaced with the Copernican, or *heliocentric*, view according to which the earth, along with the other planets, revolved around the (relatively) stationary sun. Now pre-Copernicans would have thought that the Ptolemaic view was true. And one of the reasons was that it was highly useful—it allowed people to make predictions, for example, and to safely navigate the seas. But now we think that Ptolemy's view was simply a useful fiction, and that the Copernican view is actually true. But how do we know that Copernicus's view isn't also a useful fiction doomed to be replaced by some future theory?

This question takes us into the debate between *scientific realism* and *scientific nonrealism*. The former is the view that science can discover the truth about reality and, more specifically, that scientific theories offer accurate or near-accurate descriptions of the way the world actually is. The latter is the perspective that scientific theories do *not* offer accurate or near-accurate descriptions of reality, and that science does not (or at least should not) even aim to tell us the truth about reality. Science, for the nonrealist, has other less ambitious goals such as helping us solve practical problems.

Chapter 5 begins with a rigorous defense of scientific realism by Stathis Psillos (University of Athens). As he points out, much of the debate between realists and nonrealists concerns the status of "unobservables." These are theoretical entities that cannot be actually observed (e.g., quarks) postulated by scientific theories to explain phenomena that are observed. Psillos argues that realism, even though it postulates unobservables, provides the best explanation for the enormous success of natural science. He also claims that the historical pessimism that nonrealists exhibit toward the history of scientific advancement is exaggerated and unwarranted.

Darrell Rowbottom (Lingnan University) disagrees. He defends a version of nonrealism called *instrumentalism*. This is the view that scientific theories are merely instruments for predicting and systematizing observable phenomena. Using an extended thought experiment, Rowbottom argues that we cannot in principle judge which scientific theory is true among a set of competing theories that all appeal to unobservable entities to explain phenomena. We must be guided by experience, but experience can only tell us about observable things. However, scientific theories (even ones that postulate unobservable entities) can be useful (like Ptolemy's view of the solar system) for solving practical problems.

The Scope of Scientific Explanations

Scientists seek to explain things. For example, when some unexpected phenomenon X occurs (say, the melting of the polar ice caps), scientists will develop a hypothesis (say, manmade global warming) that, if true, would explain why X happened when it did and the way it did. An important question, though, is: *What counts as a good scientific explanation?* Perhaps a good explanation is testable in some way. Perhaps a good explanation is simple (i.e., not unnecessarily complex). These and several other proposals have been made, some widely accepted, some controversial. But one thing that many (most?) philosophers of science would say about good scientific explanations is that they appeal only to *natural causes*. That is, if any explanation for some phenomenon X is going to count as a *scientific* explanation (as opposed to, say, a pseudo-scientific explanation), then that explanation cannot involve any *super*natural causes or entities (e.g., God). Scientific explanations are limited to natural causes. This outlook is known as *methodological naturalism* (MN for short).

Robert Bishop (Wheaton College) argues in defense of MN in Chapter 6. He first provides *theological* reasons to embrace MN, contending that a proper understanding of the Christian doctrines of creation *ex nihilo* and the incarnation provide strong rationale for maintaining a sharp distinction between theological and scientific explanations, the latter permitting no invocation of divine activity. Philosophically, Bishop argues that rejecting MN would undermine the very possibility of doing natural science. Allowing supernatural causes in scientific explanations implies that scientists would have to entertain and examine every logically possible explanation for any given phenomenon, a task that cannot be accomplished.

Bruce Gordon (Houston Baptist University) makes a case for a more open approach to the scope of scientific explanations, thus defending the viability of the Intelligent Design (ID) Theory. He argues that ID theory is not, as critics claim, merely an appeal to ignorance of natural causes but is based on positive evidence for the presence of intelligent causation in nature. Moreover, it is not ID theory that creates a hindrance to scientific inquiry but rather MN: those committed to MN, Gordon claims, are guilty of the "naturalism-of-the-gaps" fallacy because they are willing to embrace even wildly implausible natural explanations to avoid the possibility of intelligent causation.

Note

[1] See Alvin Plantinga and Nicholas Wolterstorff, eds., *Faith and Rationality: Reason and Belief in God* (Notre Dame: University of Notre Dame, 1983).

1

Can We Have Knowledge?

We Can Know

Michael Huemer

Study Questions

1. What reasons does Huemer give for not arguing directly against skepticism?
2. How does Huemer define knowledge? Why do you think he calls it only an "approximate" definition?
3. What is Huemer's view of justification?
4. Why does Huemer think that rejecting phenomenal conservatism is self-defeating?
5. What is the skeptical regress argument? What problems does it have according to Huemer?
6. What is the "brain-in-a-vat" argument? What problems does it have according to Huemer?

In this essay, I am not exactly going to be arguing that it's possible for people to know things. I won't be doing this for three reasons. First, if someone really doesn't think that anyone can know anything, then I'm not sure there is anything I could say that this person might find persuasive. The position that no one knows anything is known as *global skepticism*. Would a global skeptic accept any premise that I could offer? He'd have to start out thinking that no one knew whether the premise was true. Maybe the skeptic could think that some premise was at least *plausible* or *likely* to be true? But a global skeptic would have to think that no one knew whether the premise was even plausible or likely. So I'm not sure how I could convince such a person to listen to anything I had to say.

Second, in a certain sense, I think there really are no global skeptics. There have been (a few) individuals in the history of philosophy who have apparently defended global skepticism, but I think that, in a sense, none of them has really believed it (nor has anyone else). Though some people verbally endorse skepticism, nothing else about them suggests that they believe it. The rest of their belief systems, their outward behavior, their emotional and conative reactions—none of it seems to fit with the belief that no one knows anything. For instance, when a skeptical philosopher finishes teaching about skepticism in his class, and it's time to go home, he does not behave in the way one would expect from a person who thinks he doesn't know where he lives.

Third, I think skeptics have the burden of proof. Some say that the burden of proof is on whoever asserts a positive claim. I disagree. I think that if one takes up a position that seems crazy on its face, one then has the burden of explaining one's reasons. No one believes skepticism as a default position. Everyone who purports to believe skepticism does so because of some argument or arguments that they found convincing.

So I am not going to try to prove, starting from scratch, that it is possible to know things. Instead, what I plan to do is explain on a very general level something about how I think knowledge works—how we know the things that we know. Then I'll explain where I think certain arguments for skepticism go wrong.

A Short Account of Knowledge

What is knowledge? What do you have to do to count as *knowing* some proposition, P? Roughly, I think there are four conditions:

(1) You must believe P,

(2) P must be true,

(3) Your belief must be justified, and

(4) There must be no further facts out there that, if you were made aware of them, would defeat your justification for believing P.[1]

Now, I think this actually gives only an approximate definition of knowledge, and there is much more to be said about this. But I am not going to discuss it further because space is limited and I do not want to distract from my central points discussed here.

Usually, when someone asks how you know something, what they are interested in is condition (3): they aren't asking how you believe the thing, or how it's true, or even how it fails to have defeaters. They are asking how you are *justified* in believing the thing that you claim to know. "Justification" for a belief refers to that which makes a belief reasonable, or rational, or why it *makes sense* to hold the belief. For instance, if someone asks, "How do scientists know how old the Earth is?" what they are asking for is information about the evidence and the reasoning that was used to arrive at an estimate of the Earth's age. I will henceforth focus exclusively on questions about justification.

Elsewhere, I have defended a general theory about the justification of beliefs.[2] The theory is called "phenomenal conservatism." (Why is it called that? Because the word "phenomenal" comes from the Greek word *phainomena*, which means "appearances," and the theory is about conserving appearances.) The theory holds that a person has justification for believing something whenever (*i*) it seems true to them, and (*ii*) they have no reason for doubting it. Another way to put the point is that there is a *presumption* in favor of appearances: it makes sense to start with the assumption that things are as they appear. One does not need reasons for thinking things are the way they seem to be; rather, one who doubts the appearances has the burden of providing reasons for thinking that things are *not* as they seem to be.

What is an appearance? "It seems to me that P" is not to be taken as another way of saying "I believe that P" or "I'm inclined to believe that P"; rather, I take it to report a certain kind of experience, sometimes called a "seeming" or "appearance," which is distinct from belief, which represents P to be the case, and which normally occurs prior to, and causes the belief that, P. It is possible to have such an appearance state without *believing* the appearance; for instance, if you are convinced that the pink rabbit in front of you is a hallucination, then you can have the *appearance* but not the *belief* that there is a pink rabbit there. There are several species of appearances: sensory experiences (whereby something looks, sounds, feels, and so on, a certain way), apparent memories (whereby we seem to remember a past experience or previously learned fact), rational intuitions (whereby something seems necessarily true upon intellectual reflection), and perhaps others.

Phenomenal conservatism thus explains the justification of many different kinds of beliefs. Indeed, I claim that appearances are the only conceivable ultimate source of justification that one could ever have for believing anything. That is, the reason why anyone believes what they believe (if they are rational) must ultimately come down to how things seem to that person. I think it is sunny outside now because, when I look out the window, it *looks* sunny to me; this is a species of appearance. I think that the capital of California is Sacramento, because that is what I seem to recall. I think that torture is wrong because it seems wrong to me. I don't need to provide further reasons for these things; rather, if someone thinks I should stop believing them, that person needs to give me a reason for doubting what seems to me to be the case.

This is also true of, say, our epistemological beliefs. For example, most people think that a belief cannot be justified by circular reasoning. Why do they think that? Because that is how things seem to them; circular reasoning seems bad. I claim that this is something you can see to be true by introspection: if you think about your own beliefs, you'll see that they're based on what seems correct to you. If you reflect on your current thought process, as you decide whether to accept what I am now saying, you'll see that the decision turns on whether what I am saying seems right to you.

But don't some beliefs rest on *reasoning*? Yes, but beliefs based on reasoning are still based on appearances: if an argument is to convince you of some conclusion, the premises must strike you as correct, and the conclusion must seem to follow from them. The function of arguments is to alter what seems true to you, by directing attention to other things that seem true and that seem to support a particular conclusion.

Now, how do we decide whether to believe phenomenal conservatism? The answer is that people decide this based on how things seem to them. Those who reject phenomenal conservatism are simply those to whom phenomenal conservatism does not seem right. So, those people are actually depending upon phenomenal conservatism; their rejection of phenomenal conservatism could be justified only if phenomenal conservatism is actually true. If phenomenal conservatism is false, so that appearances are not a source of justification, then all beliefs based on appearances are unjustified—including the belief that phenomenal conservatism is false. So, those who reject phenomenal conservatism are in a self-defeating position.

The Regress Argument and Its Failures

The Skeptical Regress Argument Explained

Something like the following argument goes back to the ancient skeptics; it apparently originated with Agrippa and was transmitted through Sextus Empiricus:[3]

Premise 1: A belief is justified only if the believer has a reason for it, and this reason must also be justifiedly believed.

Premise 2: No one can have an infinite series of reasons.

Premise 3: No belief can be justified by circular reasoning.

Conclusion: No belief is justified.

Premise 1 seems right for most beliefs. For example, if I claim that there are unicorns living in Kansas, you will understandably find my claim unjustified unless I have some evidence or reason for believing that there are unicorns in Kansas. And whatever reason I provide should be something that I also have justification for believing. For instance, I should not declare, "I think there are unicorns in Kansas because that is the best way of explaining why it so frequently rains gold in Kansas"—unless I have justification for believing that it really does rain gold in Kansas.

This leads to the idea that any belief must have a chain of reasoning, or a "regress of reasons," standing behind it: there is the reason for the belief, and then the reason for that reason, and then the reason for the reason for the reason, and so on. I assume that premises 2 and 3 are intuitively obvious. So the series of reasons cannot go in a circle, and it cannot go on infinitely. If the chain of reasons ends in a claim that is not itself justified, then the whole chain is unjustified (from premise 1). So, the conclusion is that no one can ever have justification for any belief.

Notice how extreme the conclusion is. The argument is not claiming that there is some specially problematic class of beliefs that we can't justify. It is not claiming that our beliefs are not absolutely certain. It is not claiming that our beliefs fail to satisfy some specially strict, highfaluting, philosophical standard of justification. The argument claims that no belief whatsoever (including this one!) has even the *slightest* degree of justification. All beliefs are *completely arbitrary*; for example, my belief that there are people living in Denver is no better than the belief that there are unicorns living in Kansas. This is because, to have *any justification at all* for *P*—even a tiny bit—one must have at least *some* reason (if only a tiny, weak reason) for believing P. That is enough to start the regress, which can never be completed.

The Regress Argument Is Silly

In one sense, I think that the regress argument is not a serious argument: it is not something that a rational person could sincerely advance as their position, nor should epistemologists spend their time discussing whether this argument is correct. Rather, epistemologists should discuss what the best analysis of the argument's flaw or flaws is.

Why do I say that? Three reasons. First, as I have indicated above, I think that no one really believes global skepticism. I think that philosophy should seek the truth, and this is best done by exchanging our thoughts about the positions we each take to be true. If philosophers advance positions that they don't really believe, and then other philosophers spend time responding to those positions as if someone believed them, then what we are doing resembles a debating game more than an effort to really understand the world.

Second, the regress argument is self-refuting. The purpose of an argument is to give someone reasons for believing something. This is what an argument is—a purported reason or set of reasons for a conclusion. The regress argument obviously cannot be a good argument because, if it were a good argument, it would provide a reason to believe its conclusion, but the conclusion itself entails that there is no reason for believing anything. So it would be a counterexample to itself. Of course, if the argument were correct, the premises of the argument also would have to be unjustified, so that again we should not accept the argument.

Third, the conclusion of the regress argument is simply too implausible on its face to be a reasonable topic of dispute.[4] In order to rationally persuade me that no one knows anything, the skeptic would have to start with some premises that I am initially inclined to accept (or that seem true to me when I consider them). Furthermore, these premises would have to seem *more obvious* to me (more certain, more clearly correct) than the assumption that at least someone knows something. If it is more initially plausible that *someone knows something* than it is that the skeptic's premises are correct, then it would be more rational to reject the skeptic's premises than to reject the assumption that someone knows something. But, prior to entering philosophical discussion, the proposition that someone knows something seems about as obvious as anything. So it is difficult to see how there could ever be a rationally persuasive argument against it.

A Diagnosis of the Regress Argument

So where does the regress argument for skepticism go wrong? On my above account of justification, the regress argument goes wrong at the first step: the argument assumes that every belief requires a reason, otherwise we are not justified in holding that belief. In other words, it assumes that the epistemological default position is suspension of judgment. I see no reason for assuming this. On my account, the epistemological default position is to take appearances at face value. This is not to say that the appearances are always correct—sometimes there is a good reason for doubting them. The point is that the doubt requires a reason.

Another way to think about why the regress argument fails is to say that premise 1 wrongly assumes that a belief can only be justified by another belief. In my view, a belief can be justified by an appearance. The appearance itself cannot be either justified or unjustified; it is simply an experience that we have. So, the putative regress ends when we come to appearances.

Premise 1 claims that every belief needs a reason. So surely we would need a reason for believing premise 1 itself. What reasons can be offered? Most who endorse premise 1 either assert it without any reason or provide only an obviously question-begging reason—for example, they declare that a belief is "arbitrary" unless one has a reason for it. (What does "arbitrary" mean? If it just means "unjustified," then this argument begs the question. If it means "not supported by a reason," then the argument again begs the question.)

The best I have heard in support of premise 1 is the appeal to examples, of the sort mentioned earlier: if I believe for no reason that there are unicorns in Kansas, then my belief is unjustified. One might be tempted to generalize from cases like this to the conclusion that *any* belief unsupported by reasons is unjustified. The problem with such appeals to examples is that it is easy to overgeneralize. If one thinks a little longer, one may be able to find examples in which it seems that one does *not* need a reason in order to be justified in a belief. In that case, the proper conclusion would seem to be that *some* beliefs require reasons, while others do not.

Suppose I go to see the doctor. "Doctor," I say, "I think I have arthritis." "Why do you think you have arthritis?" the doctor asks. This would be a very reasonable question. Suppose I reply, "I think I have arthritis because I'm feeling pain in my wrists." And suppose the doctor replies, "And why do you think you are feeling pain?" Now that is not a reasonable question. How should I reply to a doctor who says that? "Huh? What do you mean?"

This illustrates that some beliefs ("I have arthritis") require reasons, while others ("I am in pain") do not. The idea that all beliefs require reasons is a hasty generalization that—like many philosophical theses—can seem plausible only when stated purely in the abstract, when we fail to attend to the specific exceptions. As soon as we look at specific examples, the generalization is obviously false.

Cartesian Skepticism and Its Failures

The Cartesian Skeptical Argument Explained

Probably the most popular kind of skepticism is Cartesian skepticism, named after René Descartes. Descartes wondered about such things as: How do I know that I am not dreaming? And, how do I know that God is not planting false sensory images in my mind—causing me to have hallucinations of physical objects around me that don't really exist? (Aside: In the end, Descartes thought that he could prove both that God existed and that God would not allow us to be systematically deceived when we use our cognitive faculties correctly.[5] But hardly anyone other than Descartes ever found Descartes's arguments on that score persuasive, so I will not discuss them further.)

The modern version of the Cartesian skeptical argument is the "brain-in-a-vat" argument: what if scientists in some advanced society learned how to keep a brain alive, suspended in a vat of nutrients? And what if they had the technology for stimulating the brain electrically, with exactly the pattern of electrical stimulation that would normally be produced by impulses coming from a person's sense organs? The brain would then have sensory experiences just like those of a normal human being. Wait, how do you know that you are not a brain in a vat, right now? (See the popular movie *The Matrix* for a similar theme.) This leads to an argument like the following (to avoid confusion with the argument from the previous section, I will start numbering at premise 4):

The Brain-in-a-Vat Argument

Premise 4: Your beliefs about the world around you are justified only if you have justification for believing that you are not a brain in a vat.

Premise 5: You have no justification for believing that you are not a brain in a vat.

Conclusion: You have no justified beliefs about the world around you.

Notice, by the way, that the conclusion this time is not global skepticism: this argument is not claiming that we cannot know anything. It is only claiming that we cannot know what the physical world around us is like. This view is known as *external-world skepticism*. External-world skepticism is not self-refuting (as global skepticism is), because "you can't know about the physical world around you" is not itself a claim about the physical world around you.

I assume that premise 4 is fairly intuitively compelling. What about premise 5? Why should we think that we cannot know whether we are brains in vats? The basic idea is that to know that you aren't a brain in a vat, you would have to have some evidence that would enable you to distinguish between being a brain in a vat and being a normal human being. Your sensory experiences don't give you any such evidence, because any sensory experience you have could just as well have been fed to you by the scientists controlling the brain in the vat. And you don't seem to have any evidence other than your sensory experiences to go on.

Notice also that the claim is not that you are *not absolutely certain* that you aren't a brain in a vat. The claim is that you have *no evidence at all* that you aren't one. (If you disagree, try to name some evidence—even a tiny bit of evidence—of your non-brain-in-a-vat-hood.) And therefore, it seems, you have *no justification* for thinking that the world around you is as it appears to be.

A Diagnosis of the Brain-in-a-Vat Argument

I think the external-world skeptics have got two things wrong. The first is, again, a mistake about the burden of proof: skeptics think that we must start with a state of suspension of judgment, and then it is the burden of someone who has determinate beliefs to refute all alternative possibilities, such as the brain-in-a-vat hypothesis, the dream hypothesis, or the deceiving God hypothesis.

I believe, on the other hand, that it is rational to begin with the assumption that everything is the way it appears, and it is the burden of the skeptic to provide reasons for doubting this. The brain-in-a-vat hypothesis does not count as a reason for doubting the appearances, because there is no actual evidence of our being brains in vats. Merely *hypothesizing* that we could be radically deceived is not giving a reason for thinking that we are so deceived.

In other words, the skeptic claims that, to justifiably form beliefs about the world around you, you would have to first come up with some independent evidence of your not being a brain in a vat. I claim, on the other hand, that you are by default justified in forming beliefs about the world around you that match the way things appear to you, *until* you have evidence of your *being* a brain in a vat.

The second mistake I think the skeptic makes has to do with the nature of evidence and reasons for belief.[6] The Cartesian skeptic thinks that we have no evidence against the brain-in-a-vat theory because any sensory experience we have *could* be had by a brain in a vat. Now, it is true that any sensory experience could be had by a brain in a vat. But this is actually one of the things that is wrong with the brain-in-a-vat theory: the theory is unfalsifiable, because it is consistent with any possible set of experiences. No matter what happens, you could always explain it by saying, "Well, the scientists decided to program that experience."

The alternative theory we can call the "real-world hypothesis": this is the theory that we are normal human beings who are correctly perceiving the world around us. The real-world hypothesis is more falsifiable than the brain-in-a-vat hypothesis, because the real-world hypothesis makes a prediction (albeit a very broad one) about our experiences: we should have *coherent* experiences. What I mean by this is roughly that we should have experiences that could be interpreted as accurately representing a world of lasting physical objects obeying consistent laws of nature. This prediction is not exactly *entailed* by the real-world hypothesis; it is just what we would generally expect. By contrast, the brain-in-a-vat theory makes no such prediction. If you are a brain-in-a-vat, there is no obvious reason why you should have coherent experiences rather than incoherent ones. Maybe the scientists decided to program coherent experiences, but they could just as well decide to program incoherent experiences; there is no reason to assume they would do the former.

So the real-world hypothesis makes more specific predictions than the brain-in-a-vat hypothesis. So what? In general, a theory is supported when it makes specific predictions that are borne out; the more specific the prediction, the stronger the support. A theory that makes no predictions will never be refuted, but it is also never supported. A theory that only makes very weak, vague predictions can only be weakly, vaguely supported. These points can be precisely formulated using theorems of probability theory; however, in consideration of readers with mathophobia, I will simply give an example to illustrate the point.

Let's say that you visit two psychics to check out their powers. Psychic Lilith, after consulting her crystal ball, predicts that next week's winning lottery numbers are 2, 23, 41, 53, and 63. The following week, the numbers are announced, and they turn out to be just what Lilith predicted. Then you go to Psychic Uri. Uri looks into his crystal ball, closes his eyes, and says, "Is there someone in your life named . . . Stephen?" You reply, "Oh yes, I have a co-worker named Stephanie!"

Which psychic is more likely to actually have psychic powers? Obviously, Lilith. Why? Uri only made a vague, weak sort of "prediction." Lilith made a much more specific prediction, which she was therefore much less likely to get right by chance.

Now, it may seem as though the prediction made by the real-world hypothesis—that of a coherent set of experiences—is only slightly more specific than the non-prediction made by the brain-in-a-vat hypothesis, so that the real-world hypothesis would be only slightly better supported by our sensory evidence. But as a matter of fact, the prediction that we should have a coherent set of experiences is, in the sense that matters, *much, much more specific* than merely the prediction that we should have some set of experiences or other. The reason is that, of all possible sets of experiences, only a tiny, negligible fraction are coherent. Another way of saying this is to say that a randomly chosen set of experiences would almost certainly be incoherent.

Here is a simple example to illustrate the point. Imagine having a computer generate a random image: for each pixel on the screen, the computer assigns it a random color from all colors that it is capable of displaying. What would the resulting image look like? I once actually programmed a computer to do this. (I knew what the result would be, but I wrote the program so I could tell other people I had done so.) The result is an image that looks like static—it does not look like a picture of anything, it does not show any noticeable patterns; if viewed from a distance, it looks like a gray square. If you have the program generate a million images, every single one will be like that. What this illustrates is that almost every possible image is incoherent. In a similar way, *almost every possible set of experiences is incoherent.* So the prediction that we should have coherent experiences is actually, in the relevant sense, an extremely specific prediction. Less than one in a million possible experiences are coherent; perhaps less than one in a googol. This is why the real-world hypothesis is much better supported than the brain-in-a-vat hypothesis.

Conclusion

There are cases of real, reasonable epistemological disputes about what we are justified in believing. For instance, people have reasonable disagreements in advanced physics about whether string theory is adequately justified (because, for example, it lacks direct experimental tests). Then there are cases of borderline-reasonable disputes, such as the dispute about whether we are really justified in believing in global warming (because, say, climate scientists could be biased). And then there are frivolous disputes, such as a dispute about whether I know how many fingers I have, or about whether we are justified in thinking that the Earth rests on the back of a giant turtle.

Skepticism erases these distinctions: it says that everything is just like the giant turtle theory. String theory, Copernican astronomy, the belief that the world contains more than four people—all of these, according to the skeptic, are just like "the Earth rests on the back of a giant turtle." And that is just obviously false. I think such a position is not a genuine attempt to account for the subject matter. (I sometimes think that if philosophers started doing biology, soon the leading theories in the field would be (1) that all living things are the same, and (2) that there are no living things at all.)

The task of an epistemologist, in my view, should be to explain the differences between theories like "the Earth rests on the back of a giant turtle" and theories like "the Earth was formed by accretion from a solar nebula"—not to declare that there is no difference. The epistemologist should help resolve reasonable disputes, such as whether string theory is justified, by providing realistic criteria for justifying a theory—not carry on insincere disputes about such things as whether I know how many fingers are on my left hand.

Having said that, I believe that skepticism is worth discussing, because it provides a test for an epistemological theory: one test for a theory about knowledge or justification is that the theory should give a satisfying account of where skeptical arguments go wrong. The theories discussed here try to do this. They provide general principles about justification that help explain why paradigm cases of justified beliefs are justified, or paradigm cases of unjustified beliefs are unjustified. In brief, the principles are:

a) It is rational to assume that things are as they appear, unless and until one has specific reasons for doubting the appearances.

b) A theory that makes specific predictions is better supported by the verification of those predictions, than a theory that makes weaker, vaguer predictions.

The regress argument goes wrong because it assumes, contrary to (a), that it is rational to start out doubting the appearances until we have a proof that the appearances are accurate. The brain-in-a-vat argument wrongly assumes that merely citing a hypothetical alternative counts as giving a reason for doubting the appearances. In addition, it assumes, contrary to (b), that a theory that can accommodate any possible set of evidence is a reasonable potential explanation of our actual evidence.

In brief, the theory that we are normal people perceiving the real world is the most plausible theory on its face: it provides the best explanation for our experiences, and we have no actual reasons for doubting it. This is why we can know things about the external world.

Notes

1 See Peter Klein, "A Proposed Definition of Propositional Knowledge," *Journal of Philosophy* 68 (1971): 471–82.

2 See Michael Huemer, *Skepticism and the Veil of Perception* (Lanham, MD: Rowman & Littlefield, 2001), ch. 5. See also my article "Phenomenal Conservatism" in the *Internet Encyclopedia of Philosophy* (2013), http://www.iep.utm.edu/phen-con.

3 What follows in the text is my reconstruction of the argument suggested by the selection from Sextus Empiricus in this volume.

4 This argument is from G. E. Moore, "Proof of an External World," *Proceedings of the British Academy* 25 (1939): 273–300; "Hume's Theory Examined," 108–26 in *Some Main Problems of Philosophy* (London: Allen & Unwin, 1953).

5 These arguments appear in Descartes's third through sixth *Meditations*, which are much less often discussed than his first two. See René Descartes, *Meditations on First Philosophy* in *The Philosophical Writings of Descartes*, vol. 2, eds. John Cottingham, Robert Stoothoff, and Dugald Murdoch (Cambridge: Cambridge University Press, 1984).
6 The following argument in the text derives from my "Serious Theories and Skeptical Theories: Why You Are Probably Not a Brain in a Vat," *Philosophical Studies* 173 (2016): 1031–52.

We Can't Know

Markus Lammenranta

Study Questions

1. What are the various kinds of skepticism that Lammenranta distinguishes? What kind does he defend?
2. How does Lammenranta characterize Descartes's two skeptical hypotheses? How does he "modernize" the second one?
3. What are the "good" and "bad" cases that the skeptical hypothesis implies? What are the three possible ways the skeptic might show that we don't know the good case is the case?
4. How does Lammenranta formulate the skeptical argument? What three principles does this argument presuppose?
5. What are the problems that Lammenranta raises for fallibilism?
6. What is the "ordinary language" response to skepticism?
7. What skeptical argument does Lammenranta offer on the assumption that fallibilism is true? What principles is it based on?
8. How does Lammenranta explain our ordinary uses of the word "know"?
9. How, according to Lammenranta, does the Academic skeptic avoid the dangers of both Pyrrhonism and dogmatism?

Sextus Empiricus starts his *Outlines of Skepticism* by distinguishing three kinds of people: (1) Those he calls dogmatists believe that they have discovered the truth and thus know the truth; (2) Academics believe that the truth cannot be discovered and thus known; and finally (3) Skeptics are those who suspend belief about the question of whether or not knowledge can be attained. They continue inquiry about the matter.[1]

Sextus suggests that genuine skeptics suspend belief.[2] Academics are really dogmatists because they defend the belief or dogma that knowledge is impossible. Nowadays, it is common to distinguish between two kinds of skeptics: *academic skeptics* defend the claim that knowledge is impossible, while *Pyrrhonian skeptics* suspend belief on the question as well as other matters. However, Sextus may be unfair. The members of Plato's Academy—whom he calls Academics—were not themselves committed to the dogma that knowledge cannot be attained. They argued that their opponents, the Stoics, were committed to it, because it follows from the Stoic theory of knowledge that knowledge is impossible. Their arguments for the thesis that knowledge is impossible should therefore be understood as *ad hominem* arguments, which rely on premises that their opponents accept.[3]

I will defend a form of Academic skepticism that denies just our knowledge about the external world—the world outside our own minds. It is also called *Cartesian skepticism* because it relies on the kind of skeptical hypotheses that René Descartes (lat. Renatus Cartesius) describes in *The First Meditation*.[4] My argument for Cartesian skepticism is meant to be an *ad hominem* argument that relies on our ordinary epistemic concepts and practices and aims therefore to show that we—the dogmatists—are committed to its skeptical conclusion. However, because we also believe that the conclusion is false—that we do know—we are led to a paradox: intuitively plausible premises entail a conclusion that we take to be false. Though the premises and the denial of the conclusion are all intuitively plausible, they are inconsistent and cannot therefore all be true. I will argue that accepting the skeptical conclusion rather than denying one of the premises is the best way of resolving this paradox.

Cartesian Skepticism

Cartesian skepticism denies that we can have any perceptual knowledge of the external world. In *The First Meditation*, Descartes argued against the possibility of this sort of knowledge. Two of his arguments relied on skeptical hypotheses describing possible situations in which we have similar perceptual experiences as we normally have; but our beliefs about the external world, based on those experiences, are false. Because our experiences do not rule out those possibilities of error, they do not give us knowledge of the external world.[5]

Ever since Descartes, philosophers have tried to respond to these arguments by trying to show either that we do have knowledge of the external world or that the skeptical reasoning is based on some false premise—without significant success. We still lack an uncontroversial and widely accepted answer to Cartesian skepticism. Perhaps the reason for this is that the skeptical reasoning is valid and based on compelling premises. I will try to show that this is the case.

In *The First Meditation*, Descartes describes two skeptical hypotheses: (1) *the dreaming hypothesis* describes the possibility that I am asleep and just dreaming that I am now typing this essay; and (2) *the evil demon hypothesis* describes the possibility that I am a disembodied mind deceived by an evil demon who produces all my experiences about the external world. I will use the latter hypothesis. However, because many philosophers no longer believe that disembodied minds are metaphysically possible, I will rely on a modernized version of it.[6]

Let us assume that the brain could be removed from the skull and then be electronically fed stimuli like those we receive normally through our own senses. This brain would have similar experiences and beliefs to ours; only these beliefs would be false. Indeed, it is quite possible that I am myself in such a situation:

> *The brain-in-a-vat hypothesis*: I am a brain in a vat wired to a computer that stimulates it so that I have the experiences and beliefs I have now but these beliefs are false.

If this hypothesis were true, my beliefs about the external world would be false and I would therefore lack knowledge of it. The Cartesian skeptic tries to show that, although I am not in fact in such a situation, the mere possibility that I could be shows that I have no knowledge of the external world. How does she try to show this?

The skeptical hypotheses draw attention to two possible situations in which I have the same experiences and beliefs. We may call them the good case and the bad case:

> *The good case*: Things are the way I think they are. I have hands, for example, and it does not just appear that I have.
>
> *The bad case*: I am a handless brain in a vat, and it merely appears to me that I have hands.

Because my experiences are the same in both cases, everything appears the same irrespective of the situation. It is clear that in the bad case, I do not know that I have hands, because I do not have hands. The skeptic argues that I do not know this even in the good case. To show this, she must assume something about the nature of knowledge. There are three sorts of considerations she can appeal to:

A. My evidence does not rule out the possibility that I am a handless brain (infallibilism).
B. I do not know that I am not a handless brain. If I do not know this, neither do I know that I have hands (the closure principle).
C. My evidence does not favor the hand hypothesis over the handless hypothesis (the underdetermination principle).

Recent discussion in epistemology focuses on the last two strategies. However, it is the first one that has been dominant in traditional philosophy, and I will defend it. The skeptical argument can thus be formulated as follows:

(CS1) If I know that I have hands, my evidence rules out the possibility that I am a handless brain.

(CS2) My evidence does not rule out the possibility that I am a handless brain.

(C) Therefore, I do not know that I have hands.

A similar argument can be given against any beliefs about the external world. So, it seems that we can have no knowledge about the external world. The argument is clearly logically valid: necessarily, if the premises are true, so is the conclusion. The question is whether the premises are true. They do appear to be true. They are based on epistemic principles that were widely accepted in the history of epistemology. I will call them Cartesian because something like them were accepted by Descartes and many other early modern philosophers.

The Principles of Cartesian Epistemology

All three skeptical strategies presuppose evidentialism and internalism.

Evidentialism: S knows that *p* only if S's evidence supports *p*.

Alternative ways of expressing the same idea is to say that S has good reasons for *p* and that S has justification for *p*.

Internalism: S has the same evidence in the good case and in the bad case.

If internalism is true, evidence must consist of something that is internal to the subject or something that she can be reflectively aware of: experiences, intuitions, and beliefs or facts about these. It does not matter exactly how we understand evidence. It is just important that S has the same evidence in both cases.

If I have the same evidence whether I am in the bad case or the good case, the evidence does not rule out the possibility that I am in the bad case, and thus does not guarantee that I am in the good case. It does not rule out the possibility that I am a handless brain. It is compatible with this possibility.

Internalism does not in itself lead to skepticism. We must also assume that knowledge requires evidence that guarantees truth and thus rules out all error-possibilities:

> *Infallibilism*: S knows that p only if S's evidence guarantees the truth of p (in other words, S's evidence rules out all alternatives to p, that is, the possibilities in which not-p).

If infallibilism is true, (CS1) is true, and if internalism is true, (CS2) is true. Together infallibilism and internalism lead to Cartesian skepticism: knowledge of the external world is impossible.

Internalism is a very popular view in contemporary epistemology. It is supported by the intuition that my beliefs are equally justified in the good case and in the bad case. Infallibilism, on the other hand, is very unpopular. Almost all philosophers reject it because it leads to skepticism. However, we should not reject infallibilism simply because it leads to skepticism. First, although fallibilism (the alternative to infallibilism) may avoid skepticism (which is far from clear), it has other problems that infallibilism avoids. Second, it may be possible to explain why people say and believe they know things about the external world, although it is in fact not the case.

Problems with Fallibilism

In this section, I will explain four problems with fallibilism that make infallibilism much more plausible. Then I will address reasons to embrace skepticism even on the assumption that fallibilism is true.

The Madness of Fallibilism

Fallibilism says that I can know that p even though my evidence does not guarantee the truth of p. So, if fallibilism is true, sentences of the following forms should appear quite natural and acceptable, but they do not:

I know that *p*, but *p* may be false.

I know that *p*, but it is possible that *q* (where *q* entails not-*p*).

For example, it would be very odd to say "I know that it is Tuesday, but I may be wrong" or "I know that the animal in the cage is a zebra, but it is possible that it is a painted mule." However, such sentences just express the fallibilist idea that knowledge is fallible. There should be nothing odd in such sentences, if fallibilism were true, but there is. So fallibilism is false.

Infallibilism, on the other hand, explains easily the oddness of such sentences. They are simply contradictory. This is how David Lewis makes the point:

> It seems as if knowledge must be by definition infallible. If you claim that *S* knows that *P*, and yet you grant that *S* cannot eliminate a certain possibility in which not-*P*, it seems as if you have granted that *S* does not after all know that *P*. To speak of fallible knowledge, or knowledge despite uneliminated possibilities of error, just *sounds* contradictory.[7]

So, the first problem is that fallibilism is unable to explain the oddness of sentences that both attribute knowledge and concede the risk of error. It is no problem for infallibilism which entails that those sentences are contradictory.

The Gettier Problem

This is the traditional analysis of knowledge:

> S knows that *p* if and only if (1) *p* is true, (2) S believes that *p*, and (3) S is justified in believing that *p*.

In 1963, Edmund Gettier published a short paper, in which he described two counterexamples to this analysis.[8] Both presupposed the fallibilist view that a justified belief may be false. After Gettier's original paper, similar counterexamples proliferated. They are all cases of true and justified beliefs that are intuitively not cases of knowledge. This is because they are cases in which a justified belief is true by good luck or accident. Here is one by Alvin Goldman:

> *Fake barns*: Henry drives in the countryside and sees a barn. Because his sight and the lighting conditions are good, his belief that the object is a barn is justified. He has thus a true and justified belief. Assume, however,

that there are barn facades around and that Henry cannot distinguish a real barn from the fake ones. In these conditions, we would not say that he knows that the object is a barn, because he was just lucky to form a true belief. He might as well have looked at a facade and formed a false belief.[9]

Cases like this pose a problem for fallibilism. If a justified belief may be false, it is possible to imagine a situation, in which a justified belief is luckily or accidentally true. For example, assume that Henry looks at a fake barn and forms a false and justified belief that it is a barn. Now change the situation so that he looks at the only real barn around and forms a true and justified belief. This belief is true just by good luck.[10]

The Gettier problem is avoided by infallibilism: if justification guarantees truth, it is not a matter of luck that a justified belief is true.

The Lottery Problem

Fallibilism can be formulated in probabilistic terms:

> S can know that p even if the probability of p given S's evidence is lower than 1.

Probability is represented by real numbers between 0 and 1. If the probability of p is 1, p is certain: there is no chance that p is false. If the probability is less than 1, there is some chance that it is false. According to fallibilism, S can know that p even if there is a chance that p is false.

Assume that I have bought a lottery ticket. There are 100,000 tickets in the lottery, and only one ticket will win. The chance of winning is very low, 0.00001, and the chance of losing is very high, 0.99999. Can I then know that my ticket will lose? We have a strong intuition that I cannot know any such thing. The problem is not that the degree of probability is too low. We can make the number of tickets larger, yet the intuition remains the same.[11]

If a fallibilist wants to deny the intuition and to claim that I can know that my ticket is a loser, she faces a serious problem. In this case, I can know on the same grounds of every losing ticket that it will lose. From this knowledge, I can then easily deduce that the one that is left is the winning ticket. But this is absurd. I cannot know before the lottery takes place which ticket will win. Otherwise, I would be a very rich man.[12]

According to fallibilism, a high probability given the evidence should be sufficient (given the other relevant conditions) for knowledge, but it is not. Fallibilism is therefore false.

The Threshold Problem

Even if fallibilism could solve the lottery problem, there would still be a threshold problem. If knowledge does not require certainty, then how strong must the evidence or justification be? What is the degree of justification needed for knowledge on a scale from 0 to 1? Any threshold less than 1 seems arbitrary. Why should a threshold of 0.95 be high enough when 0.94 is not? It seems that the only nonarbitrary answer is 1. Justification or evidence needed for knowledge must be conclusive. If this is the case, fallibilism is false.[13]

Skepticism and Ordinary Language

Fallibilism thus has many serious problems that infallibilism easily avoids. Why then has infallibilism been so unpopular in recent epistemology? The main reason is that it leads to skepticism. Many philosophers think, like David Lewis, that if they must choose between skepticism and fallibilism, they will choose fallibilism.[14] In the mid-twentieth century, it was also common to appeal to ordinary language. In everyday life, we talk about knowing things all the time. Indeed, "know" is one of the ten most often used verbs in English. If skepticism were true, our positive knowledge attributions would be false. This would be very odd.

Rather than accepting skepticism, it may be more tempting to follow John L. Austin, and other ordinary language philosophers, and to take our ordinary use of "know" at face value. Then the fact that we correctly attribute knowledge to subjects, who do not satisfy the Cartesian standards of knowledge, shows that these standards are too stringent. Our ordinary standards are less demanding. Austin also pointed out that we do not normally require of a person who claims to know something that she can rule out the possibility that she is sleeping or that she is just a brain in a vat.[15]

If Austin, Lewis, and other fallibilists are right, the first premise of the skeptical argument is false: to know that I have hands, I need not have evidence that rules out the possibility that I am a handless brain. It is enough that my evidence rules out the alternatives that are relevant. At least, in everyday contexts, skeptical hypotheses do not describe relevant alternatives, which need to be ruled out.

The Closure-Based Skeptical Argument

If fallibilism is true, the skeptical problem that is based on infallibilism is avoided. However, there are skeptical arguments that do not presuppose infallibilism. Let us assume that fallibilism is true and I can know that I have hands even though my evidence does not rule out the alternative that I am just a handless brain. It seems that I must still know in some fallible way that I am not a handless brain. How can I know that I have hands, if I do not know that I am not a handless brain? And it seems that I cannot even fallibly know this. We then get the following skeptical argument:[16]

(CP1) If I know that I have hands, I know that I am not a handless brain.

(CP2) I do not know that I am not a handless brain.

(C) Therefore, I do not know that I have hands.

The first premise is based on a very plausible principle:

The closure principle: If S knows that p and S knows that p entails q, S is in a position to know that q.

We get the first premise from this principle together with the assumption that I know that if I have hands, I am not a handless brain. How could I not know this? Propositions that I have hands and that I am a handless brain are obviously logically inconsistent. If the former is true, the latter is false. Surely, I know this.

Also the second premise is quite plausible. Now it is not required that my evidence rules out the possibility that I am a handless brain (in a sense of its being inconsistent with this possibility). Yet, it is hard to see how I could even know fallibly that the possibility does not obtain. After all, if it did obtain and I were a handless brain, I would have the same evidence as I have now.

The intuitiveness of the second premise can be explained by appealing to the following also very plausible principle:

The underdetermination principle: If S knows that p and q describe incompatible possibilities, and S's evidence does not favor p over q, then S does not know that p.

I have the same evidence in the good case, in which I have hands, and in the bad case, in which I am a handless brain. So, it seems that my evidence does not favor the option that I am in the good case rather than the option that I am in the bad case. The choice between these two options is underdetermined by my evidence. So, assuming this principle, I do not know that I have hands.

The skeptical argument could be formulated just by using the underdetermination principle without appealing to the closure principle at all.[17] There is a dispute about the best way of formulating the fallibilist skeptical argument,[18] but we need not bother about it. It is important that fallibilism must be able to give a plausible response to both arguments, and it is far from clear that it can do this: there are wide disagreements among fallibilists about the right way of resolving either sort of skeptical paradox. It seems that all attempts to do this must give up some intuitively plausible principle.[19]

It is not possible to discuss here in detail all fallibilist responses to Cartesian skepticism. It is enough to point out that they all have some costs in addition to the problems of fallibilism already mentioned. Infallibilism, in contrast, avoids all these problems. The only serious problem it does have is this: it makes our positive knowledge attributions false. What I try to do now is to show that this is not a serious cost, because it is possible to explain why we make these false knowledge attributions. If this is the case, infalliblism, even if it leads to skepticism, is overall the best attempted resolution of the Cartesian skeptical paradoxes.

The Pragmatic Explanation of False Knowledge Attributions

If Cartesian skepticism is true, our positive knowledge attributions concerning the external world are false. Why do we then make such attributions? The simple answer is that we believe that they are true and that we have knowledge of the external world. But how can we believe this, if we have the intuition that knowledge requires evidence that eliminates all possibilities of error? Is it not obvious that we do not have such evidence?

It is quite possible that ordinary people who have not taken epistemology courses typically believe that our evidence for external-world beliefs often rules out all chances of error and therefore guarantees their truth. Our ordinary knowledge attributions are made in a context, in which many things are taken for granted. They are made against mutually accepted presuppositions.[20] Together with these presuppositions our evidence may very well eliminate all possibilities of error. Because people are not typically conscious of these presuppositions, they may very well think that it is the evidence alone that does all the work and guarantees truth. This is a mistake, though a natural one, because it is only together with the presuppositions that evidence rules out all possible errors.

What about we who are aware of skeptical error-possibilities? Should we stop making positive attributions of knowledge? Not at all. It is still true that, in everyday contexts, people accept presuppositions that are incompatible with these possibilities of error. So, we do not mislead them when we say that we can rule out all alternatives even though we cannot rule out the skeptical ones. These alternatives are already ruled out by the mutually accepted presuppositions. They are not open or live possibilities for us. For example, when we speak about my perceptual knowledge about my hands in an everyday context, we typically presuppose that things are as they perceptually appear to me. This presupposition is incompatible with the possibility that I am a handless brain, which is not an open possibility in that context.

At the same time, we convey something useful to the audience, namely that my evidence rules out the open or relevant possibilities of error, the possibilities left uneliminated by our presuppositions, such as the possibility that I have stumps instead of hands. To use Paul Grice's distinction between what is said and what is meant or implicated by uttering a sentence,[21] when we attribute knowledge to me, we *say* that my evidence rules out all possibilities of error, which is false. But we *mean* or implicate that it rules out the relevant ones, which may be true.[22]

The infallibilist skeptic can therefore explain our ordinary uses of the term "know" as well as the fallibilist. The fallibilist explains them by assuming that what is said and what is meant are both typically true. The infallibilist explains them by assuming that what is said is false, while what is meant is typically true. It is what is meant that is important in communication, and here the infallibilist skeptic and the fallibilist dogmatist agree: when we attribute knowledge to someone, we mean that her evidence rules out the relevant alternatives.

The Utility of Skepticism

If both infallibilist skepticism and fallibilist dogmatism can explain our ordinary uses of "know," is there any practical difference between them? In the final section of his *Enquiry Concerning Human Understanding*,[23] David Hume considers the utility of skepticism and dogmatism respectively. He notes that no good comes from excessive Pyrrhonian skepticism. Indeed, if everybody were a Pyrrhonist and nobody had beliefs, the whole human race would become extinct, because people need to act to satisfy their basic needs and action is not possible without belief. But dogmatism also has its dangers:

> The greater part of mankind are naturally apt to be affirmative and dogmatical in their opinions; and while they see objects only on one side, and have no idea of any counterpoising argument, they throw themselves precipitately into the principles, to which they are inclined; nor have they any indulgence for those who entertain opposite sentiments. To hesitate or balance perplexes their understanding, checks their passion, and suspends their action.[24]

Hume thinks that what he calls academical or mitigated skepticism avoids the dangers of both Pyrrhonism and dogmatism. I think this is also true of the kind of Academic Cartesian skepticism defended here.[25]

As Sextus describes them, the dogmatists are people who believe that they know the truth and have therefore no need to continue inquiry. It seems that one who believes that she knows that p is inclined to reason in these ways:

A. I know that p. If I know that p, I also know that all evidence against p is misleading. So, I need pay no attention to the evidence against p. (Misleading evidence is evidence against something that is true.)[26]

B. I know that p. If I know that p, I also know that anybody who disagrees with me about the truth of p, is wrong. So, I need pay no attention to those who disagree with me about the truth of p.

C. I know that p. If I know that p, I may use p as a reason for action. So, I may use p as a reason for action.

All these ways of reasoning are based on plausible principles. The first two of them are based on the closure principle (discussed earlier), and the last one on the principle that knowledge is actionable. They explain the perils of dogmatism, as Hume sees them: dogmatists ignore evidence and arguments against their view, do not tolerate those who have opposite views, and are inclined to act rashly.

An Academic Cartesian skeptic avoids the opposite dangers of Pyrrhonism and dogmatism. First, she has beliefs and is able to act. Second, she believes that she does not know that p. So, she has not terminated the inquiry about p and is sensitive to further evidence both for p and against p, including evidence provided by other people. And, finally, she considers carefully whether her evidence for p is sufficient for action. If there is practical value in these sorts of attitudes toward one's own beliefs, Academic Cartesian skepticism has practical value that Pyrrhonism and dogmatism fail to have.

Notes

1 Julia Annas and Jonathan Barnes, *Sextus Empiricus: Outlines of Scepticism* (Cambridge: Cambridge University Press, 2000), 3.

2 There are three possible doxastic attitudes to any proposition *p*: (1) we may believe that *p*, (2) we may believe that not-*p*, or (3) we may suspend belief (or judgment) about the truth of *p*. If *p* is <God exists>, the theist believes that God exists, the atheist believes that God does not exist, and the agnostic suspends belief about the question whether God exists. According to Sextus, the agnostic is the only skeptic here; the theist and the atheist are dogmatists.

3 Gisela Striker, "Academics Versus Pyrrhonists, Reconsidered," in *The Cambridge Companion to Ancient Scepticism*, ed. Richard Bett (Cambridge: Cambridge University Press, 2010), 195.

4 John Cottingham, Robert Stoothoff, and Dugald Murdoch, *The Philosophical Writings of Descartes: Volume 2* (Cambridge: Cambridge University Press, 1985).

5 Cottingham, Stoothoff, and Murdoch, *The Philosophical Writings of Descartes: Volume 2*, 13–15.

6 Robert Nozick, *Philosophical Explanations* (Cambridge: Harvard University Press, 1981), 198; Hilary Putnam, *Reason, Truth, and History* (Cambridge: Cambridge University Press, 1981), 5–8; Michael Huemer, *Skepticism and the Veil of Perception* (Lanham, MD: Rowman & Littlefield Publishers, 2001), 2.

7 David Lewis, "Elusive Knowledge," *Australasian Journal of Philosophy* 74 (1996): 549.

8 Edmund Gettier, "Is Justified True Belief Knowledge?," *Analysis* 23 (1963): 121–23.

9 Alvin Goldman, "Discrimination and Perceptual Knowledge," *Journal of Philosophy* 73 (1976): 772–73.

10 Linda Zagzebski, "The Inescapability of Gettier Problems," *Philosophical Quarterly* 44 (1994): 65–73.

11 John Hawthorne, *Knowledge and Lotteries* (Oxford: Oxford University Press, 2003), 3–7.

12 Laurence BonJour, "The Myth of Knowledge," *Philosophical Perspectives* 24 (2010): 60–70.

13 Fred Dretske, "The Pragmatic Dimension of Knowledge," *Philosophical Studies* 40 (1981): 363–64; BonJour, "The Myth of Knowledge," 60–63.

14 Lewis, "Elusive Knowledge," 550.

15 John L. Austin, "Other Minds," in *Philosophical Papers*, 3rd ed. (Oxford: Oxford University Press, 1979), 84. See also Barry Stroud, *The Significance of Philosophical Scepticism* (Oxford: Oxford University Press, 1984), 39–57.

16 Nozick, *Philosophical Explanations*, 197–204.

17 Jonathan Vogel, "Skeptical Arguments," *Philosophical Issues* 14 (2004): 426–55.

18 Anthony Brueckner, "The Structure of the Skeptical Argument," *Philosophy and Phenomenological Research* 54 (1994): 827–35; Stewart Cohen, "Two Kinds of Skeptical Argument," *Philosophy and Phenomenological Research* 58 (1998), 143–59; Duncan Pritchard, "The Structure of Sceptical Arguments," *Philosophical Quarterly* 55 (2005): 37–52.

19 Juan Comesaña, "There Is No Immediate Justification," in *Contemporary Debates in Epistemology*, 2nd ed., eds. Mathias Steup, John Turri, and Ernest Sosa (Oxford: Blackwell, 2013), 222–35; Anthony Brueckner, "Skeptical Mystery Tour," in *Current Controversies in Epistemology*, ed. Ram Neta (New York: Routledge, 2014), 119–29.

20 See Robert Stalnaker, "Assertion," *Syntax and Semantics* 9 (1978): 315–32.

21 Paul Grice, "Logic and Conversation," in *Studies in the Way of Words* (Cambridge: Harvard University Press, 1967), 41–58.

22 Jonathan Schaffer, "Skepticism, Contextualism, and Discrimination," *Philosophy and Phenomenological Research* 69 (2004): 138–55; Wayne Davis, "Knowledge Claims and Context: Loose Use," *Philosophical Studies* 132 (2007): 395–438.

23 David Hume, *Enquiries Concerning Human Understanding and Concerning the Principles of Morals* (Oxford: Oxford University Press, [1777] 2014), 161–62.

24 Hume, *Enquiries Concerning Human Understanding and Concerning the Principles of Morals*, 161.

25 See also Allan Hazlett, *A Critical Introduction to Skepticism* (London: Bloomsbury Academic, 2014), 182–83.

26 See Saul Kripke, *Philosophical Troubles: Collected Papers, Vol. 1* (Oxford: Oxford University Press, 2011), 39–49.

RESPONSES

Response to Huemer

Markus Lammenranta

Study Questions

1. What does Lammenranta consider to be the "real problem"?
2. What argument does Lammenranta offer in response to Huemer? What premise in the argument would Huemer deny? Why?
3. What two problems does Lammenranta raise for Huemer's response to the "brain-in-a-vat" argument?
4. What are the four other "dogmatist responses" to the skeptical argument? Why does Lammenranta think they won't work?

Michael Huemer starts his defense of dogmatism by noting that he does not try to show the global skeptic that we do have knowledge. Such an attempt would be hopeless because the global skeptic would not accept any premises. It is the skeptic who has the burden of proof, he thinks. Yet the skeptic, too, faces a hopeless task if the opponent is a Moorean dogmatist whose response to every skeptical argument is that he is more certain that its conclusion is false than he is that its premises are true. It is impossible to convince such a dogmatist.

However, as I understand the problem of skepticism, it is not a matter of who has the burden of proof. The real problem is the existence of a valid skeptical argument that at least appears to have intuitively true premises. Such a skeptical argument can be understood as a paradox: the intuitively plausible premises together with the denial of the implausible conclusion cannot all be true. Both the skeptic and the dogmatist have the same task: to resolve the paradox. The skeptic must explain why both the premises and the conclusion are true even though the conclusion may initially appear implausible. The dogmatist must explain why at least one of the premises is false even though it may initially appear plausible. The one who has a better explanation wins.

Huemer's Response to Cartesian Skepticism

In my defense of skepticism, I appealed to the doctrines of internalism and infallibilism, which explain the truth of the premises and the conclusion of the Cartesian skeptical argument. Then I gave a pragmatic explanation of the initial implausibility of its conclusion. Huemer's dogmatic epistemology accepts internalism but denies infallibilism. I argued that we should not reject infallibilism too easily because fallibilism has many severe problems that infallibilism avoids. Furthermore, his epistemology has its own Cartesian skeptical problem that does not presuppose infallibilism. I will now assess whether internalist fallibilism and Huemer's epistemology in particular can solve this problem.

The following argument for external-world skepticism does not presuppose infallibilism:

(CP1) If I am justified in believing that I have hands, I am justified in believing that I am not a handless brain.

(CP2) I am not justified in believing that I am not a handless brain.

(C) Therefore, I am not justified in believing that I have hands.

I use the phrase "to be justified in believing" in the same way as Huemer uses the phrase "to have a justification for believing." The sort of justification they express is called *propositional* because I can have this sort of justification for believing a proposition I do not in fact believe.

Instead of infallibilism, the first premise (CP1) is based on the *justification-closure principle*: If S is justified in believing that p and p entails q, then S is justified in believing that q. Let's stipulate that p and q are contingent propositions and that the entailment is obvious to S. With these restrictions, the principle is very plausible. Huemer accepts it as well as the first premise (CP1). His response is to deny the second premise (CP2). Why this premise is false is supposed to be explained by his theory of justification that he calls *phenomenal conservatism*:

(PC) If it seems to S that p and S has no reason to doubt p, then S has justification for believing that p.

Now, it is not quite clear how Huemer thinks this principle explains the falsity of CP2. He says that the skeptic makes the mistake of assuming that, to justifiably form beliefs about the external world, I must first be justified in believing that I am not a brain in a vat. He thinks that no such independent justification is required. It follows from PC that, if it perceptually seems to me that I have hands and I have no reason to doubt this, I am justified in believing that I have hands. The mere possibility that I am a brain in a vat is no reason to doubt that I have hands. So, I am justified in believing that I have hands.

But what makes me then justified in believing that I am not a brain in a vat? Huemer's answer appeals to inference to the best explanation: the real-world hypothesis is a better explanation of the coherence of my sensory experiences than the brain-in-a-vat hypothesis. So, I am justified in believing that the real-world hypothesis is true and that the brain-in-a-vat hypothesis is false. I think there are two major problems with this answer.

The first problem is that the answer presupposes that I am justified in believing that my experiences are coherent. Otherwise, the inference from the coherence of my experiences would not give me justification to believe the explanatory hypothesis. It seems, though, that I do not have such justification. The coherence of my experiences is a matter of my experiences at different times fitting together. To be justified in believing in it, I must at least remember my earlier experiences. But when I try to recall such experiences, all I seem to remember are facts about the external world. Thus, if I cannot even remember my past experiences, it is clear that it does not seem to me that there is a coherence between my past and present experiences. And what else than it seeming to me that there is such a coherence could justify me in believing that there is? Indeed, Huemer thinks that seeming is the only source of justification. Furthermore, because my sensory experiences depend on my bodily movements and other external facts, there may not even be genuine regularities—or coherence—at the sensory level.[1] For example, when I rapidly turn my head, I first have an experience of there being a tree in front of me and then an experience of there being a dog. Yet, there is no regularity between tree experiences and dog experiences.

The second problem is Huemer's claim that the brain-in-a-vat hypothesis is a poor explanation of my experiences because it does not predict them at all. The hypothesis is unfalsifiable, because it is compatible with any possible set of experiences. However, this is true only if we understand the skeptical hypothesis in an unusual way. This is the way I formulated the hypothesis and, I think, the typical way of formulating it:

> *The brain-in-a-vat hypothesis*: I am a brain in a vat wired to a computer that stimulates it so that I have the experiences and beliefs I have now but these beliefs are false.

This hypothesis surely predicts that I have exactly those experiences I actually have, because it entails that I have those experiences. As Huemer understands the hypothesis, it does not say anything about the nature of my experiences. It leaves open what kind of experiences I am caused to have. I think Huemer is quite right about his skeptical hypothesis: it is a poor explanation of my experiences. But this is beside the point because we are concerned about a different hypothesis.

Other Dogmatist Responses

If PC is true, there are other ways of responding to the skeptical argument. Indeed, Huemer himself has elsewhere[2] defended some of them. One possibility, suggested by Fred Dretske,[3] is to think that the evidence that it seems to me that I have hands justifies me in believing that I have hands, but that this evidence does not justify me in believing that I am not a handless brain. The cost of this suggestion is the rejection of the plausible justification-closure principle, which is why it has not been popular recently.

The second option is to think—contra Dretske—that the fact that it seems to me that I have hands justifies me in believing both that I have hands and that I am not a handless brain. The problem with this suggestion is that it violates the following *entailment principle*: if h entails e, then e cannot justify S in believing that not-h. If hypothesis h entails evidence e, then e confirms h (raises the probability of h). How could e then justify S in believing that not-h? The brain-in-a-vat hypothesis entails that it seems to me that I have hands. So, the fact that it seems to me that I have hands confirms the hypothesis and cannot justify me in believing that it is false.

The third option, suggested by Peter Klein,[4] is to concede that my evidence that it seems to me that I have hands does not justify me in believing that I am not a handless brain, but to insist that it does justify me in believing that I have hands and that the proposition that I have hands justifies me in believing that I am not a handless brain. This suggestion has been described as "epistemic magic" and pulling the rabbit out of the hat. If my evidence does not justify me in believing that I am not a handless brain, how could the addition of a mere lemma—that I have hands—create the justification. If this were true, inference could create rather than just transmit justification from the premises to the conclusion.

The fourth option is to concede that I have no perceptual evidence against the brain-in-a-vat hypothesis but to claim that I have *a priori* justification for denying it. Let's grant I can have this sort of justification for necessary truths, such as the proposition that $2+2=4$, but the skeptical hypothesis and its denial are contingent. How could there be *a priori* justification for denying such a hypothesis?

I'm sure Huemer and other internalist fallibilists have much to say about these options and would try to make some of them look better. My present point is that they all have costs in denying something intuitive. Considering the other problems of fallibilism, Cartesian skepticism fares better.

Notes

1. William Alston, *The Reliability of Sense Perception* (Ithaca: Cornell University Press, 1993), 70–71.
2. Michael Huemer, "Direct Realism and the Brain-in-a-Vat Argument," *Philosophy and Phenomenological Research* 61 (2000): 397–413; *Skepticism and the Veil of Perception* (Lanham, MD: Rowman & Littlefield Publishers, 2001), 175–96; "The Problem of Defeasible Justification," *Erkenntnis* 54 (2001): 375–97; "Serious Theories and Skeptical Theories: Why You Are Probably not a Brain in a Vat," *Philosophical Studies* 173 (2016): 1031–52.
3. Fred Dretske, "Epistemic Operators," *Journal of Philosophy* 67 (1970): 1007–23.
4. Peter Klein, "Skepticism and Closure: Why the Evil Genius Argument Fails," *Philosophical Topics* 23 (1995): 213–36.

Response to Lammenranta

Michael Huemer

Study Questions

1. Why does Huemer think that the dispute between Lammenranta and the non-skeptic is merely semantic?
2. What is Huemer's view of what definitions are and how they work? Why does this show that the skeptic's use of the word "know" cannot be correct?
3. How does the anti-skeptic understand the word "know"?
4. Why, according to Huemer, does the fact that the level of justification required for knowledge is vague and variable not lead to skepticism?
5. Why does Huemer think, contrary to Lammenranta, that skepticism has no practical benefit for avoiding dogmatism?

The Present Dispute Is Semantic

It turns out that my central disagreement with Markus Lammenranta is a *semantic* dispute, not a substantive one. We agree on the underlying nonlinguistic facts. For instance, Lammenranta agrees with me (i) that we are not brains in vats, (ii) that the brain-in-a-vat hypothesis is extremely improbable, and (iii) that we should generally continue to hold the ordinary beliefs about the external world that we have formed based on our sensory experiences. What, then, do we disagree about? We disagree about what "know" means in English, and hence about whether the agreed-upon nonlinguistic facts make the sentence "I have knowledge of the external world" true.

This emerges in the section where Lammenranta distinguishes what we are *explicitly saying* when we ascribe knowledge from what we *implicitly mean* when we ascribe knowledge. On his view, to say "S knows that P" is (explicitly) to say that S has evidence that rules out, with 100 percent certainty, every logically possible alternative to P. However, what we implicitly mean when we say "S knows that P" is only that S's evidence rules out all the *relevant* alternatives to P. (I assume that "relevant" alternatives are ones that are sufficiently plausible or realistic. Skeptical scenarios such as the brain-in-a-vat scenario are too remote to be relevant.)

Lammenranta goes on to tell us that "what is said is false, while what is meant is typically true." In other words: when I say that I know I have hands, I *have* ruled out all the *relevant* alternatives to my having hands, but I have *not* ruled out all the *logically possible* alternatives. I agree with Lammenranta on this (as do nearly all other philosophers). Lammenranta just disagrees with most philosophers about whether this situation is correctly described with the sentence "I know that I have hands." Most philosophers think that "I know I have hands" is true when I have ruled out all the relevant alternatives to my having hands; Lammenranta thinks it is true only if I have ruled out all logically possible alternatives. What Lammenranta thinks the sentence only *implies* is what other philosophers think the sentence *says*. That is a semantic debate.

How to Judge Semantic Disputes

At least some semantic questions have determinate answers. For example, there are facts about what "know" means in English. What determines this is how the word is used in our linguistic community (the community of English speakers), and the intentions of typical speakers when they use the word. There is nothing else out there to fix word meanings.

In general, the purpose of most words in a natural language (such as English) is to group together things that members of the linguistic community are familiar with. We frequently encounter objects (or properties, situations, or whatever) that resemble each other, and we decide to group them together and put a common label on the category, so that we can communicate with each other about things of this type. For instance, we have the word "cat" because there are many furry creatures that resemble each other in certain ways, and it is useful to be able to talk about them.

That is how things are with most terms in English, including "know." We have the word "know" because we repeatedly encounter certain situations that resemble each other. For instance, there is my relation to the fact that the sky is blue when I go outside and see it; there is the relation that my students bear to the due date of the term paper, after I have told them that date (and before they've forgotten it); there is the relation mathematicians stood in to the Pythagorean theorem after a proof of it was discovered; and so on. All these situations resemble each other. Because we keep encountering situations like this, we group them together and give them a label—"knowledge."

A definition is an account of a word's conventional meaning. We start with the cases—the situations that ordinary English speakers have grouped together and labeled with a common term—and from there we try to describe, using other words, what those situations have in common that makes us group them together.

It follows from all this that a skeptical semantic theory cannot be correct. That is, an account of the meaning of "know" on which almost none of the things we call "knowledge" count as knowledge cannot be correct. Such an account, ipso facto, fails to capture what the things we group together have in common. This is not a minor disadvantage in the account; it is a radical failure in the central function of an account of meaning.

An Anti-skeptic's Semantic Theory

I think "know," in English, refers to something like this: highly justified, true belief, with no defeaters. That is, I know P when: (i) I believe P, (ii) P is true, (iii) my belief that P is sufficiently justified, and (iv) there are no facts out there that, if added to my beliefs, would render me no longer justified in believing P. This is not a perfectly complete and accurate definition, but it is close enough for our present purposes.

How much justification for P is "sufficient"? Roughly, I need enough justification that it makes sense for me to disregard alternative possibilities—not to further investigate them, not to take account of them when I reason from P to further conclusions, and so on.[1] This level of justification is vague and variable with context (it depends on what the proposition is, how easy it is to investigate, how important the truth about this proposition is, and other features of the situation), so no single, precise number can be given as the required level of justification. This is not particularly strange or problematic, nor does it mean that we never really have knowledge. Compare how things work with the following familiar words:

   a) "Old": Exactly how long must a thing have existed for it to count as old? There is no single, precise answer to that. It depends on what the thing is (old cities are older than old shoes), and even within a given category of thing the borderline is vague (there is no precise second at which one becomes an old person). It would not be a superior semantic theory to claim that nothing is ever old, or that only a thing that has existed forever (a thing that is as old as possible) is truly old.

   b) "Large": Exactly how many cubic millimeters must an object occupy to count as large? Again, there is no single, precise answer to this. It depends on what kind of thing we are talking about (large houses are larger than large cakes), and even for a given type of object, there is no precise cutoff point for being large. It would not be a superior semantic theory to claim that nothing is ever large, or that only a thing of infinite size (the largest possible) is truly large.

   c) "Know": Exactly how certain must P be in order to qualify as known? There is no single, precise answer to this. It depends on the proposition, and even for a given proposition, there is no precise cutoff. But, again, it would not be a superior semantic theory to claim that nothing is ever known, or that only things with the highest possible certainty are truly known.

Skepticism Has No Practical Benefit

In his last section, Lammenranta suggests that skepticism has practical value because it prevents people from being dogmatic, that is, from dismissing alternatives to their beliefs that should not be dismissed. I disagree.

Suppose two people agree that all the relevant alternatives to P have been eliminated, and they agree that not all the logically possible alternatives have been eliminated. But they disagree about whether, in virtue of these facts, a certain *word* applies to P. Person A thinks that "torf" applies to P in virtue of the fact that all the relevant alternatives have been eliminated. Person B, by contrast, thinks that "torf" only applies when all the logically possible alternatives have been eliminated. Surely this dispute has no practical import. It does not follow from this situation, for example, that A will be dogmatic about P and B will be open-minded. That is how it is with my disagreement with Lammenranta; just substitute "knowledge" for "torf."

You can see that this sort of dispute lacks practical import because we could avoid the dispute simply by introducing two terms with stipulative definitions. Let "torf" refer to knowledge in my sense, and let "borf" refer to knowledge in Lammenranta's sense. Then everyone can agree that we *torf* many facts about the external world, and also that we *borf* nothing about the external world. I happen to think that "know" in standard English refers to "torfing," but so what?

Keep in mind that anti-skeptics are not people who claim that we know *everything* that we believe. They are people who think we know *some things* about the external world. Anti-skeptics such as myself do not hold that one should, in general, dismiss any alternatives to one's present beliefs. We only recommend dismissing outlandish, skeptical alternatives, such as the brain-in-a-vat scenario.

Is this dogmatic? No, it isn't. It is dogmatic to dismiss reasonable alternatives. It is not dogmatic to dismiss alternatives that are irrational or absurdly unlikely; rather, to do so is merely sensible. For instance, if a physicist, in our current situation, refuses to consider string theory as a possible account of quantum gravity, that physicist is being dogmatic. But if the physicist refuses to consider the theory that the Earth rests on the back of a giant turtle, that physicist is not thereby being dogmatic; he is simply being rational.

In life, we cannot and should not seriously consider every logically possible alternative. Some alternatives are simply too remote to be worth entertaining. Those are the only alternatives that anti-skeptics tell us to ignore. This isn't a flaw in the anti-skeptical view; it is an advantage.

Note

1 For more on the attitude of disregarding alternatives, see the discussion of dismissal in my "Epistemic Possibility," *Synthese* 156 (2007): 119–42, at pp. 131–33.

Questions for Reflection

1. Is Huemer correct that the skeptic bears the burden of proof? Why?
2. Does knowledge require that we have absolute certainty (infallibilism) or not (fallibilism)? Why?
3. Do you agree with Lammenranta that the skeptical hypothesis (e.g., the possibility that you are a brain-in-a-vat) is no worse (or better) an explanation of your experience than the non-skeptical hypothesis? Why?

2

How Are Beliefs Justified?

Beliefs Can Be Justified by Experience

Daniel Howard-Snyder

Study Questions

1. What is the distinction between basic and nonbasic beliefs? Given these definitions, what is foundationalism?
2. What four preliminary clarifications does Howard-Snyder make? Why are these important?
3. What two arguments does Howard-Snyder give on behalf of foundationalism?
4. What are Davidson's arguments against experience justifying beliefs? How does Howard-Snyder respond to these arguments?
5. What is the Sellarsian Dilemma? What problems does Howard-Snyder raise against it?

Foundationalists distinguish basic from nonbasic beliefs. To say that a belief of a person is *basic* is to say that it is justified and that it owes its justification to something other than (i) her other beliefs or (ii) any features of the relations between them. (For simplicity's sake, I will leave (ii) aside in what follows.) To say that a belief of a person is *nonbasic* is to say that it is justified and not basic. Two theses constitute *foundationalism*:

   a. *Minimalism.* There are some basic beliefs.
   b. *Exclusivism.* If there are any nonbasic beliefs, that is solely because they (ultimately) owe their justification to at least one basic belief.

Minimal Foundationalism affirms Minimalism but not Exclusivism. *Experiential Foundationalism* affirms that experience can justify basic beliefs.

In this chapter, I will do three things: (i) clarify the terms and theses that I just introduced, (ii) argue for foundationalism, and (iii) assess four famous objections to Experiential Foundationalism.

Preliminary Clarifications

First, foundationalism is about the *epistemic justification* of belief. What is epistemic justification? Some philosophers say that (i) for a belief of a person to be epistemically justified is for it to be held in such a way that, by virtue of holding it in that way, the belief is likely to be true. So, for example, people tend to think that most of the beliefs that help them navigate their immediate environment are based on something, for example, perceptual or sensory experiences of the objects around them, and by virtue of being based on such experiences, those beliefs are likely to be true. Others say that (ii) for a belief of a person to be epistemically justified is for it to be held responsibly, that is, without the person violating any *epistemic obligations* with respect to acquiring true beliefs and avoiding false ones (e.g., *believe something only if you have considered all the evidence that is available to you*, and the like). Yet others affirm both (i) and (ii). You can be a foundationalist and endorse any of these views.

Second, foundationalism is a theory about the *structure* of a system of justified beliefs, that is, how the beliefs in a system of justified beliefs must be related to each other. It does not specify how a belief is justified. It only specifies how a system of justified beliefs is structured. Notably, it says that such a system must have basic beliefs (Minimalism), and any nonbasic beliefs will, ultimately, owe their justification solely to basic beliefs (Exclusivism).

Third, foundationalism is not a theory about the *activity* of justifying beliefs, that is, *showing* that they are justified. Rather, foundationalism is a theory about beliefs having the *property* of justification, their *being* justified. It is easy to see the difference between the activity and the property of justification. Consider an analogy. Suppose you challenge me with respect to how I have raised my children over the years. I would justify my past behavior by showing how it was morally justified. That is, I would try to show how my child-rearing behavior was morally justified; I would display a property that my behavior had prior to your challenge and prior to my justifying it. Similarly, suppose you challenge me with respect to my long-standing belief that God exists. I would justify my belief by showing how it was epistemically justified; I would try to display a property that my belief had prior to your challenge and prior to my justifying it. Just as the actions of a person can be morally justified without their having shown that those actions are morally justified, a person's beliefs can be epistemically justified even if they have not shown that those beliefs are epistemically justified. Why is this important? Because sometimes people criticize foundationalism for failing as a theory about the *activity* of justifying beliefs, and then they infer that it fails as a theory about the *property* of being justified.[1] This is a mistake: foundationalism is not about justifying; it's about being justified.

Finally, you might ask: if a person's basic belief does not owe its justification to other beliefs they have, to what, then, does it owe its justification? Foundationalists offer different answers. One popular answer is that basic beliefs owe their justification to *experience* (Experiential Foundationalism). For example, its *looking* to you as though you have a bellybutton can justify your belief that you have a bellybutton, and its *sounding* to you as though there's a crow cawing can justify your belief that there's a crow cawing. And the same goes for other perceptual or sensory experiences.

On Behalf of Foundationalism

What might be said on behalf of foundationalism? At least two things, I submit. First, according to commonsense, at least some of our beliefs are justified, but not by our other beliefs. Suppose I just spent the last three days hiking the 70 miles from Rainy Pass to Manning Park on the Pacific Crest Trail in the North Cascades. I ache all over and I feel hungry. I justifiedly believe that I feel achy and hungry. Are there some other beliefs of mine from which I infer these things? Not so far as I can tell. Rather, I feel achy and hungry, and so naturally I believe that I feel achy and hungry. Now, have I done something *wrong* in believing that I feel achy and hungry on the basis of my feeling achy and hungry? No. Have I believed that I feel achy and hungry on the basis of something that makes it *likely* that my belief is true? Yes. It seems, then, that however we fill in the details, my belief that I feel achy and hungry is justified and my belief owes its justification to something other than my other beliefs, namely my *feeling* achy and hungry.

And the same goes for other sorts of beliefs, not just beliefs about how I feel. Suppose that at Hart's Pass I hitch a ride to Mazama in order to resupply. As I stand by the side of the road with my thumb out, I justifiedly believe that I am hitching a ride to Mazama in order to resupply. There seem to be no other beliefs of mine from which I infer that I am hitching a ride to Mazama in order to resupply. Moreover, it seems that what justifies my belief is its *introspectively seeming* to me that that is my reason for hitching a ride. That is, I look within my mind, so to speak, and *see* what my reason for hitching a ride is: in order to resupply. Or suppose that, near the end of my hike, I imagine eating a huge, juicy steak and a crisp green salad, and drinking several pints of IPA. (Reportedly, food is the most popular thing that long-distance hikers fantasize about. Can you guess what the second is?) While I am imagining this feast, I justifiedly believe that I am imagining a feast. There seem to be no other beliefs of mine from which I infer that I am imagining this feast. Moreover, it seems that what justifies my belief that I am imagining this feast is its *appearing* to me, in my imagination, as if I'm having a feast. Or suppose the sign in front of me says, "Canadian Border: 60 miles." I justifiedly believe that the sign says this. Are there some other beliefs from which I infer that the sign says this? It seems not; I believe it simply because of the way it *looks* to me and the way it looks to me seems to be what justifies my belief that this is what the sign says. When my wife dropped me off at the trailhead this morning, she said she was driving to Winthrop. Much later, I justifiedly believe she said this. There seems to be no other belief of mine from which I infer that she said this. I simply recall her having said it, and my difficult-to-describe experience of recalling it seems to justify my believing that she said she was driving to Winthrop.[2] In each of these cases, I am doing nothing wrong in holding the belief in question on the basis of the experience in question; moreover, I hold the belief on the basis of something that makes the belief very likely to be true: experience.

Of course, what I have just said is the epitome of commonsense. Yet, commonsense is not always a reliable guide to truth. So despite what commonsense suggests in the cases I have described, *perhaps* there is some hidden belief to which these seemingly experience-based beliefs owe their justification. Even so, we can't simply neglect how things seem. And things seem congenial to both Minimal Foundationalism and to Experiential Foundationalism.

Second, foundationalism arguably provides a satisfying solution to *the regress problem*. Suppose Frances is one of us, a typical human adult; and suppose that her belief that it is cloudy outside is justified. Furthermore, suppose Frances believes that *it is cloudy outside* on the basis of an inference from two other beliefs of hers, her belief that *if it is raining, then it is cloudy outside* and her belief that *it is raining outside*. Finally, suppose her belief that *it is cloudy outside* owes its justification to these other two beliefs of hers via this inference. A simple question arises: How can this be? How can Frances's belief that it is cloudy outside owe its justification to her other two beliefs via her inference? How is inferential justification possible?

Could it be that her belief that it is cloudy outside owes its justification to her inference from those other two beliefs of hers even though neither of them is justified—*the unjustified justifier option*? Or could it be that her belief owes its justification to them since they are justified and they owe their justification to some further beliefs of hers, and those further beliefs owe their justification to some other beliefs, and so on, so that her belief that it is cloudy outside eventually owes its justification to itself—*the circular justification option*? Or could it be that her belief owes its justification to those two beliefs since they are justified and they owe their justification to some further beliefs of hers, and they, in turn, owe their justification to some other beliefs of hers, and so on, for infinitely many nonrepeating beliefs of hers—*the infinite regress option*? Each of these three options seems untenable. The unjustified justifier option seems untenable because no belief can owe its justification to other beliefs from which it is inferred unless the other beliefs are justified. The circular justification option seems untenable because no belief can owe its justification to itself. The infinite regress option seems untenable because none of us can hold infinitely many beliefs of the required sort.[3] That leaves exactly one option: Frances's belief that it is cloudy outside owes its justification to her inference from her other two beliefs, both of which are justified, and they, in turn, owe their justification, ultimately, to something other than her other beliefs—*the basic belief option*. This conclusion is congenial to Exclusivism.

Epistemological nihilists will reject this argument because it presupposes that some beliefs are justified and, says *nihilism*, no beliefs are justified. Epistemological coherentists will reject this argument because it presupposes that some beliefs are justified on the basis of an inference from other beliefs and, says *coherentism*, no belief is justified on the basis of an inference from other beliefs; a belief is justified *solely* because of its membership in a coherent system of beliefs.[4] Elsewhere, I explain why neither of these options is plausible.[5]

Notice that foundationalism's solution to the regress problem leaves us with a question: what makes basic beliefs justified, and why does it end the regress of justification? One popular view is that perceptual or sensory experience can justify basic belief and it can end the regress of justification. Moreover, recall that the first consideration in favor of foundationalism (the appeal to commonsense) says that experiences of various sorts can justify basic belief. Some people, however, object. No experience can justify belief, they say; nor can an experience stop the regress of justification. Let's assess some famous objections along these lines.

Davidson on Experiential Foundationalism

Donald Davidson gives two arguments for concluding that experience cannot justify belief.[6]

First argument. Experience causes beliefs; but a causal explanation of a belief does not show how or why it is justified; so experience cannot justify belief.

The problem with Davidson's first argument is that the conclusion does not follow from the premises. Sure enough, the fact that experience causes belief cannot all by itself explain why experience justifies belief; but no one ever said it did. Rather, experience justifies belief *only when certain additional conditions are satisfied*: for example, one would not have the experience if the belief were false, or the experience makes the belief likely to be true, or one has no good reason to think that the experience is illusory, or one satisfies the relevant epistemic duties, or the experience is the input of a reliable belief-forming process, or one exhibits intellectual virtue in holding the belief on the basis of it. The list goes on and on. Naturally, foundationalists disagree over what's on the list. But the point remains: experience does not justify belief unless some additional condition is satisfied. So we can't draw Davidson's conclusion from his premises.

Second argument. If an experience can justify belief, then the experience makes it likely that the belief is true. An experience makes it likely that a belief is true only if the experience has propositional content. But experience lacks propositional content. So experience cannot justify belief.[7]

To assess this argument, two clarifications are in order. First, suppose it looks to you right now as if there is a page of words in front of you. Its *looking* to you as if there is a page of words in front of you is a visual experience. Naturally enough, you also *believe* that there is a page of words in front of you. Now notice: your visual experience is not the same thing as your belief. That's because you can have the one without the other. For example, you can have the experience without the belief when you know that you are hallucinating, and you can have the belief without the experience when someone tells you that there is a page of words in front of you but you have your eyes closed. Second, notice also that what you believe is the proposition that *there is a page of words in front of you*. We call that proposition the *propositional content* of your belief. That's what your belief is about. It's about there being a page of words in front of you. And the same goes for beliefs more generally.

Now let's return to Davidson's second argument. Many people disagree with the third premise: just as belief has propositional content, so does experience. You see that there is a page of words in front of you and so, naturally, you believe that there is a page of words in front of you. What you see is what you believe. In experience, you "take in" the fact that there is a page of words in front of you; in belief, you affirm that there is a page of words in front of you. Your experience and your belief have the same propositional content.[8]

Many other people disagree with the first premise: an experience *can* justify belief even if the experience does not make the belief likely to be true. In this connection, they ask you to imagine that it *looks* to you as if there is a page of words in front of you but, unbeknownst to you, you're in the matrix, stuck in a pod with your brain being directly manipulated so that it looks to you as if there is a page of words in front of you when in fact there isn't. You aren't doing anything wrong to hold that belief. After all, you have no reason to be suspicious; so what else could you do? In that case, your belief is surely justified.[9]

But even if the first and third premises are both true, the second seems surely false. Experience can make a belief likely to be true even if it lacks propositional content. To see why, note that pains, tickles, itches, and other *purely qualitative states*, as philosophers call them, lack propositional content. They are not about anything in the way that beliefs are about the propositions that are their contents. So then: the pain I now feel lacks propositional content. Nevertheless, it makes it extremely likely that my belief that I am in pain is true. Likewise, even if its looking to me as if the wall is white lacks propositional content, that visual experience makes it very likely that my belief is true. Perceptual and sensory experiences can confirm beliefs.

The Sellarsian Dilemma

Davidson targeted the claim that experience can justify basic belief. Wilfred Sellars targets the claim that experience can stop the regress of inferential justification discussed earlier. We can put Sellars's argument succinctly like this:

Sellarsian Dilemma
1. Either an experience has propositional content or it doesn't.
2. If it does, then it is in need of justification itself.
3. If it doesn't, then it cannot contribute to the justification of a belief.

4. An experience can end the regress by justifying a belief only if (i) the experience is *not* in need of justification itself, and (ii) it *can* contribute to the belief's justification.

5. So, an experience cannot end the regress by justifying a belief.[10]

The argument is logically valid, but what about the premises, especially premises 2 and 3? Let's begin with premise 3. Two popular ways to defend it appeal to arbitrariness and articulability.

The Problem of Arbitrariness

Some people argue that if an experience lacks propositional content, then it's arbitrary whether it contributes to the justification of one belief rather than another. For example, suppose the wall's visually appearing white to me lacks propositional content. In that case, there is nothing about my visual experience that renders it fit to justify my belief that the wall is white rather than my belief that the price of gold in the US is currently $1,258 per ounce. It's just arbitrary to pick one over the other.[11]

We may well puzzle over how it is that an experience without propositional content can be nonarbitrarily "matched," so to speak, with a belief that has a particular content. But perhaps foundationalists can develop a couple of suggestions. For example, they might develop the idea that because there is a lawlike connection between my visual experience and my wall belief, but no such connection between my visual experience and my gold belief, my visual experience makes my wall belief very likely to be true, but it does not make my gold belief very likely to be true. Alternatively, they might develop the idea that, although my visual experience lacks propositional content, it represents the propositional content of my wall belief in a way *analogous* to the way in which a photo represents a scene or a map represents a terrain. No photo or map has propositional content. Nevertheless, a photo of your face represents your face better than a steam engine, and a map of Mt. Adams represents Mt. Adams better than the sole of your shoes. Provided that my visual experience of a white wall represents the wall I'm looking at better than the price of gold in China and other arbitrarily chosen things, there might be a way to "match" it with my wall belief in a nonarbitrary fashion.[12]

The Problem of Articulability

Some people argue that if an experience lacks propositional content, then it cannot provide an articulable reason for holding a belief. (A reason for a belief is articulable just when one can say it. So, for example, if my reason for believing that there are some hands is the fact that I have hands, then I can say "I have hands.") But if experience cannot provide an articulable reason for holding a belief, it cannot contribute to the justification of the belief. Thus, if an experience lacks propositional content, it cannot contribute to the justification of the belief.[13]

What should we make of this argument? Well, which premise deserves our attention depends on what sort of thing we take a reason for holding a belief to be. In common parlance, a reason for holding a belief is *anything* offered on its behalf, where it's left open what sorts of things might be so offered. In academic philosophy, however, it's often not left open: only *propositions* are reasons, we are told. Let's consider each option in turn.

Suppose that a reason for holding a belief is anything offered on its behalf. Then the premise that if an experience lacks propositional content, then it cannot provide an articulable reason for holding a belief is better understood as the claim that *if experience lacks propositional content, it can provide nothing articulable for holding a belief*. This understanding of the first premise might be thought to be dubious. Consider my belief that I now feel pain in my right shin. Suppose you ask me what reason I have to hold that belief. I answer: "My reason is the pain I feel in my right shin." If our current understanding of the first premise (in italics) is true, I have provided nothing articulable for holding my belief. But surely I have. For although I have not expressed a proposition but only used a noun clause to identify my reason, that suffices for providing something "articulable" for holding my belief—I did use words to refer to it, after all. We can say something similar for beliefs about sensory experience, for example my belief that the wall before me *appears* white. Suppose you ask me what reason I have to hold it. I answer: "My reason is its appearing white." Again, I have provided something articulable for holding my belief. What about my belief that the wall *is* white? Suppose you ask me what reason I have to hold it. My answer is the same as before: "My reason is the wall's appearing white." Once again I have provided something articulable for holding my belief. It seems, then, that the premise under discussion is false if it is understood in the way indicated earlier (in italics).

Now let's turn to academic philosophers, many of whom insist that only propositions can be reasons. In that case, the premise that if experience cannot provide an articulable reason for holding a belief, then it cannot contribute to the justification of the belief, is better expressed as the claim that *if an experience cannot provide an articulable proposition for holding the belief, it cannot contribute to the justification of the belief*. This understanding of the second premise might be thought to be dubious also. That's because even if the pain I now feel in my right shin cannot provide an articulable proposition for holding my belief that I feel pain there, it can contribute to my belief's justification by virtue of making the content of my belief vastly more likely than its denial. Likewise, even if the wall's appearing smooth cannot provide an articulable proposition for holding my belief that it appears smooth or holding my belief that it is smooth, it can contribute to the justification of both beliefs by virtue of making the content of each belief much more likely than its denial. That's not to say that nothing more is needed for these beliefs to be justified; but it certainly seems that, if an experience makes a belief much more likely than its denial, then it counts as a contribution to a belief's being justified, and a significant one at that.

We might also worry about premise 2 of the Sellarsian Dilemma, the claim that, if experience has propositional content, then it is in need of justification. Here's why. It goes without saying that something is in need of justification only if it is the sort of thing that can be justified or unjustified. That's why dogs and donut holes are not in need of justification; they aren't the sorts of things that can be justified or unjustified. So then: if experience is in need of justification, then it's the sort of thing that can be justified or unjustified. It follows that, *if* premise 2 is true, then, *if an experience has propositional content, it is the sort of thing that can be justified or unjustified*.

And therein lies the trouble: it's false that *if an experience has propositional content, it is the sort of thing that can be justified or unjustified*. That's because having propositional content is not enough to make something justified or unjustified. For example, my imagining how my life will be after retirement has all kinds of propositional content; I imagine that I will hike in the woods more, that I will make new friends, that I will see new places, and so on. But my imagining these things is not the sort of thing that is either justified or unjustified; and so my imagining these things is not in need of justification. The same goes for wondering, entertaining, and so on. These *mental states*, as philosophers call them, have propositional content, but that's not enough to make them be the sort of thing that can be justified or unjustified, and so having propositional content is not enough to make them be in need of justification. The same goes for perceptual and sensory experience. An experience's having propositional content is not enough to make it the sort of thing that can be justified or unjustified, and so its having propositional content is not enough to make it be in need of justification.

The upshot is that the Sellarsian Dilemma gives us little reason to deny that experience can contribute to the justification of a belief, and do so in a way that solves the regress problem in the experiential foundationalist's favor.

Conclusion

I am under no illusion that I have defended foundationalism adequately in this chapter. That would take quite a bit more work. I hope, however, to have taken a significant step toward exhibiting its attractiveness and resilience.[14]

Notes

1. See, for example, Jonathan Kvanvig, "Coherentist Theories of Justification," in *Stanford Encyclopedia of Philosophy*, ed. Edward N. Zalta (http://plato.stanford.edu/entries/justep-coherence).
2. Cf. Carl Ginet, "Infinitism is not the Solution to the Regress Problem," in *Contemporary Debates in Epistemology*, eds. Matthias Steup and Ernest Sosa (Oxford: Blackwell Publishing, 2005), 142–43; and James Pryor, "There is Immediate Justification," in *Contemporary Debates in Epistemology*, 184–85.
3. For a defense of Infinitism, see Peter Klein, "Human Knowledge and the Infinite Regress of Reasons," *Philosophical Perspectives* 13 (1999): 297–325; Jeanne Peijnenburg and David Atkinson, "The Emergence of Justification," *Philosophical Quarterly* 63 (2013): 546–64; and John Turri and Peter Klein, *Ad Infinitum: New Essays on Epistemological Infinitism* (New York: Oxford, 2014). For criticism, see D. Howard-Snyder and E. J. Coffman, "Three Arguments against Foundationalism: Arbitrariness, Epistemic Regress, and Existential Support," *Canadian Journal of Philosophy* 36 (2006): 535–64.
4. For defenses of Coherentisim, see L. Bonjour, *The Structure of Empirical Knowledge* (Cambridge, MA: Harvard, 1985); Susan Haack, *Evidence and Inquiry* (New York: Blackwell, 1993); and Ted Poston, *Reason and Explanation: A Defense of Explanatory Coherentism* (New York: Palgrave Macmillan, 2014).
5. See my response to Kevin McCain and Ted Poston in this volume (pp. 90–94).
6. Donald Davidson, "A Coherence Theory of Truth and Knowledge," in *Truth and Interpretation: Perspectives on the Philosophy of Donald Davidson*, ed. Ernest LePore (Oxford: Blackwell Publishing, 1986), 311; "the relation . . . is justified."
7. Cp. Nicholas Everitt and Eric Fisher, *Modern Epistemology* (New York: McGraw-Hill, 1995), 84.
8. John McDowell, *Mind and World* (Cambridge, MA: Harvard University Press, 1994). For critique, see Pierre Le Morvan, "Sensory Experience and Intentionalism," *Philosophy Compass* 3:4 (2008): 1–26.
9. Richard Foley, "What's Wrong with Reliabilism?," *The Monist* 68 (1985): 188–200.

10 Wilfred Sellars, "Empiricism and the Philosophy of Mind," in *Minnesota Studies in the Philosophy of Science, Volume I: The Foundations of Science and the Concepts of Psychology and Psychoanalysis*, eds. Herbert Feigl and Michael Scriven (Minneapolis: University of Minnesota Press, 1956), 253–329. See also, L. BonJour, *The Structure of Empirical Knowledge*, chapter 3.
11 Pryor, "There is Immediate Justification," 192–93.
12 And there other avenues to explore as well; see William Alston, "Back to the Theory of Appearing," *Philosophical Perspectives* 13 (1999): 198–201.
13 J. McDowell, *Mind and World*, 165–66; cf. Pryor, "There is Immediate Justification," 193–94.
14 For comments on an earlier draft of this chapter, I thank my students Alana Bomberger, Kane Dickerson, Wes Eason, James Hyde, Robert King, Miranda Levine, Sean Mittelstaedt, Emily Robertson, and Sara Wold.

Beliefs Are Justified by Coherence

Kevin McCain and Ted Poston

Study Questions

1. What is the basic idea of coherentism in contrast to foundationalism?

2. What are the three "cases" McCain and Poston describe that provide intuitive support for coherentism?

3. How do McCain and Poston understand the nature of coherence? What are the views of coherence that they reject?

4. What is the "problem of the regress of reasons"? What are the four options for responding to this problem? What is unique, according to McCain and Poston, about the last of these?

5. What two arguments do McCain and Poston offer against foundationalism?

There's real news, and there's fake news. But news reports don't come tagged with labels "real" and "fake," and even if they did come tagged, the labels themselves may be real or fake. What should we believe? This question is at the heart of epistemology. It is a question that preoccupied the father of modern philosophy, René Descartes (1596–1650), in his *Meditations*. It is a question that is of the utmost importance to every individual today. We are constantly bombarded with information that various groups or persons want us to believe. We need a view about what makes a claim worthy of belief in order to figure out what we should believe. The debate between foundationalists and coherentists is a debate over the properties that make a claim worthy of belief.

When we reflect on the question of what we should believe, two facts spring to mind. The first is that we have many beliefs. The second is that sometimes we find that our beliefs are false. We all desire to believe the truth and avoid error. But, how do we decide which of our beliefs are true and which are false? Can we go through our beliefs one by one and sort out the true ones from the false ones? Given our vast number of beliefs, that task is impossible.

Even if we can't evaluate all of our beliefs individually, it does seem that we can generally distinguish between beliefs that we have good reason for and those that we don't. Suppose you believe that the president is in New York. Is your belief true? You believe it because the news reported it. But you ask yourself "why should I take the news reporting such a thing to be a good reason to believe the President is in New York?" Suppose you had a "magic" eight ball and asked it whether the president was in New York.[1] If "yes" floated up in the window, you wouldn't take this as a good reason for really thinking that the president is in New York. Well, what's the difference? When you think about this you soon realize that you have lots of other beliefs about the news, the role of the president, New York, and so on, all of which support your belief that the news can be trusted on this matter. The key insight is that when we think about the reasons for our beliefs we see that our reasons stretch out to a vast number of beliefs that collectively support other beliefs.

Okay, so we see that some reasons are good reasons for believing and others, such as "magic" eight ball answers, aren't. Furthermore, we see that our beliefs work together to support others. But how do we answer our question about what we should believe? Do we try to do this for each of our beliefs individually? Descartes attempted to determine which beliefs he should have by examining all of his beliefs at once. He aimed to suspend judgment on anything he could call into question until he figured out which beliefs are worth having and which should be abandoned. His goal was to find a secure foundation for his beliefs that offered him assurance that each of his beliefs was true. The search for a foundation is quite natural. If you are calculating a large sum and get a result that seems odd, it's best to reduce the large sum to a series of smaller sums that you are sure of and then use those results to recalculate the larger sum.[2] The assurance of the smaller sums provides a base for calculating the larger sum. But the crucial question is whether there is, in general, a foundation for all our beliefs. Foundationalists say "yes"; coherentists say "no."

According to *coherentism*, we can't set aside *all* our other beliefs while we evaluate some particular belief. We must rely on some beliefs to evaluate others. As a result, there is no foundation of the kind Descartes sought.[3]

Instead, we start with the beliefs we have and revise them in a piecemeal fashion as we reflect and learn new things. Otto Neurath (1882–1945) helpfully compared the process of evaluating our beliefs with the repairing of a ship at sea. A sailor cannot take the ship entirely apart at sea but must, rather, replace the bad parts by relying on the other parts of the ship to stay afloat.[4] Similarly, we can't overhaul our entire system of beliefs at once and start over with a firm foundation; we have to work with the beliefs that we find ourselves with and make modifications as we go. This insight lies at the heart of coherentism. According to coherentism, the beliefs we should have (those that are justified) are the ones that fit together into the best overall system of beliefs, and these justified beliefs get their justification by cohering with the other beliefs in this system.

Intuitive Support for Coherentism

As we saw, coherentism fits well with the fact that we must evaluate our beliefs from some existing perspective. There isn't a point where we think about what we should believe without already having some beliefs. We cannot start from scratch by laying a foundation and then building a structure on a secure base. The only way to proceed is to start with one's own perspective and adjust it to make that perspective both broader and more coherent. In this section we offer three intuitive cases to support coherentism.

Case 1: Scientific Practice

Consider how scientists reason when a well-confirmed theory seems to conflict with a given observation. Do they scrap the theory and start over? No. They double-check the measurements to ensure the correctness of the problematic observation. If the observation is accurate, they modify the theory or auxiliary assumptions to restore coherence.

The planet Neptune was discovered by coherence reasoning. Newton's theory predicted an orbit for Uranus that differed from astronomical observations. Two nineteenth-century British astronomers restored the coherence between Newton's theory and these observations by positing that a planet existed with a certain mass and distance that would account for the otherwise problematic orbit of Uranus. When they trained their telescopes in the direction of where this planet should be, they discovered Neptune.

Crucially, this process of adjustment proceeds toward finding the best fit between the observation, the theory, and the rest of one's beliefs. Similarly, when we evaluate our beliefs we don't scrap them anytime we become aware of a conflict. In this sort of situation, we determine which of the conflicting beliefs is the poorest fit with our other beliefs and change it.

Case 2: Rumors

Consider another situation. Suppose you have a friend that you've known for years. Recently, some people have begun to spread vicious rumors about his character. Given everything you believe about him, you judge that the rumors must be false. You are asked to give your reasons: while you can offer a good argument based on past experience, you are hard-pressed to offer reasons that are unquestionably true such that the proponents of the rumors would be forced to accept them. Rather, you appeal to your thousandfold experiences with your friend to dismiss the rumors. In other words, you have a set of beliefs and experiences about your friend. When you learn about the rumors, your new beliefs are in tension with your other beliefs. The rumors can't be true given what you believe about your friend, but, if the rumors are true, your beliefs about your friend's character must be false. So, how should you revise your beliefs? Well, it would be wrong to scrap all of your beliefs about your friend and start from ground zero. No, you consider which set of beliefs is the most coherent—the one that couples your beliefs about your friend together with the belief that the rumors are true or the other that couples your beliefs about your friend together with the belief that the rumors are false. It turns out that the latter is the more coherent set. That's why you dismiss the rumors about your friend as just that—merely rumors. This is reasonable to do, and the beliefs that you are left with are ones that are justified.

Case 3: Eyewitness Agreement

Suppose you hear from an acquaintance that a very surprising event occurred. On the night of a recent election, a large comet appeared at the stroke of midnight and its sonic boom was loud enough to shake the dormitory. You find this doubtful. This person may be making it up or misperceiving a fireworks celebration. So, you reject this claim. But a curious thing happens. More and more people begin to report this event. There was a streak of light followed by a sonic boom. As more and more people begin to report this event, you are compelled to accept that it is true.

C. I. Lewis (1883–1964) pointed out that when we discover that independent witnesses agree with one another about what happened, it gives us very strong reason to think that the event really happened in the way that they say.

It is the coherence of the reports that provides the reason, not the individual reports themselves, each of which is not believable on its own. Coherentism applies this thinking to our beliefs in general. When our beliefs cohere with one another, the coherence of our beliefs gives us strong reason for thinking that our beliefs are true.[5]

The Nature of Coherence

So far we have described some of the intuitive reasons in support of coherentism. These reasons support two crucial coherentist claims. First, there is no secure foundation upon which to assure ourselves of the truth of the rest of our beliefs. Second, coherence among our beliefs and experiences can provide an excellent reason to think our beliefs are true. A crucial issue about the second claim concerns the nature of coherence. We haven't yet said what exactly coherence is. This is obviously a critical concept when it comes to coherentism, so we will turn to this now.

An early attempt to spell out the nature of coherence was in terms of logical entailment. Brand Blanshard (1892–1987) wrote: "Fully coherent knowledge would be knowledge in which every judgment entailed, and was entailed by, the rest of the system."[6] A. C. Ewing (1899–1973) weakened this so that each proposition in a system only had to be entailed by the rest.[7] C.I. Lewis weakened the requirement even further by shifting from logical entailment to probabilistic support with his notion of *congruence*:

> A set of statements . . . will be said to be congruent if and only if they are so related that the antecedent probability of anyone of them will be increased if the remainder of the set can be assumed as given premises.[8]

Ultimately, though, these early approaches are problematic, so they have been abandoned for a much more promising approach.[9] The most plausible way of understanding what it means for beliefs to cohere is in terms of explanatory relations. The explanatory approach to coherence is the idea that beliefs cohere with one another by forming an explanatory system—that is, they help explain one another and new information that we encounter. Consider the case of eyewitness agreement discussed earlier. The truth of the reports is the best explanation of the fact that so many independent eyewitnesses report the same event. Laurence BonJour (1943–) provides a clear statement of coherence in terms of explanatory relations. His list of principles explicating the nature of coherence gives an important role to explanation:

(1) A system of beliefs is coherent only if it is logically consistent.

(2) A system of beliefs is coherent in proportion to its degree of probabilistic consistency.

(3) The coherence of a system of beliefs is increased by the presence of inferential connections between its component beliefs and increased in proportion to the number and strength of such connections.

(4) The coherence of a system of beliefs is diminished to the extent to which it is divided into subsystems of beliefs that are relatively unconnected to each other by inferential connections.

(5) The coherence of a system of beliefs is decreased in proportion to the presence of unexplained anomalies in the believed content of the system.[10]

Explanatory coherence is an intuitive way of understanding justification. At its root, explanatory reasoning aims to fit together a group of claims that otherwise appear disconnected. In the most simple case, we have a surprising claim, q, and we note that if p, then q *because p*. That is to say, we recognize that the truth of p would provide an explanation of the truth of q that is both simple and fits with our background information. In such a case, accepting p and q as well as the fact that q *because p* increases the coherence of our system of beliefs.

Humans are in the business of explaining things. We engage in explanatory reasoning all the time. As we noted earlier, we use explanatory reasoning to determine whom to trust—our friend or the rumormongers. We use explanatory reasoning to solve crimes, diagnose illnesses, and simply function in our daily lives. According to some psychologists, there is evidence from across cultures that explanatory reasoning is involved in "our activities from the most simple and mundane . . . to the most sophisticated and unusual."[11] In fact, there is reason to think that our explanatory reasoning begins at a very young age, perhaps infancy.[12] We employ explanatory reasoning so often and so routinely that if we don't stop to reflect carefully on how we are reasoning, we are apt to not even notice. This is how we manage our beliefs, and, when we do it well, the coherence of an explanatory system yields justification.

The Structure of Justification

Up to this point we have given three intuitive cases for coherentism and discussed the nature of coherence. It is widely recognized that coherence can provide a good reason for a subject to believe a claim. What is more controversial is whether there is a foundation for belief. In this section and the next, we give several powerful considerations that there are no foundations.

Coherentism is one of several views about the structure of justification. These views have been discussed since antiquity by Aristotle (384–322 BC) and Sextus Empiricus (AD second or third century), and likely many others.[13] The structure of justification is the structure of reasons for our beliefs, a structure made clearer by consideration of the *problem of the regress of reasons*. The regress problem begins with a natural question about a particular belief, say, your belief that *p*. The question is: why do you believe *p*? Or, put another way, what's your reason for believing *p*? You might respond that some other proposition, *q*, is your reason for *p*. So there's a path from *p* to *q* such that your right to believe *p* depends on your right to believe *q*. But, what's your reason for *q*? To this you might respond, *r*. But, what's your reason for *r*? It's easy to see that in addition to being annoying this series of questions could go on indefinitely.

The regress *problem* is that it seems that we can't have good reason to believe anything because the regress leads to skepticism. Here's why. Assume that your belief that *p* is justified. Since it is, you must have a good reason for believing *p*. Call this reason *q*. In order for *q* to be a good reason for believing *p*, *q* must itself be justified. This means that you must have a good reason for believing *q*—call this reason, *r*. But, *r* will have to be justified too, so you will have to have good reason for believing *r*. And so on. It seems at this point we are left with three possibilities: (a) the regress of reasons ends—there is some justified reason which doesn't itself require a good reason for accepting it, (b) the regress circles back on itself—so, *r* is your reason for *q*, *q* is your reason for *p*, and *p* is your reason for *r*, or (c) the regress never ends—it's infinite.

We'll use diagrams to make this clearer.[14] The arrows represent the path of reasons. An arrow from *p* to *q* indicates the reason for *p* is *q*. Thus, *p*'s justification depends on *q*.

Option A: The Regress Ends at a Foundation

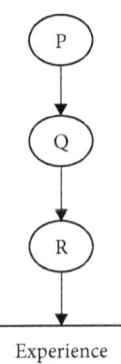

The graph labeled "Option A" shows that there is a path of reasons from beliefs (in circles) to experience (the rectangle). The belief that *p* is supported by the belief that *q*, which is supported by the belief that *r*, which itself is grounded in an experience. According to *foundationalism*, the regress of reasons ends with something that is not a belief and is capable of supporting a belief. The foundationalist claims that experience is an appropriate stopping point to the regress because (1) experience can support belief and (2) experience doesn't itself require support.

Option B: The Regress of Reasons Circles on Itself

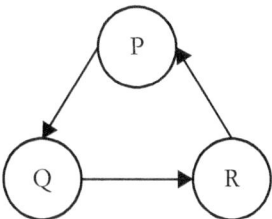

Option B illustrates a chain of reasons in which each claim depends on the next. The belief that *p* is supported by the belief that *q* which is supported by the belief that *r*, and this belief is supported by the belief that *p*. Aristotle noted that, although some philosophers have endorsed such reasoning, it is inadequate because it would prove anything and thus fail to distinguish between claims we have good reasons for and claims we do not have good reasons for.

Option C: The Regress of Reasons is Endless

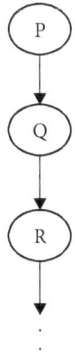

In Option C ". . ." indicates that the regress of reasons goes on forever; every proposition is supported by another without end. On this option, there is no foundation and every claim is defended by a distinct claim.

The skeptic claims the regress of reasons leads to skepticism. Against foundations, the skeptic argues that any reason that supports another must itself be supported and thus stopping the regress with unsupported experience is not adequate because justification rests on an unsupported posit. Against circles, the skeptic argues that p can't be part of the chain of reasons that justify p. Against an infinite regress, the skeptic argues that there's never any justification to get started—it's like saying that the next person in line will pay the dinner bill; if the line of customers is infinitely long the restaurant will never get paid! So, the skeptic claims that our initial assumption that your belief that p is justified must be false. But this problem afflicts all of your purportedly justified beliefs. Hence, the skeptic claims, none of your beliefs are justified!

Coherentism offers an elegant response to the regress of reasons. All three options, (a) foundation, (b) circle, and (c) endless regress, assume that the relation of support proceeds in a straight line from one proposition to another. In other words, the regress of reasons rests on the unchallenged idea that when p is justified for you, it is because of your reason q which, in turn, is justified because of r, and so on. Coherentism denies this assumption. According to coherentism, your belief that p is justified because it fits well with everything else you believe. The skeptical response to the regress of reasons takes it for granted that justification must be *linear*, but the coherentist claims that it can be *holistic*.

Coherentism: There is No Regress at All

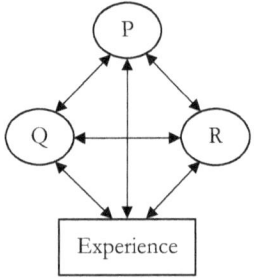

This graph offers a picture of perfect holistic coherence in which each node of beliefs and experience is supported by each other node. The thought here is that p is justified because p is part of a system of beliefs and experiences that fit together in such a way that the overall system is coherent.[15] The same is true of *q* and *r*. On this picture, there is no regress of reasons. Instead, justification occurs when there is sufficient coherence among the members of the set of beliefs and experiences. Let us underscore the fundamental point: *it is the entire system of beliefs and experiences bearing the appropriate relations of mutual support that ultimately gives us a reason for accepting* p (see BonJour's definition of the coherence relation).

A few additional remarks. The coherentist argues that ultimately justification isn't a matter of a chain of reasons at all; it's the coherence of the entire system that generates justification. In contrast, the foundationalist holds that we can stop the regress of reasons by anchoring the chain in experiences, which they claim provide reasons without requiring reasons for themselves.[16] The next section will show that there are serious problems for the foundationalist's reliance upon experiences to stop the regress of reasons.

Two Related Arguments for Coherentism

Two arguments, related to the regress of reasons, challenge the foundationalist's reliance on experience. Since they expose problems for coherentism's chief rival without posing similar problems for coherentism, these arguments provide additional support for coherentism.

The first argument is what we might call the *problem of experience*. This argument comes from the work of Wilfred Sellars (1912–1989).[17] Here's the argument:

1. Experience provides a subject with a reason for believing that *p* only if experience supports the belief that *p*.
2. Experience supports a belief that *p* only if experience has in part the content that *p*.
3. If experience has in part the content that *p* then the content of that experience can be either true or false.
4. If the content of the experience can be true or false, then either one has a reason to believe the content is true or accepting the truth of the content of the experience is arbitrary.
5. If one has a reason to believe the content of the experience is true, then the experience does not provide an end to the regress of reasons.

6. If accepting the truth of the content of the experience is arbitrary, then the experience does not provide an end to the regress of reasons.

7. Therefore, experiences do not provide an end to the regress of reasons.

The heart of the *problem of experience* is that foundationalists claim that the regress of reasons ends with experiences. Foundational beliefs are justified directly by experiences. However, the *problem of experience* makes a strong case for thinking that the experiences themselves either require reasons in order to provide justification for beliefs or relying on them to stop the regress is picking an arbitrary stopping point. Either way foundationalism seems to be in serious trouble.

This is not a problem shared by coherentism. According to coherentism, experiences can support beliefs and there is a good reason to trust experience. Our perspective with respect to beliefs based on experience includes a vast store of beliefs about the correctness of experiential beliefs. Nevertheless, coherentism doesn't commit to the idea that an experience can justify beliefs on its own. As a result, coherentism doesn't allow that experience can stop the regress of reasons, but as we've already noted, it doesn't need to stop the regress. The holistic perspective of coherentism doesn't allow the regress to get started in the first place.

The second argument exposing an advantage of coherentism over foundationalism, we might call the *problem of arbitrariness* as it rests on what Peter Klein (1940–) calls the *Principle of Avoiding Arbitrariness (PAA)*.[18] Here's the argument:

1. A belief that *p* is justified only if there is some good reason available to the subject for *p (PAA)*.

2. A foundational belief implies that there is no available reason for the subject for that belief.

3. Therefore, foundational beliefs are not justified.

The problem for the foundationalist is that whichever beliefs form the foundation, which is supposed to be the stopping point for the regress of reasons, appear to be arbitrary from the perspective of the subject with those beliefs. It is hard to see how foundationalism can both stop the regress of reasons and respect the *PAA*. Presumably, foundationalists must deny the *PAA*, but this is an intuitively plausible principle. As a result, the *problem of arbitrariness* is a significant problem for foundationalism.

Again, coherentism doesn't share this problem. Coherentists can accept the *PAA* while avoiding the regress of reasons. As we noted earlier, coherentists deny a key assumption of the regress of reasons (an assumption that foundationalists accept). Consequently, coherentism responds to the regress of reasons without incurring *the problem of arbitrariness*.

Conclusion

Coherentism is a plausible solution to the regress problem. It is vitally important that we reflect on the reasons for our beliefs and decide which beliefs are to be trusted and which are to be doubted or abandoned. This challenging task forces us to acknowledge the way in which beliefs and experiences fit together to support or challenge another belief. If we are honest with ourselves we all know that our beliefs are not fully coherent. There are tensions among our beliefs that we hope to work out. Moreover, we all know that there are many important areas that we want to have true beliefs about. According to coherentism, we ought to continue to inquire, aiming for the goal of a complete and coherent body of beliefs about matters of vital interest. As we bring our beliefs into coherence and expand our beliefs on important matters, we aim to achieve a deep human goal: understanding.[19]

Notes

1. For readers unfamiliar with the "magic" eight ball, these are plastic balls made to look like an eight ball from a billiard set. There is a small clear viewing space in the eight ball. Inside of the eight ball is an object, which is suspended in water, with various things written on it such as "yes, definitely," "outcome uncertain," "don't count on it," and so on. The way the "magic" eight ball works is that you ask it a question and give it a shake, then you read the answer to your question.
2. See D. Hume, *A Treatise of Human Nature*, ed. L. A. Selby-Bigge, 2nd ed. revised by P. H. Nidditch (Oxford: Clarendon Press, 1975/1739–1740), 1.4.1.
3. A key problem for Descartes is known as the *Cartesian Circle*. Descartes proposed that any belief that is not clearly and distinctly perceived is doubtable, and a belief that is clearly and distinctly perceived to be true is true. But Descartes wondered whether the criterion of clear and distinct perception was itself clear and distinct. If not, then it's not a good criterion for evaluating beliefs. But if it is, then it appears to support itself. Descartes actually thought that one could be deceived about whether something was clearly and distinctly perceived. So, it's far from clear how Descartes's clear and distinct rule could do the work that he needs for his project of finding a secure foundation. For more on the *Cartesian Circle*, see J. Van

Cleve, "Foundationalism, Epistemic Principles, and the Cartesian Circle," *Philosophical Review* 88, no. 1 (1979): 55–91.

4 See O. Neurath, "Protocol Sentences," in *Philosophical Papers 1913–1946*, eds. R. S. Cohen and M. Neurath (Dordrecht: Reidel, 1983/1932).

5 Of course, not everyone accepts this sort of connection between coherence and likelihood of truth. See E. J. Olsson E. J., *Against Coherence: Truth, Probability, and Justification* (Oxford: Oxford University Press, 2005). But for a compelling response in support of coherentism see also M. Huemer, "Does Probability Theory Refute Coherentism?" *Journal of Philosophy* 108, no. 1 (2011): 35–54.

6 B. Blanshard, *The Nature of Thought* (London: Allen & Unwin, 1939), 264.

7 A. C. Ewing, *Idealism: A Critical Survey* (London: Methuen, 1934).

8 C. I. Lewis, *An Analysis of Knowledge and Valuation* (LaSalle: Open Court, 1946), 338.

9 See chapter 5 of K. McCain, *The Nature of Scientific Knowledge: An Explanatory Approach* (Switzerland: Springer, 2016) for an accessible discussion of some of the problems plaguing these early approaches to coherence.

10 L. BonJour, *The Structure of Empirical Knowledge* (Cambridge, MA: Harvard University Press, 1985), 95–99. For recent defenses of explanatory approaches to justification that are similar to, but importantly different from, BonJour's see K. McCain, *Evidentialism and Epistemic Justification* (New York: Routledge, 2014); and T. Poston, *Reason and Explanation: A Defense of Explanatory Coherentism* (New York: Palgrave Macmillan, 2014).

11 R. A. Wilson and F. C. Keil, "The Shadows and Shallows of Explanation," in *Explanation and Cognition*, eds. F. C. Keil and R. A. Wilson (Cambridge, MA: MIT Press, 2000), 87.

12 See W. F. Brewer, C. A. Chinn, and A. Samarapungavan, "Explanation in Scientists and Children," in *Explanation and Cognition*, 279–98; and F. C. Keil and R. A. Wilson, "Explaining explanation," in *Explanation and Cognition*, 1–18. T. Poston (*Reason and Explanation*, 74–76) argues that the concept *because* is a primitive concept and one that occurs very early in cognitive development.

13 See Aristotle's *Posteriori Analytics* I.2; and Sextus Empiricus's *Outlines of Skepticism* Book I.xv.

14 For more detailed graphical depictions of coherentism and other views of the structure of justification, see S. Berker, "Coherentism via Graphs," *Philosophical Issues* 25 (2015): 322–52.

15 A common misunderstanding concerning coherentism is that only coherence among beliefs matters. Coherentism isn't restricted in this way, however. Although they don't justify beliefs on their own, experiences are an integral part of the best explanatory system. For a thorough discussion of this point, see J. Kvanvig and W. Riggs, "Can a Coherence Theory Appeal to Appearance States?" *Philosophical Studies* 67, no. 3 (1992): 197–217.

16 The coherentist distinguishes local from global justification. On a local level—that is, in a specific context—justification is like the foundationalist

says but with justification ending in a contextually agreed upon stopping point. But on a global level, foundationalism is wrong.

17 See in particular W. Sellars, "Empiricism and the Philosophy of Mind," in *Science, Perception, and Reality* (Atascadero, CA: Ridgeview Publishing Co, 1963), 127–96. Sellars's argument is known as *The Sellarsian Dilemma*. For discussion and defense of this dilemma, see T. Poston, *Reason and Explanation,* Ch. 5.
18 See P. Klein, "Human Knowledge and the Infinite Regress of Reasons," *Philosophical Perspectives* 13 (1999): 297–325.
19 Thanks to Samuel Baker, Anne Jeffrey, Kevin Meeker, and Isaiah Poston for helpful comments on a previous draft.

RESPONSES

Response to Howard-Snyder

Kevin McCain and Ted Poston

Study Questions

1. What mistake do McCain and Poston think Howard-Snyder makes regarding the role of experience in justification?
2. How do McCain and Poston respond to Howard-Snyder's positive case for foundationalism?
3. Why do McCain and Poston think that Howard-Snyder's response to the problem of arbitrariness is inadequate?
4. What is the problem, according to McCain and Poston, with Howard-Snyder's analogy between experiences and other mental states like imagining and wondering?

Daniel Howard-Snyder's essay is admirably clear and helpful for getting a handle on some of the key issues concerning the structure of epistemic justification. In fact, we agree with one of Howard-Snyder's key points: experiences play a central role in justifying beliefs. However, we also disagree with him on several points.

How Should We Understand Coherentism and Foundationalism?

As we noted in our opening essay, coherentism is often mischaracterized. At its core, coherentism is the view that a belief's justification is justified by its coherence with some body of information. This information may be restricted to beliefs, but it may be understood to include beliefs and experiences. Howard-Snyder's initial description of a justified "basic" belief is one that "owes its justification to something other than (i) her other beliefs or (ii) any features of the relations between them" (p. 61). Given Howard-Snyder's conditions, if experience contributes at all to the justification of one's belief, that belief is basic. This is problematic because a belief that the liquid is acidic is not basic even though it is justified by the combination of an experience of the litmus paper turning red and a belief that if the paper turns red then the liquid is acidic. Moreover, it presupposes too narrow a view of coherentism because it entails that coherentism must hold that experiences play *no role whatsoever* in justifying one's beliefs. As we explained in our opening essay, this is a common, but mistaken, understanding of coherentism. Coherentists can, and should, claim that experiences play an important role in justifying one's beliefs. Recall, the basic idea of coherentism is that a belief that *p* is justified because *p* is part of a system of beliefs and experiences that fit together in such a way that the overall system is coherent.

The disagreement between coherentists and foundationalists doesn't come down to *whether* experiences play a role in justification, but *how* experiences contribute to the justification of beliefs. Coherentists claim that experiences contribute to the justification of belief only when they are part of a coherent system of other experiences and beliefs; foundationalists claim that an experience can justify belief *all by itself*. This is the real issue between coherentism and foundationalism, and it is the heart of our disagreement with Howard-Snyder. We'll now turn to explaining where we think Howard-Snyder's case for foundationalism falters.

Howard-Snyder's Support for Foundationalism

Howard-Snyder begins his positive case for foundationalism by appealing to commonsense. More specifically, he presents examples of justified beliefs where it is intuitive that experiences play a role in justifying those beliefs. As he says, each of these cases is such that the subject "hold[s] the belief on the basis of something that makes the belief very likely to be true: experience" (p. 64). As a result, Howard-Snyder takes these cases to provide clear support for foundationalism.

This isn't correct, though. The cases that Howard-Snyder presents illustrate the necessity of experience for the justification of certain beliefs, but they don't show that experience, all on its own, is sufficient for justification. His first example mentions his justified belief that he feels achy and hungry. He rightly notes that his experiences of feeling achy and hungry play a central role in justifying this belief. The misstep though is to infer that these experiences do all of the justifying work. It isn't just the experiences that justify Howard-Snyder's belief—he also relies on background information (other beliefs and experiences that he has). For instance, at a minimum, Howard-Snyder relies on his beliefs about what it feels like to be achy and hungry. After all, if Howard-Snyder didn't already believe that *this* is what achy feels like and *that* is what it feels like to be hungry, he wouldn't be in a position to identify the feelings he currently experiences as "achy and hungry experiences." Without these background beliefs, Howard-Snyder would have no reason to believe that his present experiences are of being achy and hungry rather than, say, itchy and satisfied. Similar points apply to Howard-Snyder's other examples. As a result, although these examples help make it clear that experience plays an important role in justifying beliefs, they fail to demonstrate that experiences can justify beliefs on their own. Hence, they provide no reason to accept foundationalism over coherentism. In fact, when we think carefully about the examples, they provide reason to accept coherentism because we see that experiences justify only when combined with background information (i.e., experiences justify only when they are part of a coherent system of beliefs and experiences).[1]

The other component of Howard-Snyder's positive case for foundationalism involves arguing that foundationalism solves the regress problem. We pointed out in our opening essay that the "solution" foundationalism offers to the regress problem is problematic because of the *problem of arbitrariness* and the *problem of experience* (Howard-Snyder treats both of these problems as part of the "Sellarsian dilemma"). Instead of repeating our previous discussion here we'll turn our attention to critiquing Howard-Snyder's attempts to avoid these problems.

The Problem of Arbitrariness

Howard-Snyder's response to the arbitrariness problem boils down to the idea that experiences can make the truth of the relevant belief likely because of a "matching" between the experience and the belief. He offers two suggestions for what this matching might be. First, Howard-Snyder considers that foundationalists might claim that there is a "lawlike connection" between certain experiences and beliefs. As a result of this lawlike connection, he maintains that such an experience could make the appropriate belief "very likely to be true" (p. 68). Second, Howard-Snyder proposes that foundationalists may go with the idea that experiences represent content "in a way *analogous* to the way in which a photo represents a scene or a map represents a terrain" (p. 68). He suggests that just like maps may match terrains, experiences may match certain beliefs, and this match allows the former to justify the latter.

Both ideas are interesting, but neither solves the basic problem. The flaw in both instances is that whether or not an experience matches a belief, a belief based on that experience is still arbitrary from one's perspective unless one is aware of the matching. Suppose that you have a visual experience of a 7 × 9 dot matrix, your favorite number is 63, and you believe that this visual experience is of 63 dots. Even though the experience matches the belief, the experience does not directly justify the belief. You need to know that this experience is an experience of 63 dots. But the fact that you need this extra information means that the experience isn't justifying alone. Thus, it seems that either beliefs based on experience are arbitrary or beliefs based on experience are justified because of their fit with other beliefs and experiences. Either way, foundationalism fails to solve the regress problem.

The Problem of Experience

A major challenge for foundationalism arising from the problem of experience is to account for how an experience with content that matches belief can justify without requiring justification itself. That is, the foundationalist has to explain how an experience with content that can be accurate or inaccurate can justify without itself being justified. Howard-Snyder's response to this problem is straightforward. He argues that just because an experience has content it doesn't mean that the experience has to be justified. To support this claim he mentions several other mental states that have content but aren't the sort of things that can be justified. Among these mental states are imagining, wondering, and entertaining. These states aren't the kind of states that are justified or unjustified. He claims that experience is in the same boat as these mental states. So, Howard-Snyder maintains that experiences aren't the sort of things that can be justified.

Howard-Snyder is certainly correct that mental states like imagining, wondering, and entertaining aren't the sort of things that can be justified. Nevertheless, this doesn't solve the problem of experience. Any argument by analogy (such as Howard-Snyder's) is only as strong as the analogy upon which it relies. While experiences and these other mental states (imagining, wondering, and entertaining) are alike in some ways, they are different in one very important respect: experiences can provide justification for beliefs, but these other mental states can't. So, it's not merely that experience is like other mental states with content. Experience is a mental state with content that helps justify beliefs. This makes it very different from the other mental states that Howard-Snyder considers. Consequently, we can't conclude from the fact that these other mental states can't be justified/unjustified that experiences can't be.

Conclusion

Howard-Snyder's essay is a virtuous defense of foundationalism. Unfortunately, it's a fight that can't be won—justification is built upon the brick and mortar of experience and belief.

Note

1 For elaboration of this point see Ted Poston's, "Framework Account of Reasons" in his *Reason & Explanation: A Defense of Explanatory Coherentism* (New York: Palgrave Macmillan, 2014), 56–61.

Response to McCain and Poston

Daniel Howard-Snyder

Study Questions

1. Why does Howard-Snyder think that PAA does not pose a problem for basic beliefs?
2. What problem does Howard-Snyder raise for McCain and Poston regarding the notion of "availability" contained in PAA and EC?
3. What is the "truth-conduciveness conception" of justification? What problem does Howard-Snyder raise for EC-minus on this view of justification?
4. What is the "responsibility conception" of justification? What problem does Howard-Snyder raise for EC-minus on this view of justification?

McCain and Poston endorse (a modified version of) Peter Klein's PAA, namely this:

> (PAA) S's belief that p is justified only because there is some good reason available to S for p.

McCain and Poston (MCP) also endorse *Explanatory Coherentism*, according to which

> (EC) S's belief that p is justified because and only because p is a member of an explanatorily coherent set of propositions that are, together, the objects of all of S's beliefs and experiences, and that set is available to S.

What should we make of these two principles?

Two Problems

An Obstacle to Basic Beliefs?

First, let's note that MCP assert that PAA poses a difficulty for the idea that there are some basic beliefs. That's because, by their lights, you can't have a good reason available to you for p if you have a basic belief that p. This is false. The good reason available to you might be an experience, under the appropriate conditions. Moreover, even if the good reason available to you is, for example, the proposition that the experience is a reliable indicator of the truth of your belief that p, and even if you believe that proposition, your belief that p might still be basic since you might base your belief that p on the experience and not on your belief that the experience is a reliable indicator of the truth of your belief that p.[1]

A Problem for "Availability"

Second, notice that both principles speak of something being *available* to S. What does that involve? As Klein makes tolerably clear, what it is for a good reason to be available to S is for S to be in position to become aware of it and its goodness. Likewise, then, what it is for an explanatorily coherent set of propositions to be available to S is for S to be in a position to become aware of the set and its explanatory coherence.

And there lies trouble. No human being is in a position to become aware of the set of propositions that are the objects of *all* of their beliefs and experiences (at a given time); moreover, no human being is in a position to become aware of the explanatory coherence of that set of propositions (at that time). So MCP must relinquish either PAA or EC—unless they wish to embrace epistemic nihilism. Alternatively, they might relinquish the availability constraint. That's what I recommend.

More Problems for EC

So, then, let's focus on EC absent the availability constraint:

> (EC-minus) S's belief that p is justified because, and only because, p is a member of an explanatorily coherent set of propositions that are, together, the objects of all of S's beliefs and experiences.

Now recall from my initial essay that the relevant sort of justification in question is *epistemic* justification. Epistemologists think of epistemic justification in two broad ways. First, for a belief of a person to be epistemically justified is for it to be held in a truth-conducive fashion—that is, held in such a way that, by virtue of holding it in that way, the belief is likely to be true. Call this *the truth-conduciveness conception* of epistemic justification. Second, for a belief of a person to be epistemically justified is for it to be held responsibly—held in such a way that, by virtue of holding it in that way, the person does not violate any epistemic obligations. Call this *the responsibility conception* of epistemic justification. Let's consider EC-minus in light of each of these conceptions.

Truth-Conduciveness

Is it true that—*because* (and so *if*) the proposition p that S believes is a member of an explanatorily coherent set of propositions that are, together, the objects of all of S's beliefs and experiences—S holds the belief that p in such a way that p is likely to be true? Put the question another way: Is it true that *mere* "coherence among our beliefs and experiences can provide an excellent reason to think our beliefs are true?" (p. 76). A third way: Is it true that, *all by itself*, "the coherence of an explanatory system yields justification" (p. 77) where justification is understood as truth-conduciveness? I suspect not. Let me explain.

Imagine the propositional contents of the beliefs and experiences of some fictional character, say, Bilbo Baggins, at a particular time in the middle of *The Hobbit*. In the world of the story, that middle set of contents followed another set of contents that followed another set of contents and so on back to Bilbo's initial set of contents. Also, in the world of the story, that middle set of contents preceded another set of contents that preceded another set of contents and so on all the way to Bilbo's last set of contents (supposing there was a last). So we might well imagine Bilbo's *complete* set of contents, the series of momentary sets of contents successively laid out, from start to finish, changing over time as Bilbo's life unfolds, including the contents that weren't expressed in the telling of *The Hobbit*. Something similar can be imagined about nearly every character in just about any piece of fiction that ever has been written or ever will be written. Indeed, something similar can be said about the characters in the infinitely many merely possible never-to-be-written pieces of fiction. In each case, we might well imagine a character's complete set of contents in the way we imagined Bilbo's. Now let's imagine *your* complete set of contents. Fortunately, that series of momentary sets of contents has yet to be completed, but we can idealize away from that happy fact and imagine it anyway.

Notice three things about this infinity of complete sets of contents. First, notice that they can't all be true. Indeed, notice that if yours approximates the truth, then all the others are thoroughly false—including Bilbo's and Harry Potter's. And if Bilbo's approximates the truth, then all the others are thoroughly false—including yours and Harry Potter's. And if Harry Potter's approximates the truth, then all the others are thoroughly false—including yours and Bilbo's. And so on. Second, notice that each of these complete sets of contents is, for the most part, as explanatorily coherent as yours, at least for long stretches of time. Third, imagine some supermind popping into existence and, before viewing the world for itself, taking in before its mind's eye each of these infinitely many complete sets of contents, and their enviable explanatory coherence, all in one fell swoop. Notice that despite this information and despite its powers, our supermind would be unable to tell what world it was in. The supermind might think to itself: "Am I in Bilbo's world? Or Harry Potter's? Or _____ [fill in the blank with your name]?" And it would say the same thing about each of the other infinitely many worlds associated with each explanatorily coherent complete set of contents that it held before its mind's eye.

The moral of this imaginative exercise is clear. It is obviously false that *mere* explanatory coherence can provide an excellent reason for you to think your beliefs are true. It is obviously false that *all by itself* the coherence of an explanatory system yields justification, where justification is understood as truth-conduciveness.

Responsibility

Now let's turn to the second way of thinking about epistemic justification. Is it true that—*because* (and so *if*) the proposition p that S believes is a member of an explanatorily coherent set of propositions that are, together, the objects of all of S's beliefs and experiences—S holds the belief that p in such a way that S violates no epistemic obligations? Well, that depends on what other propositions S believes. Suppose that S wisely believes that mere explanatory coherence provides absolutely *no* reason to think that *any* of S's beliefs are true—as I think S should. Then, if S has their wits about them, S will also think that, *all by itself*, the fact that p is a member of an explanatorily coherent set of propositions is a lousy reason to think that p is true. Given that S has no other basis for believing p, then, if S goes ahead and believes p anyway, S will violate the epistemic obligation: *Don't believe something when, by your own lights, all you've got to go on to believe it is a lousy reason to think that it is true*. Therefore, it is false that the coherence of an explanatory system yields justification, where justification is understood as responsibility.

I suspect, therefore, that EC-minus is false. And what goes for EC-minus goes for any other version of coherentism. Simply because the content of a system of beliefs and experiences is structured in an explanatorily coherent way, it does not follow that some belief whose content is a member of that system can enjoy epistemic justification.

Note

1 For more on Klein's PAA, see D. Howard-Snyder and E. J. Coffman, "Three Arguments Against Foundationalism: Arbitrariness, Epistemic Regress, and Existential Support," *Canadian Journal of Philosophy* 36 (2006): 535–64 (available online).

Questions for Reflection

1. Who provides the more satisfying solution to the regress problem—the foundationalist or the coherentist? Why?

2. How strong is the Sellarsian Dilemma? Does it undermine foundationalism or not? Why?

3. Is there a way, contrary to Howard-Snyder's claim, for an explanatorily coherent system to yield epistemic justification? If so, how?

3

Must the Grounds of Knowledge Be Accessible to the Knower?

The Grounds of Knowledge Must Be Accessible

Ali Hasan

Study Questions

1. How does Hasan characterize the internalist/externalist debate?

2. How does Hasan define internalism and externalism? How does the Gettier Problem impact the debate between these views?

3. What does Hasan mean by "good grounds," "access," and "based on" in his definition of doxastic justification? How does his view contrast with that of reliabilism?

4. What are the two initial cases Hasan presents in defense of internalism? How do they support internalism? Why do they pose a difficulty for reliabilism?

5. How might the reliabilist amend his view to accommodate the evil demon case? Why does Hasan find this unsatisfactory?

6. What other cases does Hasan present to bolster his claim that external conditions are necessary for justification?

7. How does Hasan defend the claim that external conditions are not sufficient for justification?

8. What alternative response might the reliabilist give to the evil demon and fairy cases? How does Hasan reply to this response?

Knowledge and Justified True Belief

I believe that a man named René Descartes wrote the *Meditations on First Philosophy*. Knowledge requires belief: if I do not believe that Descartes is the author of the *Meditations*, I do not know it. Knowledge also requires *truth*: if it turns out that Descartes never wrote the *Meditations*, I might *think* I know that Descartes wrote the *Meditations*, but I would not, in fact, know this.

Having a true belief is not, however, sufficient for knowledge. I might believe that Descartes is the author of the *Meditations* because I heard it from Harry, despite the fact that trustworthy sources have told me that Harry is a pathological liar. My belief, though true, would not be knowledge. Or suppose I believe that there is an even number of stars in our galaxy, but only because I like even numbers and, irrationally, think that the universe is constructed to my liking. Or I might believe it for no reason at all—it might simply be the result of a brain malfunction or of getting hit on the head. Even if this belief is true, it does not count as knowledge. So, true belief is not sufficient for knowledge.

What else does knowledge require? As some epistemologists put it, the above beliefs are "unjustified" or "unwarranted." It is difficult to deny that, intuitively, there is some positive property that is missing in my initial examples and others. Beliefs that result from mere wishful thinking, fear, biases, or hasty generalization are intuitively not justified, not warranted, not well-founded, or not epistemically proper, even if they happen to be true. Moreover, beliefs based on careful observation and good reasoning are intuitively justified, warranted, well-founded, or proper, even if they happen to be false. There seems to be some positive property (whether we call it "justification" or something else) that the former beliefs lack and the latter beliefs have, that is necessary for knowledge. However, these terms seem to be little more than placeholders for whatever is missing from such cases. Indeed, the term "warrant" is sometimes used in epistemology to stand for whatever condition(s) must be satisfied in order for a true belief to count as knowledge. We need a more informative and illuminating account.

Here's a start. We just saw that the mere truth or falsity of a belief does not determine whether the belief has or lacks the positive property. But we should not conclude from this that justification has nothing to do with truth. Indeed, the reason the initial cases of true belief mentioned earlier do not count as knowledge is that such beliefs are not related, in the right sort of way, to the truth. This is only a start, though, for the interesting question is *what counts as the "right sort of way."* Nevertheless, it helps us frame the debate between the internalist and the externalist. Let us take the *justification* of a belief to stand for this property that a belief must have for it to count as knowledge, a property involving some appropriate relation to the truth of one's belief. We can now understand the internalist/externalist debate as a disagreement about what this property requires. Whether epistemologists actually use the term "justification" or some other term to refer to this sort of property does not matter.

Roughly, according to the *internalist*, having a justified belief requires that something relevant to the truth, or probable truth, of one's belief must be internal to, or accessible from, the subject's first-person perspective. More specifically, the subject must have first-person access to good grounds or evidence for belief—that is, reasons to think that the belief is (probably) true. A natural way to think of the internalist view is to say that it identifies justification with *rationality*. Intuitively, a belief of mine is rational only if I have some good reason to think it is true, and I can have such a reason only if I have some sort of internal access to it. The internalist claims that the above beliefs are not justified because they are not rational. My belief that Descartes wrote the *Meditations* is based on bad grounds, the testimony of someone I have good reasons not to trust; my belief that there is an even number of stars is based on another irrational belief, or has no basis at all (because it is due to a brain malfunction).

For *the externalist*, something about the belief or the way it is formed must be appropriately related to the truth for the belief to be justified. There must be some non-accidental connection—some lawful, causal, or other probabilistic connection—to the truth of what one believes. But the subject need not have first-person access to grounds to think there is such a connection.[1] Perhaps the subject has access to good grounds for belief in some cases, but, says the externalist, it is not strictly and always *needed* for justification or knowledge. In this paper, I defend a form of internalism.[2]

The internalist-externalist controversy is complicated by the *Gettier problem*. I would like to briefly discuss this problem before clarifying and defending my view. Edmund Gettier argued quite persuasively that justified true belief is not sufficient for knowledge.[3] To use one of Gettier's own examples—I might be justified in believing that Jones owns a Ford, which would also justify me in believing something this entails: that either Jones owns a Ford or Brown is in Barcelona. But suppose, despite my having excellent reasons to believe that Jones owns a Ford, he actually doesn't, and it just so happens that Brown is in Barcelona. The belief would be a justified true belief, but not knowledge. Or consider a different example: I believe, on the basis of looking at my watch, that it is 10:00 p.m. I have very good reasons to trust it. But my watch is just stuck and has been stuck for 24 hours without me noticing. I have a justified true belief, but not knowledge.[4] Thus, even if knowledge requires justified true belief, these conditions are not sufficient for knowledge.

Where does this leave us with respect to the internalist-externalist debate? The internalist might say that knowledge still requires access to good reasons. The Gettier cases don't give us a reason to reject that, though they arguably do show that something more is required. For example, perhaps there needs to be some sort of non-accidental connection between one's evidence for the belief and its truth, a connection that is typically if not always inaccessible to the subject. It's important to see that internalists can and typically do accept that what we might call "external conditions" are necessary for knowledge. Let us define an *external condition* relative to the subject's belief that p as any condition that could fail to obtain even when the subject has access to good grounds for believing that p. The truth of one's belief is, at least typically, an external condition. The existence of a non-accidental connection between my reasons and the truth of my belief might also be an external condition. Contemporary internalists accept that some external conditions are necessary for knowledge, but they deny that external conditions are *sufficient* for knowledge. Alternatively, the internalist might accept a form of "infallibilism" about knowledge: knowledge requires a kind of absolute certainty; our justification must guarantee the truth of what we believe. I want to leave open what further condition might be required for knowledge, including whether knowledge requires some kind of certainty or infallibility. My focus will be on whether or not we can dispense with the requirement of access to reasons.

The externalist claims that knowledge does not require belief based on internally accessible grounds. We should *replace* the internalist requirement with some strong, objective connection to the truth or probability of the belief. If there is a solution to the Gettier problem, it lies in finding the right combination of external conditions to avoid further counterexamples. However, coming up with the right conditions remains a significant challenge, even for the externalist. And if externalists come up with "Gettier-proof" conditions, internalists can build these external conditions into the account of knowledge, but still insist on an internalist account of epistemic justification. The Gettier problem thus seems to have little to do with the internalist-externalist debate.[5]

Internalism

According to the sort of internalist account I am defending here, knowledge requires justified belief, where a belief that p is justified if and only if the subject (a) has good, accessible grounds or evidence for believing that p, (b) believes that p on the basis of these grounds, and (c) does not have "defeaters," that is, good grounds to think p is false, or that the source of the belief is unreliable.

By "good grounds" for believing that p, I mean good reasons to believe that p, where the reasons are *epistemic* reasons rather than *prudential or moral* reasons—roughly, reasons relevant to the *truth* of one's belief that *p* rather than reasons relevant to the personal or moral goodness of believing that *p*.[6] For example, if a lawyer's believing that his client is innocent will improve his ability to defend him in court, that may give the lawyer a reason to believe that he is innocent, but it's not an *epistemic reason*, or *epistemic justification*, for the belief.[7] It is not *grounds* or *evidence* for belief, even if it provides some other sort of reason or justification to believe.

What do I mean by "access"? This is difficult to spell out precisely. For now I will just add that the relevant sort of access involves either *an actual* or *a potential awareness*. One need not actually access or be aware of evidence *E* at some time in order to be justified in believing that *p* on the basis of *E* at that time, but *E* must in some sense be accessible to the subject by reflection alone. For example, I take it that you know or are at least justified in believing that Descartes wrote the *Meditations*. But you rarely, if ever, turn your attention to your reasons for believing this. Intuitively, your belief could still be justified so long as you have good grounds or evidence to believe that Descartes wrote the *Meditations*, grounds that you can access, and whose relevance to this belief you can appreciate.

Justified belief is belief that is *based on* good grounds. It is not enough that I *have* good grounds to believe that some proposition *p* is true; I must also *base* my belief on good grounds. Suppose I believe that Descartes wrote the *Meditations*, and I actually have access to good evidence for this, but I believe it only because I heard this from Harry, despite knowing that he is a pathological liar. Intuitively, my belief is not justified, even though it easily *could* be. As some epistemologists put it, I *have justification to believe* this proposition—I have "propositional justification"—but I do not have a *justified belief* in the proposition—I do not have "doxastic justification."

The externalist claims that certain external conditions are necessary and sufficient for justification. Various externalist accounts have been proposed, but it will help to focus on a popular form of externalism for purposes of illustration: process-reliabilism.[8] Very roughly, *reliabilism* says that a belief is epistemically justified *only if* it is produced by a type of process that is *reliable*, in the sense that it has a tendency to produce true beliefs more often than false ones, or in the sense that "in the long run" most beliefs produced by this type of process are true. Reliabilists standardly add something like a "no defeaters" condition to avoid obvious counterexamples (in my own account given earlier, it's condition (c)): a belief is epistemically justified *if and only if* it is produced by a reliable process, and the subject has no access to defeaters. For example, suppose that I look outside my window and I seem to see a unicorn. Let's stipulate that I really do see a genuine unicorn, and that my belief that this is a unicorn is produced by a highly reliable perceptual process. But suppose that I have excellent (though misleading) reasons to believe that there are no real unicorns. Or suppose that my doctor has warned me that my medication causes hallucinations in a small percentage of cases. I would surely not be justified in believing that this is a unicorn, despite the fact that I form the belief on the basis of a reliable perception.

Notice that the "no defeaters" condition is itself an external condition. It is one thing to require that I *not possess* reasons to think my belief is *false* or the source *untrustworthy*; it is quite another to require that I also *possess reasons* to think my belief is *true*. The internalist accepts the latter as a requirement for justification, while the externalist rejects it.

Defending Internalism

Why do I think internalism is true? Basically, because it is, upon reflection, intuitively correct. Part of the motivation for internalism has already been given earlier: many examples seem to show that true belief is not sufficient for knowledge, and that some positive epistemic property, which we called "epistemic justification," is also required. And, as we reflect on the possible cases, what seems to be missing from them is *rational* belief. Intuitively, in order for my belief to be rational, or for me to be rational in holding it, I must have good reasons to take the proposition to be true.

But this is, at best, an inconclusive defense of internalism, for one might claim that the problem in the examples discussed so far is not a lack of, or defect in, rationality, at least not in any sense of the term that requires access to good grounds. Rather, the problem is that these beliefs have no lawful, causal, or objective connection to the truth.

However, upon further reflection, we see that internalism yields intuitively correct classifications for various cases we can think about, cases that externalism, in contrast, has trouble with. I do not want to claim here that these examples constitute conclusive support for internalism, or that externalists cannot or have not given interesting and potentially plausible responses to them. However, when we consider such examples as a whole, we see that the motivation for internalism is both straightforward and powerful, and that a plausible treatment of such cases is a significant challenge to those who deny internalism. First, consider the following case:

Normal Perception: René is sitting by a fire, holding and reading from a book of philosophy, and has the corresponding experiences: he seems to be sitting, seems to see and feel the warmth of the fire, seems to see and feel the book in his hands, is reading such-and-such words, and so on. His perceptual and cognitive faculties are all in good, functioning order. René believes, on the basis of these experiences or appearances, that he is reading a book by the fire. (He is thus very much like you.)

From a commonsense standpoint, René is justified in his beliefs. He holds the sorts of ordinary beliefs that you do, and on a similar basis. It seems that externalists are able to account for the fact that René's beliefs are justified, for he satisfies the standard external conditions for justification: his beliefs are the result of perceptual and cognitive processes that are in good working order, and so the belief-forming processes are reliable. Internalists, too, are apparently able to account for the fact that René's beliefs are justified, for he seems to satisfy the internalist conditions: much like you, René has access to his perceptual states, to the visual sensations of the fire and the book, to the feeling of heat and the feeling of the book in his hands, and these provide strong reasons for his beliefs.

But now compare the following case:

Evil Demon: René has exactly the same experiences or apparent perceptions as in the Normal Perception case. He believes, on the basis of these experiences, that he is reading a book by the fire. But all René's perceptual beliefs are false, for he is the victim of a powerful and evil demon who produces misleading perceptual experiences in him. (He is thus "internally" exactly like the René of the Normal Perception case, and "internally" very much like you.)

René's belief that he is reading by the fire is surely just as justified in this case as in the first. It may help to put yourself in his situation, and imagine an undetectable switch from the Normal Perception case to the evil demon case: suppose that a powerful demon or alien has abducted you in your sleep and is now manipulating your brain directly, giving you the apparent perceptions you now have. Nothing would ever seem different from your own point of view, for the demon produces in your brain just the changes that are normally present when you wake up, have coffee, sit in a chair to read a book, and so on. And suppose that you suddenly wake up in the middle of reading this sentence or the next, and you seem to see a demon or alien before you, and the pod that he has kept you in. You are not justified *now* in believing you *were* reading a book; but surely, you *were* justified in believing it back when you were having those experiences.

The internalist can make good sense of our intuitions in this case: in the normal case, and initially in the evil demon case, you have access to good reasons to believe that you are reading by a fire, and you have no defeaters—no clear reasons to disbelieve or suspend belief about this. Then there occurs a significant change in the sorts of experiences you have access to, and so it is not surprising that there is a change in what you are and are not justified in believing at that point.

Skeptical concerns can, of course, be raised, even in ordinary or normal cases: as the challenge of responding to skeptical arguments reflects, it is difficult to explain why our reasons for our ordinary beliefs are as good as we initially or commonsensically take them to be. But to the extent that René's belief is justified in the Normal case, it is justified in the second case; to the extent that his justification is shaky or defeated in the one case, it is in the other. And the internalist can explain why: what René has access to in the two cases is the same.

The reliabilist is in a more difficult position. The external conditions that the reliabilist takes to be necessary and sufficient for justification are satisfied in the Normal Perception case but not in the evil demon case. René's belief that he is reading by the fire is the result of a reliable belief-forming process in the first case, but not the second. Reliabilism thus seems to imply that the belief is justified in the first case but not the second case, and this is counterintuitive. It may help once again to put yourself in René's position, and imagine that there is a transition from the Normal case to the demon case. Reliabilism seems to imply that you go from being justified in believing that you are reading by the fire to being unjustified, despite the fact that nothing at all changes from your own perspective. In fact, you could go from being justified to being unjustified in the middle of reading this sentence, if the demon suddenly decides to abduct you while continuing to manipulate your brain directly, causing in your brain just the states and processes normally caused by the continued activity of reading. Intuitively, your belief would be just as justified, even though it is no longer produced by a reliable belief-forming process.[9]

It might be tempting to amend the reliabilist view to accommodate the evil demon case in the following way: a belief is justified *if and only if* it is produced by a process that is reliable *in our world*, and the believer has no defeaters.[10] So, to find out if René's belief is justified in the evil demon case, we should ask whether it is produced by a process that is, in fact, reliable in our world. If it is, then we can treat René's belief in the hypothetical case as justified as well. However, there are two problems with this account. First, it seems we should allow for the possibility, in principle, that *our* world turns out to be a demon world. Perhaps the demon has been uninterested in deceiving us up until now. Our ordinary perceptual beliefs would go from being justified to being unjustified according to the account, and that is counterintuitive. Second, we surely want to allow for the possibility that some beliefs be justified even though they are formed by processes that do not exist, or are not reliable, in our world. Perhaps certain creatures could have existed whose belief-forming processes are nothing like the processes that are reliable in our world; we don't want to just rule out even the possibility that any such beliefs be justified!

Let us consider another pair of cases:

Reliable Testimony: Jude would like to go fishing. He believes, on the basis of Leila's testimony, that there are some largemouth bass in the neighborhood pond. Leila is generally very reliable when it comes to such things. Jude has no reasons to distrust Leila; in fact, he has very good reasons to trust her.

Unreliable Testimony: Jude would like to go fishing. He believes, on the basis of Leila's testimony, that there are some largemouth bass in the neighborhood pond. Jude has no reasons to distrust Leila; in fact, he has very good reasons to trust her. But Leila is actually not at all trustworthy when it comes to such things, or, indeed, much else. She likes to make things up and impress people, and is quite good at seamlessly weaving truths and lies, and picking her lies selectively so that they are hard to disprove. Only about half of what she says is true.

Intuitively, Jude is equally justified in the two cases. And once again, the internalist has a straightforward explanation: Jude has access to the same reasons for belief, and no access to defeaters. His first-person perspective on matters is the same in both cases. He may come to have some reason to distrust Leila's testimony, or lower his confidence in her trustworthiness, if he finds out that there are no largemouth bass in the pond. But absent defeaters, it seems he is justified in his belief.

Skeptical concerns can, of course, be raised with respect to our reliance on testimony. Perhaps there are skeptical arguments that seem to show that our reliance on testimony is on shaky ground, and that our epistemic reasons for trusting others' testimony are not as good as we might initially think. But to the extent that Jude's belief is justified in the Reliable Testimony case, it is justified in the Unreliable Testimony case; to the extent that Jude's reasons are shaky or too weak in the one case, they are in the other. Internalism thus makes good sense of the intuition that Jude is equally justified (or unjustified) in the two cases.

If, on the other hand, an external condition like reliability were necessary for justification, we would have to say that Jude's belief is unjustified in the second case. The reliabilist might attempt to avoid the problem by saying that testimony of this sort is a generally reliable way for Jude to form beliefs, even if *Leila's* testimony is not.[11] But we can imagine a more extreme case of unreliable testimony, where all the people Jude talks to are unreliable testifiers, but they conspire to keep Jude in the dark, much as Truman Burbank's family, friends, and neighbors (in the movie *The Truman Show*) manage (for a while) to keep him in the dark about the fact that he is the star of a popular TV show.

Intuitively, Jude's belief would be just as justified as in the Reliable Testimony case, despite not satisfying the external condition of reliability.

The cases discussed seem to undermine the claim that reliability (and similar external conditions) are *necessary* for justification, and they support the sufficiency of the internalist's proposed conditions.[12] Let's now consider a case that seems to show that external conditions are *not sufficient* for justification, and so supports the necessity of access to reasons.[13]

> **Wishful Thinking:** Some of Aria's beliefs are due to wishful thinking. For example, she believes that she will live to be over a hundred years old (she is presently forty), and has the belief only because she really wishes it were true. She has no reasons for or against the truth of the belief, and no reasons for or against the claim that her belief is produced by wishful thinking.

Aria is unjustified in her belief. For the internalist, the problem is that Aria's belief is not based on any good reason to think she will live that long. For the externalist, her belief is not the output of a reliable belief-forming process. But now consider this case:

> **Fairy:** As in the case discussed, Aria believes that she will live to be over a hundred years old, and has the belief only because she really wishes it were true. She has no reasons for or against the truth of the belief, and no reasons for or against the claim that her belief is produced by wishful thinking. Unbeknownst to her, however, there exists a powerful fairy intent on making Aria's wishes come true.

Intuitively, Aria's belief is not justified. We can imagine that her belief went from being unreliable to being reliable because the fairy took a liking to her, and decided to grant her wish by ensuring her longevity. But Aria's belief is unjustified nonetheless. So the satisfaction of external conditions, like reliability and the absence of defeaters, are not sufficient for justification. Internalists can explain why: Aria never had good reasons for her belief, and still doesn't.

The reliabilist might attempt to avoid the problem by saying that a belief is justified *if and only if* it is produced by a process that is reliable *in our world*, and the subject has no defeaters. Since wishful thinking is not reliable in our world, when we consider the hypothetical case we could say that this belief is not justified. But we have already critiqued this suggestion earlier in discussing the evil demon case.[14]

Finally, externalists might attempt to give a different response. They might claim that our intuitions in the evil demon and Fairy cases are misleading because we are confusing *responsibility or blame* with *epistemic justification*. In the evil demon case, René is *not to blame* for his beliefs; in the fairy case, Aria *is to blame* for believing on the basis of wishful thinking. But these beliefs are not epistemically justified.[15]

However, this still doesn't seem to get things right. Compare René's situation in the evil demon case with another demon victim, George, who is caused to have false beliefs directly, without having any perceptual experiences or cogent reasoning. We should not blame George for his beliefs—he doesn't have much, if any, control over them. Both René and George are blameless, and their beliefs are not based on reliable processes. But René is intuitively justified in his belief while George is not. Internalists would point out that René has, either within his perspective or accessible from it, good reasons to believe, while George does not. Once again, reflecting on these cases, we see that internalism—but not externalism—provides a plausible, intuitively correct account of epistemic justification.

Conclusion

Internalist and externalists tend to agree that knowledge requires what I have called "epistemically justified" belief, that is, belief that is appropriately related to the truth or probability of one's belief, but they disagree about what this relation to truth or probability involves. The internalist claims a belief is justified if and only if it is based on good, accessible grounds—that is, good reasons to think the belief true or probable—and the subject has no defeaters. The externalist claims that a belief is epistemically justified if and only if certain external conditions are satisfied. We focused on reliabilism for illustration, according to which a belief is justified if and only if it is produced by a reliable or truth-conducive belief-forming process, in the absence of defeaters; no condition of access to grounds is necessary. We found that when we reflect on a range of cases and ask whether the subjects are epistemically justified, internalism yields intuitively correct answers for those cases, while reliabilism and, arguably, other forms of externalism, yield some strongly counterintuitive results. We should therefore conclude that justified belief requires rational belief, belief based on good, accessible grounds.[16]

Notes

1. For a highly influential defense of a view of this sort, see Alvin Goldman's "What is Justified Belief?" in *Justification and Knowledge*, ed. George Pappas (Dordrecht, Holland: Reidel, 1979), 1–25.
2. I defend a form of "access internalism" according to which justification depends essentially on the reasons one has access to. It should be distinguished from "mentalism" or "internal state internalism," according to which one's justification depends only on what is mental or inside the mind (e.g., experiences and other mental states, and relations between these

states). I do not have space here to discuss mentalism and its relation to access internalism.

3   Edmund Gettier, "Is Justified True Belief Knowledge?" *Analysis* 23, no. 6 (1963): 121–23.

4   Bertrand Russell gave a similar example to show that true belief is not sufficient for knowledge, though it works just as well to show that justified true belief is not sufficient for knowledge. See his *Human Knowledge: Its Scope and Limits* (New York: Simon and Schuster, 1978), 70.

5   Linda Zagzebski has argued that the Gettier problem is inescapable for any account, whether internalist or externalist, so long as the account accepts the assumption that the justification required for knowledge does not guarantee truth (see her "The Inescapability of Gettier Problems," *Philosophical Quarterly* 44, no. 174 [1994]: 65–73). Some might take this to be a good reason to accept the analysis just discussed in the text, according to which knowledge is (roughly) conclusively or infallibly justified belief. Others might take the lesson to be that we should give up and take knowledge to be a fundamental, unanalyzable concept. I do not have space to discuss these views further here.

6   This isn't quite right. Suppose believing you will get well makes it likely that you will get well. Believing you will get well would then be a reason relevant to the likelihood of the belief's being true, but it's still not an epistemic reason. We may need to add some condition to the effect that the subject is able to grasp or appreciate the relevance of the reason to the truth.

7   This example is from Stewart Cohen's "Justification and Truth," *Philosophical Studies* 46, no. 3 (1984): 279–95.

8   See A. Goldman, *Justification and Knowledge,* for a defense of reliabilism.

9   S. Cohen raises this "new evil demon problem" for externalism in his "Justification and Truth."

10 Goldman (*Justification and Knowledge*) considers this revision to the view, though as a response to a different sort of case—the fairy case—that we'll discuss below. He anticipates and attempts to address the first of the objections raised here, but not the second.

11 This raises difficult questions for the reliabilist: at what level of generality should we think of the processes that are responsible for the belief? Which is the relevant process type: Leila's testimony regarding fish? Leila's testimony in general? The testimony of people in my neighborhood? The testimony of people in general? But let's assume that this "generality problem" can be solved somehow. For more on this, see Earl Conee and Richard Feldman's, "The generality problem for reliabilism," *Philosophical Studies* 89, no. 1 (1998): 1–29.

12 As we have seen, the "no defeaters" condition is an external condition that internalists and externalists accept.

13 For other counterexamples to the sufficiency of external conditions for justification, see Laurence BonJour, "Externalist Theories of Empirical Knowledge," *Midwest Studies in Philosophy* 5, no. 1 (1980): 53–73.

14 A. Goldman (*Justification and Knowledge*) tentatively suggests this sort of revision to the view. See related note 10 above.

15 For a response of this sort, see Alvin Goldman, "Strong and Weak Justification," in *Philosophical Perspectives 2: Epistemology*, ed. James Tomberlin (Atascadero, CA: Ridgeview Publishing, 1988), 51–71.

16 I am grateful to Richard Fumerton and Steve Cowan for helpful comments on an earlier draft.

The Grounds of Knowledge Need Not Be Accessible

Stephen Hetherington

Study Questions

1. What conception of knowledge does Hetherington find in Plato's *Meno* and which is challenged by Gettier? What notion of evidence is usually presupposed in this conception of knowledge?

2. What are the two forms of internalism? What two claims are made by the first form?

3. What is Hetherington's generic characterization if externalism? What is the less generic form that he presents?

4. What is BonJour's thought experiment presented in defense of internalism? What is the thought experiment supposed to show?

5. Why does Hetherington think that internalism is too demanding? What is the dilemma apparently facing internalism?

6. What is the "improved" version of internalism that Hetherington discusses? Why does he think that this "improvement" should lead us to adopt externalism?

7. How does Hetherington respond to the internalist requirement that one *know that one knows*?

Ancient Intimations of Modern Epistemic Internalism

Prepare for a journey through time and space, to ancient Greece. We will arrive there around 400 BCE to hear a famous conversation between the philosopher Socrates and a young man, Meno.

Then again, we could read the conversation in Plato's dialogue *Meno*. There, we find Socrates and Meno pondering a journey to Larissa. What (they wonder) is needed for traveling successfully to a destination? Does one need *knowledge*—such as of the correct path to follow? Yes, argued Socrates: otherwise, one would be wandering—perhaps not aimlessly, but at least randomly.

Meno was asking whether it is enough to have a *belief* (an opinion) as to the correct path, if the belief is *true* (accurate). Socrates replied:

> True opinions, as long as they remain, are a fine thing and all they do is good, but they are not willing to remain long, and they escape from a man's mind, so that they are not worth much until one ties them down by (giving) an account of the reason why. And that, Meno my friend, is recollection, as we previously agreed. After they are tied down, in the first place they become knowledge, and then they remain in place. That is why knowledge is prized higher than correct opinion, and knowledge differs from correct opinion in being tied down.[1]

So, according to Socrates, knowing includes having "an account of the reason why." Contemporary philosophers interpret him as saying that knowing includes having helpful *evidence*. We are thus presented with this proposed conception of knowledge:

> A belief's being knowledge includes its being true (accurate) and well supported by evidence.

This is what philosophers call a *justified true belief* conception of knowledge. Since 1963 they have devoted much energy to assessing the merits of that form of conception. Edmund Gettier famously argued that a belief's being true and justified is insufficient for its being knowledge.[2] Many have agreed with him. Few, though, have doubted that a belief's being true and justified is *needed* for its being knowledge. If we are to understand knowledge, therefore, we must understand *at least* its apparently required justification component.

The justification in question is *epistemic* justification. The evidence is for the belief's supposed *truth* (rather than for its being a practical belief to have). Truth-directed justification is said to be needed if a true belief is to be knowledge. (The word "epistemic" reflects this. The ancient Greek word for knowledge is *epistēmē*.) Socrates would have said that *evidence* plays this role.

So, what *is* evidence? Socrates would also have said—as do most contemporary philosophers—that it is somehow within the would-be knower's thinking. Either she is *aware* of the evidence, or she *can easily* be aware of it. (She might be attending to something else, yet could easily bring the evidence to her consciousness.) The evidence is thought of as giving the person a *rationally based reason* for her to have the belief. She has what epistemologists call epistemically *internalist* justification for the belief.

Epistemic internalists say that this is the only way to have an epistemically justified belief. Supposedly, epistemic internalism can take either of two general forms: *awareness* (or *accessibility*) internalism and *mentalism*. This chapter will focus on the former. (Later, I will explain why mentalism may be set aside as not being true to internalism's motivating spirit.) Internalism says that a belief is epistemically justified if the believer has in mind, or has easily available to her mind, some good evidence or reason. Such evidence is often called the belief's (epistemic) *ground*. Then epistemic internalism makes two main sorts of claim:

(1) Any justified belief is grounded in good evidence or reason, either present to the believer's awareness or easily able to be so.

(2) The belief's being grounded in that way is something of which the believer is, or could easily be, aware.

Introducing Epistemic Externalism

The previous section portrays modern epistemic internalism as having ancient roots, with its underlying thinking having long been with us. Is such thinking also correct? Or should we favor epistemic *externalism*?

Epistemic externalism generalizes (1), while denying (2).

The Generalization. When a belief is justified, externalism allows that *something*—perhaps evidence, but also perhaps not—is somehow supporting the truth of the belief.

The Denial. Externalism allows, however, that the believer *need not* be either actually or easily able to be aware of whatever—via the generalization of (1) — is making her belief justified.

That is a generic characterization of externalism, as (1)-generalized-plus-(2)-denied. Let us make it less generic. The most influential contemporary externalist idea is *reliabilism*.[3] Consider some belief of yours. How did it come into being? Did it arise reliably—in what is also called a *truth-conditionally* reliable way? This is the question of whether the belief was formed in a way that was sufficiently *likely* to yield a true rather than false belief. A typical externalist suggestion is that if your belief is formed reliably, then it is epistemically justified (provided that you have no independent reason for distrusting it). For it was likely to be true, given its way of coming into being.

That is externalist thinking because the reliability is allowed to contribute to one's justification simply by *existing*. The believer is not required to be, or even easily able to be, *aware* of the reliability. A justified believer need only *be* forming her belief reliably, such as by thinking well and carefully; she need not *reflect on* her doing so. That history behind the belief's coming into existence is not epistemically internal to the person. And why (we will be asked by externalists) should she do more than that, if a belief of hers is to be justified?

An Internalist Objection to Externalism

Internalists might ask, in return, whether externalism is demanding *enough* in what it expects from would-be justified believers. Internalists might reach for a much-discussed kind of thought experiment from Laurence BonJour.[4]

BonJour imagined someone's having a reliable—but unnoticed-by-her—power of *clairvoyance*. Here is a simple version of one kind of case that he describes. Suppose that—suddenly, without forethought or reasoned grounding—this person believes that the US president is in New York City (NYC). This belief is a product of her unwitting-yet-reliable capacity for clairvoyance. The belief is true: the president *is* in NYC. So, the belief is true *and* produced reliably (it was likely to be true, given how it has been formed). Still, because the believer is unaware of being clairvoyant, isn't she rationally *unjustified* in maintaining the belief about the president? Her subjective perspective—the totality of whatever she is, or could easily be, aware of at this time—gives her no consciously accessed or easily accessible reason to accept her belief. The belief's being formed reliably thus remains epistemically *external* for her: she has no awareness of the reliability nor could she easily gain such awareness at that time. Surely, therefore, the belief is unjustified, regardless of being formed reliably.

Internalists see this imagined case as being widely instructive. It shows (they say) that a belief's being justified *always* requires the believer to be actually, or at least easily able to be, aware of whatever is making her belief justified. Forming a belief reliably without being either actually, or easily able to be, aware of that reliability would never suffice to make a belief justified.

An Externalist Objection to Internalism

The previous section argued, in an internalist spirit, that we should be somewhat demanding in our conception of what it takes to have a justified belief. But is internalism *too* demanding? Is it requiring *too much* actual or potential reflection by any would-be justified believer? It does not *say* at the outset that it requires an especially large amount of self-reflection. Nonetheless, upon reflection, should we say that its key idea is implicitly committed to that confronting result?[5]

Imagine forming a belief, in a normal way via news reports, that the US president is in NYC. You have what feels like good and normal evidence supporting your belief. Is that enough (on internalism) to make the belief justified?

We saw earlier that internalism makes two sorts of demands: not only must you have good evidence but you must also be either aware or easily able to be aware of having it. Indeed, you must be either aware or easily able to be aware of having it *and* of its being good evidence. Otherwise, the evidence and its pertinent goodness *may as well be an epistemically external circumstance for you*. The situation would be relevantly like one where you have a belief that is formed reliably without your being aware or easily able to be aware of that reliability. And that other situation, we saw, is one where only *externalists* would grant that your belief can be justified (in virtue of that reliability). Hence, in order to distinguish itself clearly from externalism, internalism must insist that—if your evidence is to justify your belief—you are either aware or easily able to be aware of the evidence and of its being good.

That might sound like a reasonable requirement by internalism. But let us reflect on that internalist demand. When saying "aware" (on behalf of internalists), I mean at the very least that you do or could easily *seem*, to yourself, to have good evidence for your belief. However, what if that actual or easily available seeming-to-you is an illusion—inaccurate and misleading without giving you any indication that it is? Mere wishful thinking, for instance, might be making it seem to you that you have good evidence for your belief. I say "might" because I am describing at least a *possibility*. Still, how can you remove this disturbing possibility—setting it aside as *merely* a possibility? Here is a constraint upon any such attempt: you need to remove the wishful-thinking possibility *rationally*, not with wishful thinking. But internalism must therefore require you, when making that attempt, to have or to be easily able to have a *further* awareness—a rationally supported one, amounting to either actual or easily available good *evidence* that the previous actual or easily available awareness was not mere wishful thinking. This new actual or easily available awareness would need to *justify* your thinking that the initial actual or easily available awareness was to be trusted when telling you that you have good evidence for your belief about the president.

Yet how can the internalist analysis guarantee that this reflection is enough? Instead, doesn't the core internalist demand continue and continue and continue? After all, *any* new actual or easily available awareness is no more guaranteed to be accurate than the previous one was. Maybe *each* new one is wishful thinking: you might deeply and inescapably—even if always unwittingly—wish to be a rational thinker. This desire could be so strong that the wishful-thinking worry recurs and recurs. How *ever* could it be removed in a way of which internalism approves? Internalist thinking could *never* cease requiring you to have either actual or easily available awarenesses, each new one reflecting on the previous one—yet each subject to a recurring worry about whether, unwittingly, *it* is wishful thinking. In short, internalist attempts to understand your situation could never end by accepting that you have done enough reflecting to have justification for your initial belief.

Here, again, is the problem:

> No matter how good *in fact* is the support provided by a believer's evidence (of which she is or can easily be aware), she must be either actually or easily able to be aware *of* that good support's being provided, so that it is not merely wishful thinking, say. (If the believer is neither aware, nor easily able to be aware, of its being present and good, then she is merely *trusting* that she has a justified belief. This seems like dogmatic—not justified—believing.) Accordingly, we are plunged yet again—then again and again, ever again—into requiring the believer to engage, or be easily able to engage, in continued self-awareness and reflection. All of this, in order to understand her as having even a single justified belief about where the president is.

This sequence of reflection cannot ever be ended, which is another way of saying that, on internalism, *you must always do more* if you are to have even a single justified belief.

In practice, of course, you would stop reflecting at some point. Yet internalism must regard this as your stopping simply when it is practical for you to do so, with your epistemic task still unfinished. For, *by* stopping, you would be *neither actually, nor easily able to be, aware of whether your reflecting until then—no matter how extensive it has been—is actually good*. Perhaps an externalist—but no internalist—could accept this as part of your initial belief's being justified (e.g., if your thinking so far had been done reliably).

That is *epistemic internalism's dilemma*. It claims that internalism imposes upon would-be justified believers an unsatisfiable commitment—a need at least to be easily able to undertake what is, in a hidden way, an *unending* quest for evidence of which one is or could easily be aware, even to have a single justified belief. The cost of having evidence *not* like that would be one's satisfying at most an externalist but not an internalist requirement for justification. Perhaps, then, we *should* interpret in epistemically externalist terms the possession of justification for a belief. We would, it seems, be working with a more realistic—and, in principle, a satisfiable—account of justified belief.

Importantly, this dilemma applies to the purportedly internalist story told by *mentalists* (mentioned earlier).[6] On mentalism, a belief is justified only by appropriate inner (mental, cognitive) states of the believer that contribute appropriately to producing her belief. Need she also be actually, or easily able to be, aware of these states and their role in helping her belief to be formed? Not according to mentalism. Yet that mentalist response allows the believer to be in a situation strikingly akin to one where a belief is formed reliably, say, without the believer being actually or easily able to be aware of this; and, again, only on an *externalist* interpretation could that reliability's presence justify the belief. Mentalism allows that helpful states and belief-forming processes are present, but does not require the believer to have either actual or easily available awareness of them. Thus, mentalism fails to satisfy at least the classic internalist thinking bequeathed to us by Socrates. We may set it aside.[7]

An Improved Epistemic Internalism?

Internalism's interpretive potential continues to be debated.[8] The central question—made more urgent by epistemic internalism's dilemma—remains that of whether a belief's being justified *has* to involve good supportive evidence of which the believer is or could easily be aware. Internalism says that it does; externalism denies so. How can we settle this matter?

This section presents an improved version of epistemic internalism. But the following section then shows that even this version should give way to an epistemic externalism. We will thereby have a further argument for accepting externalism: if even a more plausible version of internalism should be replaced by externalism, this is a reason for regarding only externalism as potentially being correct about the nature of justified belief.

My initial aim is therefore to understand internalism as fairly as possible. I will begin by highlighting an aspect of its underlying motivation that is more deeply explanatory of internalism's appeal than what we have encountered so far.

We met Socrates and Meno earlier, as they were contemplating traveling to Larissa. Socrates said that knowing includes having "an account of the reason why" an opinion is true, if the opinion is to be knowledge. That suggestion was internalist in its conception of what, we now appreciate, was a recognition of the importance of a belief's being justified if it is to be knowledge. Yet if we are to evaluate Socrates's suggestion, we must interpret his recommendation carefully. Specifically, we must interpret it as asking Meno not merely to *have* evidence—by *having* that "account of the reason why." Expecting Meno to have such evidence would be a step, it could seem, toward giving internalist thinking some prima facie plausibility. But it would not be enough. The same is true of expecting Meno to have either an actual or an easily available awareness of the evidence. What else is needed, then? I suggest that what also needs to be seen by internalists as mattering is the evidence's being available, via actual or potential awareness, *as a fit tool or instrument to be used* by the believer.

Only then can we view the believer's possessing the evidence as part of her *bearing responsibility* for having and maintaining the belief;[9] and internalists (such as BonJour himself, mentioned earlier) have often thought of one's having justification for a belief *as*, at least partly, one's believing in an intellectually responsible way. Only then, too, can the believer *take* responsibility for having the belief, by wittingly putting the evidence to use in relevantly responsible ways—posing or answering questions, guiding associated inquiry or movements, reassuring herself when she feels unsure, and so on. As Meno travels to Larissa, his evidence—of the correct path to follow—should be actually or easily able to be part of his accompanying mental *activity*, as he thinks about where to go. What matters is not merely his *being* aware of the correct path to follow. His being aware has to serve a further purpose: it is needed *so that he could use* his evidence wittingly and aptly.

I propose that this is the underlying point of internalism's requiring each justified belief to rest upon good evidence of which the believer is or could easily be aware. It explains why we might ever be tempted to impose that internalist requirement. We should only ever insist—as internalism does—on a person's evidence or reasons being actually or easily able to be accessed by her awareness (if her belief is to be justified), if she either does or could proceed to *use* them in whatever ways the justified belief itself would need to be used. So, epistemic internalism, understood more fully, could usefully be called an epistemically *active* internalism (or "active-internalism").

Externalism Refined

Now we will see why even the previous section's improved conception of why one might at least initially be tempted by internalism—conceiving of it as active-internalism—is ultimately better interpreted as motivation for an active-*externalism*.

First, the talk of *using* one's evidence does not mandate an internalist construal. One can use evidence rationally in an externalist way: one need only act in ways that *accord with* the evidence, rather than ways that consciously call upon it as a self-aware story accompanying one's actions. Here we might reach for Ernest Sosa's evocative distinction between animal knowledge and reflective knowledge.[10] The latter includes being self-aware in an internalist way; the former does not. Although animal knowledge requires reliability in thought, no reflection upon the reliability is required. One just *is* believing reliably; no actual or easily available awareness is needed of one's doing so. And that distinction between two kinds of knowledge may be applied to uses of evidence. Distinguish animal evidence from reflective evidence. One could use evidence rationally by acting in ways that *accord with* it—just as many animals act by moving efficiently and directly in their environments, in accord with what their senses tell them about their surroundings. So, to use evidence rationally is not to be fundamentally different from other animals. Hence, just as we do not expect them to reflect upon whatever is justifying their beliefs or kindred cognitive states, we should not expect people to do so. (Someone might respond, of course, by saying "But people, unlike other animals, can be expected to do so, since they *could* do so." Not if epistemic internalism's dilemma is correct!)

Second, upon understanding that internalism should become active-internalism, we should accept that internalism is needlessly limiting in its conception of justified belief. There are many ways to believe rationally, only some of which include the self-aware use of good evidence by reflecting, or easily being able to reflect, consciously *on its being good evidence*. Once more we can usefully compare ourselves with other animals. When constructing a dam, a beaver has and uses good evidence, I take it. But presumably it is not using good evidence *of which it is, or could easily be, aware as being* good evidence. Equally, although we might say that a child has good evidence of a particular person's being her mother, we would never say that she must appreciate this good evidence *as being* good evidence.

To those claims, however, someone might reply thus: "You admit that the beaver and the child can have, and be in accord with, what is actually good evidence. Isn't this all that the active-internalist asks of them?" Not quite. Internalism requires that good evidence be present, but also that its presence *as good evidence* be actually or easily able to be noticed by the believer, not only so that her belief is justified but also so that it is justified *by her using* (or at least her being easily able to use) the evidence. For example (and as active-internalism implies), the believer would need to have actually, or been easily able to have, guided her belief into existence, in part by calling upon her awareness of the evidence's being good. Or she would at least need to be able to evaluate and defend her belief rationally, again in part by noticing and appreciating her good evidence. However, this is where the internalist story has become less realistic. What it demands is not what reflection on the beaver and the child reveals as happening in their cases: when forming their respective beliefs, they can be acting in *accord with* their good evidence—without having been easily able to *guide themselves consciously* toward having that belief, or being easily able to evaluate and defend it rationally, by appreciating that good evidence *as being* good evidence.

So, active-externalism—like active-internalism—can welcome a believer's using evidence. But active-externalism need not interpret her as having *had* to be using evidence, in guiding or evaluating or defending her believing (or by being easily able to do so) via her awareness of the evidence's being good. Like internalism, externalism allows us to say that good evidence can be useful within justified believing. Externalism says, however, that internalism *overstates* that potential role for evidence within justified believing.

Internalism is sometimes prompted by the thought that having knowledge always includes one's *knowing that* one knows—and so that having a justified belief always includes one's knowing that one does. You would believe justifiedly that you are sitting on a chair, partly by being able to reflect on your sensory evidence of sitting there: it feels to you that you are sitting there. And its feeling to you that you are doing so would be something of which you are or could easily be aware. By having, and knowing that you have, the sitting-on-a-chair feeling, you could thereby know that you have a justified belief that you are sitting on a chair. If you could *not* have that knowledge of your evidence, something would be missing from whatever is needed for you to believe justifiedly that you are sitting on a chair: for instance, your sitting-on-a-chair feeling would be insufficiently clear and present to you for it to be justifying your belief that you are sitting on a chair.

Again, though, that internalist thinking is needlessly strong; externalism's competing analysis of the situation suffices. We need only say (as externalism does) that the ability to be aware of one's sensory evidence can be welcome and useful—without having been *needed* for that sensory evidence to be giving you a justified belief that you are sitting on a chair. You can have and use that sensory evidence in ways that need not include your reflecting on its goodness *as* sensory evidence. You can reach the same belief (that you are sitting on a chair) in a cognitively reliable way. And your belief can be justified even if you were unable to be self-consciously guiding yourself toward it by reflecting explicitly on your sensory evidence's quality as evidence.

The externalist's basic point is simple. An active-externalist may allow that being aware of having good evidence for a view can be useful when one aspires to having a justified belief. But she is not committed to saying that having, or even being easily able to have, that awareness is *needed* if one's belief is to be justified. Being aware of the quality of one's evidence can help one's beliefs to be justified in such a way that they are available in a self-aware way for confidently inquiring, answering questions, posing questions, reassuring, and so on—all of which could be welcome to one as a believer. Yet this does not entail that a belief *has* to be attended by an ability to engage in self-conscious reflection on one's evidence if the belief is to be justified. Reaching for evidence in a self-aware, let alone a self-guiding, way need not be the only way to have justified beliefs, even helpfully usable justified beliefs.

We might say that externalists strive to understand the nature of justified belief in what they would regard as a more realistic way than is envisaged by internalists. Maybe internalism is an ideal. Maybe it describes what rational justification for a belief would be like *if* we could reflect endlessly on our evidence and its quality. But that ideal is unsatisfiable. And although we generally encourage people to satisfy various ideals, we do not generally deny people *all* measure of achievement once they fall short of satisfying those ideals. Is having a justified belief an achievement? Is it an achievement attainable in less-than-ideal ways? Epistemic externalism invites us to answer those questions with "yes," encouraging us to regard rational justification in a humanly forgiving way, possibly by stressing what is shared by a far wider world of believers and potential believers—animals, children, and, yes, reflective human adults. Details await us. Already, though, we have some reason to accept externalism's being basically correct in how it tries to understand what it is for a belief to be rationally justified.[11]

Notes

1 *Meno* 97e–98a. The translation is by G. M. A. Grube, *Plato: Five Dialogues* (Indianapolis: Hackett Publishing, 1981), at p. 86.
2 "Is Justified True Belief Kknowledge?" *Analysis* 23 (1963): 121–23.
3 This is a view advocated especially by Alvin Goldman. See, for example, "What Is Justified Belief?" in *Justification and Knowledge: New Studies in Epistemology*, ed. G. S. Pappas (Dordrecht: D. Reidel, 1979), 1–23; and *Epistemology and Cognition* (Cambridge, MA: Harvard University Press, 1986).
4 See chapter 3 of *The Structure of Empirical Knowledge* (Cambridge, MA: Harvard University Press, 1985).
5 We are about to meet what I and Michael Bergmann refer to as *epistemic internalism's dilemma*. Elsewhere, we present more complex formulations of it. See my "Epistemic Internalism's Dilemma," *American Philosophical Quarterly* 27 (1990): 245–51; and "On Being Epistemically Internal," *Philosophy and Phenomenological Research* 51 (1991): 855–71. For Bergmann, see *Justification without Awareness: A Defense of Epistemic Externalism* (Oxford: Clarendon Press, 2006); and "A Dilemma for Internalism," in *Knowledge and Reality: Essays in Honor of Alvin Plantinga*, eds. T. M. Crisp, M. Davidson, and D. vander Laan (Dordrecht: Springer, 2006), 137–77.

6 Defenders of mentalism include J. L. Pollock and J. Cruz, *Contemporary Theories of Knowledge*, 2nd ed. (Lanham, MD: Rowman & Littlefield, 1999), 130–42; and E. Conee and R. Feldman, "Internalism Defended," in *Epistemology: Internalism and Externalism*, ed. H. Kornblith (Malden, MA: Blackwell, 2001), 231–60.

7 For a similar assessment, see H. Kornblith, *On Reflection* (Oxford: Oxford University Press, 2012), 35–37. For more detailed discussion, see M. Bergmann, *Justification without Awareness*, ch. 3.

8 For such debate, see B. Coppenger and M. Bergmann, eds., *Intellectual Assurance: Essays on Traditional Epistemic Internalism* (Oxford: Oxford University Press, 2016); M. Steup, "Does Phenomenal Conservatism Solve Internalism's Dilemma?" in *Seemings and Justification: New Essays on Dogmatism and Phenomenal Conservatism*, ed. C. Tucker (New York: Oxford University Press, 2013), 135–53; and M. Bergmann, "Phenomenal Conservatism and the Dilemma for Internalism," in *Seemings and Justification*, 154–78. For earlier surveys, see the following: W. P. Alston, "Internalism and Externalism in Epistemology," *Philosophical Topics* 14 (1986): 179–221; S. Hetherington, *Knowledge Puzzles: An Introduction to Epistemology* (Boulder, CO: Westview Press, 1996), chs 14, 15; H. Kornblith, ed., *Epistemology: Internalism and Externalism*; and B. J. C. Madison, "Epistemic Internalism," *Philosophy Compass* 5 (2010): 840–53.

9 See Baron Reed on what he calls *attributabilism*—the idea that a belief is knowledge only if, presumably through the person's responsible use of evidence, the belief's being present and true is sufficiently attributable to what *she* does, rather than too much to the role of some external force: "The Long Road to Scepticism," *The Journal of Philosophy* 104 (2007): 236–62. For discussion of Reed, see S. Hetherington, "The Extended Knower," *Philosophical Explorations* 15 (2012): 207–18.

10 See, for example, chapter 7 of his *Reflective Knowledge: Apt Belief and Reflective Knowledge, Vol. II* (Oxford: Clarendon Press, 2009).

11 Thanks to Brent Madison for helpful comments on a draft of this chapter.

RESPONSES

Response to Hasan

Stephen Hetherington

Study Questions

1. Why does Hetherington think, contrary to Hasan, that the person in the evil demon case is *not* justified?
2. According to Hetherington, what is (and is not) the appropriate moral of Hasan's fairy story?
3. How does Hetherington retell the fairy story so that Aria's beliefs turn out to be justified on externalist grounds?

When deciding whether some belief is epistemically justified it might feel natural to ask what *evidence* is being used consciously to support the belief, or that could easily be cited to support it. This is the *internalist* instinct. And Ali Hasan argues in support of that internalist instinct. Whatever makes a belief justified, he urges, is *only ever an evidential reason* that is at least easily accessible to the believer's mind when she forms and maintains the belief.

How does Hasan argue for this picture? He appeals to imagined *cases* and our *intuitions* about them. First, Hasan offers his case "evil demon" as one where a belief *is* justified although there is an external circumstance that externalists would take to preclude justification. This case is intended to show that being in an apt external circumstance is not *needed* if one's belief is to be justified. Second, Hasan offers his case "fairy" as one where a belief is *not* justified although there is an external circumstance that externalists would take to make the belief justified. This case is intended to show that being in an apt external circumstance is not *sufficient* for making one's belief justified. Between these two cases, external circumstances are being claimed to be irrelevant to whether a belief is justified. All that matters, argues Hasan, is a believer's having internally accessible evidence—her (epistemic) *reasons* for her belief.

Hasan's *Evil Demon* Case

In one of philosophy's most famous pieces of writing—his 1641 "Meditation I"—René Descartes contemplated the possibility of there being an evil demon (genius, spirit) who continually deceives him, rendering his beliefs false. How could he ever know that this possibility is *not* obtaining? Given how clever the demon is imagined to be, Descartes could never *notice* his being deceived by the demon. Hence, he could never notice a *difference* between when this is, and when it is not, happening to him. Whether or not it is happening would be an external circumstance, unnoticed by his internal evidence.

Now we encounter Hasan's "evil demon" case—a version of what, he acknowledges, is called the *new* evil demon problem. Imagine two people, one of whom is sensing the world in a normal way (in Hasan's "Normal Perception" case), the other of whom (in the "evil demon" case) would describe her inner experiences as being about the world in that same way—yet who is being deceived by an evil demon. The latter person's beliefs are false—thanks to the evil demon. Even so, claims Hasan, this deeply deceived believer is "surely just as justified" in her beliefs as is the other person, who is having normal sensory experiences and thereby normally justified beliefs about the surrounding world. Even those demon-deceived beliefs are justified—no matter that, presumably, they fail a simple externalist criterion for being justified. (That criterion would be something like "Not being formed in a way that leads to rampant mistakes.") So, internalism suffices as a general framework for how we should conceive of what is needed if a belief is to be justified.

But how can Hasan be so sure that those two believers—the normally perceiving one and the demon-blighted one—are equally justified in their beliefs that are ostensibly about the surrounding world? Near the end of his chapter, Hasan denies that what is constituting this (internalist) justification is "*responsibility or blame.*" He is denying that what makes the two beliefs equally justified is each believer's being equally *blameless* when trusting and believing in response to how the world seems to her. What, then, *is* Hasan's internalist explanation of why even the demon-blighted believer—like the normally perceiving one—has justified beliefs? Unfortunately, he does not offer that explanation; he merely "intuits" both of them have justified beliefs.

Let us investigate this ourselves. How might an externalist respond to Hasan's case? The externalist needs to explain why those demon-deceived beliefs are *not* justified (contrary to what Hasan claims). How might she do this? She could begin by noting that justification's presence or absence should reflect *something* about *truth's* presence or absence. Even if a particular belief can be justified yet false, we might wonder how justification can ever be present if *all* of one's beliefs are false. Shouldn't a belief's being justified include at least the possibility of its being true? Here, too, we might remind ourselves of how Hasan introduces the general idea of what makes a ground for belief a good *epistemic* reason: we are talking of "reasons relevant to the *truth* of one's belief that *p.*"

Consider also the following point. We are asked by Hasan to accord justification to those demon-deceived beliefs, based as they are on inner-but-deceived experiences, *quite irrespectively* of whether the experiences are accurate and the beliefs are true. Justification is thereby attributed *simply because of the semantic content* in front of, or accessible to, the believer's mind. Yet this is a literally shallow or superficial analysis. What would be *constituting* the justification? In answering that question, urges externalism, we must look *beyond* mere semantic content. After all, what would make an inner experienced content (e.g., "That looks like a cat") *good* evidence supporting another inner experienced content (e.g., "That is a cat")? *From where* does that justificatory goodness come? Surely not from merely the inner semantic content; surely, at least, from that content *plus* facts about the world beyond. We rely—usually silently and unconsciously—on the world *being normal* when we take "That looks like a cat" to justify "That is a cat." And to accept this interpretation of how we think, and how our beliefs are thereby justified, is to presume an *externalist* interpretation of the case. In which event, we are not entitled to assume, as Hasan does with "evil demon," that the demon-deceived beliefs are justified—merely, it seems, because they have the same inner semantic *content* as do the beliefs in the "Normal Perception" case.

Hasan's *Fairy* Case

As Hasan indicates, internalists often imagine situations where someone forms a belief in a way that we would standardly regard as inadequate for justifying the belief—yet where, due to a remarkable external circumstance, the belief satisfies what externalists might regard as an apt criterion for being justified. Hasan's "fairy" case is one such situation. It includes a belief ("I will live to be more than one hundred years old!") being formed by Aria through wishful thinking. It also includes a "powerful fairy intent on making Aria's wishes come true." Whereas the evil demon made beliefs false, this fairy makes beliefs true—Aria's, at any rate. Her belief is true—reliably so. Nonetheless, insists Hasan, "intuitively, Aria's belief is not justified."

Hasan interprets this case as illustrating the *insufficiency*, for being justified, of a belief's satisfying a natural externalist criterion, namely, being formed in a way that *reliably* produces true beliefs. In Hasan's view, the belief is unjustified because that reliability is not accompanied by the believer's being able to access it (being able to be aware of the reliability).

In response, compare the following two situations: (i) Hasan's "fairy" case: a belief arises through wishful thinking—no supportive evidence being used in forming it—yet it is made true by a hidden and besotted fairy. (ii) A belief is formed by using supportive evidence, yet the person has no capacity—perhaps she lacks the concept of good evidence—ever to be aware of that evidence's being supportive.

There is a substantial epistemic difference between those two cases: even if we concede justification's absence from case (i), we need not make the same concession for case (ii). This is significant because in *each* situation the belief is supported in an externalist way: in each, *part of the reason why* the belief is justified is inaccessible to the believer. Nevertheless, this does not reflect poorly upon externalism per se. It means only that we must distinguish between better externalist theories and poorer ones. In (ii), there is evidence; and it is accessible in that it can be *used* by the believer in ways in which evidence should be used. Still, its *being* good evidence, let alone whatever *makes* it good, is inaccessible to the believer: she cannot reflect in those conceptual terms upon the evidence she is using. Still, this is no reason to deny her justification. We should allow that her belief is justified, albeit in an externalist way, within case (ii).

Again, the moral is simple: there are better, and there are worse, versions of externalism. Hasan's "fairy" case reflects poorly only on a less subtle, more extreme, version of externalism. This is partly why my initial chapter suggested an *improved* form of internalism (active-internalism), along with a correlatively improved form of externalism (active-externalism).

In accord with that suggestion, imagine Aria's *using*—not merely having—her belief (within an expanded telling of Hasan's "fairy"): her belief is a product of wishful thinking, but it matters to her, and so she will apply it in various settings, such as when planning aspects of her future life. Given how Hasan presents his case, the friendly fairy will remain vigilant, manipulating the world to allow Aria's belief to be true. This implies that Aria will continue receiving favorable *feedback* from the world, in response to her future actions using the belief. That is, she will receive evidence supporting her belief. Even so, active-externalism allows us to interpret this evidence in an externalist way: Aria is not able to reflect on her evidence to access its quality *as* evidence, for example. She uses it, and, in fact, it is good—even if she cannot access *why* it is good. Surely this will still suffice to make her belief justified over the course of its life. In which event, no longer is the case one like Hasan's "fairy" that includes an *un*justified belief satisfying what could otherwise be seen as a prima facie adequate form of externalism. Once we view the case anew—through the lens of a prima facie adequate form of externalism—we need not regard it as threatening externalism per se about the nature of epistemic justification.

Response to Hetherington

Ali Hasan

Study Questions

1. What is the internalist's dilemma? What does it imply if internalism is true?

2. How does Hasan respond to the internalist's dilemma? How does he illustrate his response?

3. What two potential objections to his response does Hasan anticipate? How does he respond to these objections?

In his essay, Stephen Hetherington presents a challenging dilemma for the internalist that turns on a question: Does epistemic justification require that the subject have internal access to—that is, be aware, or at least be able to become aware, of—some evidence *and of its being good evidence*? Whatever the answer, it seems to lead to trouble for the internalist.[1]

The Apparent Internalist's Dilemma

If the internalist answers "no"—for example, by requiring access to the evidence but not to its being good evidence—then the view does not satisfy classical internalist thinking and is not interestingly different from externalism. As Hetherington puts it, "the evidence and its pertinent goodness *may as well be an epistemically external circumstance for you*" (p. 111).

If the internalist answers "yes," then the requirement becomes so demanding that *none* of our beliefs would be justified, for we could never do enough reflecting to satisfy the requirement. The problem arises from the fact that it might *seem* to me that I have good evidence for some claim or proposition *P* when, in fact, this "seeming" is an illusion. In order to be justified, I must be able to rule out this possibility, or at least set it aside as *mere* possibility, an *unlikely* possibility. Of course, if I am to do so rationally and not just dogmatically, I need good evidence to think that *I have good evidence to think that P*. But, again, it might merely *seem* to me that I have good evidence to think this. This need for good evidence will keep recurring at every one of an endless hierarchy of levels. Our finite minds cannot satisfy such a requirement. Hetherington concludes that "internalism imposes upon would-be justified believers an unsatisfiable commitment" (p. 112). In short: if internalism is true, then global skepticism, the thesis that none of our beliefs are justified, is true.

Why is this bad news for internalism? Though Hetherington doesn't directly answer this question, one straightforward answer is that global skepticism is false: I am now justified in believing at least *some* things (e.g., that something exists, that I exist, that 1+1=2, that there are no square circles). It follows that internalism is false.

Notice that the argument is not just that if internalism is true, then very young children, animals, and any beings without the ability to access and appreciate their evidence don't have epistemically justified or rational beliefs—an implication many internalists are happy to accept. Nor is the argument just that if internalism is true, then we are not justified in believing anything about the world outside our own minds. This external-world skepticism is a radical form of skepticism, but it is still not as obviously false as global skepticism. Moreover, internalists have argued that we have access to good grounds to reject external-world skepticism.[2]

However, if Hetherington is right that internalism implies that *no belief* can be justified, that would be a clearer, stronger reason to reject internalism. I will therefore focus on this argument, though some of what I say may suggest responses to these other versions of the objection that internalism is too demanding.

Responding to the Dilemma

In defending internalism, I characterized the access required for justification in terms of actual or potential awareness (i.e., ability to become aware) of good grounds, grounds whose relevance to the belief the subject can appreciate. So, I do accept something at least roughly like Hetherington's characterization of internalism as the view that justification requires access to good evidence *and to its being good evidence*. We have just seen an argument that this leads to an utterly unsatisfiable standard. How do I reply?

First of all, I don't require that the justified subject have a seeming or awareness *that the evidence is good evidence*. An appreciation of the relevance of evidence to what one believes, or an appreciation of the evidence's pertinent "goodness" for some belief, need not involve literally applying the concept of *good evidence*. All that is required is that the subject be aware of something's *making true* or *making probable* what one believes. Now, in a sense, to be aware of something's making true or making probable what one believes *just is* to be aware of its being good evidence for what one believes! I do take justification to require access to the fact that one's evidence is good evidence in this sense. But I don't want to require, in addition to this, that the subject must also have and apply a concept of "good evidence." Moreover, "good evidence" is often used to mean something different or something more. For example, we might use it to mean something that is publicly accessible, or that would be accepted as true in legal or scientific contexts, or that is a reliable source of knowledge. I don't want to claim that the justified subject must be aware of having good evidence in any of these senses.

It will help to consider the following examples of awareness of something's making true, or making probable, what one believes: (a) I am experiencing a taste, and am directly aware of this taste's *matching, fitting, or corresponding to* my concept *salty*. I am thus aware of this taste's making it true that *this is salty*. (b) I am having thoughts and experiences, and I am aware that my having thoughts or experiences *requires* the existence of a self; the fact that I have thoughts or experiences *implies, entails, or makes true* that I (some person or self) exists. (c) I seem to be hearing and (successfully) singing along to a song, and I am aware that this *makes it probable that* I've heard it before. Our awareness of these relations can make a difference to our perspective on the truth or probability of what we believe. In these cases, the evidence and its pertinent goodness are *not external circumstances* for the subject, even if they don't literally involve the subject's conceiving of the evidence as "good evidence."

Hetherington might grant much of this, at least for the sake of argument, but claim that it doesn't avoid the sort of problem he is raising. For it might *merely seem* to me that something makes true or makes probable what I believe. This possibility must also be set aside, which would require further evidence, and so lead to a similar, unsatisfiable regress.

However, an internalist can deny that the sort of awareness required for justification must take the form of a seeming or appearance state that could possibly be illusory. A seeming or appearance state is a representation or involves a representation, and as such it can go wrong. It seems to me that I see a coffee mug on the table, but it is possible that it is a mere illusion, or that I am dreaming. But a long tradition of internalists holds that awareness can take a non-representational form. To be directly (non-representationally) aware of something is to stand in a real relation to it. When it comes to a real relation, it can't exist without its "relata" or the things related. I cannot, for example, be aware of my having a headache without the existence of the headache. This applies to awareness *of relations*: I cannot be directly aware of a relation of correspondence, entailment, or probability without this relation actually existing. I cannot be aware, for example, of my experience's corresponding or fitting with my concept of a headache without the experience's actually corresponding to the concept. If our awareness of the evidence and its pertinent goodness can take this form—being a *direct, non-representational* awareness of a *making-true* or *making-probable* relation—then it cannot be illusory in the way representational states can. This allows us to challenge the objection that internalism's requirement is *unsatisfiable*.

One might object that even if I do have a direct awareness of this sort, don't I also need to be aware that I have this direct awareness, or know that this awareness is not illusory, is not a mere seeming, and so on? I don't think so. Internalism requires that the subject be able to be aware of some evidence and (on my view) its pertinent goodness; it does not, or need not, require that one be aware *of the fact that one is aware* of the evidence and its pertinent goodness. Although some forms of internalism have claimed that justified subjects must be aware or know that they satisfy conditions of knowledge or justification, an internalist can coherently reject that requirement, including any requirement that subjects know or be aware that they satisfy *internalist* conditions of knowledge.

Notes

1 For a similar dilemma, see Michael Bergmann's *Justification without Awareness: A Defense of Epistemic Externalism* (Oxford: Clarendon Press, 2006). For a reply, see my "Classical Foundationalism and Bergmann's Dilemma for Internalism," *Journal of Philosophical Research* 36 (2011): 391–410.
2 See Laurence BonJour's, "Foundationalism and the External World," *Philosophical Perspectives* 13 (1999): 229–49; Michael Huemer's, "Serious Theories and Skeptical Theories: Why You are Probably Not a Brain in a Vat," *Philosophical Studies* 173 (2016): 1031–52; and my "Skepticism and Spatial Objects," (forthcoming), *International Journal for the Study of Skepticism*.

Questions for Reflection

1. Has Hetherington adequately addressed the problems posed for externalism by the evil demon and fairy cases? Why?
2. Can the internalist respond to the charge that internalism makes it impossible for young children and higher-order animals to have justified beliefs? If so, how?
3. How serious is the internalist's dilemma? Has Hasan adequately answered it? Why?
4. Is there a difference between *justifying a belief* and a belief *being justified*? If so, what is it? If not, why not? What difference, if any, would this distinction make to the internalism/externalism debate?

4

Do Religious Beliefs Require Evidence?

Religious Beliefs Require Evidence

Trent Dougherty

Study Questions

1. How does Dougherty first define evidentialism? How does he later modify the definition and why?
2. What are the two kinds of epistemic justification? How are they related? What, then, is Dougherty's evidentialist thesis about knowledge?
3. How does Dougherty understand the idea of "fit" between belief and evidence? What third definition of evidentialism follows from this discussion?
4. What are the traditional sources of evidence or "cognitive faculties"? How does Dougherty connect them to evidentialism?
5. What is the "best bet," according to Dougherty, concerning what counts as a religious belief? Why does this imply that religious beliefs should not be exempt from evidential standards?
6. What argument does Dougherty consider against evidentialism about religious belief? How does he respond to this argument?
7. How does Dougherty respond to the objection that his view makes justification too easy?

8. Why does Dougherty reject the idea that religious beliefs are not meant to represent objective features of the world but simply express emotional states or values?

9. What two alternatives to evidentialism does Dougherty address? How does he respond to them?

In this brief essay, I defend a view called "evidentialism" about religious belief. The view I will defend is in a family of views that march under the evidentialist banner. The view is frequently misunderstood, so I will have to spend some time saying not just what the view is but also what the view isn't. Evidentialism is a view that applies to all beliefs, not just religious beliefs. Accordingly, that evidentialism applies to religious beliefs is just a consequence of its applying to all beliefs. Some people seem to think religious beliefs are somehow special in a way that exempts them from the requirements that evidentialism proposes. I will question this exemption and say something about why I reject it. Toward the end, I will briefly discuss some alternatives—or at least apparent alternatives—to evidentialism. I find them all to be either unmotivated or not actually alternatives to evidentialism.

Evidentialism: A Sketch of a Version

So, first, what is evidentialism? At a first approximation, evidentialism is the following thesis:

(E1) You should always believe in accordance with the evidence.

This may sound so much like common sense that you may wonder how anyone could ever doubt it. I myself think that (E1) is what we might call a "conceptual" truth: a proposition that is true just in virtue of the concepts involved. Plausibly, what distinguishes beliefs from other mental states is that they are in some way aimed at truth. Beliefs are, first, a kind of mental "representational state." That is, they are mental states that represent the world as being a certain way. But our minds are not directly connected to the external world; we are aware of the world through the various senses. The senses "give testimony" that the world is such and such, then the mind interprets those signals and forms a hypothesis, if you will, about the nature of the thing causing those sensory stimulations. These sensory stimulations we can for now call our "empirical evidence," though later I will want to qualify that. The qualification is that, technically, sensory states are the *cause* of our having evidence, which consists in a special kind of mental state (nothing

I say here hangs on that, however) I'll call a "seeming." The external world is not the only thing we form beliefs about, but we'll focus on it for now as a paradigm case. Via our empirical evidence, we form an idea of what the world is like, called a "belief." That image can turn out to be accurate or inaccurate to varying degrees.

So beliefs are *ultimately* aimed at truth (something in a sense "outside" us), but they are *immediately* responsive to our empirical evidence, which are the signs—sometimes reliable, sometimes regrettably not—of how the world is. Perhaps you've experienced an illusion or a hallucination. In such cases, the testimony of your senses was false. However, if the belief you formed matched that empirical evidence, then there's nothing to complain about in your belief-forming process, though you may need to file a complaint with your senses. Of course, it could be that your senses are working fine, but the part of the brain that ties them together into a mental image is malfunctioning. Then the complaint should be filed against that mechanism, but so long as the belief matches the mental image, then there's nothing to complain about in the belief-forming mechanism. When this match occurs, many philosophers apply the term "epistemic justification" to apply to the belief. We can thus formulate evidentialism as a thesis about epistemic justification:

(E2) A belief is epistemically justified when it matches the evidence.

This sense of "justified" may share some things in common with *moral* "justification" but a better way to understand it is to think about what it means for a paragraph of text to be justified: it lines up exactly with the margins, it fits just right. Moral justification concerns actions. Epistemic justification concerns beliefs. Beliefs are not actions. You can't just believe something by trying. Don't believe me? Try!

Above, I've used the terms "in accordance with," "matches," and "fits." It is high time to flesh that out a bit more, since without saying more about these notions, evidentialism remains intuitive but more vague than is desired here. First, though, let me distinguish between two kinds of epistemic justification. Then, after extending the notion of evidence a bit, I'll address the application to specifically religious beliefs.

Two Kinds of Epistemic Justification

The word "justification" applies to different kinds of things, and its meaning depends on which kind of thing one is applying it to. The most basic kind of justification is *propositional justification*. Both beliefs and, say I, experiences have propositions as contents. Some philosophers seem to believe that experiences don't have contents, but it's hard to see what they are getting at, and I won't discuss that view. When the senses "testify" that the external world is such and such, *that the world is such and such* is the content of their testimony. The "*that the world is such and such*" phrase names the proposition that is their content. My senses may testify to me that there is a red mug in front of me. *That there is a red mug in front of me* is the propositional content of that experience. Under normal circumstances, that experience will give rise to a belief that there is a red mug in front of me. There is a perfect match between the contents of the experience and the content of the belief. Propositional justification, then, can be defined in the following manner:

> (PJ) Some target proposition P is *propositionally justified* relative to a body of evidence E when P matches E.

It's tempting to think that if E is your total evidence, then if E supports P, it would be right for you to believe P. But that would be mistaken. For you might have E as evidence and yet come to believe P on the basis of wishful thinking, superstition, or because of a brain lesion you develop due to a burst of gamma rays from Alpha Centauri. In this case your belief with content P wouldn't be justified for you even if you had E as evidence and E supported P, because your evidence E would *play no role* (or the *wrong* role) in your coming to form the belief that P. When E plays the right role in your coming to believe P, we say that your belief that P is properly *based on* your evidence E. Putting this together, we get the following definition (from the Greek word *doxa*, meaning belief or opinion):

> (DJ) Some target belief B is *doxastically justified* by E when E supports P and the belief that P is properly based on E.

Note that while (PJ) is a thesis about propositions, (DJ) is a thesis about beliefs. Beliefs have propositions as their contents. That is, beliefs are mental states with propositional content, propositions are not mental states. In neither case are *people* the objects of evaluation. People can be the objects of moral evaluation or psychological evaluation, but people are not the subjects of evaluation for the evidentialist. Some theorists evaluate people in a way they call "epistemic" when they evaluate that person's practices of inquiry. For instance, we can evaluate the conditions under which I should take the time to inquire and to what degree I should pursue my inquiries. But such evaluations are just a function of what other interests I have and what is at stake. As such, they are not properly epistemic, but rather a species of moral evaluation. So doxastic justification is propositional justification *plus proper basing*. But what is proper basing?

I can't give a general account of proper basing, but it's easy to see the kinds of things that can exclude it. In the broad sense I intend here, proper basing is ruled out if one or more of the following were to occur: cognitive malfunctions, too much of the wrong kind of luck, bizarre causal chains, flawed chains of assumptions, and more. We can use the above notions to yield an evidentialist thesis about knowledge.

(EK) Some target belief B of some person S counts as an item of knowledge when:

(i) B has P as its content;

(ii) S has E as evidence;

(iii) P fits E;

(iv) S properly bases B on E; and

(v) P is true.

Knowledge isn't the only, or the most important, kind of belief, but in ordinary circumstances the concept of knowledge can often be useful (so long as it doesn't distract us from more important states like understanding and wisdom, and as long as we realize that sometimes knowledge isn't good enough to act on in high-stakes cases). Now the only thing required to complete my brief survey of evidentialism is that promised discussion of "fit" and a brief extension of the notion of evidence.

"Fit" and Evidence

The first aspect of "fit" falls pretty easily out of the discussion: fit in content. A belief fits an experience when they have the same content, or when the content of the experience logically entails the content of the belief. When an experience testifies that we feel water, the belief that we feel water is thereby justified; or at least it is justified to some *degree*. The next aspect of fit we may call "strength" (previous philosophers have called it "vividness," "liveliness," "vivacity," and other things). For it might *really* seem that we feel water, or it might *kind of* seem like we feel water, with lots of stops in between. And, of course, not only do the experiences that support our beliefs come in varying degrees but our beliefs themselves also come in varying degrees. So this second aspect of fit has to do with the strength of belief matching the strength of the evidence. In order to apply these notions to evidentialism, we need to abandon the tripartite notion of belief/disbelief/suspension of judgment and talk about "doxastic attitudes," which span degrees of strength from 0 to 1 (or to 100 percent certainty, which is the same thing). This allows us to derive the following evolved notion of evidentialism here.

> (E3) S's doxastic attitude toward P is justified when there is a match in content and strength with the experiential evidence E that S has for P.

Sources of Evidence

Thus far I have only spoken of "empirical evidence" or the "testimony of the senses." But I did note along the way that we form beliefs about things other than the external world. For example, we form beliefs about nonempirical metaphysical truths as well as the contents of our own mind and our past. The traditional term for our ability to grasp abstract truths like those in math, logic, and metaphysics is "Understanding" with a capital "U" or "Reason" with a capital "R" or "Rational insight/intuition." Add to this Memory and Introspection, and we have the traditional sources of evidence—Sensation, Understanding, Memory, and Introspection. Each of these sources bears testimony to the realm of truth relevant to it. Sensation tells us that there is a cat on the roof. Understanding tells us that numerical equality is transitive. Memory tells us what we had for breakfast. Introspection tells us what we experience and believe. Each of these sources sometimes speaks with conviction and sometimes it speaks more tentatively. None are infallible. Further, this may not be an exhaustive list of sources of evidence, but this is a thought we will come back to later. For now, it would be nice to find a way to speak of all these sources taken together (and note that Sensation is itself a bundle of at least five sources).

Without assuming too much metaphysical baggage, let's say that the genus to which these kinds of sources belong is a "cognitive faculty." Now consider the following thesis I call *Reasons Commonsensism* (RC):

> (RC) If you have a cognitive faculty that says that P, then you thereby have a reason for P.

Your evidence for a proposition just consists in all the reasons you have for that proposition taken together. When you weigh up all those reasons you get the "evidential probability" or "epistemic probability" that proposition has for you. I'll call the outputs of these cognitive faculties, for lack of a better word, "seemings." It's perhaps easiest and best to understand seemings from considering some examples (in the end, you can call them whatever you want, the examples are primary and all assume the absence of cognitive malfunction for the sake of convenience of expression). When you look right at a ripe banana it seems that there is a yellow object in front of you. When you look at a simple truth of mathematics it seems that it is true. When you remember what you ate for breakfast, it seems to you that you had toast (or whatever). When you introspect to see how strongly you believe evidentialism, it seems that it is very likely to be true (or so I hope!). Seemings are always seemings *that* something is such and such. That is, they are propositional attitude states. They are distinct from beliefs, because in rare cases of malfunction, seemings and beliefs can come apart, but seemings are so intimately tied to beliefs as their immediate causes that under ordinary circumstances there is no discernible gap between them and they are thus essentially indistinguishable. Still, one is the *report* and the other the *response*. A justified response is one that matches—in strength and content—the report to which it is responding. We can now express (RC) and evidentialism more economically:

(RC*) If it seems to you that P, then you thereby have a reason to believe that P, in proportion to the strength of the seeming.

Reasons commonsensism illuminates (E3) above, and I mean for the latter to be read as informed by the former. This completes my sketch of evidentialism.

Application to Religious Belief

As I mentioned above, evidentialism is meant to apply to religious beliefs just because it is meant to apply to all beliefs. But some have sought an exemption from evidentialism for religious belief. In this section I evaluate and reject this idea. There are a few preliminary difficulties that need to be addressed, however, before we can turn to the relationship between evidentialism and religious belief.

What Is Religious Belief?

The first difficulty is in having even a vague notion of what a religious belief is. I am myself quite skeptical that there is any very helpful notion answering to the phrase "religious belief." Here's why. The best bet for a theory of what counts as religious belief is based not on the content of the belief but the attitudes associated with it. For the belief that there is a God, for example, was held by both Aristotle and Thomas Jefferson, neither of whom were religious by a mile. For many, the belief that there is a God is, intuitively, a religious belief, but for Aristotle and Jefferson, it was not. The difference between theists and nonreligious theists isn't theism but rather what it means to the individual emotionally and practically. Aristotle famously said that humans and God can't be friends because they are too different. Jefferson thought it beneath the deity to interfere in worldly affairs.

But if an account of what counts as religious and what does not is based not on content but on attitudes, then there is no reason to exempt religious belief from evidential standards, because belief aims at truth, not emotional satisfaction or practical usefulness. This is not to say, of course, that religious beliefs do not feature prominently in our emotional lives and practical activities. Rather, it is simply to say that the evaluation of a belief as such has nothing to do with satisfaction. It would be very satisfying to believe I was the most popular man on YouTube, but unless there is evidence that this is true, it would be an inappropriate belief.

Justified Religious Belief

Here is one argument against evidentialism about religious belief:

P1: Some strongly held religious beliefs are justified.

P2: No religious beliefs have strong evidence.

C1: Therefore, evidentialism is false.

More generally, one might simply think there are some religious beliefs that have more justification than they have evidence. Fortunately, there is no threat here to evidentialism if one also holds the common sense reasons theory of evidence expressed in RC*. For RC* is unprejudiced with regard to contents. Whatever the faculty producing the seeming or whatever the lower-level experiences causing the seeming—in the way that red sense-experiences cause it to seem to us that there is a red thing—it is the having of the seeming that constitutes the evidence. The cause is part of a different story, not the story of justification. What causes you to have that evidence is part of the story about knowledge. If the red mug in front of you looks green because you have a color spectrum inversion disorder caused by a burst of gamma rays from Alpha Centauri, and it's looking blue causes it to seem to you that it is blue, then you are justified in believing it is blue; but, since it is not blue, you do not know it is blue. And even if it does look red and its looking red causes it to seem to you that it is red, but it does so because, due to—you guessed it—a brain lesion caused by a burst of gamma rays from Alpha Centauri, which makes you think that it is an elephant and that all elephants are red, your true belief that there is a red thing, though it be in the end based on the appearance of a red thing, is caused in the wrong sort of way to count as something you know.

So, suppose the experience of seeing a sunset or a newborn child causes it to seem to you that there is a God. You are thereby justified in believing there is a God. Or, if the experience of praying the Prayer of Contrition makes it seem to you that God has forgiven you, you are justified in believing that God has forgiven you (with a strength proportional to the strength of the experience). If atheism is true, that justified belief doesn't count as knowledge. If the process is too affected by, say, wishful thinking, then it won't count as knowledge. But evidentialism is first and foremost a thesis about justification, not knowledge. It is, after all, confidence levels that drive and explain behavior.

Medieval theologians sometimes talked of a cognitive faculty they called the "oculi contemplationis" (or "eyes of contemplation") whereby individuals had the ability to perceive God. If there is such a faculty, then when it functions properly it can produce not only evidentially justified belief—via the production of evidence, its seeming that God exists—but also knowledge. If there is not such a cognitive faculty, then many religious believers are misled by their evidence and have justified false beliefs. But there is no problem at all about having justified religious beliefs in accordance with evidentialism. And, of course, there is a rich tradition of arguments in support of religious belief. Some people may not find these arguments convincing, but that doesn't count against the justification of those who do find them convincing. In short, there is no conflict whatsoever between evidentialism and the justification of religious belief.

One objection to this view is that it makes justification too easy. One reply to that objection is that justification *is* easy! It's a pretty low-grade epistemic good compared to other high-grade epistemic goods like understanding and wisdom. Not every epistemic good has to be hard to come by. There are lots of ways justified beliefs can fall short of ideal beliefs.

Another reply is that all I've argued is that we can have strong, direct or indirect evidence for religious beliefs (which for now I'm just taking to denote beliefs key to systems that are typically called religions). How hard it is to be justified on the whole will differ by context. Some people live in environments epistemically friendly to religious belief, such as healthy religious communities. The life experience of individuals in such a context is often a conduit of much evidence for religious belief. Others live in environments epistemically hostile to religious belief, such as highly secularized societies. The life experience of individuals in such a context is often a conduit of much evidence against religious belief. Religious believers in such a context will need to have extra evidence or answers for the arguments against their beliefs, which believers in more friendly environments will not need. How hard it is to have well-justified religious beliefs will depend entirely on the context in which they arise. But again, the concerns with difficulties such as these do not threaten RC* or E3.

One way to state the problem I've just addressed is to say that people often misunderstand what is meant by the word "evidence." The term tends to invoke the kind of evidence at play in paradigmatic scientific or legal contexts people are familiar with, whether real or fictional. The kinds of evidence that dominate our ordinary discourse (in the developed West) are those involved in biology, medicine, and the courtroom. There may well not be any obvious evidence of the kinds used there that directly relate to the justification of religious belief. But as indicated, the notion of evidence is vastly more broad than that. This is so even in the more complicated cases found in science, medicine, and law. Certainly the kind of evidence theoretical physicists marshal on behalf of the existence of, for instance, the top quark or the Higgs Boson are much more varied than we ordinarily think of. Our toy cases of looking at red mugs certainly aren't going to cut it when it comes to theoretical entities. Also, we have justified beliefs about morality for which the evidence consists in simple intuitions. We all know that genocide is wrong. We all know that rape is wrong. We all know that racism is wrong. These are, in fact, among our most well-justified beliefs. I believe we have discovered some planets outside our own solar system. However, I am much, much more sure that racism is wrong. The evidence for moral beliefs consists in simple, vivid intuitions, insights into the nature of the moral. In this respect, our evidence for moral principles is similar to our evidence for logical principles. We all know that if $A = B$ and $B = C$, then $A = C$, when "=" expresses numerical identity. What is your evidence for this belief? It is a simple, vivid intuition, an insight into the nature of logical reality.

Some people whose notion of evidence is too influenced by the medical and legal dramas they watch on television, or by silly junior-high notions of the "scientific method," look down on intuitions as evidence. But such people are left with no good theory of the justification they so obviously have for many of their moral and mathematical beliefs. Our evidence for our very important beliefs about the mental states of others is similarly intuitive. Religious beliefs are often justified similarly to moral, mathematical, and mental beliefs. If one holds a theory of evidence that is broad enough for our moral, mathematical, and mental beliefs, then there is no problem at all in consistently holding that religious beliefs are justified and that religious beliefs must live up to the same evidential standards of all other beliefs.

Exempting Religious Belief?

The above clarification regarding evidence notwithstanding, some people think religious beliefs stand in stark discontinuity to other kinds of beliefs. They may or may not hold that this is true for moral beliefs. The basic idea is that such beliefs are not intended to represent any objective features of the world. Rather, this line of thinking goes, religious (and, usually, moral) beliefs are meant to express emotional states or values or something along those lines. Sometimes something like the following justification is offered. Our language evolved in response to the advantages of discoursing about the natural world. But religious and moral beliefs are not about the natural world, so we can't even talk about those worlds, much less form cognitive beliefs about them. I reject these views on the grounds (among others) that they would equally undercut the justification of mathematical beliefs and beliefs about theoretical physics. And the idea that religious beliefs are not intended to objectively represent the world is a relatively new thought in the history of ideas. It didn't gain much currency until the nineteenth century, and I don't see much of anything going for it.

Alternatives to Evidentialism?

Moderate Fideism. A view called "moderate fideism" (*fide* is the Latin word for "faith") does not assert a radical discontinuity between religious beliefs and other beliefs. It therefore does not exempt them from evidential standards entirely. However, it does claim that because of the *moral importance* of religious beliefs, there is a special exemption for religious belief when the evidence leaves the situation indeterminate. In other words, if there is definitive evidence against religious belief, then to believe would be wrong. If there were definitive evidence for religious belief, then not to believe would be wrong. But if the evidence is indefinite in either direction, it is permissible to believe, because of how important it is to believe.

While this is a much more reasonable proposal than exempting religious belief entirely from rational scrutiny, it is based on a confusion between two different kinds of justification. Because belief is a truth-oriented (or, better, accuracy-oriented) attitude, an attitude that "aims" at truth (or accuracy), it's justification—whether propositional or doxastic—is based on what is truth-indicative: evidence. But acting *as though* a belief is true—whether you believe it or not—is rational when it has the greatest expected consequences of the choices available to one. It can be irrational to act on the belief that the snake is nonvenomous because the cost of being wrong is too high. And it can be rational to act as though you believe you can beat an illness, even though you don't believe you can, in order to increase the odds of your doing so. When no moral duty is involved, actions are rational or not dependent on consequences. But beliefs are always rational or not based on evidence. Moderate fideism confuses these two.

Reformed Epistemology. So-called Reformed epistemology is often touted as an alternative to evidentialism. The basic idea behind Reformed epistemology is that because God has designed us to form religious or religiously relevant beliefs in certain circumstances, when we form those beliefs in those circumstances, they can count as knowledge. This is an interesting proposal, but it has literally nothing to do with evidentialism, either pro or con, apart from a theory about the relationship between evidence and knowledge. Evidentialism is about epistemic justification, the intuitive "rightfulness" of holding a belief just based on what beliefs *are*: accuracy-oriented mental states. Maybe knowledge entails a particular relationship with evidence and maybe it doesn't. I am personally inclined to think it does, but maybe there are some kinds of knowledge, similar to what your dog or cat may have, that doesn't require the kind of evidential state humans are capable of. As indicated by my earlier characterization of evidence, even when someone "just knows" that something is true but can't explain how they know it, they are still responding to evidence, which in such cases consists in a kind of self-impelling intuition similar to those that give rise to mathematical, mental, and moral knowledge.

The fact is, Reformed epistemology arose in opposition to the idea that one needed *explicit arguments* for religious beliefs or that religious beliefs needed to be grounded in self-evident and certain truths. Even the casual reader will have noticed that I make no mention of self-evidence or certainty or explicit arguments. Maybe we have some of these some of the time, maybe sometimes we have all of them, maybe we never have any of them. Nothing in what I've said rules out or commits me to anything about these notions, the avoiding of which were the inspiration for Reformed epistemology.

Conclusion

In the previous section I argued that evidentialism is first and foremost a thesis about the justification of beliefs. Particularly, I defended both evidentialism (E3) and reasons commonsensism (RC*) as plausible theses regarding the doxastic justification of our beliefs on the one hand and the sources of evidence for those beliefs on the other.

I also argued that religious beliefs are no different in nature from moral and logical beliefs, for example. Specifically, I think it the case that if one thinks that beliefs of those sorts are eligible for justification, then one has no good reason to think that religious beliefs should receive exemption from the demands placed on other sorts of beliefs.

To conclude, then, if, on the basis of some cognitive faculty, it seems to you that P—say, "*that God exists*," for example—then you thereby have a reason to believe that P, in proportion to the strength of the seeming.

Religious Beliefs Do Not Require Evidence

Thomas D. Senor

Study Questions

1. What are the different things it might mean to say that it's wrong to hold religious beliefs without evidence? What do epistemologists typically mean by it?
2. How does Senor characterize evidentialism about religious belief? What are the two kinds of "good evidence"?
3. Why does evidentialism seem to be bad news for the "person in the pew"?
4. What is the "Faith above Reason" approach to responding to evidentialism? What reasons have people given for holding this view? Why does Senor reject it?
5. Instead of the "Faith above Reason" approach, what strategy does Senor prefer for responding to evidentialism?
6. What is "dual-systems" theory"? What does it suggest regarding how our beliefs are justified?
7. In light of dual-systems theory, how does Senor think that religious beliefs are justified?
8. What potential objection to his view does Senor raise? How does Senor respond to the objection?

There is a straightforward sense according to which the assertion in the title of this chapter is clearly true: people sometimes have religious beliefs for which they have no evidence. So we must begin by separating the *psychological* claim that people who believe in God don't always have evidence for their convictions from the *normative* thesis that it is *all right* or *not a bad thing* to have religious beliefs even if you don't have evidence for them. It is the latter, normative understanding that we will be concerned with in this chapter.

What are we asserting, then, when we say that it is all right or not a bad thing to hold religious beliefs without having evidence for them? One thing we might mean is that such believers are doing nothing *morally* wrong in believing as they do. So, for example, if you believe that "God loves all people" but you lack evidence for this claim, you can't be reasonably thought to have violated any ethical duty or principle. Or can you? Some think so. Philosopher W. K. Clifford thinks that when you believe anything in the absence of sufficient evidence, you are committing a sin against humanity! That seems pretty extreme. Why should you think such a thing? Furthermore, if you believe that God loves everyone, even without good evidence, you might be more likely to treat people well, and where's the sin in that? While I won't be providing much by way of argument for it, I'm going to assume from here on out that the primary issue does not concern morality. Believing without evidence might be a bad idea for other reasons, but it isn't (primarily, anyway) because it is morally wrong to do so.

If it isn't a violation of an ethical duty to believe without evidence, then in what sense is it "not all right" or "a bad thing"? The answer most epistemologists (that is, philosophers who study questions of knowledge and rational belief) would give is this: it is irrational or unreasonable to believe a proposition that you lack evidence for. It's not that you are doing something that is a violation of *moral* principles, but rather that you are doing something in violation of rational or *epistemic* principles. The general assumption is that beliefs are successful when they are true. In some minimal sense, when you have a belief that is false, things haven't gone as they should; you've not gotten things right. The question, then, is how we can bring it about that our beliefs are (mostly) true. A plausible strategy is to try to make sure that you believe something only if you have good reason for believing it. We know from experience that when we base our beliefs on good reasons, then our beliefs tend to be true. If I believe that Mary will come to my party just because I really want her to, I have no good reason to think she'll show up and my belief might well be false. But if I believe it because Mary told me that she'd be there, and I've always known her to do what she says she'll do, then I will very likely be right in my belief.

Evidentialism

On the perspective we are now exploring, having a "good reason" for holding a belief is to have solid evidence that the belief is true. And the person who thinks that it is "not all right" or " a bad thing" to hold a belief without evidence is committed to the following epistemic principle (EP):

> EP: Religious beliefs are epistemically justified only if they are based on good evidence.

To fully understand what EP implies, we'll have to understand more about what "good evidence" comes to.

What Is "Good Evidence"?

While philosophers have offered varying accounts of what evidence is, to streamline our discussion, I'm going to assume that when it comes to evidence for our beliefs there are two fundamental kinds. First, there is *experiential evidence*. If I see a cardinal in my birdbath, and thereby come to believe that there is a cardinal in my birdbath, my evidence is my visual experience. Or if I smell the distinctive smell of popcorn as I walk into the office, I'll come to believe that someone is having popcorn because of what I smell. In these cases, the evidence for belief is experiential. While the five senses provide a great deal of our experiential evidence, we also have experience of our own thoughts and feelings. I notice that I'm dragging, and upon reflection, I realize that I'm feeling sad. This might naturally lead me to believe that I'm feeling a bit down today. Even more straightforwardly, if I wake up and feel a pain in my elbow, I might (naturally enough) believe that I have a pain in my elbow.

The other fundamental kind of evidence that we have for beliefs is *our other beliefs*. Suppose that I believe that my favored candidate for the upcoming election for the US Senate will almost surely lose. Now this belief is unlikely to be grounded in anything that I directly experience: it's not that I can literally see or hear or smell that she is going to lose. Rather, it is based on other beliefs I hold. In particular, it is based on my belief that the statewide electorate is strongly disposed to elect candidates of Party A whereas my candidate is from Party B. Also, my candidate is running against a relatively popular incumbent, and such incumbents rarely lose. Finally, I've seen a head-to-head poll that shows that my candidate trails by fifteen percentage points. Now given that I believe all of these other things (and have no other relevant beliefs about the election), it is clear that I have very good reason to think my candidate will lose. So the second kind of evidence comes in the form of other things we believe.

Two additional points should be made here. First, the beliefs that I have as evidence for my belief that my candidate will lose will only be *good* evidence (that is, will only justify me) if I have good reason to believe them. If I'm just a very pessimistic person, and I believe the poll numbers are bad, that incumbents usually win, and that my state generally votes the other party only because I just expect things to go against my wishes, then I don't have good evidence that my candidate will lose. On the other hand, if I believe these other three things because I pay attention to the political reporting of reliable sources, then those beliefs will be justified (because they are backed by good evidence) and they will justify me in thinking my candidate will lose. So when a belief is justified by another belief (or beliefs), the latter *justifying* beliefs must be justified as well.

The final point about evidence that I want to make here is that sometimes beliefs are grounded by a combination of the two types we've been considering. If I hear the grandfather clock strike three chimes and I come to believe that it is three o'clock in the afternoon, my belief will be based in part on what I heard. But it will also be dependent on my background belief that those chimes represent the current time, and that it is daytime, and so the three chimes mean that it is 3:00 p.m. rather than 3:00 a.m. So "good evidence" for a belief will come directly from experience, from beliefs, or a combination of the two.

Let's call the position that EP ("Religious beliefs are epistemically justified only if they are based on good evidence") is true *evidentialism*. We've seen earlier that there is something initially plausible about it. For it seems that beliefs that are grounded in good evidence are likely to be true. So why would anyone care to deny EP? And even if you wanted to, what could you say to defend yourself?

Evidentialism and Religious Belief

Let's begin by noting that EP would seem to be bad news for the rationality of the religious belief of common folks or "the person in the pew." For if EP is true, then only beliefs that are based on good evidence are justified. What are the prospects that religious beliefs will pass this test? Although exactly what is required for "good evidence" hasn't been made explicit, we've seen that typical cases of good evidence involve perception or reasoning from justified beliefs. So let's take the belief that God exists. What is the average person's "good evidence" for this? Does she have anything akin to perceptual experience? Many people will claim they hear a "still, small voice" or feel comforted in times of hardship or feel a sense of call or leading when making difficult decisions. I have no doubt that such reports are genuine and don't deny that the experiences really are of God. But none of these experiences has anything like the justifying force that seeing a blooming redbud tree gives you in believing that you are seeing brightly colored blossoms. Moving from the content of the experience that "I feel comforted" to the belief that "God exists" is not something that religious experiences justify you in doing.

So how about the other standard way of justifying beliefs? Maybe the standard believer is justified by some kind of argument or body of evidence that she knows (or is justified in believing). Note that it is not enough that *there is* a good argument or body of evidence for the existence of God in order for the believer to satisfy EP. That evidence can justify her belief only if she possesses that evidence—only if she is justified in believing that evidence. So what body of evidence might the average religious believer have that would justify her belief that God exists? Clearly, we don't have the space here to look seriously at the possibilities. But I can report that even among theistic professional philosophers, there is no consensus that *any* of the traditional arguments provides adequate justification for believing that God exists. Furthermore, the standard theist won't know those arguments anyway. At best, she might say that the universe is an amazing place, and she can't see how all this complexity and beauty could happen without God as its explanation. Even if there is the making of a decent argument here, to get from the complexity and beauty of the universe to the existence of God requires a number of intermediate steps that those without philosophical training will be unlikely to provide.

In short, it looks as though EC will be bad news for the average believer. Perhaps there is good reason to believe in God known by certain theologians and philosophers, but that will be of no use to those who aren't up on the academic literature.

Responding to Evidentialism

Broadly speaking, there are two ways to reasonably avoid the point of the evidentialist position. First, you might grant that EP is true, but insist that religious beliefs aren't supposed to be epistemically justified, and that it would be a bad thing if they were. The point in this reply is not to deny EP, but rather to burst its bubble. For if it is a good thing that religious beliefs *aren't* justified, then evidentialism is more or less irrelevant. The second way to respond is to deny that religious belief needs to be based on good evidence in order to be justified. That is, you might argue that EP is false. We'll look at these two responses in order.

Faith above Reason

There is an ancient tradition in Christianity that maintains that faith and evidence do not work well together. It's not that, generally speaking, we shouldn't try to have good evidence for our beliefs, but only that in the realm of faith you shouldn't look for reasons and evidence. Why would people think this? Some have thought that this is what Jesus was suggesting when he told Thomas, "Have you believed because you have seen me? Blessed are those who have not seen and yet have come to believe" (Jn 20:29, NRSV). This has suggested to some that it is better to have simple faith or trust, and that believing *without* good evidence is religiously preferable. Another New Testament reference that leads some to think that faith should eschew rationality is when the apostle Paul writes that the young church's teaching about Christ is "a stumbling block to Jews and foolishness to Gentiles" (1 Cor. 1:23, NRSV). In saying that the Gospel is "foolishness to Gentiles," he is sometimes understood as saying that if you try to make rational sense of the Christian message, it will appear ridiculous. Indeed, early Christian philosopher Tertullian (*c.* 155–*c.* 240 CE) famously said "I believe because it is impossible!"

Nineteenth-century philosopher Soren Kierkegaard argued that the goal of faith is absolute commitment to God.[1] But if belief in God requires evidence like other kinds of beliefs do, then we should proportion the degree of conviction we have with the strength of our reason. In normal contexts, if you have only modest reason to believe something, and you are being reasonable, you won't believe it very confidently, if at all. On the other hand, if you have great evidence, your confidence should be stronger. If I believe that Omar was at the party because Abdul said that he *thought* he saw him there but he wasn't sure, then my belief will be hedged. On the other hand, if I believe that Omar was at the party because I spoke with him there, then my belief will be fully confident.

Kierkegaard's objection to basing religious belief on evidence is grounded in the conviction that if faith requires evidence, then you can only be absolutely committed to God (that is, have complete conviction) if you have absolute proof that God exists. And if you ever begin to think that your evidence is not superstrong, then you should dial back your commitment. And that struck Kierkegaard as antithetical to the nature of religious faith. So, even if EP is true, religious commitment should not be grounded in evidence and so it is appropriate that it is epistemically unjustified.

While it is hard to argue with Kierkegaard's conception of religious faith as involving (at least ideally) ultimate commitment, the idea that faith *should* be unjustified or irrational is problematic. After all, religious people want not just to have faith but they want to have *true* beliefs about God. But if faith is epistemically unjustified, then what reason do we have for thinking that it is true? Furthermore, if evidence isn't needed, what's to stop us from having faith in absolutely anything? Why have Christian faith as opposed to Hindu faith or faith in astrology? It is for these reasons that I think we should not accept the Kierkegaardian position on the relation of faith and reason.

Reasonable Faith

Earlier I said that there were two ways to not be an evidentialist about religious belief. The first, as we've seen, is to accept the evidentialist principle, agree that belief in God doesn't measure up to its standard, yet insist that this is a virtue rather than a vice. The second is to claim that the rationality of religious belief doesn't depend on one's having good evidence of its truth. And there are two ways one might go about this. On the one hand, one might argue that while EP is a good epistemic principle for many kinds of belief, religious convictions are a special sort and that the standards of rationality are different for them. This position is distinct from the Kierkegaardian perspective we just discussed because it insists that religious beliefs are rational whereas the Kierkegaardian position denies this (and says it's a good thing that they are not). On the other hand, one might think that while EP is initially plausible, it turns out not to be a good general principle of rationality. In the remainder of this essay, I'll be taking the second tack: I'll argue against the truth of EP as a general rule.

One of the most striking findings in contemporary cognitive science is what has become known as "dual-systems" theory.[2] According to this perspective, each of us contains two independent, although highly interactive, cognitive systems known as System 1 and System 2. In what follows, I briefly introduce dual-systems theory and then explain why I think it casts EP into serious doubt.

System 1 acts automatically and quickly, and it isn't under voluntary control (that is, it will function whether or not we want it to). It is continually observing our immediate environment and producing beliefs and answering very simple questions that require no reflection. Some of the processes that System 1 makes use of are innate: if I see a person with a bright smile, I will believe that the person is happy (even if that thought doesn't consciously cross my mind). This is not a learned inference; we are born with the disposition to "see" certain emotions in facial expressions. System 1 is at work when we answer simple, and obvious questions like "What is your name?" or "What year is it?" As the examples we have seen indicate, some of what happens in System 1 is innate but some of it is what has been learned and become automated.

In contrast to System 1, System 2 is relatively slow, to a significant extent under our conscious control, and the system we use when we are explicitly trying to figure things out or learn new skills. To get a quick feel of the distinction between the systems, recall what it was like to learn to drive. The first few times you take the wheel, you are paying explicit attention to so many things: depressing the accelerator, moving the steering wheel so that the car stays in the lane, the traffic in front of you, your speed, and so on. There is so much to think about in your early driving days that you could never have also carried on a conversation about college or even listened to the words of your favorite song. But now that you've been driving for a few years, the great majority of what you do when you drive happens automatically. System 1 has taken over for System 2. Now you can carry on even intellectually demanding conversations as you drive because System 2 is only minimally involved in your standard driving routine. But that its role has been greatly diminished doesn't mean that it isn't still there. For instance, as you are driving through an area you know to be a speed trap, you might decide to both pay more attention to your speed and be on the lookout for a police car. Each of these requires cognitive attention to specific things. System 1 is good at paying general attention to what one might encounter; System 2 is required to pay special attention to specific things.

System 2 is what we might think of as the rational system. If I ask you what the sum of 123 and 42 is, System 2 will kick in and you'll perform the sum in your head according to the rules that you learned long ago. If I ask you to tell me, roughly, the percentage of your philosophy class that wears glasses, you will recall faces of those in your class that come to mind, reflect on that, make a judgment about how many people are in the class in total, and either perform the basic division to get a number or use your background knowledge that, say, 5 out of 25 is 20 percent.

Now you might be wondering how this all relates to the justification of religious belief and EP. I can begin to explain this by noting that System 1 and System 2 bear only the slightest resemblance to the way we assumed beliefs were formed when we marked the distinction between beliefs that are justified by experience and beliefs that are justified by other justified beliefs that support them. As described earlier in this essay, a belief that there is a cardinal in my birdbath might be justified by my seeing a cardinal there. In such a case, the content of the belief ("there is a cardinal in the birdbath") is directly related to the content of what I see—that is, a cardinal's bathing in the bath. For beliefs that are justified by other beliefs, they get their justification by those other beliefs via a good inductive or deductive argument for them. In the example I gave earlier, my belief that my favored candidate for the Senate would lose was justified by my beliefs that legitimate polls showed her behind, that my state rarely elects members of her party to national office, and that she is running against an incumbent who is popular. These beliefs can easily be strung together to provide a very good inductive argument to the conclusion that my favored candidate will lose the election.

Both of these examples will satisfy EP. So if System 1 tended to work by forming beliefs that have the same or very similar content to what I perceive, then it would obey the evidentialist edict. But that's not the way that System 1 standardly works. System 1 is the product of our evolutionary history and, as we saw with the example involving facial expressions and anger, it is hardwired to pick up on certain features of the environment and form beliefs that may have little to do with the content of what one actually perceives. There is little direct connection in content between seeing someone with an open mouth and squinting eyes and forming the belief that the person is mad. Of course, over time we might learn that such judgments are generally true and so then have good evidence that the person is angry. But those background beliefs have nothing to do with why we form the belief in the first place. The belief that the person is angry is not based on good evidence but rather on a natural disposition to form a belief about a person's mental state based solely on her facial expression.

We might think that things are better when it comes to System 2. And certainly in some cases they are. In my example above, if my belief that my favored candidate will lose really is the result of my rationally considering the evidence, then System 2 will have produced a belief that EP will deem justified. But in many cases, even once System 2 becomes involved, my belief will not be based on solid logical or probabilistic reasoning. According to repeated studies, people often tend to believe a given candidate will win or lose an election not because of what they've read about the likelihood of the candidates' winning but rather because the candidate has certain facial features that produce confidence or that produce a lack thereof. Of course, we aren't conscious of the role that these features play in grounding our beliefs about likely candidate success; nevertheless, they often play an important part in our believing as we do. Also, when we do try to consider what our background experience has to say about a topic, our memory will tend to produce a relative few examples (often examples that confirm whatever it is that we are considering) and we will believe on the basis of only a small sample of what our total evidence is (psychologists call this the "availability heuristic").

So what is the upshot of all of this? My point is that it is naïve to think that our beliefs tend to be grounded either in perceptual experience that has the same or very similar content to the beliefs thereby formed, or in reasoning processes that make use of the relevant background beliefs to construct either logically valid or probabilistically sound arguments for the beliefs in question. Our processes are much more intuitive and rough-and-ready than that.

A better way to understand justification in light of the foibles of human psychology will imply that some natural ways that we tend to form beliefs are justification-conferring—and some not. A plausible way to distinguish the good from the bad processes is to say that justification-conferring processes are reliable (that is, tend to produce true rather than false beliefs). Furthermore, if a given belief is the natural product of innate cognitive processes that have a long evolutionary history (and are perhaps part of the cognitive design that

God has given us), then we aren't in any way blameworthy for believing as we do.

So it is my contention that, like other beliefs, religious belief will be justified if it is produced by processes that are reliable; and people who have religious beliefs that are grounded in innate processes are believing in an acceptable (i.e., not blameworthy) way. Of course, this isn't to say that beliefs that are grounded in good evidence aren't justified too. But EP says that *only* beliefs grounded in good evidence are justified. So, if EP is true and what contemporary cognitive and social psychologists tell us is true too, then humans will have very few justified beliefs. On the other hand, if we adopt, a broadly reliabilist account of justification, religious beliefs (both of the academic and of the ordinary fold) may be justified even if the devout lack good evidence for them.

At this point, one might object to what I've said as follows: "Suppose the reliabilist is right. So, if the processes that produce religious belief are reliable, then those beliefs are justified. But how are we supposed to know that those processes are, in fact, reliable? The fact is that we have no idea if they are reliable or not. And if we are clueless about their actual reliability, then we are clueless about whether those beliefs are justified. We will have made no progress at all in determining the rationality of religious belief."

This is an important objection. It is true that if you opt for a reliabilist (or any brand of externalism)[3] theory of justification, it might be difficult to know how to assess the rationality of religious belief. In reply, I'd like to note two things: first, it is not only religious beliefs that will be hard to assess. It turns out that showing that even perceptual processes are reliable is also an extremely difficult task. Suppose you want to check the reliability of vision. You seem to see an apple in front of you and so to test your vision you reach out and touch it. Sure enough, you feel its smooth skin. Your vision has been vindicated, but only by assuming that your tactile sense is reliable (i.e., you were just trusting your sense of touch to test your vision). So then how would you test your sense of touch? You could lean in and take a whiff. If it smells like an apple, then that corroborates what you have seen and felt. But, again, at this point you are just assuming that your olfactory sense is reliable. And now you can see the problem: if the goal is to show that your senses are reliable, you can't simply assume that some of them are. You've got to show that they *all* are reliable. And it is very hard to see how that can be done.[4]

My second response to the objection that if reliabilism is true, then we won't know if our beliefs are justified is that things aren't a whole lot better if one accepts an evidentialist theory like EP. For on that account, one is justified only if one has sufficient evidence. But in anything other than simple perceptual cases, it is hard to know exactly what one's evidence is for a belief. And even if you knew for sure what the precise evidence set is, figuring out that your evidence adequately supports the belief in question is a complicated (and controversial) task.

Conclusion

In this chapter, I've argued that religious beliefs do not require evidence to be rational. While the evidentialist principle we considered is initially plausible, in the end it is not the standard by which we should judge our beliefs—religious or otherwise. Let me conclude by offering an olive branch to my evidentialist friends. While a belief doesn't require positive evidential support to be justified—its being formed by a reliable process is all the positive support it needs—if, on the whole, there is strong reason to think that a belief is false, then that makes the belief unjustified all things considered. Put in terms of current epistemology, evidence against the truth of a belief can defeat the justification or rationality of a belief. That means that even if good arguments for the existence of God are not necessary for having rational theistic belief, good arguments for the *non*existence of God might well be sufficient to defeat the rationality of the belief for those who know the arguments. So, even from the perspective of a reliabilist, there is a lot of work to be done to make belief in God rational on the whole. For example, if the problem of evil is a good argument for atheism, then the rationality of belief in God will be undermined.[5]

So I have not been arguing that the sober, careful consideration of evidence is irrelevant to the rationality of religious belief. Instead, I have argued only that the evidentialist principle is not true and positive evidential support is not necessary for rational belief in God.

Notes

1 See Soren Kierkegaard, *Concluding Unscientific Postscript*, trans. David F. Swenson and Walter Lowrie (Princeton University Press, 1968).
2 A fascinating popular book on this is Daniel Kahneman's *Thinking, Fast and Slow* (FSG Publisher, 2011).
3 For arguments for and against externalism in epistemology see the essays by Ali Hasan and Stephen Hetherington in Chapter 3 of this volume.
4 For an extended discussion of this point, see William P. Alston's *The Reliability of the Senses* (Ithaca: Cornell University Press, 1996).
5 For a discussion of the problem of evil, see the essay by Bruce Russell and the response by Joshua Rasmussen in this volume.

RESPONSES

Response to Dougherty

Thomas D. Senor

Study Questions

1. What are the three characterizations of epistemic justification? Which one does Dougherty have in mind? Why, according to Senor, is this relevant?
2. What unclarity does Senor find in Dougherty's claim that religious beliefs are no different than logical and moral beliefs? How does Senor clear up the confusion?
3. How are Dougherty's and Senor's understanding of evidentialism similar? How do they differ?
4. What objections to Dougherty's (RC) does Senor have?

Trent Dougherty argues for the following claims: (i) evidentialism is the right theory of justified belief; (ii) religious beliefs are no different in nature from moral and logical beliefs—so if those beliefs require evidence for justification, then so do religious beliefs; and (iii) "if on the basis of some cognitive faculty it seems to you that P—say, '*that God exists*' for example—then you thereby have a reason to believe that P, in proportion to the strength of the seeming." In this response, I'll mostly take issue with Dougherty's third, and primary, thesis but I also want to consider reasons to be dubious of the other two.

Is Evidentialism the Right Theory of Justified Belief?

As I wrote in my essay on this subject, the title of our debate raises the question: "*Require* for what?" Dougherty makes it clear what he thinks evidence is required for—epistemically justified belief. But what is that? In order to see if evidentialism is a plausible account of justification, we need to have some general characterization of the concept or property of which we are giving a theory. There are three distinct characterizations that have been given for epistemic justification, and it is an open question whether any one theory can account for more than one of the characterizations—much less account for them all.

One thing philosophers have in their sites when they talk about justification is the central epistemic component of knowledge. Nearly all epistemologists think that in order for a person to know something (e.g., that the earth is the third planet from the sun) the person must believe it, or in more colloquial language, she must "think that it's true." If she doesn't have an opinion about it, she doesn't know it. Second, it must actually *be* true. But true belief isn't sufficient for knowledge since her belief might just be a lucky guess. So epistemologists think that in order to have knowledge there must be something that ties together the belief and the truth of the belief. And that is what justification is. Justification, on this perspective, is what takes true belief and makes it knowledge (or at least very close to knowledge). So, for example, when I see that the car is blue and on that basis come to believe that the car is blue, my perceptual state is the key (and justifying) link between the belief and what makes it true.

A second way of thinking about justification sees it as synonymous with rationality. For a belief to be justified in this sense, it must be rational. Does the person have whatever is necessary for a rational person who is in her position to believe the proposition? Put another way, are the person's reasons enough to make the belief rational?

Finally, some epistemologists have thought of epistemic justification of belief as a lot like moral justification of action. To be morally justified is to have done your duty; it is to be blameless in acting as you do. Similarly, a belief is justified in this sense if it has been arrived at in a way consistent with one's epistemic duty; the belief is justified because the subject is blameless in forming it.

So, when Dougherty explains his evidentialist account of justification, which characterization does he have in mind? It seems clear that it is primarily the second: to be justified requires that the belief be the right response to one's evidence; to believe against one's evidence is akin to believing irrationally.

I go through the above to note that even if Dougherty's evidentialism is the correct theory of the second conception of justification, there are other answers to the question "Does religious belief require evidence in order to be justified?" that are also epistemically important given the different ways justification can be characterized. In other words, even if evidentialism is *a right* theory of belief, that is by no means equivalent to its being *the right* theory of justified belief.

Are Religious Beliefs No Different from Moral and Logical Beliefs?

I'm in agreement about this. Or at least I think I am. I'm a little unclear about precisely what this second claim is. I'd have thought that Dougherty's position was that *all beliefs* require evidence for being justified—and so that all beliefs are on a par in this regard. But the claim in his conclusion is that religious beliefs are to be treated as "moral and logical" beliefs, not necessarily beliefs in general. A way to reconcile these claims is to say that all beliefs require evidence, but that some beliefs (like moral and logical beliefs) have mostly *intuitive* evidence, rather than the more robust evidence that we get from the senses. So religious beliefs are justified as are moral and logical beliefs in that the evidence for them doesn't trace back (typically) to sensory experience.

Do Seemings Justify?

It is his third, and most significant, conclusion that I strenuously object to. In order to see just what my objection is, however, let's review the ways he and I define evidentialism. For the version of evidentialism that I think is plausible as a theory of epistemic rationality is quite a bit different from the version he ends up with.

As I defined it, evidentialism regarding religious belief says that such beliefs are justified only if they are based on good evidence. The basic idea of evidentialism, as both Dougherty and I understand it, is that a doxastic attitude is justified to the degree that it fits the evidence one has. So, loosely, if you have no reason to think that P is true and also no reason to think it is false, then you shouldn't believe P; if you have pretty good reason to think P is true and no reason to think it is false, then you should have moderate confidence that P is true. The big question is, of course, what counts as evidence?

Here again there is a lot of agreement between Dougherty and myself. When I look outside and see leaves covering my lawn, I believe that the lawn is covered in leaves. My evidence for my belief is my visual state (or "percept") that represents the lawn as leaf-covered. When I look outside and see that the flag on the mailbox is now down, I believe that the mail has come. This is based both on my seeing that the flag is down and on my remembering that I put it up earlier in the day, together with believing that a lowered flag on a mailbox is a sign that the mail has arrived. Perceptual states, introspective states, memories, and beliefs can all provide evidence for belief. So far, so good.

In addition to the evidential states just listed, Dougherty adds another: "seemings." Now some varieties of seemings are unproblematic. To take one of his examples, when I look at a ripe banana, it seems that there is a yellow object in front of me. If the seeming here just is the visual state—call sensory states from all of the senses "perceptual seemings"—then it is clear both how the seeming provides *evidence* and how, in normal contexts, it provides *good* evidence for my belief that there is a yellow object in front of me.

However, Dougherty thinks perceptual seemings aren't the only kind of seemings that confer justification. Recall the thesis that he calls *reasons commonsensism*: "If it seems to you that P, then you thereby have a reason to believe that P, in proportion to the strength of the seeming." What kinds of seemings other than perceptual seemings does he have in mind? He clearly thinks moral and logical seemings are evidentially significant. And I suppose many others would be willing to include such things. But (RC) doesn't stop there. It is *perfectly general*. Any seeming of any kind gives you a reason for belief—gives you evidence of the truth of that belief. Furthermore, the stronger the seeming, the stronger the evidence. So for any proposition at all, if it really, *really* seems to you that it is true, then you have really, *really* good reason to believe it.

I have two objections to (RC). First, I don't see what it has to do with evidentialism. Some seemings provide good evidence because they are reliable signs of the truth of their content. My visual experience of a ripe banana is good evidence that there is a yellow object in front of me because almost always (always?) when I have that experience there is a yellow object before me. But, notoriously, not all seemings are like that. The more we learn about implicit bias, for example, the clearer it is that some seemings provide no reason at all for belief. It may genuinely seem to the racist, upon seeing a man of a disliked race, that he is dishonest and lazy. But that is not good reason to believe because the seeming is grounded in racism. Or it might seem to the sexist that the resume of the male applicant is superior to the resume of the female applicant even though the resumes are, in fact, identical. But because the seeming is a product of implicit bias, it isn't good evidence (no matter how strong the feeling is).

My second objection is one that Dougherty mentions himself: it makes justification too easy. Boy does it! Suppose I look at my leaf-covered lawn and it *really* seems to me that there are precisely 2,397 leaves there. I haven't counted the leaves, and I have no special leaf-counting perceptual faculty. If (RC*) is correct, then I have very good reason—good evidence— for thinking that there are 2,397 leaves on my lawn. But if that is all there is to justification, then there's no reason to be interested in it since *anything* can be justified for anyone if only it *seems* to them to be true. Surely when people sincerely wonder if belief in God is justified, they won't be satisfied by being told that since it really seems to some people that God exists, then the belief is justified.

So while evidentialism is a plausible theory of rationality, commonsensism is not. And if all that can be said for religious belief is that it is justified because it *seems* to some people to be true, then there is little to recommend it from an epistemic perspective.

Response to Senor

Trent Dougherty

Study Questions

1. What is the precise version of the Problem of the Person in the Pew? Why does Dougherty think the argument is trivial?
2. What kind of good evidence does Dougherty think the person in the pew has which undermines the first premise of the argument?
3. What does Dougherty say in response to Senor's discussion of "System 1 thinking"?
4. How, according to Dougherty, has Senor misread the New Testament? What additional data does he offer for an evidentialist reading of Scripture?

In my response to Tom Senor, I will focus on what I take to be the two principle critiques that he makes of the role of evidence for religious beliefs. First, I will respond to his concern for the epistemic justification of the "person in the pew." Second, I will offer an objection to his understanding of what the New Testament suggests regarding the justification of religious beliefs.

The Person in the Pew

In my opening essay, I anticipated a line of argument that Senor in fact ends up using. We can call it the *Problem of the Person in the Pew*:

(P1) If evidentialism is true, then the person in the pew isn't justified in their religious beliefs.

(P2) But the person in the pew *is* justified in their religious beliefs.

Therefore,

(C1) Evidentialism is false.

I think the anti-evidentialism argument I canvased is actually more precise than this one, but it'll do. First, though, we'll have to make it a bit more precise. For there are all kinds of people in all kinds of pews. I'm sure Senor is aiming at something like this.

(P1') If evidentialism is true, then no naïve believer is justified.

(P2') Some naïve believers are justified.

Therefore,

C1 Evidentialism is false.

Though this argument is undoubtedly valid, it will be hard for it to be cogent because it's hard to read "naïve believer" in any way other than "believer who lacks positive evidence for their religious beliefs." This reading makes it a pretty trivial argument. For the argument not to be trivial, Senor needs there to be witnesses in the pews who really do lack positive evidence *in the relevant sense*. However, that's just what I deny.

I spelled out carefully in my opening essay the kind of evidence any person in the pew can have. On the broad view of evidence I described—one, it should be noted again, that is neutral with respect to religion—there is no good reason to believe P1'. For the broad evidentialism I defended doesn't put any remotely unreasonable requirements on the person in the pew. For it countenances a broad notion of evidence beyond mere sense perception on the one hand and formal reasoning on the other. As I pointed out in my opening remarks, our justifications for our basic memory, introspection, and mathematical beliefs don't fit tidily in Senor's taxonomy.

Specifically, to answer Senor's question, the average person's good evidence that God exists is her awareness that life just makes the most sense when viewed from a framework that includes a belief in God. They see the world *as* the product of some kind of plan. "Seeing as" is a common phenomenon. For instance, when we judge people's emotional states, we see them as happy or sad or excited or whatever. There is a characteristic look they have, which we recognize. The evidence, technically, consists in the state of awareness and recognition of that look. That's the positive indicator or sign of the emotion.

Likewise, the believer recognizes the characteristic fingerprint of God on the universe. There is no more need for the believer to have explicit arguments for God's existence than for the average person to have explicit arguments connecting facial expressions to emotions. Thus, it is strange to me that Senor thinks that "System 1" thinking bypasses evidential considerations. What's true is that it bypasses *inferential* considerations. But experiential evidence doesn't need to be inferential (as even Senor admits early in his essay), nor do our beliefs need to be "grounded either in perceptual experience that has the same or very similar content to the beliefs thereby formed, or in reasoning processes that make use of the relevant background beliefs to construct either logically valid or probabilistically sound arguments for the beliefs in question" (p. xx). There is a middle ground between these two sources of justification in the kind of awareness that a belief just makes sense of our general experience. I have tried to capture this picture of evidence in my opening remarks in my principle (RC*). It doesn't have to be too sophisticated. There is no problem here for the person in the pew.

Evidence and the New Testament

What I have said is more than enough to answer Senor's anti-evidentialism. Nevertheless, I think it is worth some space to address his misreading of the New Testament. When the post-resurrection Jesus says to Thomas, "Blessed are those who have not seen and yet have come to believe," he is by no means recommending belief with no evidence. Rather, he is commending belief on the basis of the evidence the apostles already had. It is widely understood that Jesus expected the disciples to know from his prior words and deeds, as well as prophesy from the Hebrew Scriptures, that he would rise from the dead. Thomas's problem wasn't that he wanted evidence or that he was wanting for evidence; quite the contrary: he was being rebuked *because he had failed to appreciate the evidence he had been given.* And the notion that the Gospel is "foolishness to the Gentiles" is simply that God inverts the "logic" of the world: instead of putting oneself first, one puts God and others first.

Jesus's interaction with Thomas is far from a lone instance of scripture attesting to the importance of evidence for religious beliefs. Consider, for example, the opening prologue to the Gospel of St. Luke (Lk. 1:1-4). In the prologue, Luke, a well-educated, trained physician, writes to Theophilus that he has compiled the following "narrative" regarding the life and works of Jesus. There are several aspects of the prologue worth noting that have a bearing on my defense of evidentialism. First, Luke references that he is only one of many individuals to have undertaken the work of compiling such a historical narrative, thus opening himself up for refutation by contrary evidence or further confirmation by corroborating evidence. Luke is referencing not only first-order evidence but also clearly evincing an appreciation of the dynamics of evidential confirmation.[1] Theophilus was not the only person for whom such an account was written. Even the average people in the early church desired and were thus given evidence for their beliefs. Second, the information contained within Luke's narrative was drawn from eyewitnesses of Christ's work. The point of emphasis for Luke, here, is that these sources had experienced firsthand what he will recount and, thus, that they are credible. Finally, Luke writes that his work was done so that Theophilus "may have certainty concerning the things that [he has] been taught" (Lk. 1:4). That is, Luke clearly considers his work as playing an evidentiary role for Theophilus's beliefs.

Many additional passages might easily be brought to bear on the issue, but I think what has been said is sufficient.

Notes

1 To see that this understanding was not anomalous in the ancient world, see J. Franklin, *The Science of Conjecture: Evidence and Probability before Pascal* (Baltimore, MD: The John Hopkins University Press, 2001), 1–11.

Questions for Reflection

1. Should religious beliefs be exempt from being justified by good evidence, contrary to Dougherty's claim? If so, why? Would you agree with Senor that they should at least be reasonable or justified in some sense, contrary to Kierkegaard? If not, why?

2. Is Senor right that Dougherty's brand of evidentialism is far too permissive in what counts as good evidence? Can Dougherty respond to this charge? How?

3. Would the "person in the pew" have more sympathy for Dougherty's view or Senor's? Why?

4. How would someone who, unlike both Dougherty and Senor, thinks that religious beliefs are irrational or unjustified respond to Dougherty? How would he respond to Senor?

5

Can Science Discover the Truth about Reality?

Science Discovers the Truth about Reality

Stathis Psillos

Study Questions

1. Why are scientific theories born false? Why does Psillos think this is a harmless kind of falsity?
2. What two assumptions have become part and parcel of science since the scientific revolution? What view of science has been made possible by these assumptions?
3. What is the instrumentalist conception of scientific theories? How does Osiander illustrate this view?
4. What are the three theses of scientific realism? Which does Psillos claim is the one presently at issue?
5. What is the "No Miracles Argument" in defense of scientific realism? How does Psillos illustrate it?
6. What fallacy might the skeptic charge the No Miracles Argument with? How does Psillos answer the charge?
7. What "local arguments" does Psillos give for realism? How, according to Psillos, do the local and global arguments for realism reinforce each other?
8. What is the "historical pessimism" argument against realism? Why does Psillos think that this argument does not seriously damage realism?

9. What is the challenge to realism presented by the "underdetermination of theories by evidence"? How does Psillos respond to this challenge?

10. How does Psillos respond to suspicion for the unobservable? What does he think is the real issue? Why?

Scientific theories are born false. This is due to the fact that the reality they aim to represent is, typically, very complex; hence, theories indispensably employ idealizations and abstractions. As a result of this, they typically fail to accurately map the worldly phenomena in their full complexity. But this is a harmless kind of falsity, since, strictly speaking, a false theory can nonetheless be partially, or significantly, or even approximately, true. Science can and does discover significant truths about reality even if, strictly speaking, scientific theories are false due to the vagaries of scientific representation. Those who deny that science tracks the truth, or those who are simply skeptical about this, are not, as a rule, driven by the trivial fact that scientific theories fail to map the world in its full complexity. They would be denialists or skeptics even if scientific theories were, somehow, capable of representing the world fully and accurately. Their motivations are, by and large, driven by epistemological concerns about knowledge of the unobservable. But why should there be a problem with knowing what is not given to us in our immediate experience?

The philosophical issue at stake relates to the fact that, at least after the scientific revolution of the seventeenth century, two important assumptions have become part and parcel of science. The *first* is that there is a distinction between appearance and reality. The *second* is that this reality (beyond or behind the appearances) is by and large unobservable to the naked eye; it is composed of unobservable entities, processes, and mechanisms such that all observable phenomena and empirical laws are accounted for on their basis. These two assumptions made it possible to view science as an activity that aims to map the reality over and above the appearances, thereby discovering the hidden micro-constitution of the world. The denialists then deny that there is a reality behind the appearances to be mapped out, whereas the skeptics claim that, even if there is one, it cannot be known.

Historically, this kind of stance was epitomized in the preface to Nicolaus Copernicus's famously revolutionary book *On the Revolutions of the Heavenly Spheres*. Posthumously published in 1543, the book offered an account of the planetary motions based on the hypothesis that the sun is immobile and that the rest of the planets move around the sun. Contrary to the appearances, and to established scientific theory inherited from Aristotle, Copernicus famously ascribed "certain motions to the terrestrial globe [i.e., Earth]," rendering it one of the planets. Based on the assumption of the mobility of the Earth, Copernicus was aiming to find "sounder explanations" "for the revolution of the celestial spheres" than those of his predecessors.[1] The preface to the book was anonymous and was penned by Andreas Osiander, a Lutheran priest. In it, it was boldly stated that

> it is the duty of an astronomer to compose the history of the celestial motions through careful and expert study. Then he must conceive and devise the causes of these motions or hypotheses about them. Since he cannot in any way attain to the true causes, he will adopt whatever suppositions enable the motions to be computed correctly from the principles of geometry for the future as well as for the past . . . for these hypotheses need not be true nor even probable. On the contrary, if they provide a calculus consistent with the observations, that alone is enough.[2]

Although Osiander talks only about astronomy, this is one of the most accurate descriptions of what came to be known as an *instrumentalist* conception of scientific theories: theories are not, even in principle, maps of a hidden reality; they are mere tools for classification, prediction, and control: that is, for *saving the phenomena*. I will use "instrumentalism" as a generic term to refer to either denialists or skeptics.

Opposing instrumentalism is *scientific realism*. In my view, scientific realism comprises three theses or stances:[3]

The Metaphysical Thesis: The world has a definite and mind-independent structure.

The Semantic Thesis: Scientific theories are truth-conditioned descriptions of their intended domain. Hence, they are capable of being true or false. The theoretical terms featuring in theories have putative factual reference. So, if scientific theories are true, the unobservable entities they posit actually populate the world.

The Epistemic Thesis: Mature and predictively successful scientific theories are well confirmed and approximately true. So entities posited by them, or, at any rate entities very similar to those posited, inhabit the world.

What is presently at issue is the third thesis (aka *epistemic optimism*). According to this thesis, science has succeeded in tracking (partial, approximate) truth. Science, in other words, has revealed substantial parts of the unobservable structure and nature of the world. In light of the fact that modern science is so much immersed in a description of the world in terms of hidden-to-the-naked eye entities and structures, why should there be philosophical doubt about its ability to offer a truth-like account of the world? More positively put, what are the main reasons for taking science as tracking significant truths about the world?

The Positive Case for Realism

There are two types of argument in defense of scientific realism: one is global and the other is local. The global argument has come to be known as *The No Miracles Argument* due to its first formulation by Hilary Putnam. According to him, "The positive argument for realism is that it is the only philosophy that does not make the success of science a miracle."[4] This figurative talk of miracles is meant to illustrate the main thrust of the argument, namely, that accepting theories as approximately true is the best explanation for their empirical and predictive successes and especially of their tendency to yield novel predictions. The alternative explanations of the empirical successes of theories are deemed simply inadequate or worse than the realist one.

Take, for instance, a rival view that the unobservable entities whose existence is implied by the truth of a theory are not real, but useful fictions. This is known as *fictionalism* and was defended by the philosopher Hans Vaihinger in *The Philosophy of As If*. For him what is meant by saying that matter consists of atoms is that matter must be treated *as if* it consisted of atoms; that is, that "empirically given matter must be treated as it would be treated if it consisted of atoms."[5] It should be obvious that this "as-if" story offers no genuine explanation for the successes of the atomic theory of matter; at best, it is a fallback position whose own intelligibility is parasitic on the atomic theory of matter.

Actually, it's no accident that the first versions of the No Miracles Argument were formulated in the midst of the philosophical and scientific battle concerning the truth of the atomic theory of matter. Nor is it an accident that this kind of argument swayed many skeptics or instrumentalists to realism (or some form of it, anyway). The French physicist and philosopher of science Pierre Duhem, for instance, noted that admitting that theories are simply "racks filled with tools" which organize and classify empirical laws, without thereby revealing some hidden parts of the nature and structure of reality, cannot account for how theories can be "prophets for us." This "clairvoyance" of scientific theories would be unnatural to expect—it would be a "marvelous feat of chance"—if "the theory was a purely artificial system" which "fails to hint at any reflection of the real relations among the invisible realities."[6] But this same "clairvoyance" would be perfectly natural if the principles of the theory "express profound and real relations among things." If, that is, what the theory asserts of the unobservable reality is truth-like, it is natural to expect that it will yield predictions of novel phenomena, that is, of phenomena that have not been observed before the theory predicts them.

A truth-like theory can anticipate fresh experiments and observations and not merely accommodate known ones. A historically significant case was the confirmed prediction of Fresnel's wave theory of diffraction of light-rays—that if the light from a source is intercepted by an opaque disk, a bright spot will appear at the center of the shadow of the disk. But theories can, and do, get support from explaining already known facts. For instance, Einstein's General Theory of Relativity (GTR) was supported by the fact that it accounted for the anomalous perihelion on Mercury—an anomaly that had plagued Newton's theory of gravity. According to astronomical observations, the precession of the perihelion of Mercury, versus the fixed stars, was 575.1 arc-seconds per century. Simon Newcomb accounted for 531.7 arc-seconds from the gravitational perturbations of the other planets on Mercury, leaving an unexplained discrepancy of 43.4 arc-seconds per century. It was this discrepancy that was accounted for by Einstein's theory of gravity, resulting in what he took to be "convincing proof of the correctness of [his own] theory."[7] What's important to add is that this prediction of the already known discrepancy counted in favor of Einstein's theory precisely because information about it was *not* used in the construction of GTR, but "was borne," as it were, naturally out of it.

The No Miracles Argument relies on more concrete types of explanatory reasoning which occur all the time in science. It relies on the fact that certain theories are accepted as approximately true, at least in the respects relevant to their theory-led predictions, based on their predictive and empirical successes. But its own scope is a lot broader. It is not *just* a generalization over the scientists' abductive-explanatory inferences. It aims to defend the thesis that *Inference to the Best Explanation* (IBE), a *type* of inferential method extensively used in science, is reliable. Now, this might create a tension. The No Miracles Argument itself is an explanatory argument; it is an instance of IBE. How, then, it might be asked, can it be used to justify the reliability of IBE as an inferential method? Isn't this approach circular? As I have argued in detail elsewhere,[8] there is some sort of circularity here but it is benign as opposed to malign: it is "rule-circularity" as opposed to the vicious "premise-circularity." Indeed, it turns out that any attempt to offer a rule-based justification of the basic inferential methods (being deduction or induction) will have to be rule-circular; that is, it will have to employ at the *meta-level* the rule of inference that is being justified at the object-level. The alternative is either to admit a rather problematic immediate (non-inferential) justification of the basic modes of reasoning or to succumb to skepticism. In this sense, the NMA-based justification of IBE is in good company: if it fails, deduction and induction will turn out to be unjustified too.

It might be argued that the No Miracles Argument is inductively fallacious.⁹ That is, it might be taken as a probabilistic argument that moves from the fact that a chance agreement with the facts predicted by a theory T is very improbable (i.e., that the probability of empirical success of the theory T given that T is *false* is extremely low), to the conclusion that T is very likely to be true given its empirical success. Now, this *kind* of argument would be inductively fallacious. It would commit the so-called base-rate fallacy, since it has neglected the prior probability of T being true independent of its empirical success. Yet, there is no good reason to think that this is the right way to formulate the No Miracles Argument. This formulation obscures the role of explanatory considerations in accepting an empirically successful theory as true. But even if we were to admit a probabilistic version of the No Miracles Argument, we could always render it inductively cogent by admitting prior probabilities of theories (that is, the probability of a theory being true prior to the evidence coming in) based on considerations of initial theoretical plausibility (e.g., simplicity and explanatory power).¹⁰

How about then providing more local arguments for realism? It should be noted that the right question to ask is not how likely it is that an *arbitrary* (randomly selected) theory T be true, given that it has been successful. This question would require unavailable statistical information about the rates of truth and falsity among theories and hence it would be unanswerable. Instead, the right question to ask is: How likely is it that a certain *specific* theory T be true, given that it has been successful? This second question can certainly be answered by looking into the actual case history, namely, the *particular* successes of individual theories—for example, the discovery of the structure of the DNA molecules, or the explanation of the anomalous perihelion of Mercury. What then matters for the probability of the truth of a specific theory, for example, the double helix model, is that there is lots of first-order scientific evidence about the structure of the DNA molecule to convince the scientists that the double helix model is approximately true. Approximate truth is a relation between the specific theory and its domain (a relation of approximate fit). It is a local relation which can be examined by looking at the initial plausibility of this theory and the evidence there is in its favor from its explanatory and predictive (especially novel predictive) successes.

In this respect, the establishment of the atomic theory of matter, thanks to the work of the French physicist Jean Perrin, is instructive. In 1901 he published a paper in *Revue Scientifique* under the title *The Molecular Hypothesis*. Ten years later, in 1911, he published another paper in the same journal with the title *The Reality of Molecules*. The conclusion of this article was that "the objective reality of molecules" had been demonstrated. What had happened in between? Perrin had shown how a well-established phenomenon known as Brownian motion (the incessant and irregular agitation of small (invisible) particles suspended in a liquid) could be accounted for only on the basis of the atomic conception of matter—that is, on the theory that matter has an essentially granular structure. Perrin rested on causal-eliminative reasoning to render as initially plausible the hypothesis that the cause of the Brownian motion was internal to the liquid and not due to external factors. He then devised a specific theoretical model of the observed exponential distribution of the Brownian particles in a cross-section of the liquid based on the kinetic theory of gases, and was able to predict with great accuracy Avogadro's number N, namely, the number of molecules in a gram-molecule of a gas. This is a huge but finite number. As Perrin noted, on the alternative hypothesis that matter is continuous, the number N would be either 0 or infinity. On his atomic theory, however, the observed value of N was very close to the one predicted by the theory. As Perrin put it: "That, in the immense interval [0, infinity] which *a priori* seems possible for N, the number should fall precisely on a value so near to the value predicted, certainly cannot be considered as the result of chance."[11] His argument for the reality of molecules makes it very likely that molecules exist and cause the Brownian motion. Not just that. He consolidated the proof by showing what he called "*le miracle de concordances*," namely, that all known ways to predict Avogadro's number (from a diverse array of phenomena) are in considerable agreement. This "concordance" would be hard to explain if it were not accepted that there are molecules which are actually measured. Reflecting on Perrin's experiments, Henri Poincaré, who was initially skeptical of the reality of molecules, noted in 1912: "The brilliant determinations of the number of atoms computed by Mr Perrin have completed the triumph of atomism. What makes it all the more convincing are the multiple correspondences between results obtained by entirely different processes . . . . The atom of the chemist is now a reality."[12]

It might be thought that Perrin's case, which is far from atypical, shows that only local arguments for realism might have any hope for success. This wouldn't be right. For one, Perrin himself did not see his argument as sui generis about the reality of molecules. He saw it as an instance of a general methodological pattern. He wrote in 1916 (about what he called "the intuitive-deductive method," which was none other than IBE):

> To divine in this way the existence and properties of objects that still lie outside our ken, *to explain the complications of the visible in terms of invisible simplicity* is the function of the intuitive intelligence which, thanks to men such as Dalton and Boltzmann, has given us the doctrine of Atoms. This book [*Les Atomes*] aims at giving an exposition of that doctrine.[13]

Perrin's point concerned the credibility of a type of method that aims to explain the visible in terms of the invisible—and this is what IBE (in essence) is about. For another, the method that aims to explain the visible in terms of the invisible is a genus: *ampliative explanatory inference. qua* genus, it has species and instances. Scientists might use explanatory considerations and explanatory models in ampliative inference in various ways. But all these ways have an underlying abstract form: they *explain* the visible in terms of the invisible. Hence, there is a dialectical relationship between the various local arguments for realism and the global one.[14]

To see this, do note that scientific realism is a view about science-in-general and its epistemic credentials. Hence, its content, *qua* a philosophical thesis, exceeds a conjunction of claims such as "electrons exist & protons exist & . . . & DNA molecules exist." Scientific realism is not a list-like thesis, whose content can be captured by a sum of cases. It's an *explanatory* thesis, which asserts something about science-in-general and its method—namely, that science is in the truth-business (not merely as an aim but as an actual cognitive achievement), and scientific methodology (significantly in those aspects of it that promise to reveal to us the unseen blueprint of the world) is reliable. Precisely because of this, the defense of realism should combine the global and the local perspectives, which reinforce each other.

The Negative Case for Realism

Evidence for the existence of atoms and other entities is (and should be) evidence for realism. Scientific evidence that science can reveal to us the atomic structure of the world is evidence that science can offer us knowledge of the world. But note that this kind of evidence is not about atoms in particular. It is about *unobservables* in general—whatever is posited by successful scientific theories. The existence of atoms lends credence to the methods used to arrive at them—and the methods might well be operative in other domains of inquiry.

But there is more global evidence to be taken into account. Science has a history, and the history of science has been taken to undermine the basic realist thesis that science is in the truth-business. One important reason to lower the epistemic sights of science is that science has had a poor track record: it has gone through so many radical revolutions, so many dramatic theory-changes, that there is reason to believe that what is currently accepted will be overturned in the near future. Defending realism and the claim that science delivers truths about the world requires blocking this *historical pessimism*.

Pessimistic arguments from the history of science have become prominent twice over: toward the end of the nineteenth century when the scientific image of the world was in turmoil, and toward the end of the twentieth century when the realist turn in the philosophy of science was in full swing. On both occasions, the key claim was that, given the past record of failed scientific theories which emerged triumphantly only to be abandoned at a later stage, there is reason to expect that at least some if not most of the presently accepted theories will have the same fate. Unless, of course, we are entitled to suppose that currently accepted theories "form an exception," as Leo Tolstoy—the first author of this argument—put it.[15] Yet, he added, this is a supposition which "we have no right to make." In its second incarnation, this kind of argument was taken to be broadly inductive. As Newton-Smith put it on behalf of the instrumentalist:

> Indeed, there is inductive support for a pessimistic induction: any theory will be discovered to be false within, say 200 years of being propounded. We may think of some of our current theories as being true. But modesty requires us to assume that they are not so. For what is so special about the present? We have good inductive grounds for concluding that current theories—even our most favourite ones—will come to be seen to be false.[16]

Larry Laudan gave this argument prima facie historical credibility by putting forward the historical gambit, viz., a longish list of actual past theories which were supposed to be predictively successful but turned out to be false and were abandoned. He guessed a certain 6 to 1 ratio of false to true theories: "I daresay that for every highly successful theory in the past of science which we now believe to be a genuinely referring theory, one could find half a dozen once successful theories which we now regard as substantially non-referring."[17]

How damaging for realism is this kind of argument? It turns out that it's not too much—though care should be taken by realists in its light. There are various ways to discredit this historical argument. For instance, it might be argued that the sampling of theories which constitute the inductive evidence is neither random nor otherwise representative of theories in general: radically different theories developed in radically different periods, and with varying rates of success have been grouped together. It might be stressed that only very few past theories were robust enough to yield novel predictions. Be that as it may, the best defense of realism in the face of the historical argument is the one outlined by Ludwig Boltzmann and (independently) by Poincaré at the beginning of the twentieth century. Replying to the "historical principle," according to which theories are essentially insecure because they tend to be abandoned and replaced by other, "totally different" ones, Boltzmann argued that there is enough continuity in theory-change to warrant the claim that some "achievements may possibly remain the possession of science for all time, though in a modified and perfected form."[18] In a similar fashion, Poincaré argued that the history of science shows that there is continuity at the level of mathematical equations, which he took to express theoretical relations among things. The history of the development of physics, Poincaré stressed, shows that "new relations are continually being discovered between objects which seemed destined to remain forever unconnected."[19] Hence, the history of science is replete with elements of invariance in theory-change, theoretical hypotheses and laws that have stood the test of time. The key point is that the pervasive invariant elements in theory-change suggest that, as science grows, more and more elements of the hidden reality are correctly identified and mapped out: the growing and evolving scientific image paints a truer picture of the unobservable world.

Hence, against historical pessimism, it can be argued that there is a nontrivial pattern of retention in theory-change: elements of past theories have been retained in subsequent theories and are part of the current scientific image. We may then draw the optimistic conclusion that a lot of what is currently accepted by scientists will "remain the possession of science for all time," such as atomism, Newton's law of gravity, Maxwell's equations, Dalton's laws, and many other components of past theories that are still with us as part and parcel of the scientific image. The result of all this is that realists should be more selective in what they are realists about. I have dubbed this realist selectivity as the *divide et impera* strategy.[20] As Philip Kitcher[21] and I[22] have argued, there are ways to distinguish between the "good" and the "bad" *parts* of past abandoned theories and to show that the "good" parts—those that enjoyed evidential support, or were not idle components and the like—were retained in subsequent theories. This kind of response suggests that there has been enough theoretical continuity in theory-change to warrant the realist claim that science is "on the right track." The emergence of an evolving-but-convergent network of theoretical assertions is best explained by the assumption that such assertions are, by and large, approximately true.

How about the epistemic challenge to realism coming from the so-called *underdetermination of theories by evidence*? Here the argument is based on the claim that for each and every scientific theory T, there are empirically equivalent rivals—alternative theories that have exactly the same observational consequences as with the given theory T. It is then further claimed that no evidence can distinguish between T and its rivals. Is then epistemic pessimism warranted? Note that this kind of thesis, in all its generality, is not proven. It's far from established that each theory has nontrivial, that is, scientifically respectable, empirically equivalent rivals. A recent attempt to substantiate the actuality of underdetermination is problematic. According to Kyle Stanford,[23] at any given stage of inquiry, there have been hitherto unconceived but radically distinct alternatives to extant scientific theories. When, in the fullness of time, these alternatives came to be formulated, they were equally well confirmed by the then available evidence; they came to be accepted by scientists in due course; and eventually they replaced their already existing rivals. This is a condition that he calls "Recurrent Transient Underdetermination." If theories are subject to this predicament, Stanford argues, belief in their truth is not warranted.

Suppose, for the sake of the argument, that we grant all this. It should be immediately noted that realism about theories would be in jeopardy *only if* the argument based on historical pessimism were sound. Unless historical pessimism is warranted, Stanford's argument does not suffice to show that the new and hitherto unconceived theories will be radically dissimilar to the superseded ones. But we have already found reasons to resist historical pessimism. In fact, Stanford's argument misfires against scientific practice, for a retentionist strategy is part and parcel of this practice. Hence, the conceptual space of unconceived alternatives is constrained by existing theories and the need to retain those parts of the theories that account for their successes. This is because the retained parts add credence (and truth-content) to the new theory, by transferring their own evidential support to the new theory. As suggested already, Einstein could clearly identify the sources of success in Newton's theory of gravity independently of his own alternative theory, and it is precisely for this reason that he insisted that he had to recover Newton's law of attraction (a key source of the Newtonian success) as a limiting case of his own GTR. He could then show that his new theory could do both: it could recover the (independently identified) sources of success in Newton's theory (in the form of the law of attraction) *and* account for its failures by identifying further causal factors (the curvature of space-time) that explain the discrepancies between the predicted orbits of planets (by Newton's theory of gravity) and the observed trajectories.

Why, we may ask, is there epistemic suspicion for the unobservable? Why are they taken to be epistemically inaccessible? This is not a normal scientific suspicion. Isaac Newton, for instance, was not driven by it. In his famous third rule of philosophizing, he had no problem in extending to all objects (no matter how small or big) the properties found by experiments to be possessed by some objects.[24] The key issue is not observability—which is parochial and anthropocentric. Rather, the key issue is the explanatory role, and in particular the legitimacy of the methods (or the bridge principles) that permit us to close the supposed epistemic gap between the seen and the unseen. As modern science shows, the distinction between observables and unobservables is simply irrelevant to coming to have a justified belief in the reality of an entity. What matters is whether this belief is confirmed by the relevant evidence (and the indispensably relevant theoretical virtues) and becomes a stable part of the scientific image. And that's how it should be. There is no reason for double standards in confirmation, simply because the ways in which assertions about unobservables are confirmed are the ways in which assertions about observables are confirmed.

Notes

1. See Nicolaus Copernicus, *On the Revolutions*, trans. Edward Rosen (Baltimore and London: Johns Hopkins University Press, 1978), 3, 5.
2. Copernicus, *On the Revolutions*, xvi.
3. Stathis Psillos, *Scientific Realism: How Science Tracks Truth* (London and New York: Routledge, 1999), xvii.
4. Hilary Putnam, *Mathematics, Matter and Method,* Philosophical Papers, vol. 1 (Cambridge: Cambridge University Press, 1975), 73.
5. Hans Vaihinger, *The Philosophy of "As If,"* trans. C. K. Ogden (London: Kegan Paul, Trench, Trubner and Co, Ltd., 1911/1935), 93.
6. See Pierre Duhem, *The Aim and Structure of Physical Theory,* trans. P. Wiener (Princeton, NJ: Princeton University Press, 1906/1954), 27–28.
7. Albert Einstein, "The Foundation of the General Theory of Relativity," reprinted in A. Einstein, *The Principle of Relativity* (Mineola, NY: Dover, 1932), 145.
8. See Psillos, *Scientific Realism*, 80ff.; and Stathis Psillos, "The Scope and Limits of the No-Miracles Argument," in *The Philosophy of Science in a European Perspective*, vol. II, ed. F. Stadler, et al. (New York: Springer, 2011), 23–35.
9. See, for example, Colin Howson, *Hume's Problem* (New York: Oxford University Press, 2000).
10. See Stathis Psillos, *Knowing the Structure of Nature* (London: Palgrave Macmillan, 2009); and Richard Dawid and Stephan Hartmann, "The No Miracles Argument Without the Base Rate Fallacy," *Synthese* (forthcoming).
11. Jean Perrin, *Brownian Movement and Molecular Reality,* trans. F. Soddy (London: Taylor and Francis, 1910), 46.
12. Henri Poincaré, *Mathematics and Science: Last Essays* (New York: Dover, 1913), 90.
13. Jean Perrin, *Atoms,* trans. D. I Hammick (London: Constable & Company, Ltd., 1916), vii.
14. See Stathis Psillos, "Moving Molecules Above the Scientific Horizon: On Perrin's Case for Realism," *Journal for General Philosophy of Science* 42 (2011): 339–63.
15. Leo Tolstoy, *Essays & Letters*, trans. Aylmer Maud (New York: Funk and Wagnalls Company, 1904), 105.
16. W. H. Newton-Smith, *The Rationality of Science* (London: RKP, 1981), 14.
17. Larry Laudan, "A Confutation of Convergent Realism," *Philosophy of Science* 48 (1981): 35.

18 Ludwig Boltzmann, "The Recent Development of Method in Theoretical Physics," *The Monist* 11 (1901): 253.
19 Henri Poincaré, "Sur les Rapports de la Physique Expérimentale et de la Physique Mathématique," in *Rapports Présentés au Congrès International de Physique*, vol. 1 (Paris: Gauthier-Villars, 1901), 23.
20 Psillos, *Scientific Realism*.
21 Philip Kitcher, *The Advancement of Science* (Oxford: Oxford University Press, 1993).
22 Psillos, *Scientific Realism*.
23 P. K. Stanford, *Exceeding Our Grasp: Science, History, and the Problem of Unconceived Alternatives* (Oxford: Oxford University Press, 2006).
24 See Isaac Newton, *Mathematical Principles of Natural Philosophy*, trans. Andrew Motte, revised by Florian Cajori (Berkeley, Los Angeles, and London: University of California Press, 1934), 398–99.

Science Does Not Discover the Truth about Reality

Darrell P. Rowbottom

Study Questions

1. What is the "fallacy of appealing to consequences"? Why is it a fallacy?
2. What feature of science does Rowbottom invite you to believe in? In what sense does this feature both concern and not concern reality?
3. How might science be good at predicting how observable things behave even while making false claims about unobservable things?
4. What is the Parable of the Alien Artifact? How would you answer the questions that Rowbottom asks at each stage?
5. What conclusion about science does Rowbottom draw from his discussion of the parable?
6. What value does science have, according to Rowbottom?

The Fallacy of Appealing to Consequences

I have the unfortunate task of arguing for a view that most well-educated people think is crazy. I once thought it was crazy, too, back when I was studying physics as an undergraduate, although I also knew that some great scientists, like Lord Kelvin and Niels Bohr, held it. In fact, I became a philosopher in order to argue that science *does* discover the truth about reality! I tried. But there came a point at which it seemed to me that the arguments against this view were stronger than the arguments for it. I then had a nasty epiphany: most of what I believed about the fundamental nature of the world was based on scant evidence, and perhaps even faith.

I begin with this tale to encourage you to open your mind. This is exceptionally difficult when you're faced with a possibility that you don't want to be an actuality. You probably don't want to believe—and probably don't even want to seriously entertain the possibility—that your partner is sleeping with your best friend behind your back. Similarly, you probably don't want to believe that you know—and, indeed, that humanity as a whole knows—relatively little about how the world *really* is. Yet these claims might, I'm sorry to say, be true. Whether they are true doesn't depend on what we want, and it's a fallacy to argue that something is true simply because it is desirable for it to be so. This fallacy has a special name: *appeal to consequences*.

Prediction, Reality, Observability, and Discovery

But allow me to soften the potential blow of accepting the possibility I'll argue for, by pointing out a desirable state of affairs concerning science that I won't ask you to doubt. In doing so, I'll also explain what "reality" and "discover" refer to in the title, and clarify what I'll argue for in the remainder of this essay.

Let's begin with a key feature of science that I invite you to believe in. Science reliably assists us in making numerous successful *predictions*. It helps us to determine when natural phenomena like eclipses and high tides will occur. It has repeatedly enabled us to do new things, from generating electricity to constructing lasers. It has also helped us to improve how we do things we've done for time immemorial: we have used it to improve our running and throwing techniques, for instance.

These predictions *do* concern *reality* in one everyday sense of the word. They are about the empirical world of our sensations: things we can touch, see, hear, smell, and feel. However, they don't directly concern "reality" in another sense of the word, namely as it refers to something more fundamental, beyond or underlying the empirical realm. These predictions don't, that's to say, directly concern the (ultimate) reality behind the appearances. It's reality in that ultimate sense that science does not discover the truth about. Or so I will argue.

Some examples will help to make this (ultimate) sense of reality clearer. Consider mundane *observable* objects like iron and steel bars. Grant that they're real material things, which exist independently of us. Now think about what contemporary science tells us about them. On the one hand, it tells us how they will (observably) behave in response to *observable* changes in conditions—for example, when they interact with other *observable* objects—in a vast array of circumstances. It tells us how they will alter in size in response to changes in temperature, how much force is required to bend or break them, how they'll rust on exposure to air and water, their resistances to electrical currents, and so on.[1] On the other hand, science involves claims about the *unobservable* composition and structure of those objects. It tells us that iron bars are composed of a single kind of atom, whereas steel bars are composed of more than one kind of atom. It also tells us there are tiny things called electrons, which are freed (or "dissociated") from the atoms and able to move around in these substances.[2] The presence of a "sea of electrons" in these metals is said to be responsible for their relatively high electrical and thermal conductivities. Such seas are said not to be present in considerably better insulators, like wood.

Now it's easy to see that science might be an excellent tool for predicting how observable things (observably) behave despite making false, and even wildly inaccurate, claims about unobservable things like electrons. Indeed, much past science was predictively useful despite involving theories about unobservable things that modern science says do not exist. A substance called caloric was once thought to be responsible for heat, for example. And theories involving caloric were used for many successful predictions: one of the most remarkable, by Pierre-Simon Laplace, concerns how the speed of sound varies according to temperature.

The history of science similarly shows that it's possible to have false theories about *some* observable things—often ones that haven't been observed—that are exceptionally useful when it comes to predicting other observable things. For example, it's easy to predict how many heavenly bodies move in the night sky by imagining that the Earth is a stationary sphere, and that the sun and a giant fixed "sphere of stars" rotate around it on different axes. The Ancient Greeks knew this well.[3]

What's more, some philosophers think there's a significant chance that we're living in a computer simulation (such as the one depicted in *The Matrix*). Although this seems like a wild idea, at first sight, it's worth thinking about what evidence we could have, if any, that we are *not* in such a simulation.[4] That's to say, how could contemporary science have convincingly ruled that out? And if it hasn't, why should we think it has discovered the truth about *reality*, as distinct from the truth about a *simulated* reality? I won't pursue these questions any more here, but they're worth bearing in mind. If nothing else, they suggest that giving a *complete* argument for the view that science discovers the truth about reality is an extraordinarily tough task.

Before I begin my argument, I must also say something about *discovery*. As hinted earlier, this has to be based on evidence: it can't be a matter of mere guesswork. Imagine it's true, for example, that the physical things we encounter in our daily lives—tables, chairs, cups, saucers, and so on—are made of atoms. Democritus had this idea back in ancient Greece, and he believed it was true.[5] But he didn't *discover* it. It was a hypothesis for which there was no significant experimental evidence, insofar as it wasn't connected with experience (and thus predictions).

Similarly, I think that modern scientists may sometimes make lucky guesses about how unobservable things are. However, I deny that they can discover—or, at least, that they can *typically* discover—facts about the unobservable, that is, even though modern scientists *do* use their hypotheses to make successful predictions.

The Parable of the Alien Artifact

I will now begin my argument. I will proceed by using a number of thought experiments, and by relying on analogies involving concrete examples. I have two main reasons for doing this. First, it makes it easy to understand what is at the core of the debate on whether science can discover the truth about reality, and to judge what one thinks about it. Second, it's more fun than discussing things at an abstract level—involving "theories," "observation statements," and so on—or than working through a detailed case study from the history of science.

I'll ask you to think about what the scenarios show. You may prefer different responses from those that I think are right. But that's fine, as long as you can find an argument for your response. Ultimately, my job here is to give you a sense of why I think the way I do, and to encourage you to see that it's reasonable.

The Parable: Part I

Without further ado, let the parable begin. Imagine an alien spacecraft crash-lands on Earth. There are no survivors, and almost everything is smashed to smithereens. But an artifact is discovered in the wreckage which seems to be intact and functional. It's a cylinder, made of an unknown kind of material. It has a small screen on the top—or bottom?—on which different colored symbols appear over time.

The artifact is investigated for several years. Various attempts are made to get inside it, but to no avail; it's made of a material harder than anything we've ever encountered. Attempts are also made to scan it—that is, to work out what's inside it by using x-rays, ultrasound, and other such techniques. But all of these also fail. We aren't able to look inside, hear inside, or in any way detect what's inside. We can't even work out what the shell is made of.

However, this doesn't stop one bold scientist, Sarah, from speculating about what's inside the alien cylinder. She records how the symbols change over time, and considers what they might represent. (She uses a video recorder, so that the data can be stored for later examination.) Eventually, she comes up with the idea that her object of study is a clock. She proposes that changes of the symbols and their colors represent changes in units of time, although the units of time involved are different from ours. Color changes happen around every 15 seconds, and symbol changes happen around every 5 minutes. The colors complete a full cycle over the 5-minute period too (i.e., the color pattern repeats every 5 minutes). The symbols complete a full cycle every 10 hours or so.

Sarah doesn't stop there. She goes on to build a cylinder clock that looks highly similar to the alien one on the outside, although its outer casing and screen are made of different materials. She then puts her cylinder alongside the alien one and shows her fellow scientists how the patterns are identical and almost perfectly synchronized (at least over relatively short time periods). The scientists are impressed. Sarah goes on to declare that science now has a great idea of what's inside the alien cylinder: "It's highly probable that it's approximately the same as what's inside the cylinder that I made!"

This is a good opportunity for you to pause to think about this. Is there something wrong with Sarah's reasoning? What is it, if so? Or maybe you think it's good? If so, you have strong sympathy with the view that science can easily discover the truth about reality. But perhaps you will change your mind, as the story continues.

The Parable: Part II

Enter a second scientist, Jean, who disagrees with Sarah's verdict. Jean argues that the mechanism used by Sarah can be improved upon in many ways, while still being responsible for the same external effects. In particular, Jean is convinced that the mechanism could perform exactly the same function while being a lot simpler and more elegant in construction.

Not content merely with arguing this, Jean builds her own cylinder. On the outside, it is almost indistinguishable from Sarah's; it's made of the same materials, and its display changes in almost the same way in the lab. But on the inside, it has a much more elegant mechanism. There are fewer cogs, and the mechanism is more efficient, insofar as there's less friction as a result. It's also much more pleasing to the eye. It's beautifully made.

Jean argues that the mechanism in her cylinder is (probably) approximately the same as that in the alien cylinder. A dispute ensues between Sarah and Jean because both agree that only one of their two mechanisms could be approximately the same as the one in the alien cylinder. That's because their two mechanisms are different from one another in several ways that they consider significant.

Jean argues that the aliens must be smart, and would clearly prefer a simple and elegant construction for the hidden mechanism. Sarah argues that the aliens might have a different notion of beauty from ours, and might construct their devices with entirely different principles in mind from the ones we use. So she thinks their two theories about what's in the cylinder are at least as good as each other.

Again, this is a good time to think about where you stand on this disagreement. Who is right? Is there any principled way to choose between the two theories/models? It will help, when you consider your answer, to be aware of a significant disanalogy between the story here and the situation that scientists often face. They tend to deal with natural phenomena that might *not* be the result of design. And assuming that such phenomena aren't the result of design—for example, by God or another such powerful being—then the dispute would concern whether there are reasons to expect *nature* to be simple rather than complex, or beautiful rather than ugly, on the unobservable level.

The Parable: Part III

Jean and Sarah eventually agree that it might be possible to settle their dispute by gathering new evidence because each of their cylinders behaves in somewhat different ways. For example, Jean's cylinder runs on battery power, and the cells occasionally need replacing. On the other hand, Sarah's more complex cylinder runs on solar power. Thus Sarah's model makes the novel prediction that the alien cylinder will cease to work in a dark environment, although Jean's cylinder would continue to function in the dark. In reply, Jean can only offer the (admittedly vaguer) prediction that the alien cylinder will cease to function at some point, and won't be able to function again without having the cells (or some kind of fuel) replaced.

A test is performed. The alien cylinder is shielded, as best as we can shield it, from e-m radiation (like light). Lo and behold, the display switches off. And when it's removed from the shielded room, the display quickly comes back on again. The cylinder has also "lost time," (i.e., behaves as if an internal time-keeping mechanism wasn't functioning in the dark). Sarah declares victory! Her model made a novel prediction that the other didn't, and this surely means that hers is approximately true, or *at the very least nearer to the truth* than that of her adversary! Or so she claims.

However, Jean isn't impressed. She points out the following. The alien cylinder could still be battery powered. But it could have a light detector, and a mechanism that switches the display off in the dark. She adds that it might be a device for measuring time spent in light environments, or for recording the total time that it's exposed to light. Jean also adds that the mechanism in her cylinder, plus this minor modification, would still be simpler than the mechanism in Sarah's!

Sarah fires back that Jean is a sore loser, because now she's just changing her ideas to suit what happened. The only thing the two sides can agree on is that the new data should be accounted for somehow.

Yet again, I invite you to think about this situation. Does the order that the evidence comes in make any difference? Is Sarah's theory/model clearly better? To help you to judge, imagine that it was instead known from the beginning that the alien cylinder switched off in the dark. Imagine also that Jean instead used a light detector switch coupled with a battery in her initial model. Should this change our view of the two models? Why? (Or why not?)

The Parable: Part IV

A third scientist, Clara, has been watching the dispute between Sarah and Jean with considerable interest. She decides the time is right to intervene, because she thinks not only that Sarah and Jean are wrong but also that the dispute between them is rather unscientific.

First, Clara points out that Sarah and Jean have only outlined a few different ways that the mechanism in the alien cylinder might be. So, even imagining high simplicity indicates truth-likeness, she asks, why be confident that there aren't *much* simpler ways the internal mechanism could be, which haven't yet been thought of? Maybe some such simpler ways are even beyond our ability to conceive of, given our current constraints, Clara goes on to suggest. After all, the aliens' brains and cultures could be very different from our own. To strengthen her case, she points out all the different ways that clocks have worked in Earth's history.

Second, Clara adds that a lot of extra complexity is sometimes required to improve the accuracy of a device. And that means getting close-to-accurate predictions (of visible external parts, for example, dial movement) may be possible with a much simpler model (of internal parts) than that necessary to get highly accurate predictions. She points out that increasing the accuracy of pendulum-based clocks involved introducing lots of features: arrangements designed to keep the center of mass of the pendulum roughly constant through a range of temperature changes; flasks containing vacuums to reduce air friction; and so on.[6]

Third, Clara points out that the other scientists have only outlined a few different theories about the purpose of the alien device, and that there could be lots of things inside the cylinder that they haven't yet learned about. Maybe the cylinder is a bomb, she speculates. "What evidence does anyone have that it isn't?" she asks. She adds that it might not even have a clock as a part. Perhaps the changing symbols on the face measure the rate of change of something else, and the rate of change of that thing happens to have been constant over the period during which the device has been examined. Maybe there's a creature inside in a relatively dormant state, and the readout shows that its heart is beating regularly (or even just approximately regularly), for example. Or perhaps its *twin* hearts are beating regularly.

Fourth, Clara declares that the inability of science to determine what's in the cylinder—or even what's *probably approximately* in the cylinder—isn't something that scientists should be upset about or ashamed of. "It's not as if science is worthless if it can't let us know what's beyond the realm of experience!" she insists. She points out that we might prefer Jean's model to Sarah's on pragmatic grounds. It's a simpler and more attractive way *to think of what's inside the cylinder* from the point of view of: (a) gaining a *subjective sense of understanding* of what happens on its display; and (b) having a *memorable way to predict* what's expected to happen on its display in the future (and what likely happened for some time into the past).

In evaluating Clara's point of view, recall the fallacy of appealing to consequences. To help us to be mindful of this, let's add that Clara really doesn't *like* her conclusion. She dearly wishes she could know what was inside the cylinder, because she's intensely curious. But she is also hard-headed. Her desires don't affect her judgment.

You might also like to consider whether many real scientists would find Clara's view convincing. Would they be inclined to agree, and simply try to get more data on how the cylinder behaved (perhaps by exposing it to different environments), for example? A word of warning is in order, even if this is true. It's possible for scientists to be wrong about how best to do science, and what science can ultimately tell us. After all, they tend to spend most of their time doing science, rather than thinking about the philosophical issues it raises. At least, that's true nowadays. A hundred years or so ago, the situation was rather different. There were many philosopher-scientists, such as Pierre Duhem, Ernst Mach, and Henri Poincaré.[7]

The Parable: Part V

Years pass. Some scientists continue to speculate about what's inside the cylinder, and build different models of its inner workings. Other scientists say this is a waste of time, because the new models don't generate new testable predictions. It's a stalemate.

Eventually, though, there's an amazing breakthrough. A new scanning instrument is developed. It uses highly penetrating rays to form images. (Think of a medical x-ray machine. It's a bit like that but uses different rays.) The instrument wasn't developed in connection with investigating the alien cylinder, but luckily it generates images when it's used on the cylinder. Sarah and Jean agree that they're finally able to see what's inside, and rejoice! On the basis of the images, they conclude that neither of their models was even approximately right. There aren't any cogs depicted on the images, for one thing.

Jean also claims that the new findings show that Clara's view of science is wrong. But Clara is unrepentant. She responds that she never denied that *some* unobservable things might become observable, over time, as a result of technological innovations. "However," she adds, "that doesn't mean *everything* should be expected to become observable. And it doesn't follow that the most fundamental parts of reality are going to become observable. So, even if it's true that the inside of the alien device can now be seen, my position on science is not refuted!"

Clara doesn't stop there, though. She's also hesitant about endorsing the claim that the inside of the alien cylinder has really been observed. Instead, she believes only that it has been *causally interacted with in such a way as to generate an image*. She uses an analogy to make her point: "Think about a simple chest x-ray. Does this enable us to see inside someone's body? Only on a *casual* way of talking, I think. I don't doubt that the images generated *depend* on what's inside the body—after all, we can compare the images generated with what's inside the body, when operations and autopsies occur. But they have to be interpreted, and this isn't as straightforward as nonexperts might first think. Indeed, that's why specialist radiographers are needed to interpret the images. Really, one is dealing with an image where colors range from white to black. Picking out ribs is typically easy, because we recognize the shape and there's a high contrast. But there are multiple possible explanations for grey patches of varying shades in different areas, for example."

Clara also points out that judgments about what chest x-ray images show are aided by other direct observations, in a way that judgments about the scan of the alien artifact aren't. Medics have been able to look inside many people and gather data about what's there *with their own eyes*, and by using other techniques involving *direct interaction* with visible innards. They have been able to compare those findings with x-ray images on numerous occasions. But no one has looked inside the alien cylinder, in the everyday sense of "look." So it's much more troublesome to interpret the images generated. Clara puts it so:

> Imagine for the sake of argument that x-rays could penetrate the alien cylinder, and we have a 3-d x-ray image of the cylinder. How would we know what to take any grey volume to represent? We might take it to show either that something is in, or that something surrounds, that area. But even if it told us that much, it still wouldn't tell us which of those two possibilities was right. Moreover, there could be a variety of different things in a single volume with any particular shade. After all, two or more different kinds of thing may be equally as transparent to x-rays. And who knows what kinds of material the aliens have!

A Brief Conclusion

As I've already mentioned, I pretty much agree with Clara's line. I would summarize this as follows. The main way we have to work out what's in the world is experience. And experience tells us about observable things, insofar as it tells us about things that we observe. It doesn't tell us about unobservable things. On the contrary, there are many different theories about unobservable things that are consistent with what we experience—that is, the observable "facts."

We shouldn't rely on principles that *don't* derive support from our experience, like "the simpler theory is more likely be true, everything else being equal" or "the theory that gives the best explanation is most likely to be true, everything else being equal." And even if it were somehow to be shown that those exceptionally dubious principles were correct, there would still be a significant barrier to using them. Why? Because we don't seem to have any grounds—from experience or otherwise—for thinking we've conceived of the simplest theory, or the theory with the most explanatory power, or whatever else you like, in any particular case.

To put it bluntly, we are highly limited creatures. We have limited senses, limited intellects, and so forth. To think we could discover fundamental things about a reality that lies beyond our limited senses would be to think that our intellects are exceptionally powerful (and perhaps even that we have some faculty of insight by which we can eliminate some logical possibilities). Humility is more appropriate. We are men and women, not gods or angels.

This, in brief, is why I don't think science typically discovers the truth about reality. But this doesn't mean that I don't value science. On the contrary, I value it highly as a means by which to solve practical problems. I also value theories that talk about unobservable things, especially theories that are simple, that have high explanatory power, and so forth. I just think that these virtues are *pragmatic* in character. They make the theories easy to use, easy to memorize, furnish us with a subjective sense of understanding of the empirical world, and so forth. Having these things is a remarkable achievement for beings as limited as us!

Notes

1 There are many different kinds of steel, with many different properties, because steels are alloys, or mixtures of iron and other elements. Some are highly magnetic, whereas some are only slightly magnetic. Some rust easily, whereas others rust only under much more extreme conditions. And so forth.

2 In iron, contemporary science also says there is typically a well-ordered lattice structure involving the positive ions, through which the electrons move. This structure depends on the temperature and external pressure.

3 Predicting how the planets appear to move is a bit harder; "planet" comes from the Greek for "wanderer," because planets were once thought to be special kinds of stars.

4 It's plausible we could have evidence that we *are* in such a simulation; we could have weird glitch-like experiences, for example. But does the absence of such evidence constitute evidence that we're not in such a simulation? Similarly, does the fact that we haven't met any alien species constitute evidence that there aren't such species?

5 One could argue that Democritus's idea of an atom was rather different from ours. For example, he thought that atoms are indivisible. However, it's also possible to argue that he was wrong that atoms had this property, and nevertheless correct that there are atoms.

6 Look up "gridirion pendulum" and "mercury pendulum" on the internet, to get a flavor of the changes.

7 Articles on each of these philosopher-scientists appear in the *Stanford Encyclopedia of Philosophy*, which is available at the following URL: plato.stanford.edu.

RESPONSES

Response to Psillos

Darrell P. Rowbottom

Study Questions

1. According to Rowbottom, what is the relationship between the second and third theses of scientific realism?

2. What problem does Rowbottom have with the semantic thesis of realism? What example does he use to make his point?

3. What is the problem with the idea of "approximate truth," according to Rowbottom?

4. Why does Rowbottom think that Psillos cannot establish the initial plausibility of a theory?

My response has two parts. The first concerns the semantic thesis of scientific realism. The second concerns the "no miracles" argument and the property of approximate truth featuring therein.

The Semantic Thesis

Psillos characterizes scientific realism in terms of three theses, and says that "what is presently at issue is the third thesis (aka *epistemic optimism*)" (p. 160). Although this is true, Psillos's discussion tends to give the impression that the other theses don't need to be defended in order to show that the third thesis is true. But they do require defending. For example, if scientific theories are not "capable of being true or false," as the *semantic* thesis says, then they aren't capable of being approximately true. That's because all approximately true theories are false.

I'd like therefore to begin by picking on the undefended claim that "The theoretical terms featuring in theories have putative factual reference," which appears in the semantic thesis. Note first how remarkably bold it is: it's a claim about *all* theoretical terms. Note second that it's extremely implausible because it's so bold; unless we had great evidence to the contrary, we'd expect scientists to use metaphors, and sometimes talk loosely or vaguely, just like everyone else. We'd suspect that they sometimes talk about things, or properties of things, although this talk *should not* be taken literally.

Let me give you a quick example. Pick up any university-level general textbook on physics, and you'll find that electrons are said to have a property of spin. But the best textbooks explain that the idea behind attributing this property isn't *really* that electrons spin. Serway and Jewett, for example, write:

> **The Electron Is Not Spinning**
>
> Although the concept of a spinning electron is conceptually useful, it should not be taken literally. The spin of the Earth is a mechanical rotation. On the other hand, electron spin is a purely quantum effect that gives the electron an angular momentum as if it were physically spinning.[1]

In other words, these scientists are saying that it's *convenient* to think of electrons as spinning for some purposes, although this shouldn't be mistaken for a claim that they want you to evaluate the truth of. The claim "electrons spin" is figurative.

Interestingly, moreover, the story about spin doesn't stop there. That's because the claim that "the electron [has] an angular momentum as if it were physically spinning" is also extremely difficult to take literally, rather than as an extremely loose way of talking. Without wanting to bedazzle you with the intricacies of quantum theory, the reason is as follows. Angular momentum, as classically defined, involves distance; for example, a merry-go-round has angular momentum when it spins around a point, its center, which remains at a particular distance to each of its parts. Thus we may wonder which distance is (or which distances are) supposed to be relevant in the case of the electron's so-called angular momentum. Contemporary physics gives no answer to this question. And there are legitimate ways of *interpreting* quantum theory such that all the factors appearing in equations that are attributed to "electron spin" don't *really* refer to any intrinsic property of the electron. If you happen to be studying physics, look up *Bohm's theory* to find out more.[2]

In short, it's wrong to take all scientific talk involving theoretical terms at face value ("literally"). Scientists often have reasonable differences of opinion about what to take literally and what not, although typically—and this is crucial—those differences of opinion don't affect their ability to make accurate predictions about observables.

The "No Miracles" Argument and "Approximate Truth"

In the remainder of this response, I will focus on the so-called "no miracles" argument and the "approximately true" property featuring therein.

To begin with, notice how Psillos shifts talking about truth and approximate truth at various points at which he should not. For example, he says at one juncture that "the right question to ask is: how likely is it that a certain *specific* theory T be true, given that it has been successful?" (p. 163). But he starts his piece by suggesting that the answer to this kind of question will typically be "highly unlikely," when he admits that "Scientific theories are born false . . . [because] theories indispensably employ idealizations and abstractions" (p. 159). "Ok," you might think, "so Psillos wasn't as precise as he should have been." But my worry is that these little unintentional slips—if that's what they are—are liable to mislead a reader into thinking that approximately true statements have similar properties to true statements when it comes to explanation and prediction. But it's far from clear that they do, and Psillos presents no argument that they do. Let me now explain in further depth.

Almost everyone agrees that a completely true set of beliefs (including beliefs in theories) will never lead one astray in action (provided one is aware of those beliefs and their consequences): if those beliefs are true, then whatever they predict will be true. But an approximately true set of beliefs won't do the same trick. For example, it's approximately true that I am under 188 centimeters tall. But it doesn't follow that I will not bump my head when carefully walking upright under a ceiling that's 188 centimeters in height (given also some true everyday background beliefs about ceilings, walking, and so on). This would follow, though, if it were simply *true* that I am under 188 centimeters in height.

This is uncontroversial. So what Psillos presumably thinks is that predictions from approximately true beliefs are true significantly more often—much more probably—than not. But this is far from obvious. To see my point, consider now all the people who are approximately under 188 centimeters in height. (If you like, you can just consider all the *possible* heights that such people could have.) What's the probability that one of them, picked at random, will not bump their head when walking carefully under a ceiling that's exactly 188 centimeters in height? Is it pretty high? Plausibly not. There's a whole range of heights that count as being *approximately* under 188 centimeters, while being *over* 188 centimeters. And the heights that are clearly under 188 centimeters—like 187 centimeters—aren't *merely* approximately so. Think of this in terms of an interval. To be approximately under 188 centimeters is to have a height, in centimeters, between 188-x and 188+x, where x<<188. For example, x might be 0.1 centimeter. And it's easy to see that there may be as many people above 188 centimeters in height as those below 188 centimeters in height in this group.

Psillos might reply that my quick example doesn't involve "approximate truth" in the sense he meant it (perhaps because he is talking about scientific theories). But he doesn't explain what he takes approximate truth to be. All he says is that "approximate truth is a relation between the specific theory and its domain (a relation of approximate fit)" (p. 163). But what exactly does it mean for a theory to approximately fit its domain? Because we are offered no account of what fitting involves, let alone what approximate fitting involves, it's reasonable for us to doubt whether this rather mystical "approximate truth" of theories leads to probable truth of predictions using those theories. Moreover, why should we think that approximate truth is the only reasonable explanation of predictive power? How about those theories that have significant *elements* of truth in them, but fall short of being approximately true, for example?

One of the few things that *is* clear about approximate truth is that it is unobservable. It's not like red, or flowers, or Donald Trump. One has to *infer* its presence, as Psillos admits. He writes:

> It is a local relation which can be examined by looking at the initial plausibility of [a given] theory and the evidence there is in its favor from its explanatory and predictive (especially novel predictive) successes. (Ibid.)

Note the mention of "initial plausibility." What is this, and why does it matter? Psillos hints at the answer toward the end of his piece, when he mentions "the indispensably relevant theoretical virtues" in addition to "the relevant evidence." The sudden mention of "theoretical virtues" may be surprising—they are not mentioned elsewhere. But the important idea is that some theories have virtues that make them attractive *independently* of experience. They can be simple. They can be aesthetically pleasing. And so on.

But do these properties, which help to determine "initial plausibility," indicate truth, or approximate truth, more often than not? Why should we think that? Why not think that the world is extremely complex and ugly? This isn't to deny that theoretical virtues are important. I think they are, but only for *pragmatic* reasons. For instance, I think simple theories are good because they're easier for us to understand than complex theories.

Psillos thinks he knows quite a bit about how to spot invisible (and inaudible and intangible) things and properties—like approximate truth—on the basis of visible ones. I take myself to lack such fantastic powers. I am a humble animal. I have extremely limited capacities for knowing grand-scale truths (such as general rules for linking initial plausibility to probable truth-likeness). I probably can't even conceive of the fundamental nature of reality. The main thing I have to go on is my experience, and that is severely limited. I wish it were different. I wish I were Professor X. Sadly, I am not.

Notes

1 R. A. Serway and J. W. Jewett, *Physics for Scientists and Engineers with Modern Physics,* 9th ed. (Boston, MA: Brooks/Cole, 2013), 1315.
2 See S. Goldstein, "Bohmian Mechanics," in *Stanford Encyclopedia of Philosophy* (https://plato.stanford.edu/archives/sum2017/entries/qm-bohm/) for a nice summary of spin on this theory.

Response to Rowbottom

Stathis Psillos

Study Questions

1. According to Psillos, what view of scientific progress does the scientific skeptic have? How does Psillos respond to this view?
2. Why does Psillos think that the skeptic cannot be skeptical of the unobservable without also being skeptical of the observable?
3. What is the "rational kernel" that Psillos finds in Rowbottom's "fallacy of appealing to consequences"? But what might still be the case for theories that make true predictions?
4. What is science *about*, according to Psillos? What, then, is (and is not) the issue?
5. How does Psillos respond to Rowbottom's imaginary skeptical scientist?

A skeptic about X is someone who challenges the claim that facts (or truths) about X can be known. Strictly speaking, a skeptic does not assert that facts about X *are* unknowable. This would amount to a piece of knowledge. So, skeptics aim to reduce to absurdity any claim to know facts about X.

In our case, X is the realm of the unobservable. The scientific realists' claim that science reveals to us truths about the unobservable is challenged by what I call the *scientific skeptic*. Presumably, all reasons cited by a realist which aim to support the claim that science does offer at least some knowledge of the unobservable are found wanting by the skeptic. The bottom line of all skeptical challenges is that experience (perhaps aided by reason) can never prove or confirm the truth of a theory which purports to refer to unobservable entities: any serious nontrivial theory will always be a *hypothesis* relative to experience and what is directly given (to us) in it.

No Scientific Progress?

Note that for a scientific skeptic, science has no history of cognitive progress beyond the phenomena. Concerning the hidden-to-the-naked-eye behind the phenomena (if there is such a reality at all), we are as ignorant now as we were in the times of ancient Greek science. To put the point somewhat crudely: modern medical theory is just as unwarranted *qua* knowledge of causes of the symptoms of diseases as the Hippocratic medicine, and Einstein's general relativity is just as unjustified a view about the structure of the solar system as Aristotle's theory of crystalline spheres. After all, if the problem lies with the unobservable per se, that is, if the problem arises because scientific theories posit unobservables, the crystalline spheres are as unobservable as the space-time curvature. This is hardly a plausible position to take given the tremendous empirical and explanatory success of current science.

The skeptic might retort that the crystalline spheres theory is refuted by the evidence while Einstein's GTR is not. But this would be an admission of defeat since it would entail that evidence can asymmetrically bear on theories, and hence, that evidence may make one theory justifiably preferable over another.

What about Observables?

The key question regarding scientific skepticism is this: Can it be selective or, in the end, does it have to be wholesale? Can, that is, one be a skeptic about unobservables such as electrons and DNA molecules without the skepticism spilling over to observables? The typical scientific skeptic just takes it for granted that we can know things about the observable: the medium-sized material things that surround us and exist independently of us. But the observable things are not those that constitute the "empirical world of our sensations," as Rowbottom describes it, simply because the empirical world of "our" sensations is non-modal while the observable world is modal. To call Y (e.g., a table or a satellite) observ*able* is to make a modal claim about what sensations someone would have had they been in a position to observe it. Something can be observable even if no one ever actually sees it, and is thus no part of the empirical world of our actual sensations. And the world of *possible* sensations (i.e., the world of what we could *possibly* sense) is not quite empirical since what counts as a possible sensation is, at least partly, a theoretical matter.

The key point here is that the observ*able* is not the observed; hence, any claim about the observable exceeds in content any claim about the observed—in exactly the same way in which claims about the unobserv*able* go beyond claims about the observ*able*. The point that something observable *could* be observed is moot, since scientific skeptics take it that an ordinary (inductive) generalization about unobserved observables is justified independently of it being the case that the unobserved observables are actually observed. Differently put, the transition from the observed to the observ*able* exhibits the very same inferential properties (and epistemic risks) as the transition from the observable to the unobservable. If one is not a skeptic about the unobserved observables (and typical scientific skeptics are not), one cannot really be a skeptic about the unobservables.

Aren't Theories Confirmable?

The skeptic tells us that science can be an "excellent tool for predicting how observable things (observably) behave" (p. 172), despite being false about the unobservable. Here again, however, a weaker position is available: science can be an excellent tool for predicting how the *next* observed thing will (observably) behave, despite making false claims about the observable. After all, given the evidence, it is epistemically safer to infer that the next swan is white rather than that all swans are white. To adopt the stronger position, which is more akin to the empirical laws established by science, the scientific skeptic should rely on inductive inferences from the observed to the observable which, as noted already, are not much less risky than the scientific realists' inference from the observable to the unobservable.

Rowbottom puts the point crudely when he says that "it's a fallacy to argue that something is true simply because it is desirable for it to be so" (p. 171). The rational kernel of the point is that from the truth of some consequences we cannot validly derive the truth of the hypotheses from which they follow: a false theory can have true consequences. Still, it does not follow that the truth of a theory (or its partial or approximate truth) does not offer the *best explanation* of its true consequences. The best explanation of the evidence is not proved to be true but it can still be warranted by the evidence *qua* best explanation. Note, apropos, that Rowbottom's point cuts across the board:

equally we should not infer the truth of a theory about observables from its (true) consequences (about the observed). The epistemically optimist view associated with scientific realism is that a theory is confirmed by its correct predictions; or, at any rate, that it is confirmed more than its rivals. On *any* theory of confirmation but a dogmatic one (viz., one which gives zero prior probability to a theory's being true), the empirical evidence can render a theory probable, even highly probable.

Would it be rational for someone to give a theory zero prior probability? Note that this is not quite the skeptical attitude, which should at least leave it open that a theory might be true. Giving zero prior probability to any theory simply sums up the view that no evidence can have any bearing on any scientific theory.

Hence, it's hard to be a selective skeptic about the unobservable without being a skeptic about everything, unless you cite a relevant difference between knowing facts about the unobservable and knowing facts about the observable.

What's So Special about the Unobservable?

Rowbottom puts it thus: "The main way we have to work out what's in the world is experience. And experience tells us about observable things. . . . It doesn't tell us about unobservable things" (p. 179). Experience, we noted already, does not quite tell us about observables unless we fix the right modalities. More importantly, science is not *about* the observable. The observable can offer evidence and the observer can check this evidence, but the evidence sought after is about the deeper structure of the world. Science, then, is about understanding the world by gathering evidence for the various theories, most of which are such that they posit, among other things, an inner microscopic composition and structure to the various macroscopic objects (including us). If evidence is what science does and should look for, then observability per se is not the issue. Rather, the issue is experimental detectability of posited entities and confirmation of theories. Science has developed various reliable methods to detect the presence of things which are too little to be seen by the naked eye. The theoretical physicist Carlo Rovelli puts the point very nicely when he says:

> Some philosophers of science overly circumscribe science by limiting it to its numerical predictions. They miss the point, because they confuse the instruments with the objectives. Verifiable quantitative predictions are

instruments to validate hypotheses. The objective of scientific research is not just to arrive at predictions: it is to understand how the world functions.[1]

A skeptic can always argue that, say, observing through an instrument is not observing anything real but observing an *image*—which is more like a mirage or a public hallucination than an image *of* something. Rowbottom's imaginary skeptical scientist says that by employing an instrument there has been a causal interaction with the instrument "*in such a way as to generate an image*" (p. 178). Lots could be said in reply, but this might suffice.[2] The image is an image *of* something and not a mere image if various conditions are satisfied (e.g., if the same image can be seen by using different methods or instruments; or if it can be manipulated systematically by means of interventions). When Rovelli says that "we have now observed gravitational waves directly" by means of a detector, he is not merely saying that the detector produced an image but, instead, that the detector has opened up a window into quantum gravity.[3]

Notes

1. Carlo Rovelli, *Reality Is Not What It Seems: The Journey to Quantum Gravity* (London: Penguin Books, 2017), 210.
2. For more on this, see S. Psillos, "The View *from Within* and the View *from Above*: Looking at van Fraassen's Perrin," in *Representation and Models in Science: Bas van Fraassen's Approach*, ed. W. J. Gonzalez (Dordrecht: Springer, 2014), 143–66.
3. For a discussion of the connection between scientific understanding and realism, see S. Psillos, "World-Involving Scientific Understanding," *Balkan Journal of Philosophy* 9 (2017): 4–21.

Questions for Reflection

1. Do you think that Psillos can overcome the problems associated with the idea of approximate truth? How?
2. How, if at all, might Rowbottom respond to Psillos's claim that skepticism about unobservables requires skepticism about observables, too?
3. What do you think science is about and why is it valuable?

6

Are Scientific Explanations Limited to Natural Causes?

Scientific Explanations Are Limited to Natural Causes

Robert C. Bishop

Study Questions

1. What evidence does Bishop cite for the "long history" of making a distinction between theological and scientific explanations?
2. What is methodological naturalism (or MN)?
3. What theological reasons does Bishop give for MN?
4. What is the distinction between "contextual negations" and "logical negations"? How does Bishop's cookie jar experiment illustrate the difference?
5. Why do scientists not pursue logical negations? What does this have to do with MN?
6. Why, according to Bishop, does MN not imply that God doesn't exist (metaphysical naturalism) or that God is uninvolved with nature?
7. How has MN been formulated (e.g., by Gregory and Plantinga) so as to make it indistinguishable from metaphysical naturalism? Why is this a mistake, according to Bishop?

Natural science inquiry is practiced by people holding a wide variety of religious and nonreligious beliefs. Indeed, scientific inquiry's most basic assumptions are shared by the vast majority of worldviews.[1] To understand this kind of belief independence of the natural sciences, it is helpful to begin with its theological background. Historians of science have documented many contributions Christian theology made to the development of modern scientific inquiry in the seventeenth century as well as the break in positive relationship between theology and the natural sciences occurring in the nineteenth century.[2] Nevertheless, this positive relationship rarely implied that God was invoked as a direct explanatory factor in scientific hypotheses and theories.

The idea that there is a distinction between theological and scientific explanations has a long history, going back well into the medieval period and beyond, when natural philosophy was the mode of inquiry into nature. For example, David Lindberg notes that the thirteenth-century natural philosopher, Albertus Magnus, Thomas Aquinas's teacher, distinguished

> between philosophy and theology on methodological grounds and to find out what philosophy alone, without any help from theology, could demonstrate about reality . . . . [Albertus] acknowledged (with every other medieval thinker) that God is ultimately the cause of everything, but he argued that God customarily works through natural causes and that the natural philosopher's obligation was to take the latter to their limit . . . . Albertus pointed out that God employs natural causes to accomplish his purposes; and the philosopher's task is not to investigate the causes of God's will, but to inquire into the natural causes by which God's will produces its effect. To introduce divine causality into a philosophical discussion . . . would be a violation of the proper boundaries between philosophy and theology.[3]

Robert Boyle articulated the view, common among natural philosophers and clerics of his day, that God usually worked through natural laws, though this did not rule out divine interventions for special purposes.[4] Isaac Newton argued for a very similar view, going so far as to say: "Where natural causes are at hand God uses them as his instruments in his works."[5] A similar attitude was articulated by Congregational minister and geologist George Frederick Wright in an 1876 issue of *Bibliotheca Sacra*, reprinted in his book *Studies in Science and Religion*:

> It is not in accordance with what we specially value in the modern habits of thought, to cut the Gordian knot with the simple assertion, "so God has made it," . . . . Such a course would be suicidal to all scientific thought, and would endanger the rational foundation upon which our proof of revelation rests. It is superstition and not reverence, which leads us to avoid the questions concerning the order and mode of the divine operations . . . . We are to press known secondary causes as far as they will go in explanation

of facts. We are not to resort to an unknown cause for explanation of phenomena until the power of known causes has been exhausted. If we cease to observe this rule there is an end to all science and of all sound sense.[6]

Finally, consider a practical example of the focus on natural causes: in the face of a smallpox outbreak in New England in 1721, no less a divine than Cotton Mather advocated an inoculation campaign as the appropriate religious response.[7]

In recent times, this limitation to studying nature's properties and processes on their own terms without invoking God has been given the name *methodological naturalism* (MN).[8] This self-limitation of scientific inquiry to material properties and processes is purposeful, as I describe later, and has been largely the consensus view among theistic natural philosophers and scientists over the centuries (though there have always been rare exceptions). Nevertheless, some object that it places an overly narrow restriction on natural science inquiry by supposedly leaving out possibilities for Divine action in nature that might be scientifically discernable. I will argue that there are good theological and methodological reasons for the traditional restriction of natural science inquiry to material properties and processes.

Theological Reasons for Methodological Naturalism

Why did so many theists find MN compelling? In short: theology. Drawing on the history of theology and science, Thomas Torrance described the following paradox. The theological understanding of God creating the universe ex nihilo—making time, space, matter, energy, laws, and so on—means that the cosmos's existence and order is contingent on divine love, will, and power. This contingency led many theologians and natural philosophers over the course of the fifteenth and sixteenth centuries to the conclusion culminating in the seventeenth century that empirical and theoretical methods of study were the appropriate forms of inquiry for regular, repeatable natural phenomena. (Though not all natural philosophers and theologians endorsed this view; for instance, Cartesians continued to argue for reason alone as the only means for discovering truth.) Yet, virtually all natural philosophers and theologians still allowed for the miraculous. However, Torrance continues:

> Scientific investigation of this created order, rigorously in accordance with its distinctive nature, must be pursued without reference to God or any

recourse to theological reasoning. The paradox may be succinctly formulated in terms of two classic statements of Reformed theology: nothing can be established about contingence except through divine revelation . . . , and, divine creation requires us to investigate the contingent world out of its own natural processes alone; without including God in the given.[9]

According to Christian theology, all things that are not divine were created through the Son of God. This can only be known through special revelation *and* reasoning through its implications; it could not be inferred by empirical inquiry. Special revelation, however, does not include specific information about the properties and processes of nature, only that these are expressions of the contingent order God gave the creation. Coming to understand that contingent order requires exploring the properties and processes of nature on their own terms—MN (Torrance does not use the term). The empirical and theoretical methods of inquiry constructed during the sixteenth and seventeenth centuries were the theological and natural philosophic response to this situation.

Torrance went on to argue that the incarnation of the Son of God—the one through whom all created things are made—reinforced this conclusion that MN was the appropriate approach to the study of Nature:

> The interrelation between the incarnation of the Logos and the creation of all things visible and invisible out of nothing by the same Logos, called for a profound rethinking of the relation between God and the world as one in which it is recognized that the radical distinction between uncreated and created being, between the uncreated rationality of God and the created rationality of the world, far from reducing the being and rationality of the contingent world to unreality and insignificance, establishes their reality and secures their significance, not in spite of, but precisely in their contingent character. That is to say, the incarnation has the constant effect of affirming the contingent intelligibility of the creation, reinforcing the requirement to accept it as the specific kind of rationality proper to the physical world, and as the only kind capable of providing empirical grounds for knowledge of the universe in its own natural processes.[10]

Ex nihilo creation implies that there is an absolute distinction between Creator and created, between two distinct kinds of being: necessary vs. contingent. Nevertheless, contingent being is not somehow less real. Rather, the reality of contingent being is affirmed because the one who made contingent being took on that very being in the incarnation. Some of the implications of this situation theologians and natural philosophers worked out was that the processes in nature were genuine actors and that these processes were intelligible because they had a contingent rationality given by their Creator. To understand these actors required empirical and theoretical methods focused on the characteristics of these natural processes.

Torrance added one more strand to the theological argument for MN. God created freely and under no necessity or other form of compulsion, meaning that the universe exists as a loving, gracious act. This divine freedom in creation implies the contingent being and rationality of nature. Moreover, it implies God does not depend on the creation for existence, meaning, or purpose, while creation depends wholly upon God for existence, meaning, and purpose. Therefore, nature is sustained in its being by God with no logical relation between it and God. The nonlogical relationship between God and the creation is important, Torrance argues, because "if there were such a relation, knowledge of the created world and knowledge of God would be clamped together in such a way that we would derive knowledge of God necessarily and coercively from knowledge of the world, while knowledge of the world even in its natural operations would not be possible without constantly including God among the data." This would be to fall back into classical Greek natural philosophical views where the "rational forms of the Deity are immanently and materially embodied in the universe" eliminating "the conditions for the emergence of empirical science."[11] For instance, Aristotle grounded teleology—behavior directed toward an end or purpose—in the essential natures of things in the world; in contrast, Christian theological understanding of divine freedom in creation grounded teleology in God leading to a very different methodological approach to studying created things.[12]

These strands of thought, among others, provide a deep, historical-theological basis for studying the properties and processes of nature for the purposes of understanding them on their own terms—that is, without resorting to explicit reference to the Creator and/or divine activity in or through nature. As Torrance puts it, God made the cosmos in such a way that "to do it justice we are obliged to concentrate on it for its own sake . . . . If natural science is to be rigorously faithful to the universe that God has created it must bracket off the universe from God and develop autonomous modes of inquiry *appropriate to the distinctive reality of the universe* which allow it to disclose its own inherent rational order."[13] Theologically, this "bracketing" is for the purpose of understanding nature on its own terms as a creation of God—to uncover and understand the patterns and processes in the created order as actual patterns and processes of matter and energy in space and time. This is the essence of the focus on the properties and processes of nature as the explanatory locus for regular, repeatable phenomena worked out in the sixteenth and seventeenth centuries.

The force of Torrance's theological argument is as follows. The Creator-creature distinction implies God gave nature a contingent form of being distinctly different from the being of the Creator. Hence, the methods for studying nature must be designed with nature as the object of study in mind, not God. Second, the incarnation implies that the contingent being of nature was affirmed in its substantiality as well as in its divine valuation for its own sake. Therefore, methods that focus on that contingent being are called for in any study taking the creation seriously on its own terms. Third, a creation made freely through divine love, rather than necessity, and valued by that love for its own sake, can only properly be studied using methods focusing on its properties and processes. Notice that the upshot of the theological argument is that this self-limiting focus of scientific inquiry is a matter of *respect for what God has made*, not logical implication—respect for the genuine reality of nature's contingent being as a gift of God, honoring the need to treat creation as creature rather than divine.

What one can see from the theological-historical line of argument Torrance develops is that MN is *indistinguishable from natural science inquiry as it was developed in the seventeenth century and beyond*.[14] He offers an argument that MN is required by an appropriate theological attitude toward, and knowledge of, nature. Indeed, the upshot of this argument is that to deny MN is to be committed to there being a logical relationship between God and creation, which has deeply problematic theological consequences for both God and the universe.[15] At the same time, notice that MN does not imply God's nonexistence or that there is no divine activity in nature; it is a theologically well-motivated concept and practice. As Ronald L. Numbers summarizes, "scientific naturalism of the methodological kind could—and did—exist with orthodox Christianity. Despite the occasional efforts of unbelievers to use scientific naturalism to construct a world without God, it has retained strong Christian support down to the present. And well it might, for, as we have seen, scientific naturalism was largely made in Christendom by pious Christians."[16] All MN implies is that natural properties and processes are to be studied accurately on their own terms.

Methodological Reasons for Methodological Naturalism

This line of theological justification for an MN-like approach to natural science inquiry held sway well into the eighteenth century. In more recent times, methodological arguments for justifying MN have been the fashion. The most important of these has to do with the very nature of natural scientific methods.

Suppose you are conducting an experiment to determine whether there is a cookie in a cookie jar. The experimental setup is as follows: a friend is behind a screen, opens the jar, and flips a coin. Heads means place a cookie in the jar, while tails means hide the cookie somewhere else. Your friend then closes the jar and removes the screen. Now it should be possible for you to determine whether there is a cookie in the jar.

Given this setup, there are two mutually exclusive hypotheses that exhaust all the contextually relevant possibilities for the outcome of the experiment:

H_1: There is a cookie in the jar.

H_2: There is no cookie in the jar.

The hypotheses are mutually exclusive because they share all the same presuppositions of the experimental arrangement (e.g., the cookie jar and cookie are real, reason and sense experience are basically reliable, there is a truth to the matter of whether there is a cookie in the jar, seeing the cookie in the jar implies it exists, flipped coins can determine conditions for a cookie being in the jar, etc.) and the truth of one implies the other is false. Scientists formulate mutually exclusive and jointly exhaustive hypotheses when pursuing scientific inquiry because it is possible to make an observation and determine which hypothesis is confirmed. If you open the cookie jar and see the cookie within, then you have confirmed H_1.

As simple as the cookie jar experiment sounds, it illustrates the basics of more complex kinds of experiments scientists perform and report in the literature.[17] The presuppositions relevant for the experiment are in place. What counts as relevant evidence is also defined through the presuppositions underlying the experimental setup and the set of possible hypotheses. Moreover, there is an appropriate logical connection (*modus ponens*[18]) between the evidence (seeing a cookie in the jar) and the conclusion (H_1). The crucial point made clear by the simplicity of the experiment is that the presuppositions and the questions to be asked as well as how they are to be answered are linked in a *context*. The line of inquiry represents a context that fixes what the meaningful or appropriate questions are. Likewise, the possible appropriate answers to these questions are constrained by the context. In our example, the presuppositions that cookies and cookie jars exist, that seeing a cookie is a sign of its existence, that cookie jars can hold cookies, and so on, are contextually related to the question being asked. (Is there a cookie in the jar?) The limits represented by this context are how we know that H_1 and H_2 form a mutually exclusive and jointly exhaustive set for investigation.

You proceed to open the cookie jar, look inside, and see that there is no cookie. You can conclude that the most likely explanation is that the coin flip turned up tails and your friend hid the cookie somewhere else. There are only two contextually relevant possibilities, H_1 and H_2, and you have good evidence that H_1 is false. But is it not possible that the coin flip turned up heads and that your friend placed the cookie inside the jar? Perhaps the reason you saw no cookie in the jar is because God made the cookie disappear.

This leads us to the heart of the matter about MN: the reason that the two hypotheses are mutually exclusive and jointly exhaustive is that they represent a *contextual negation* of each other. Hypotheses that are contextual negations of each other share the same set of presuppositions forming the context for the line of inquiry of the experiment. The only negation is the principal contents of the alternative hypotheses. In our case, H_1 and H_2 share the presuppositions (that cookies and cookie jars exist, that cookies can inhabit cookie jars, that seeing a cookie is evidence for its existence, that coin flips can determine whether there is a cookie in the jar, etc.), but they negate each other's principal claim regarding there being a cookie in the jar.

Now consider a third hypothesis:

H_3: It is not the case that there is a cookie in the jar because God made it disappear.

This hypothesis is similar to the following hypotheses:

H_4: It is not the case that there is a cookie in the jar because flying green space monkeys from Mars stole the cookie.

H_5: It is not the case that there is a cookie in the jar because the cookie spontaneously evaporated.

H_6: It is not the case that there is a cookie in the jar because cookies only exist in dreams.

H_7: It is not the case that there is a cookie in the jar because you are a dog sleeping and dreaming you are a human observing a cookie jar.

An infinite number of alternative hypotheses such as these exist. What all have in common, and what sets them apart from H_1 and H_2 is that these alternative hypotheses are all *logical negations*. Hypotheses that are logical negations are the complete opposite of each other without regard for the context of inquiry. In our example, none of the alternative hypotheses retain the same set of presuppositions and line of inquiry—the context—of H_1 and H_2.

Scientists *do not* pursue logical negations in their scientific work for reasons similar to why in everyday life we do not seriously consider these possibilities. Think of the number of contextual—physically relevant—possibilities for the cookie jar experiment as being analogous to the size of the period at the end of this sentence. Then the number of logical possibilities would be analogous to the size of the universe! This is a loose analogy attempting to give some sense for how restricted physical contextually relevant possibility is compared with logical possibility. The universe would have to be infinite in size to more closely match the "size" of logical possibility.

Neither scientists, nor we in our everyday lives, can afford to waste resources pursuing the endless possibilities provided by logical negations. Instead, scientists focus on what is contextually relevant when trying to understand or explain something because the knowledge they are seeking is tied to that context. The basic approach scientists follow is based on *Newton's fourth rule of reasoning*[19]: any hypothesis, model, or theory established by evidence should be considered provisionally true until further relevant evidence either renders it more exact or demonstrates its exceptions. Contextually relevant physical evidence is required to either modify scientific hypotheses or come to understand their exceptions. Mere logical possibilities are not relevant to scientific inquiry and explanation.

The bottom line of this methodological reasoning is that opening the door to logical possibility actually destroys natural science inquiry because its methods are *designed to study physical possibilities tied to physical evidence*. There are no scientific methods for studying logical possibility; that is the provenance of philosophical and other forms of inquiry. Methodological naturalism reflects the scientists' self-limitation to methodologies that can explore physical reality. To relax MN allowing God as an explanatory element in scientific explanations would be to allow possibilities beyond physical relevance, opening the door to logical possibility (there is no non-question-begging way to allow H_3 without allowing all other logical negations). This is to confuse scientific with philosophical and other forms of inquiry. For scientific inquiry to do the job that it has been designed to do—and has been doing so successfully—it must self-restrict its methods of investigation to physically contextually relevant possibilities.

God and Scientific Inquiry

I suggested that the main motivation for rejecting MN is that it somehow unduly restricts scientific inquiry from considering the presence and activity of God in nature. The self-imposed limitations represented by MN in no way imply that God is not present to and working through the properties and processes of nature. This would be the implication of *metaphysical naturalism*, the philosophical belief that there is no divine or supernatural reality. Rather, the upshot of the theological background to MN is that the self-restriction on scientific methodology simply means that scientists are studying nature's properties and processes *as creation* with its own kind of being, where nature is a gift of God as much as is the creative rationality scientists employ to study nature on its own terms. Indeed, natural philosophers of the seventeenth century thought they were devising methods of study that—by focusing on nature's properties and processes as created things—would enable them to better understand God's providence in the world through those properties and processes.[20]

It was recognized for a long time that MN-like approaches to the study of nature were consistent with what theologians call the ministerial mode of divine activity in nature: forms of cooperative interaction among the features of nature such that they "minister" to each other.[21] For instance, in a review essay of *Vestiges of the Natural History of Creation* and Auguste Comte's *Course of Positive Philosophy*, *The Southern Quarterly Review* wrote:

> God generally effects his purposes, however, by intermediate agencies, and this is especially the case in dead, unorganized matter . . . . It is only in miracles that we see God interrupting the energies with which he has endowed matter. These bring about his purposes, and complete his designs without his interference . . . . God still is present; but it is in the operation of unchangeable laws; in the sustaining of efficient energies which he has imposed on the material world that he has created.[22]

Similarly, Torrance argues that laws of nature are "descriptions of autonomous normative structures in the universe," and "ultimately are as *laws* by reference to the commanding and unifying rationality of God the Creator and Sustainer of the universe."[23] Indeed, one would be hard-pressed to find a natural philosopher of the seventeenth century who, while affirming the self-imposed limits of MN, also denied that "the underlying connection, the ultimate consistency, in natural laws is grounded beyond their limits in God's creative upholding of the contingent universe" linking nature to divine rationality, constancy, and reliability "as its transcendent ground."[24] Limiting scientific methods to not asking "God questions" is fully consistent with robust theological beliefs about God's involvement with nature for its own sake.

On the methodological side, the very possibility of scientific inquiry is grounded in the self-restriction to focusing only on material properties and processes in context. In the cookie jar experiment, this excludes H_3 because the context of natural science inquiry is to understand how nature operates, not what God can do. Yet, notice that restricting inquiry to the context shared by H_1 and H_2 in no way implies that God does not exist or is not active in the experiment. Formally, MN is consistent with either theism or atheism.

Sometimes MN has been formulated in such a way that it seems indistinguishable from metaphysical naturalism. For instance, Brad Gregory has characterized MN as "the methodological postulate of metaphysical naturalism, which entails that for science to be science, by definition it can pursue, identify, and entertain only natural causes as plausible explanations of natural phenomena, with the universe as a whole regarded *as if it were a closed system of natural causes*."[25] And some authors have taken to calling MN "methodological atheism."[26] These formulations are indistinguishable from metaphysical naturalism because they already build in metaphysically naturalistic assumptions as the appropriate attitude toward scientific inquiry. Alvin Plantinga has a subtle version of this confusion. In his characterization MN is "the idea that in science we should proceed *as if* the supernatural is not given."[27] He then goes on to claim that "the evidence base of a Christian theist will include (among much else) belief in God," but MN rules out such evidence.[28] However, as we have seen, properly formulated MN does not rule out belief in God, nor does it rule out a scientist being inspired in their work by God (e.g., Michael Faraday). It is merely a focus on methods and questions for studying material properties and processes for their own sake.

Torrance warned that it is possible for scientists to so focus on MN that they are "tempted to treat the universe as a self-sufficient necessary system which does not need to be understood by reference outside of or beyond it."[29] This tendency may be called a lapse into metaphysical naturalism, and much thinking about natural science inquiry fell in just this way over the course of the nineteenth century.[30] Nevertheless, falling to this temptation does not indict MN; rather, it indicts those who fall into metaphysical naturalism due to lack of careful thought about natural science inquiry's powers *and* limits and its history. As Torrance puts it, the natural sciences' restriction "to intramundane connections and explanations" and methodological "exclusion of all reference to extramundane relations . . . does not imply that there is no reality beyond what is open to investigation through its own methods and instruments or is accessible to understanding and formalization within the limits of its own conceptual framework—otherwise it would be guilty of the fallacy of identifying the real with what is conceivable" by natural science reasoning alone.[31] Methodological naturalism's limitation is the flip side of natural science inquiry's strength. But getting carried away by the powers of scientific inquiry to the conclusion that nothing beyond material properties and processes exist is to ontologize method into metaphysics.

Notes

1 Hugh Gauch, *Scientific Method in Practice* (Cambridge: Cambridge University Press, 2003), 112–55.
2 Frank M. Turner, *Between Science and Religion: The Reaction to Scientific Naturalism in Late Victorian England* (New Haven: Yale University Press,

1974); Amos Funkenstein, *Theology and the Scientific Imagination: From the Middle Ages to the Seventeenth Century* (Princeton: Princeton University Press, 1986); David C. Lindberg and Ronald N. Numbers, eds., *God and Nature: Historical Essays on the Encounter between Christianity and Science* (Berkeley: University of California Press, 1986); R. Hooykaas, "The Rise of Modern Science: When and Why?," *The British Journal for the History of Science* 20 (1987): 453–73; Harold P. Nebelsick, *Renaissance and Reformation and the Rise of Science* (Edinburgh: T&T Clark, 1992); Toby E. Huff, *The Rise of Early Modern Science: Islam, China and the West* (Cambridge: Cambridge University Press, 1993); Richard Olsen, *Science Deified & Science Defied: The Historical Significance of Science in Western Culture*, Vol. 2 (Berkeley: University of California Press, 1995); Edward Grant, *The Foundations of Modern Science in the Middle Ages: Their Religious, Institutional and Intellectual Contexts* (Cambridge: Cambridge University Press, 1996); Ronald L. Numbers, "Science without God: Natural Laws and Christian Beliefs," in *When Science & Christianity Meet*, eds. David C. Lindberg and Ronald L. Numbers (Cambridge, MA: Harvard University Press, 2003), 265–85; Peter Harrison, *The Fall of Man and the Foundations of Science* (Cambridge: Cambridge University Press, 2007); Robert C. Bishop, "God and Methodological Naturalism in the Scientific Revolution and Beyond," *Perspectives on Science and Christian Faith* 65, no. 1 (2013): 10–23.

3 David C. Lindberg, *The Beginnings of Western Science: The European Scientific Tradition in Philosophical, Religious, and Institutional Context, Prehistory to AD 1450*, 2nd ed. (Chicago: University of Chicago Press, 2007), 240–21.

4 Rose-Mary Sargent, *The Diffident Naturalist: Robert Boyle and the Philosophy of Experiment* (Chicago: University of Chicago Press, 1995).

5 Isaac Newton, *The Correspondence of Isaac Newton*, vol. 2, ed. H. W. Turnbull (Cambridge: Cambridge University Press, 1960), 334.

6 George F. Wright, *Studies in Science and Religion* (Andover, MA: Warren F. Draper, 1882), 74.

7 Maxine van de Wertering, "A Reconstruction of the Inoculation Controversy," *New England Quarterly* 58 (1985): 46–67.

8 Paul deVries, "Naturalism in the Natural Sciences: A Christian Perspective," *Christian Scholars Review* XV (1986): 388–89.

9 Thomas F. Torrance, *Divine and Contingent Order* (Edinburgh: T&T Clark, 1981), 26.

10 Torrance, *Divine and Contingent Order*, 33–34.

11 Torrance, *Divine and Contingent Order*, 34.

12 Francis Oakley, "Christian Theology and the Newtonian Science: The Rise of the Concept of the Laws of Nature," *Church History* 30, no. 4 (1961): 433–57.

13 Torrance, *Divine and Contingent Order*, 35–36, 72, emphasis added.

14 Bishop, "God and Methodological Naturalism."

15 Torrance, *Divine and Contingent Order*; and Colin E. Gunton, *The Triune Creator: A Historical and Systematic Study* (Grand Rapids, MI: Eerdmans, 1998).

16 Numbers, "Science without God," 84.
17 For details see Gauch, *Scientific Method in Practice*, chap. 4.
18 *Modus ponens* is a deductive inference of the form: If A, then B. A. Therefore, B.
19 Isaac Newton, *The Principia: Mathematical Principles of Natural Philosophy*, trans. I. Bernard Cohen and Anne Whiteman (Berkeley: University of California Press, 1999), 796.
20 Funkenstein, *Theology and the Scientific Imagination*, and Bishop, "God and Methodological Naturalism."
21 Robert C. Bishop, Larry L. Funck, Raymond J. Lewis, Stephen O. Moshier, and John H. Walton, *Understanding Scientific Theories of Origins: with Biblical and Theological Perspectives* (Downers Gove: InterVarsity Press, in press), chap. 2.
22 "The Nebular Hypothesis," *The Southern Quarterly Review*, New Series 1, no. 1 (1856): 95–117. Compare with the quotations at the beginning of this essay.
23 Torrance, *Divine and Contingent Order*, 38 (emphasis in the original).
24 Torrance, *Divine and Contingent Order*, 38.
25 Brad S. Gregory, "No Room for God? History, Science, Metaphysics, and the Study of Religion," *History and Theory* 47 (2008): 505.
26 Nancey Murphy, "Phillip Johnson on Trial," *Perspectives on Science and Christian Faith* 45, no. 1 (1993): 33.
27 Alvin Plantinga, *Where the Conflict Really Lies: Science, Religion, and Naturalism* (New York: Oxford University Press, 2011), 170 (emphasis added).
28 Plantinga, *Where the Conflict Really Lies*, 173.
29 Torrance, *Divine and Contingent Order*, 72.
30 Bishop, "God and Methodological Naturalism."
31 Torrance, *Divine and Contingent Order*, 74.

Scientific Explanations Are Not Limited to Natural Causes

Bruce L. Gordon

Study Questions

1. How does Gordon define natural science? Why does he think that one cannot presume that natural science only allows for natural causes and explanations?

2. How does Gordon define MN? How is it contrasted with metaphysical naturalism?
3. What is intelligent design (ID) theory? How is the question of MN relevant to it?
4. What are the six reasons Gordon gives to be optimistic about ID theory?
5. Why does Gordon think that the Scientific Revolution was not characterized by MN?
6. What is the "naturalism-of-the-gaps" fallacy, according to Gordon? How does it destroy scientific rationality?
7. What is modern uniformitarianism? How is it supposed to preserve the reliability of scientific enquiry while allowing for the possibility of intelligent causation?

It is commonplace today to think that natural science is, and must be, about the business of offering naturalistic explanations of natural phenomena. "It is, after all," the advocates of this viewpoint remark, "*natural* science, not *supernatural* science." And so it is. Of course, it is called *natural* science rather than *supernatural* science because its subject matter is the study of nature, not God. It is not the case that it has received its name because the explanations it offers must, by the very nature of the subject, only appeal to natural causes. One cannot presume that the only explanations suitable to the study of nature are naturalistic (material efficient causes) without begging a crucial question about *the nature of nature* and constructing a caricature of historical scientific practice. Natural science is neither more nor less than the systematic empirical investigation and rational explanation of the natural order. An important issue in this systematic study is whether the universe is, in fact, self-contained, or instead requires something beyond itself to explain its existence and internal function, and whether answering this question is within the reach of natural science. I will argue that the question of whether our universe is self-contained and internally self-explanatory is, in fact, amenable to scientific investigation and answerable in the negative. What is more, I will argue that the project of natural science has its metaphysical foundation and modern genesis in theistic metaphysics and is rationally best grounded and sustained in this context. We must begin, however, by examining the contemporary context for this debate before tracing the historical genesis and evaluating the legitimacy of "methodological naturalism" as a procedural constraint on the scientific enterprise.

Whence Methodological Naturalism?

Broadly defined, *methodological naturalism* (MN) is the operative principle that all scientific explanations must prescind from appeals to transcendent causation (causes existing beyond and operating independently of the material universe) and invoke only immanent natural causes in attempting to give an account of natural phenomena. It is important not to confuse MN with *metaphysical* naturalism. The latter denies the very existence of transcendent causes, the former merely refuses to recognize their legitimacy as *scientific* explanations, quite independent of whether they exist or not. In other words, *when doing science*, the methodological naturalist operates *as if* metaphysical naturalism were true, whatever he or she might otherwise believe about the existence of a transcendent reality and its effects on the universe in which we live. So, while engaged in scientific research, the methodological naturalist treats the universe *as if* it were a closed system of material efficient causes because this is the only kind of causality that meets his explanatory restrictions. It is for this reason that some advocates of MN refer to it as "methodological atheism,"[1] though we will retain the standard terminology.

Intelligent Design Theory and Its Discontents

The issue of MN has been brought to public attention in the last three decades by the rise of intelligent design (ID) theory and its development as a research program among a small segment of the scientific community. Briefly put, ID theorists have developed mathematical descriptions of structures *only* produced by intelligent causes, along with mathematical models of goal-directed processes, and they have used these to argue that certain features of the universe and of biological systems (those that can be modeled by such mathematics) are *best explained* by intelligent causes rather than blind natural processes. This explanatory reorientation respecting the origin of certain natural systems both grounds and catalyzes new lines of engineering-based research in the natural and medical sciences.

Even so, the larger scientific community has not responded favorably to ID research and the banner of MN has been raised high in an effort to exclude it from science. Ironically, some of the most vociferous defenses of MN have come from theists frantic that any association of theism with ID risks the possibility of another "Galileo affair" in which belief in God is given a black eye when "science" turns out to be right and "religion" turns out to be wrong. These cautious souls think it best not to inquire after intelligent causes in nature and find that affirming MN provides just the right prophylactic to preclude the religious contamination of science and the scientific discreditation of religion.

ID theorists are unmoved by such concerns. Even philosophically astute *metaphysical naturalists* recognize that MN plays no defining role in science (it fails as a demarcation criterion) and it simply begs the question to assert that design-theoretic inferences have no scientific validity because they violate it.[2] Furthermore, not everyone *favorably disposed* to design-theoretic science is a theist—consider the atheists Bradley Monton and Thomas Nagel,[3] or the agnostics David Berlinski, Steve Fuller, and Michael Denton,[4] for example. Beyond the fact that atheists and theists can be co-belligerents on some of these issues, however, most theists in the ID community are quite sanguine about the possible falsity of any given inference to intelligent causality. There are several reasons why.

Countering the Critics

First, ID theorists understand that *design inferences are not arguments from ignorance* indicative of a "god-of-the-gaps" fallacy, whereas many of their critics do not. Design inferences do not proceed from the insufficiency of known physical processes to the conclusion that "God must have done it." Rather, design inferences are made on the basis of precise mathematical characterizations of informational structures for which intelligent agency, and *only* intelligent agency, is *known* to be a sufficient cause.[5] Inferring the likely truth of the best rationally and empirically discoverable explanation—or at least *accepting* it as the most viable working hypothesis—is standard scientific practice. In short, ID theory has a *positive* and *solid* scientific basis.[6]

Secondly, even though ID explanations are "theistically friendly," *they are neither intended nor expected to ground full-fledged theism* (and indeed are incapable of doing so). One must always be careful to distinguish the evidence that indicates design, which is something susceptible to scientific investigation, from the implications of the existence of such evidence, which is a matter for philosophical discussion and argument. ID science is concerned with the former, not the latter. In this regard, it is worth noting that design inferences in biology and cosmology *need not* be interpreted as violating MN. For instance, even though it displaces rather than solves the problem of the ultimate origin of biological and cosmological information, serious discussions have taken and are taking place in the scientific community over the hypothesis that life on earth was seeded by intelligent beings from elsewhere in the universe and on the question of whether the universe itself might be a computer simulation.[7] Both of these scenarios create metaphysical contexts in which intelligent causation not only plays a role but also may reasonably be expected to be detectable.[8] Others, distressed by the prospect of theism but impressed by the strength of the evidence for design, have turned in the direction of an *immanentistic panpsychism* as the metaphysical context for intelligent causation in nature.[9] Do such scenarios metaphysically and epistemologically underdetermine the question of whether design inferences violate MN? Maybe. More likely, empirical distinctions between immanent and transcendent ID hypotheses may be forthcoming, as well as criteria of conceptual and explanatory adequacy favoring one hypothesis over the other. Regardless, we will suppose for the purposes of the present discussion that ID theory *does* run afoul of MN and argue that this violation is inconsequential since MN has no important non-question-begging role to play as an essential constraint on scientific explanations.

Thirdly, while design theorists affirm the in-principle defeasibility of design inferences—since it is *epistemically* possible (however unlikely) that a properly grounded design explanation might someday be replaced by a better nondesign explanation if fundamentally new and presently inconceivable physical processes were discovered—*individual design inferences in separate biological and physical contexts are logically independent of each other*. This means that the alleged falsity of a design inference in one area implies *nothing* about the falsity of design inferences in an unconnected area.

Fourthly, ID is not a science-stopper; it is a science-motivator. Aside from the fact that no one in the ID research community is advocating that research based on alternative hypotheses be halted when the best available explanation for some natural structure or process is concluded to be design, there are many positive consequences that follow from the inclusion of design-theoretic methods in the scientific toolbox:

a. *The Value of Alternative Research Programs.* Those committed to other research programs will continue to press the limits of undirected processes in an effort to discover how they might explain the same phenomena. This will either sharpen our understanding of the true limits of undirected natural processes in that area of study or lead to the discovery of something currently unknown that opens new vistas of research. Those persuaded that design *is* the correct explanation for that same phenomenon, however, will be able to devote their time to other scientific research questions they regard as more fruitful. Inclusion of a rigorous design-theoretic paradigm in the sciences will free scientific inquiry from inhibitive conceptual shackles and allow mutually critical research communities to keep each other honest about what each has, and has not, achieved by way of scientific explanation. Unwavering commitment to an explanatory strategy and unwillingness to consider alternatives in the scientific community as a whole is what, more than anything else, blocks the path of inquiry.

b. *ID Can Motivate Science and MN Can Obstruct It: The Case of Junk DNA.*[10] While a dogmatic commitment to design explanations could certainly be obstructive, so can a dogmatic commitment to MN. For example, consider the effects of MN as a restriction on explanations of the origin and development of life. Darwinian explanations have mostly had free rein since theories that account for the diversity of life by undirected physical processes are the only ones acceptable to MN. One consequence of this is the expectation that the genomes for modern species are full of vestigial genetic flotsam carried along the evolutionary stream from ancestral organisms (so-called Junk DNA).[11] This understanding has been invoked by metaphysical naturalists and theistic evolutionists on multiple occasions to argue against ID.[12] As Wojciech Makalowski has observed:

> The term "junk DNA" for many years repelled mainstream researchers from studying noncoding DNA. Who, except a small number of genomic clochards, would like to dig through genomic garbage? However, in science as in normal life, there are some clochards who, at the risk of being ridiculed, explore unpopular territories. Because of them, the view of junk DNA, especially repetitive elements, began to change in the early 1990s. Now, more and more biologists regard repetitive elements as a genomic treasure.[13]

By mandating the undirected origin and evolution of organisms, MN blocked interest for many years in the functionality of the 98 percent of DNA that doesn't code for the construction of proteins, effectively serving as a science-stopper.

By contrast, as early as 1984, the first generation of modern design-theoretic scientists proposed programmatic research into the hypothesis that the origin of the biological information in DNA had an intelligent cause.[14] This perspective has motivated research into the question of whether so-called junk DNA has a function and—with the discovery that the regions of DNA that code for assembling functional proteins are not the only ones containing functional information and that DNA molecules contain nested instructions and codes that overlap each other in ways far more sophisticated than ever expected—it is looking more and more like ID is not just a reasonable explanation, but *the only realistic explanation* for the origin of the functional information in DNA. For example, even the information for constructing individual proteins is sometimes drawn from multiple locations along a DNA strand and, in addition to producing the messenger RNA that facilitates this task, generates other RNAs that are not involved in protein construction but instead part of a regulatory system crucial to the embryonic development of organisms and the specification of their body plans.[15] Furthermore, the ENCODE (Encyclopedia of DNA Elements) Project focused on identifying all the functional elements of the human genome, and the FANTOM (Functional Annotation of Mammalian Genome) Consortium have shown that these non-protein-related RNAs are constructed from *both* strands of DNA, and that RNA constructed from the strand formerly thought only to play a role in DNA replication (the "anti-sense" strand) is a major part of the transcriptome (the entirety of an organism's RNA).[16] As an international team of genome researchers concluded in 2007, the frequency of "overlapping coding regions" with highly specified functionality "is nearly impossible by chance."[17] These overlapping codes profoundly reduce the probability of beneficial mutation.[18] What is more, in the last few years it has become increasingly clear that highly specified epigenetic information (information that does not involve changes in the DNA code, but which affects the formation of RNAs and proteins and larger-scale organismal development) also plays a significant role in the formation of animal body plans.[19]

c. *The Scientific Questions ID Theory Poses*. ID theory yields different research questions than naturalistic origin theories. While critics are apt to accuse ID researchers of confusing the natural sciences with the engineering sciences, insofar as certain features of nature *are* intelligently designed, these things *are* engineered, so studying nature using engineering insights and principles *becomes* a subcategory of natural science. As usual, it all boils down to *the nature of nature*: get it wrong and MN becomes a science-stopper that shuts down empirically justifiable and fruitful lines of inquiry.

It is very important to study what undirected natural processes can accomplish, but once it is known that intelligent causation provides the best explanation for some natural phenomenon, the scientific question of origins has been answered (though questions of the significance of this discovery, which are *not* scientific, are still open for a wide-ranging discussion). The closure of an origins question by ID science then opens a wide vista of scientific questions from an engineering standpoint that draw on resources across the spectrum of the engineering disciplines: biomolecular engineering, genetic engineering, systems engineering, process engineering, computer engineering, nano-engineering, and so on, all dedicated to investigating the means by which natural complex-specified functional information is implemented, degraded, reconstructible/reverse-engineerable, optimized/optimizable, integrated and, for human purposes, imitable (biomimetics). In short, answering one scientific question opens the door for other questions to be asked. ID is not a science-stopper: when it is found to be applicable, it redirects scientific research from dead-ends into different and more fruitful paths.[20]

Fifthly, influential narratives concerning the historical interaction between science and religion are largely false. The narratives in question portray that interaction as laden with conflict, with scientific rationality overrunning religious superstition. Such narratives have enjoyed uncritical propagation in the media and entrenched status in the anti-religious diatribes of the "New Atheists" (e.g., Richard Dawkins, Sam Harris, Daniel Dennett, Christopher Hitchens, and others). But more recent historical scholarship is replacing this false narrative with an appreciation for how religious worldviews, especially theistic convictions, drove the development of modern science[21] and how the prevalence of naturalism—both metaphysical and methodological—in the scientific community is actually undermining scientific rationality.[22]

Sixthly and finally, quite apart from the issues of biological and cosmological design, *scientific rationality and explanation thrive better in the context of theistic metaphysics than naturalistic metaphysics*. Only theism provides an adequate justification for the assumptions of the uniformity of nature and its intelligibility to the human mind necessary to the scientific enterprise. It is thus not surprising that theistic conviction historically provided a powerful impetus to the development of science, for it is still the ontological and epistemic basis that makes the most sense of scientific practice. Understanding why the heuristic methodologies of science are truth-conducive, and recognizing the ontological basis for the regularity of the world, have no epistemic home in the explanatory universe of MN. Nature is regular, but it is regular *because* of transcendent causation, not in spite of it; this is what grounds the uniformitarian assumptions requisite to science.[23] But if this is so, how has MN come to dominate the contemporary conception of science?

Did Methodological Naturalism Drive the Scientific Revolution?

Robert Bishop has recently tried to argue that the embrace of MN was a primary characteristic of the Scientific Revolution—exemplified especially in the work of Robert Boyle (1627–1691) and Isaac Newton (1642–1727)—and it explains why modern science has been so successful.[24] A broader examination of the Scientific Revolution reveals this to be a dubious thesis and the accompanying story selectively designed to support a conclusion antecedently held. Even Boyle and Newton fail to fit the narrative. For example, Boyle explains the view of nature that undergirds his mechanistic approach as follows:

> When . . . I see a curious clock, how orderly every wheel and other part performs its own motions, and with what seeming unanimity they conspire to tell the hour, and to accomplish the designs of the artificer; I do not imagine that any of the wheels, etc., or the engine itself is endowed with reason, but commend that of the workman, who framed it so artfully. So

when I contemplate the action of those several creatures, that make up the world, I do not include the inanimate species, at least, that it is made up of, or the vast engine itself, to act with reason or design, but admire and praise the most wise author, who by his admirable contrivance, can so readily produce effects, to which so great a number of successive and conspiring causes are required.[25]

In short, the relationship between the Mechanical Philosophy and Aristotle's four causes is more subtle than Bishop allows. Despite their preoccupation with contact mechanisms and efficient material causality, advocates of the Mechanical Philosophy assumed a Christian metaphysics and, as a result, preserved *formal causes* in the *ID* of nature's mechanisms, and *final causes* in the *purposes* these mechanisms were designed to serve.

Isaac Newton, the poster-child for the Scientific Revolution, held views similar to Boyle's. Arguing for the ID of the solar system in the General Scholium to his *Principia*, Newton stated of the planetary trajectories:

The Planets and Comets ought perpetually to be resolv'd according to the Laws already Explain'd, in Orbs such in kind and position, as we have supposed. They will indeed be retain'd in their Orbits by the Laws of Gravity, but they could by no means at first acquire such a regular position of their Orbs by those Laws. The Six Primary Planets revolve round the Sun in Circles Concentrical to the Sun, with the same direction of their Motion, and very nearly in the same plain. The Ten Moons (or Secondary Planets) Revolve round the Earth, Jupiter and Saturn, with the same Direction of their Motion, and very nearly in the plain of the Orbs of the Planets. And all these regular Motions have not their rise from Mechanical Causes, seeing the Comets are carried in Orbs very Eccentrical, and that very freely thro' all parts of the Heaven. By which kind of Motion the Comets pass very swiftly and easily thro' the Orbs of the Planets, and in their Aphelia when they move more slowly, and are longer detain'd they are the most remotely distant from one another, and their mutual attraction by much the weakest. This most Elegant System of the Planets and Comets could not be produced but by and under the Contrivance and Dominion of an Intelligent and Powerful Being.[26]

We see here Newton's appreciation of the sensitivity of physical systems to initial conditions and perturbations and his recognition that, if laws and mechanisms in nature are to serve their *intended* purposes, the *fine-tuning* of initial and operative conditions is required. In short, Newton was no advocate of MN. Where the Mechanical Philosophy is concerned, efficient material causation is best regarded as the *phenomenological accompaniment of a formal (conceptually designed) and final (purposefully actualized) causation that is explanatorily fundamental.*

The situation in biology from 1600–1900 provides an even clearer counterexample to the MN-driven narrative. The presence of a design plan as a formal cause for species identification, and its intelligent implementation to serve a purpose in the natural order, dominated biological science prior to Darwin. Common design was the analytic principle for cataloging and classifying life in the scientific work of John Ray (1627–1705) and Carl Linnaeus (1707–1778). Gregor Mendel (1822–1884), the Augustinian monk who founded modern genetics, regarded his three laws of inheritance as indicative of design and, having read Darwin, saw natural selection as much more limited in its relevance.[27] *Even Darwin himself agreed* that the naturalistic constraints he brought to bear in his attempt to explain the origin of species amounted to a fundamental *reorientation* in the science of biology. In the Introduction to *The Origin of Species* he indicates he is going to challenge "the view which most naturalists entertain, and which I formerly entertained—namely, each species has been independently created."[28] In short, the historical locus for the purging of formal and final causation from science and for the origins of MN as a presumed constraint on scientific explanation finds its home in Charles Darwin's *The Origin of Species* (1859).

Methodological naturalism's ascent to contemporary orthodoxy began with the Darwinian Revolution, not the Scientific Revolution. But to say that science only became science when this happened, because only then did MN constrain the explanations scientists offered, is to beg the very question at issue and make a fiat declaration as unconvincing as it is historically inaccurate. The ascendancy of MN is an artifact of a conception of nature that is not intrinsic to the task of scientific explanation itself, and as we have seen, scientists *can* detect and appeal to intelligent causation as the best scientific explanation of certain features of the natural world.

Naturalism-of-the-Gaps and the Ends of Scientific Rationality

When the actual physical and biological details needing explanation cease to decide the issue and all that remains is the attitude that transcendent intelligent causation must be excluded from the explanatory toolbox of science, we are primed for the "naturalism-of-the-gaps" fallacy. The faith that undirected natural causes will eventually bridge explanatory gaps in the naturalistic story, especially in cases where what is currently unexplainable by undirected causes bears all the positive hallmarks of intelligent causation, is both unwarranted and revelatory of an *a priori* commitment to hold the naturalistic barricades, come what may. As the Harvard evolutionary biologist Richard Lewontin infamously remarked:

> Our willingness to accept scientific claims that are against common sense is the key to an understanding of the real struggle between science and the supernatural. We take the side of science in spite of the patent absurdity of some of its constructs . . . in spite of the tolerance of the scientific community for unsubstantiated just-so stories, because we have a prior commitment, a commitment to materialism. . . . Moreover, that materialism is absolute, for we cannot allow a Divine Foot in the door. . . . Anyone who could believe in God could believe in anything. To appeal to an omnipotent deity is to allow at any moment the regularities of nature may be ruptured, that miracles may happen.[29]

Ironically, this willfully blind commitment to a "naturalism-of-the-gaps" ends by destroying the very scientific rationality that Lewontin wishes to preserve.

As an illustration of this, consider the situation in which origin-of-life researchers committed to MN find themselves, a predicament given clear expression by molecular biologist Eugene Koonin at the National Center for Biotechnology Information at the National Institutes of Health:

> Despite considerable experimental and theoretical effort, no compelling scenarios currently exist for the origin of replication and translation, the key processes that together comprise the core of biological systems and the apparent pre-requisite of biological evolution. The RNA World concept might offer the best chance for the resolution of this conundrum but so far cannot account for the emergence of an efficient RNA replicase or the translation system.
>
> The MWO [Many Worlds in One] version of the cosmological model of eternal inflation could suggest a way out of this conundrum because, in an infinite multiverse with a finite number of distinct macroscopic histories (each repeated an infinite number of times), emergence of even highly complex systems by chance is not just possible but inevitable . . . . Specifically, it becomes conceivable that the minimal requirement (the breakthrough stage) for the onset of biological evolution is a primitive coupled replication-translation system that *emerged by chance*. That this extremely rare event occurred on earth and gave rise to life as we know it is explained by anthropic selection alone . . . .

By showing that highly complex systems, actually, can emerge by chance and, moreover, are inevitable, if extremely rare, in the universe, the present model sidesteps the issue of irreducibility and leaves no room whatsoever for any form of intelligent design.[30]

So, to preserve methodologically naturalistic explanations in biology, appeal to the infinite probabilistic resources of multiverse cosmology is invoked, the latter having been invented to explain away, within naturalistic constraints, finely tuned parameters in physics and cosmology. This naturalistic just-so story is jumpstarted, in turn, by conjecturing a "different physics" using an ill-defined quantization of space-time to circumvent the conclusion of Big Bang cosmology that the space-time, matter, and energy of our universe/multiverse had an absolute beginning insusceptible to physical explanation. But this "different physics," which goes under the name of *quantum cosmology*, is woefully deficient and still has finely tuned functional parameters that physics cannot explain.[31]

These broad appeals to infinite resources come at the cost of destroying scientific rationality. The inflationary string multiverse—currently the best naturalistic candidate for explaining away the fine-tuning of the initial conditions, laws, and constants of our observable universe—simultaneously explains too little and too much. It explains too little in that it has finely tuned design-parameters itself, some of which require a greater order of fine-tuning than the first-order fine-tuning supposedly explained. It thus relocates the ground of the design inference rather than eliminates it. Inflationary cosmology also explains too much because its profligate probabilistic resources induce problems that undermine scientific rationality altogether.[32] In particular, the inflationary multiverse gives rise to the "measure problem"—manifested in various guises as endlessly cloned realities, the youngness paradox, and the Boltzmann Brain paradox, to name a few—aptly summarized by theoretical physicist Max Tegmark:

> By predicting that space isn't just big but truly infinite, inflation has also brought about the so-called measure problem, which I view as the greatest crisis facing modern physics. Physics is all about predicting the future from the past, but inflation seems to sabotage this. When we try to predict the probability that something particular will happen, inflation always gives the same useless answer: infinity divided by infinity. The problem is that whatever experiment you make, inflation predicts there will be infinitely many copies of you, far away in our infinite space, obtaining each physically possible outcome; and despite years of teeth-grinding in the cosmology community, no consensus has emerged on how to extract sensible

answers from these infinities. So, strictly speaking, we physicists can no longer predict anything at all! This means that today's best theories need a major shakeup by retiring an incorrect assumption. Which one? Here's my prime suspect: ∞.[33]

Of course, the specter of infinity arose, in part, from the need for explanatory resources sufficient to preserve the constraints of MN in science. And this naturalism-of-the-gaps that invokes the very infinities that Tegmark describes as "ruining physics" is starting to ruin biology too. Taming infinity and restoring scientific rationality is going to require taking an axe to the root of the problem: *MN must go*. It turns out then, contrary to Lewontin's assertion, that rational explanations presuppose purpose, not blind chance, and it is the materialist, not the theist, who not only could believe anything but ultimately needs the conditions under which anything (except transcendent causation) can be believed.[34]

Conclusion: The Larger Toolbox Vindicated

The solid mathematical and empirical basis of design inferences and the rationally destructive consequences of trying to avoid them vindicate their place in science and their inclusion in the scientific toolbox. They can even be subsumed under the rubric of the uniformitarian assumptions requisite to science. *Modern* uniformitarianism is the idea that scientific explanations are circumscribed by uniformly operating regularities of nature or extrapolations from them: the universe exhibits a uniform and investigable causal structure that provides a stable background for scientific experimentation, observation, and theorization. Uniformitarian reasoning thus infers past causes from present effects under the assumption that the causal structure of the world has remained constant and permits reliable inferences. Since we have a very clear conception of what can happen in the regular course of nature that forms a stable background to human activity, this can be contrasted with what lies *outside* the regular course of nature in a pattern that reliably indicates the particular and directed action of an intelligent cause. Because structures and processes that exhibit a degree of complex-specified information exceeding the probability bounds of the observable universe[35] are habitually and uniformly associated with intelligent activity, intelligent causes are part of the causal structure of the world and so fall within the purview of scientific investigation both methodologically and substantively. ID explanations are therefore a species of uniformitarian analysis.

The idea that parts of nature might best be modeled by processes that have their end in view before it is achieved, or by structures that result from such processes, is eminently reasonable in a theistic context and entirely compatible with the uniformitarian assumptions necessary to science. Having set aside the false constraints of MN, and relying instead on a uniformitarian principle that permits recognition, from repeated experience, of the objective and regular characteristics of intelligent causation, it becomes entirely plausible that certain features of the universe and of biological systems exhibit purpose that is detectable and quantifiable. It furthermore becomes an entirely legitimate *scientific* enterprise to investigate this question. So *requiescat in pace*, MN—science has known thee for a spell, but never had need of thee.

Notes

1   Nancey Murphy, "Philip Johnson on Trial: A Critique of His Critique of Darwin," *Perspectives on Science and Christian Faith* 45, no. 1 (1993): 26–36.

2   Maarten Boudry, et al., "How Not to Attack Intelligent Design Creationism: Philosophical Misconceptions about Methodological Naturalism," *Foundations of Science* 15 (2010): 227–44; Martin Boudry, et al., "Grist to the Mill of Anti-Evolutionism: The Failed Strategy of Ruling the Supernatural out of Science by Philosophical Fiat," *Science & Education* 21 (2012): 1151–65; and Sahotra Sarkar, "The Science Question in Intelligent Design," *Synthese* 178 (2011): 291–305.

3   See Bradley Monton, *Seeking God in Science: An Atheist Defends Intelligent Design* (Peterborough, ON: Broadview Press, 2009); and Thomas Nagel, *Mind and Cosmos: Why the Materialist Neo-Darwinian Conception of Nature Is Almost Certainly False* (Oxford: Oxford University Press, 2012).

4   See David Berlinski, *The Devil's Delusion: Atheism and Its Scientific Pretensions* (New York, NY: Basic Books, 2009); and *The Deniable Darwin and Other Essays* (Seattle, WA: Discovery Institute Press, 2010); Steve Fuller, *Science vs. Religion? Intelligent Design and the Problem of Evolution* (Malden, MA: Polity Press, 2007); *Dissent over Descent: Intelligent Design's Challenge to Darwinism* (London, UK: Icon Books, 2008); and Michael Denton, *Evolution: A Theory in Crisis* (Chevy Chase, MD: Adler & Adler, 1986); *Nature's Destiny: How the Laws of Biology Reveal Purpose in the Universe* (New York, NY: The Free Press, 1998); and *Evolution: Still a Theory in Crisis* (Seattle: Discovery Institute Press, 2016).

5   It is important to note that biological information, including and most especially that embodied in DNA and RNA, is *functional* or *complex-specified* information, not Shannon information (a measure of mere complexity) and certainly not semantic information. Failure to understand this leads some ID critics to dismiss design-theoretic discussions of information processing

systems in biology as "metaphorical" and "misleading" (see for example the inaccurate discussion in the essay by Robert Bishop and Robert O'Connor, "Doubting the Signature," *Books & Culture*, November to December 2014 (http://www.booksandculture.com/articles/2014/novdec/doubting-signature.html)). But the fact that the gene expression system constitutes an information processing system is not even remotely controversial. Helpful clarifications obviating these kinds of confusions can be found in Section VIII of David Klinghoffer, ed. *Debating Darwin's Doubt* (Seattle: Discovery Institute Press, 2015), especially the essays by Stephen Meyer and Casey Luskin.

6 For ongoing technical research on the mathematical, computational, and observational/experimental basis of ID theory in biology and other sciences, the reader will find it helpful to consult the work of *Biologic Institute* in Seattle (http://www.biologicinstitute.org/research) and *The Evolutionary Informatics Lab* (http://www.evoinfo.org/index/) run by Robert Marks, a computational engineer at Baylor University. The following technical monographs and compendia of ID research are essential resources: William A. Dembski, *The Design Inference: Eliminating Chance through Small Probabilities* (Cambridge: Cambridge University Press, 1998); Robert Marks, William Dembski, and Winston Ewert, *Introduction to Evolutionary Informatics* (Singapore: World Scientific, 2017); Bruce Gordon and William Dembski, *The Nature of Nature: Examining the Role of Naturalism in Science* (Wilmington, DE: ISI Books, 2011); Robert Marks, Michael Behe, William Dembski, Bruce Gordon, and John Sanford, eds., *Biological Information: New Perspectives* (Singapore: World Scientific, 2013); and Luke Barnes, "The Fine-Tuning of the Universe for Intelligent Life" (https://arxiv.org/pdf/1112.4647.pdf). Popular science books dealing with these subjects are also very helpful—see various works by Michael Behe, William Dembski, Jonathan Wells, Stephen Meyer, Douglas Axe, Guillermo Gonzalez, and Luke Barnes.

7 The following resources provide good introductions: On undirected panspermia hypotheses: Chandra Wickramasinghe, "The Astrobiological Case for Our Cosmic Ancestry," *International Journal of Astrobiology* 9, no. 2 (2010): 119–29. On intelligently seeded life hypotheses: Francis Crick and Leslie Orgel, "Directed Panspermia," *Icarus* 19 (1973): 341–46; and Francis Crick, *Life Itself: Its Origin and Nature* (New York: Touchstone, 1982). On the hypothesis that the universe is a computer simulation: Jürgen Schmidhuber, (1999) "A Computer Scientist's View of Life, the Universe, and Everything" (https://arxiv.org/pdf/quant-ph/9904050.pdf); and (2000) "Algorithmic Theories of Everything" (https://arxiv.org/pdf/quant-ph/0011122.pdf); Nick Bostrum, "Are You Living in a Computer Simulation?" *Philosophical Quarterly* 53, no. 211 (2003): 243–55.

8 Another technical issue giving rise to interpretive questions is the possibility of suboptimal design. Alleged cases of suboptimal design are often thrown in the face of ID theorists by scientific naturalists apparently oblivious to the fact they are offering a theological rather than a scientific argument against ID research. This possibility is also emphasized by theists who want to use evolution as a tool in theodicy that allegedly distances God from natural evils.

A good discussion of the shortcomings of such reasoning and other related issues can be found in Jay Richards's edited collection *God and Evolution* (Seattle: Discovery Institute Press, 2010). While the claimed suboptimality of certain biological designs is interesting from the standpoint of both engineering science and theodicy, it really is a red herring as far as the viability of design inferences is concerned. Suboptimal designs—if they are in fact suboptimal—are nonetheless still *designed*, and therefore require an intelligent cause.

9   For a survey of panpsychist theories and critical responses to them, see William Seager and Sean Allen-Hermanson, "Panpsychism," *The Stanford Encyclopedia of Philosophy* (https://plato.stanford.edu/archives/fall2015/entries/panpsychism). See also Nagel, *Mind and Cosmos*.

10 This subsection is a little more technical than the rest of this essay, but readers who remember their high school biology should be able to follow it. As a reminder, recall that DNA (deoxyribonucleic acid) molecules are the basic carrier of genetic information and are found in the chromosomes of almost all living organisms. DNA has a double-helical (twisted ladder) construction in which four bases (adenine, cytosine, guanine, and thymine) attached to a sugar-phosphate backbone bond in complementary pairs (adenine with thymine, cytosine with guanine) as rungs linking the two strands of the ladder. When the molecule replicates, the two strands separate and serve as templates for the formation of new strands. RNAs (ribonucleic acids) are normally single strands that are transcribed from one or other strand of the DNA molecule (with uracil substituting for thymine as a base in RNA). Some RNAs serve as templates for the synthesis of proteins, but over the last twenty-five years or so, it has been discovered that most RNAs perform a variety of other functions that regulate cell activity and play an indispensable role in the stages of development and growth from the fertilized egg to the establishment of the body plans characteristic of different species.

11 Representative of this mindset, firmly entrenched by the 1970s, are the following references (with relevant pages indicated): Susumu Ohno, "So Much 'Junk' DNA in Our Genome," *Brookhaven Symposia in Biology* 23 (1972): 366–70; Richard Dawkins, *The Selfish Gene* (New York: Oxford University Press, 1976), 47; W. Ford Doolittle and Carmen Sapienza, "Selfish Genes, the Phenotype Paradigm, and Genome Evolution," *Nature* 284 (1980): 601–3; and Leslie Orgel and Francis Crick, "Selfish DNA: The Ultimate Parasite," *Nature* 284 (1980): 604–7.

12 For example (with relevant pages indicated): Richard Dawkins, *A Devil's Chaplain: Reflections on Hope, Lies, Science, and Love* (New York: Mariner Books, 2004), 99; and *The Greatest Show on Earth: The Evidence for Evolution* (New York: Free Press, 2009), 332–33; Douglas J. Futuyma, *Evolution* (Sunderland, MA: Sinauer Associates, 2005), 48–49, 456, 530; Michael Shermer, *Why Darwin Matters: The Case Against Intelligent Design* (New York: Holt, 2006), 74–75; Philip Kitcher, *Living with Darwin: Evolution, Design, and the Future of Faith* (New York: Oxford University Press, 2007), 57–58, 111; Jerry A. Coyne, *Why Evolution Is True* (New York: Viking, 2009), 66–67, 81.

13 Wojciech Makalowski, "Not Junk After All," *Science* 300, no. 5623 (2003): 1246–47. An excellent discussion of this development and its significance, along with an extensive guide to the technical literature, can be found in Jonathan Wells's book *The Myth of Junk DNA* (Seattle: Discovery Institute Press, 2011).

14 Charles Thaxton, Walter Bradley, and Roger Olson. *The Mystery of Life's Origin: Reassessing Current Theories* (New York: Philosophical Library, 1984), 210–11.

15 For a helpful discussion of these and related results, see chapter 3 of J. Wells, *The Myth of Junk DNA* (Seattle: Discovery Institute Press, 2011).

16 S. Katayama, et al., "Antisense Transcription in the Mammalian Transcriptome," *Science* 309 (2005): 1564–66; P. Engström, et al., "Complex Loci in Human and Mouse Genomes," *PLoS Genetics* 2, no. 4 (2006): e47; Y. He, et al., "The Antisense Transcriptomes of Human Cells," *Science* 322 (2008): 1855–57; and K. V. Morris, et al., "Bidirectional Transcription Directs Both Transcriptional Gene Activation and Suppression in Human Cells," *PLoS Genetics* 4, no. 11 (2008): e1000258.

17 W-Y Chung, et al., "A First Look at ARFome: Dual-Coding Genes in Mammalian Genomes," *PLoS Computational Biology* 3, no. 5 (2007): e91.

18 G. Montañez, et al., "Multiple Overlapping Genetic Codes Profoundly Reduce the Probability of Beneficial Mutation," in *Biological Information: New Perspectives*, eds. Robert Marks, Michael Behe, William Dembski, Bruce Gordon, and John Sanford (Singapore: World Scientific, 2013), 139–67.

19 Jonathan Wells, "Membrane Patterns Carry Ontogenetic Information that is Specified Independently of DNA," *BIO-Complexity* 2 (2014): 1–28 (http://bio-complexity.org/ojs/index.php/main/article/view/BIO-C.2014.2/BIO-C.2014.2). The extensive footnotes in Wells's article provide a helpful look into the world of epigenetic research. A broad and accessible account of ongoing epigenetic research can be found in Thomas Woodward's and James Gills's, *The Mysterious Epigenome: What Lies Beyond DNA* (Grand Rapids, MI: Kregel Publications, 2012).

20 For a lucid discussion of ID-based research in science, see William Dembski, *The Design Revolution: Answering the Toughest Questions about Intelligent Design* (Downers Grove: IVP, 2004), 310–17. See also footnote 6, above.

21 Eugene Klaaren, *Religious Origins of Modern Science* (Grand Rapids, MI: Eerdmans, 1977); Margaret Osler, *Divine will and the Mechanical Philosophy: Gassendi and Descartes on Contingency and Necessity in the Created World* (Cambridge: Cambridge University Press, 1994); Edward Grant, *The Foundations of Modern Science in the Middle Ages: Their Religious, Institutional, and Intellectual Contexts* (Cambridge: Cambridge University Press, 1996); Rodney Stark, *For the Glory of God: How Monotheism Led to Reformations, Science, Witch-Hunts, and the End of Slavery* (Princeton: Princeton University Press, 2003); David Lindberg, *The Beginnings of Western Science: The European Scientific Tradition in Philosophical, Religious, and Institutional Context, Prehistory to A.D. 1450,* 2nd ed. (Chicago: University of Chicago Press, 2007); Ronald Numbers, ed. *Galileo Goes to Jail and Other Myths about Science and Religion* (Harvard University

Press, 2010); James Hannam, *The Genesis of Science: How the Christian Middle Ages Launched the Scientific Revolution* (Washington, DC: Regnery Publishing, 2011); Bruce Gordon, "The Rise of Naturalism and Its Problematic Role in Science and Culture," in *The Nature of Nature*, 3–61; and many more sources.

22 Alvin Plantinga, *Warrant and Proper Function* (Oxford: Oxford University Press, 1993); Alvin Plantinga, "Respondeo," in *Warrant in Contemporary Epistemology: Essays in Honor of Plantinga's Theory of Knowledge*, ed. Jonathan L. Kvanvig (Lanham, MD: Rowman & Littlefield, 1996), 307–78; James Beilby, ed. *Naturalism Defeated? Essays on Plantinga's Evolutionary Argument against Naturalism* (Ithaca: Cornell University Press, 2002); Michael Rea, *World without Design: The Ontological Consequences of Naturalism* (Oxford: Oxford University Press, 2002); Alvin Plantinga, *Where the Conflict Really Lies: Science, Religion, and Naturalism* (Oxford: Oxford University Press, 2011).

23 Plantinga, *Where the Conflict Really Lies*; and Bruce L. Gordon, "In Defense of Uniformitarianism," *Perspectives on Science and Christian Faith* 65, no. 2 (2013): 79–86.

24 Robert C. Bishop, "God and Methodological Naturalism in the Scientific Revolution and Beyond," *Perspectives on Science and Christian Faith* 65, no. 1 (2013): 10–23.

25 Robert Boyle, *The Works of the Honourable Robert Boyle* [5 Volumes, London: A. Millar, 1744], vol. 1, p. 447.

26 Isaac Newton, General Scholium to the *Principia* (1687), translated from Latin by John Maxwell (1715), (https://newtonprojectca.files.wordpress.com/2013/06/newton-general-scholium-in-maxwell-1715-letter-size.pdf).

27 Harry Sootin, *Gregor Mendel: Father of the Science of Genetics* (New York: Vanguard Press, 1959); Hugo Iltis, "Gregor Mendel and His Work," *The Scientific Monthly* 56, no. 5 (1943): 414–23; Dan Graves, *Scientists of Faith* (Grand Rapids, MI: Kregel Publications, 1996), 140–44.

28 Charles Darwin, *The Origin of Species*, 6 (http://darwin-online.org.uk/Variorum/1859/1859-6-dns.html).

29 Richard Lewontin, "Billions and billions of demons," *The New York Review of Books*, January 9, 1997: 28–32.

30 Eugene Koonin, "The Cosmological Model of Eternal Inflation and the Transition from Chance to Biological Evolution in the History of Life," *Biology Direct* 2, no. 15 (2007), (http://www.biologydirect.com/content/2/1/15).

31 The details involved in this naturalistic story, all considered, are complicated and space prohibits their discussion here. For helpful and concise introductions to many of these details, the *Dictionary of Christianity and Science*, ed. Paul Copan, et al. (Grand Rapids, MI: Zondervan, 2017) is an invaluable resource. In regard to the essential place of the principle of sufficient reason in science, see Bruce L. Gordon, "The Necessity of Sufficiency: The Argument from the Incompleteness of Nature," in *Two Dozen (or so) Arguments for God: The Plantinga Project*, eds. Trent Dougherty and Jerry Walls (Oxford: Oxford University Press, forthcoming).

32. See Bruce L. Gordon, "Balloons on a String: A Critique of Multiverse Cosmology," in *The Nature of Nature*, 558–601.

33. Max Tegmark, "Infinity is a Beautiful Concept—And It's Ruining Physics," in *This Idea Must Die: Scientific Theories that are Blocking Progress*, ed. John Brockman (New York: Harper Perennial, 2015), 48–51. See also http://blogs.discovermagazine.com/crux/2015/02/20/infinity-ruining-physics.

34. See also Casey Luskin, "Just-So Stories," in the *Dictionary of Christianity and Science*.

35. Seth Lloyd, "Computational Capacity of the Universe," *Physical Review Letters* 88, no. 23 (2002): 237901 (https://arxiv.org/pdf/quant-ph/0110141.pdf). See also the discussion of universal probability bounds in William A. Dembski, *The Design Inference*.

RESPONSES

Response to Bishop

Bruce L. Gordon

Study Questions

1. According to Gordon, in what way is Bishop (rather than Gregory and Plantinga) confused about the definition of MN? What problem does Gordon find with Bishop's own definition of MN?
2. Why does Gordon think that Bishop's "disappearing cookie" argument commits the Straw Man fallacy? How does he illustrate how ID may offer the best explanation for some phenomena?
3. What is uniformitarianism? How does it allow for intelligent causation to fall under the purview of science?
4. What mistake does Gordon accuse Bishop of making regarding MN and the Scientific Revolution?
5. How does Gordon respond to Bishop's theological justification of MN?

Robert Bishop and I differ profoundly on the nature and methodology of science. In my response to his essay, I will first dissect his obfuscation of the definition of MN. Second, I will show that he has constructed a straw man in his effort to provide methodological reasons for MN. Third, I will outline the difference between MN and uniformitarianism and point out that the Scientific Revolution relied on a version of the latter that gives a role to intelligent causation in the origin of certain natural structures, thus allowing explanatory differences, when needed, between origin science and operational science. This approach serves science much better than MN. Finally, I will argue that Bishop's theological "justification" for MN is an unconvincing attempt to make a theologically counterintuitive position plausible.

What Is Methodological Naturalism?

Bishop's attempt, at the end of his essay, to clarify the meaning of MN by arguing that various thinkers—from Brad Gregory to Alvin Plantinga—are confused about its definition, has the opposite effect and obfuscates what was otherwise both correct and clear. There is a legitimate distinction between operating *as if* something were true and believing that it is, in fact, true. When making a physical calculation, for example, a physicist often will proceed *as if* a simplifying assumption were true—for example, that a surface is frictionless—even though he knows that it is not. So, when Brad Gregory asserts that MN is the practice of treating the whole universe "*as if* it were a closed system of natural causes," or Alvin Plantinga characterizes MN as the idea that science "should proceed *as if* the supernatural is not given," they are defining it as a *hypothetical stance* that is invoked as a methodological constraint on scientific investigation. MN is thus neither more nor less than acting *as if* naturalism were true for the purpose of doing science—that is, after all, why it is called methodological *naturalism*. To suppose that adopting this methodological stance involves the belief that naturalism is actually true, or that it, as Bishop implies, "rules out belief in God" or "rules out a scientist being inspired by their belief in God" (p. 200), is to confuse a working hypothesis with an actual belief—that is, to confuse methodology with metaphysics and the hypothetical with the actual. Bishop compounds this irony by quoting with approval Thomas Torrance's characterization of scientific procedure as the methodological restriction "to intramundane connections and explanations" and "exclusion of all reference to extramundane relations . . . ." In other words, MN counsels the scientist to investigate the universe solely *as if* it were a closed system of natural causes—and to exclude any reference to an extramundane reality which, of course, means excluding any reference to God. Correct or not, Torrance's description of scientific methodology is *equivalent* to Gregory's and Plantinga's definition of MN. Bishop is attempting a distinction where there is no difference and, in the process, revealing his own confusion.

Bishop has elsewhere tried to take the edge off MN's definition, distinguishing it from metaphysical naturalism as follows:

> *Metaphysical* naturalism is the philosophical belief that material reality is the only reality. There is no God, nor angels, spirit beings, or spiritual realm. In contrast, *methodological* naturalism (MN) is an approach to scientific investigation that seeks to take phenomena on their own terms, to understand them as they actually are.[1]

Unless one begs the question about the nature of nature, however, this milquetoast definition would make MN perfectly acceptable to ID theorists. After all, it is entirely possible that the phenomena "as they actually are" exhibit detectable design because they are, in fact, designed structures or processes. But Bishop will have no part of ID theory.[2] He asserts that any design there might be in nature is "signed using invisible ink."[3] Bishop's MN has, apparently, turned into the outright metaphysical assertion that, if God had any hand in nature, nature can show no evidence of it. If this is not to "ontologize method into metaphysics," I'm not sure what is.

Bishop's Straw Man ID Theory

It is thus not surprising that Bishop caricatures the idea that scientific explanations are not limited to natural causes. The *straw man fallacy* rejects a position after attacking a misrepresentation of it, and Bishop's "disappearing cookie" argument that science is not possible in the absence of MN does this by *misrepresenting* the only serious hypothesis allowing for nonnatural causes: intelligent design. To open the door to intelligent causes as explanations is *not*, as he asserts, to open the door to *mere* logical possibility. Properly understood, ID explanations *arise from the study of physical possibilities tied to physical evidence*. So the ID theorist satisfies Bishop's desiderata with respect to empirically constrained and contextually relevant physical possibilities. Broadly schematized, ID theorists are interested in *quantifying* the amount of *functionally specified information* embodied in physical and biological systems and then *evaluating* whether this amount exceeds the computational capacity of the observable universe. If it does, the information in that system exhibits a pattern for which intelligence *is the only known sufficient cause*.[4] Under these conditions, the *best explanation* is intelligent causation.

As an example, consider the origin of protein folds.[5] The protein-coding segments of DNA must produce amino acid sequences (proteins) that fold into biologically functional structures in three dimensions, but the sequence of triplet-codons along the sugar-phosphate backbone of DNA is *not determined* by any biochemical laws or self-organizational properties any more than the chemistry of ink bonding to paper explains the contents of a book. The relevant empirical study is thus evaluating how frequently *functional* protein folds occur in amino acid sequence space. Careful laboratory experimentation and analysis performed by Douglas Axe[6] has shown that, on average, a *single* protein folding domain (i.e., *one* stand-alone functional protein fold) has little tolerance for variation and a probability in amino acid sequence space of about 1 in 10^{74}. Life on earth as we know it requires around a thousand different protein folding domains, so these bare protein constituents, quite apart from their functional assemblage into actual organisms, have a probability of 1 in $10^{74,000}$ of existing at all. The computational capacity of the observable universe allows, *at best*, for the undirected generation of 10^{120} bits of functionally specified information,[7] so functionally specified structures having a probability less than 1 in 10^{120} are *best explained* by an intelligent cause, not a blind natural process.[8] This means that in the entire history of the universe we should expect to see the undirected production of no more than two protein folds (which have a joint probability of 1 in 10^{148}), yet we have—on one planet, no less—around a thousand of them.

Methodological Naturalism versus Uniformitarianism

Given the *inadequacy* of MN, is there *any* methodological principle that can serve as a guide to the construction of scientific explanations and be helpful for investigating not just the *ordinary course* of nature but also the *origin* of those natural structures whose ordinary course is being investigated? The answer is that there *is* such a principle: *uniformitarianism*. Uniformitarianism is the methodological assumption that the causal structure of the universe has remained constant throughout its history and, therefore, that *past events* may be explained on the basis of *presently operative causes*.[9] In this regard, we have a very clear conception of what can happen in the regular course of nature that forms a stable background to intelligent activity. This stable background can be contrasted with what lies *outside* the regular course of nature and *requires* the action of an intelligent cause, namely, structures and processes that exhibit a degree of functionally specified information exceeding the computational capacity of the observable universe, for these are *habitually* and *uniformly* associated with intelligent activity. This hallmark of intelligent causation *is also part of the uniform causal structure of the world* and—in accordance with uniformitarian principle—falls within the purview of scientific investigation both methodologically and substantively.[10]

If we now look back at the Scientific Revolution and consider the *full scope* of all that was said by its key figures, we discern that while they were no advocates of MN—for they understood the *origin* and *order* of the universe and of biological species in terms of intelligent design—they did believe that the universe *operated* in a regular manner that was susceptible to mathematical description and, generally, through the medium of efficient material causation. In fact, the Scientific Revolution was driven as much by the understanding that nature was *designed* as it was driven by recognition of the *uniform mathematical order discernible in its causal operation*. MN is a post-Darwinian development that Bishop anachronistically and incorrectly projects backward into the origins of modern science.

A Theological Justification for Methodological Naturalism?

Finally, a comment on Bishop's peculiar attempt to provide a *theological* justification for MN. The idea, derived from Torrance, that the Incarnation somehow justifies the idea that science should operate *as if* God only works through natural causes seems not just a *non sequitur*, but singularly inappropriate. It *does not follow* from the fact that the universe has an order revealed through its natural processes that seamless natural processes are all we should expect science to reveal. Yes, divine action may be regarded as "incarnate" in the natural order of the universe, but it is not restricted to the natural order of the universe—as the Incarnation itself makes clear. The Incarnation *begins* with extraordinary divine action—a miraculous virgin birth—*develops* with extraordinary divine action—Christ performing a variety of miracles such as turning water into wine, healing paralytics, raising the dead, and so on—and *ends* (at least in the God-with-us mode) with Christ's miraculous resurrection and ascension. If anything contradicts the expectation that God confines himself to operating through natural causes, it is the Incarnation. Bishop's theological "justification" for MN is not just a dubious piece of reasoning; it is, at its core, counterintuitive and contrary to the fundamental orientation of the biblical narrative and of Christian theology.[11]

Conclusion

As we have seen, from a philosophical and scientific standpoint, the position that scientific explanations are limited to natural causes is exceedingly weak and its denial is much more defensible. But from a specifically Judeo-Christian standpoint, *theological* attempts to justify MN are not just counterintuitive, they are completely wrong-headed. When the arguments are objectively weighed in the balance, then, it seems clear that scientific explanations *are not*, and *should not*, be limited to natural causes.

Notes

1   Robert C. Bishop, "God and Methodological Naturalism in the Scientific Revolution and Beyond," *Perspectives on Science and Christian Faith* 65, no. 1 (2013): 10–23. The quote is from page 10. In his essay in this volume, Bishop also quotes and expands upon Thomas Torrance's view as maintaining

that exploration of the contingent order of creation "requires exploring the properties and processes of nature *on their own terms*," a condition he mistakenly takes to be equivalent to MN.

2   Robert C. Bishop, "The Extended Synthesis" (Reviewing *Darwin's Doubt*: Robert Bishop, Parts 1–4 (2014)): Part 1: http://biologos.org/blogs/archive/the-extended-synthesis-reviewing-darwins-doubt-robert-bishop-part-1; Part 2: http://biologos.org/blogs/archive/two-rhetorical-strategies-reviewing-darwins-doubt-robert-bishop-part-2; Part 3: http://biologos.org/blogs/archive/meyers-inference-to-intelligent-design-as-the-best-explanation-reviewing-da; Part 4: http://biologos.org/blogs/archive/final-assessments-reviewing-darwins-doubt-robert-bishop-part-4; Robert C. Bishop "God and Methodological Naturalism in the Scientific Revolution and Beyond"; Robert Bishop and Robert O'Connor, "Doubting the Signature," *Books & Culture* (November to December 2014) (http://www.booksandculture.com/articles/2014/novdec/doubting-signature.html); and so on. For a catalog of Bishop's misunderstandings and a response to his criticisms of ID in these essays, see Paul Nelson's articles (Chapters 34 and 37), Casey Luskin's articles (Chapters 35 and 41), and especially Stephen Meyer's articles (Chapters 39, 40, 42, and 43) in David Klinghoffer, ed., *Debating Darwin's Doubt* (Seattle: Discovery Institute Press, 2015).

3   Robert Bishop and Robert O'Connor, "Doubting the Signature."

4   As mentioned in note 5 of my primary essay, in criticizing ID research, Bishop shows no awareness of the significance of the distinction among Shannon information, semantic information, and functional information, or of the uncontroversial fact that the gene expression system processes functional information.

5   The reader may find it helpful to review the discussion of "junk DNA" in my primary essay, along with its associated footnotes. For a more extensive discussion of this example, see the appendix (pp. 31–32) to my essay "The Rise of Naturalism and Its Problematic Role in Science and Culture," in *The Nature of Nature: Examining the Role of Naturalism in Science*, eds. Bruce L. Gordon and William A. Dembski (Wilmington: ISI Books, 2011), 3–61. The discussion on 27–30 is also helpful.

6   Douglas D. Axe, "Extreme Functional Sensitivity to Conservative Amino Acid Changes on Enzyme Exteriors," *Journal of Molecular Biology* 301 (2000): 585–96; "Estimating the Prevalence of Protein Sequences Adopting Functional Enzyme Folds," *Journal of Molecular Biology* 341 (2004): 1295–315; and "The Case Against a Darwinian Origin of Protein Folds," *BIO-Complexity* 1 (2010): 1–12 (http://bio-complexity.org/ojs/index.php/main/article/view/BIO-C.2010.1/BIO-C.2010.1).

7   Seth Lloyd, "Computational Capacity of the Universe," *Physical Review Letters* 88, no. 23 (2002): 237901 (https://arxiv.org/pdf/quant-ph/0110141.pdf).

8   This rough-and-ready discussion is aimed at cultivating your intuitions and motivating further exploration of design-theoretic mathematics. For the technical development of design-theoretic mathematics, I recommend the introductory probabilistic treatment in William A. Dembski, *The Design*

Inference: Eliminating Chance through Small Probabilities (Cambridge: Cambridge University Press, 1998); and the advanced information-theoretic treatment in Robert J. Marks II, William A. Dembski, and Winston Ewert, *Introduction to Evolutionary Informatics* (Singapore: World Scientific Publishing Company, 2017).

9   This is a general definition of the concept. There are different varieties of uniformitarianism. An excellent discussion of these varieties and their role in science can be found in Davis Young's and Ralph Stearley's book *The Bible, Rocks and Time: Geological Evidence for the Age of the Earth* (Downers Grove: IVP Academic, 2008), 95–100, 447–74.

10 For further clarification of the differences between MN and uniformitarianism and a defense of ID as a species of uniformitarian analysis, see my essay "In Defense of Uniformitarianism," *Perspectives on Science and Christian Faith* 65, no. 2 (2013): 1–8.

11 Note the words of the Old Testament psalmist, "The heavens declare the glory of God; the skies proclaim the work of his hands. Day after day they pour forth speech; night after night they reveal knowledge" (Psalm 19:1-2); and the Apostle Paul's declaration, "Since the creation of the world God's invisible qualities—his eternal power and divine nature—have been clearly seen, being understood from what has been made, so that people are without excuse" (Rom. 1:20). The expectation here is not one of "invisible ink," but rather of a divine design so evident that only the willfully blind could fail to see it.

Response to Gordon

Robert C. Bishop

Study Questions

1. What fallacies does Bishop think Gordon has committed in his critique of MN and why?

2. How, according to Bishop, has Gordon misread the history of science? What does he think is the most that Gordon's historical evidence shows?

3. How does Bishop respond to the charge that defenders of MN are guilty of a "naturalism-of-the-gaps" fallacy?

Bruce Gordon defends the notion that science is not limited to natural causes by offering a vigorous attack on MN. Unfortunately, his critique is guilty of several informal fallacies, confusions, and mischaracterizations, as I will show.

A Lesson in Fallacies

Gordon writes: "In other words, *when doing science*, the methodological naturalist operates *as if* metaphysical naturalism were true, whatever he or she might otherwise believe about the existence of a transcendent reality and its effects on the universe in which we live" (p. 204). This is more than a gloss on MN; it is to fundamentally mischaracterize it. Kepler, Galileo, Boyle, and Newton, for instance, did not practice MN *as if* metaphysical naturalism was true. They practiced MN as the best approach for understanding natural properties and processes *as God's creation*, since they understood these to be secondary causes through which God worked in the world. So, it is not the case that these and other scientists following in their footsteps treated the universe "*as if* it were a closed system of material efficient causes because this is the only kind of causality that meets [the methodological naturalist's] explanatory restrictions" (Ibid.). This misunderstanding transforms MN into metaphysical naturalism, leads to confusion about what really is at stake in scientific inquiry, and sets up an easily knocked-down *strawman*.

Gordon impugns the motives of theists who pursue MN as worrying that "any association of theism with ID risks the possibility of another 'Galileo affair' in which belief in God is given a black eye when 'science' turns out to be right and 'religion' turns out to be wrong" (Ibid.). This is an anecdotal, *ad hominem* charge without evidence, and tells us nothing about the merits of MN. Nevertheless, I know of no theists in the sciences who harbor this motivation and doubt any exist. Moreover, Gordon's claim exhibits the fallacy of *privileged cynicism*: adopt the most cynical motivation or reason (MN advocates are afraid of "contamination of science and the scientific discreditation of religion," Ibid.), to tarnish the view you oppose. Again, this does not deal with MN on its merits.

Turning to a defense of ID is not very helpful as a critique of MN since ID actually offers a different way of knowing, one aimed at understanding intelligent causes. We already have such agentic forms of inquiry—the social and behavioral sciences, history, archaeology, literary studies among many others (some of which, such as forensics, deploy many natural science methods with the aim of understanding and identifying agents—criminals—and their actions). We practice these forms of inquiry whenever *we already know we are dealing with intelligent agents*. For these forms of inquiry, one cannot coherently formulate MN because agents are involved.[1] Instead of *ad hominem* charges, and privileged cynicism, ID supporters should acknowledge they are advocating agentic forms of inquiry. MN simply is impertinent to these forms of inquiry. Furthermore, trying to turn the natural sciences into agentic inquiry simply confuses these distinct forms of inquiry—this is a category mistake.[2] There is no issue of the demarcation problem, here; that is a *red herring*. The objects of inquiry pick out when we need agentic forms of inquiry. ID supporters are interested in studying intelligent causes and that is OK. Let them make the best arguments they can that agentic forms of inquiry are the best ones to use in cases of biological complexity rather than natural science inquiry; we all can evaluate those arguments. In contrast, the destruction of scientific inquiry—the throwing away of MN—is not OK.

To understand why ignoring different forms of inquiry is problematic, consider Gordon's claim that DNA, RNA, and other complex biological phenomena are information processing systems (endnote 5). It does not matter that there might be a mathematically precise formulation of "complex-specified information" to apply to such biological phenomena. By itself, this does not tell us whether such phenomena actually are information processing systems. Biology and biochemistry communities do not have settled views on the phenomena in their domain as information processing systems. This fact is evidence that there currently is no objective way to determine the truth of the ontological claim that DNA and RNA are information processing systems. ID advocates are not free to assume that these phenomena are information processing systems; that simply *begs the question* (one of many problems with complex-specified information[3]). This is not a matter of "confusing" so-called complex-specified information with Shannon information. It is a matter of ontology. Here, we have an example where ID supporters first need to establish that agentic forms of inquiry are relevant because the key ID assumption is an engineering one: intelligent causes are the creators of information processing systems.

Misreading History

Gordon's quotations demonstrate that natural philosophers, such as Boyle, recognized that the properties, processes, and structures of nature were a creation of God. Nevertheless, none of this historical evidence undercuts the observation that sixteenth- and seventeenth-century natural philosophers constructed what we now call MN as the best means for understanding the secondary causes that may have produced these structures. No one disputes that these natural philosophers recognized and praised the Creator for the works of creation. Yet, this praise is perfectly consistent with MN as developed by these natural philosophers.

It is true that Newton claimed he could find no other cause than God's direct, unmediated action for explaining the exact order of the solar system.

Unfortunately, this is not a great example for Gordon's case against MN. First, Newton's *Principia*, as well as his *Optiks*, are filled with inquiry and conclusions carried out according to MN. In his comments about the intricate ordering of the solar system, Newton illustrates the practice of MN: he clearly is arguing that he believes the limits of secondary causes to produce such an impressive "clockwork" system have been exceeded and he cannot imagine any other explanation. Second, where Newton's imagination failed, Kant and Laplace showed that Newton's own laws *could explain* how God created the solar system through secondary causes (the nebular hypothesis). This is a beautiful example of MN, but Gordon's misconstruing it as metaphysical naturalism leads to misunderstanding Newton.

Gordon's biology examples fare worse. In the Western tradition, up until the publication of Darwin's (and Wallace's) work, the whole of biology operated under Aristotle's natural philosophy (there being plenty of theological framing for it after the rise of Christianity). With the publication of *The Origin of Species*, scientists largely switched to MN with a level of success that put the previous centuries of biological natural philosophy to shame (e.g., much of what had been taken to be true of organisms was shown to be wrong; levels of order and coherence were made manifest that had gone hidden for centuries). Many theists who engaged in MN studies of biology from that point on—and even theists who simply admired the results of such work—praised the Creator for such magnificent things that were being discovered; but they never confused the primary causation of the Creator with the secondary causation of the creation.[4] They were clear on the Creator-creature distinction as well as formal and final causation versus efficient causation. Gordon's conclusions that "Methodological naturalism's ascent to contemporary orthodoxy began with the Darwinian Revolution, not the Scientific Revolution," and "MN is an artifact of a conception of nature that is not intrinsic to the task of scientific explanation itself" (p. 211) are woefully unsubstantiated. The historical evidence he adduces only demonstrates that *metaphysical* naturalism was not the rule of the day.

Naturalism-of-the-Gaps?

Finally, Gordon discusses what some have called the "naturalism-of-the-gaps" fallacy. Maybe metaphysical naturalists commit such a fallacy. Nonetheless, such failures tell us nothing about MN. These are failures of *metaphysical naturalism*. Gordon's misconstrual of MN as metaphysical naturalism leads his argumentation astray again. He misreads Koonin as defending MN *at all costs*, when Koonin is describing what he takes to be a reasonable possibility for trying to understand the current state of origins of life research under metaphysical naturalism. Gordon again imputes the worst possible motives to researchers who discovered the multiverse as a consequence of string theory: the multiverse was supposedly "invented to explain away, within naturalistic constraints, finely tuned parameters in physics and cosmology" (p. 15).[5] Though a questionable move, Koonin's is not scientifically irrational.

Gordon has been arguing against metaphysical naturalism all along, but never touches MN.

Notes

1. Robert C. Bishop, "What Is This Naturalism Stuff All About?" *Journal of Theoretical and Philosophical Psychology* 29 (2009): 108–13.

2. Robert C. Bishop, *The Philosophy of the Social Sciences* (Continuum International Publishing Group, June 2007).

3. Richard Wein, "Not a Free Lunch But a Box of Chocolates: A Critique of William Dembski's Book *No Free Lunch*," The TalkOrigins Archive (2000), (http ://www.talkorigins.org/design/faqs/nfl), accessed on October 2, 2017; Joe Felsenstein, "Has Natural Selection Been Refuted? The Arguments of William Dembski," *Reports of the National Center for Science Education* 27, nos. 3–4 (2007): 20–26 (https://ncse.com/library-resource/has-natural-selection-been-ref uted-arguments-william-dembski), accessed on October 2, 2017. Aside from these technical issues, ID's specified complexity measure identifies so-called irreducibly complex systems—systems that cannot have a history of stepwise development because they need all their current components to perform their current function; remove any one component and these systems cease to function—as the product of an intelligent cause acting apart from natural processes. These identifications turn out to be false positives. See Christoph Adami, "Reducible Complexity," *Science* 312 (April 7, 2006): 61–63; Jamie T. Bridgham, Sean M. Carroll, and Joseph W. Thornton, "Evolution of Hormone-Receptor Complexity by Molecular Exploitation," *Science* 312 (April 7, 2006): 97–101; Andrea Bottaro, Matt A. Inlay and Nicholas J Matzke, "Immunology in the Spotlight at the Dover 'Intelligent Design' Trial," *Nature Immunology* 7 (May 5, 2006): 433–35; Mark J. Pallen and Nicholas J. Matzke, "From *The Origin of Species* to the Origin of Bacterial Flagella," *Nature Reviews Microbiology* 4 (October 2006): 784–90.

4. James R. Moore, *The Post-Darwinian Controversies: A Study of the Protestant Struggle to Come to Terms with Darwin in Great Britain and America 1870-1900* (Cambridge: Cambridge University Press, 1979).

5. Robert C. Bishop, Larry L. Funck, Raymond J. Lewis, Stephen O. Moshier, and John H. Walton, *Understanding Scientific Theories of Origins: With Biblical and Theological Perspectives* (Downers Gove: InterVarsity Press, in press), chap. 10.

Questions for Reflection

1. If God exists, should we presume that He would or would not intervene miraculously in the course of nature? If He did, would that undermine science? Why?

2. Do the key figures of the Scientific Revolution provide more support for Bishop's view or for Gordon's? Why?

3. What do you think is the correct or best definition of MN? On this understanding, is MN the best way to do science? Why?

4. Can the ID theorist invoke intelligent causation without violating the integrity of science? If so, how?

5. Is the advocate of MN guilty of the "naturalism-of-the-gaps" fallacy or not? Why?

6. Has Gordon really committed all the fallacies that Bishop charges him with? Can Gordon respond to any of these charges? If so, how?

Essay Suggestions

A. Consider an ordinary belief that you have such as your belief about what you had for breakfast or about some visual experience you are currently having. Using what you have learned from the debate between Huemer and Lammenranta over skepticism, write a paper in which you argue either that you know or do not know that belief. Your argument should include responses to the objections raised by the author whose view your reject.

B. A principle that plays a key role in the debate over skepticism is the *epistemic closure principle* which is stated as follows:

> If S knows that *p* and S knows that *p* entails *q*, then S knows that *q*.

Write an essay in which you argue either for or against this principle. Be sure to explain how your answer relates to the problem of skepticism.

C. Write an essay in which you trace out as thoroughly as you can the justification you might have for your belief that the earth revolves around the sun according to both the foundationalist and coherentist schemes. Explain which approach does the better job of justifying your belief, being sure to address objections that might be raised by those on the other side.

D. Write a paper in response to the Gettier Problem. What do you think are the necessary and sufficient conditions for knowledge? Defend your answer and explain whether it is more in line with internalism or externalism.

E. In the *Peanuts* comic strip, the character Linus believes that a being called the Great Pumpkin will show up in the pumpkin patch each Halloween. The Great Pumpkin never shows up but Linus keeps on believing despite having no evidence at all. According to the *Great Pumpkin Objection*, if we allow that religious beliefs are justified without evidence, we would have to grant that Linus's belief in the Great Pumpkin is justified too. Write an essay in which you argue that this objection either does or does not pose a serious problem for the view that religious belief does not require evidence.

F. In light of the debate over scientific realism versus nonrealism, do you think we should believe what modern science tells us about unobservable things? Write an essay in which you present an argument (or arguments) defending your answer to this question. Be sure to consider and respond to any arguments from the other side.

G. Suppose some astronauts are exploring a distant planet and they stumble upon what appears to be a large machine hidden in a cavern. It has lots of moving parts and electronic components, but it is composed of materials completely unknown on earth. What's more, the astronauts are unable to discern what purpose or function the object has. Write a paper in which you argue that a commitment to methodological naturalism either would or would not hinder the astronauts from drawing the conclusion that the machine was built by an intelligent alien race.

H. An issue often related to the debate over methodological naturalism is the *demarcation problem*. This is the problem of clearly distinguishing true science from pseudo-science (e.g., astrology). Write a paper in which you either (1) seek to resolve the demarcation problem by establishing criteria for what counts as science without thereby ruling out disciplines that *are* science or allowing in disciplines that you think are not science, or (2) argue that there is no clear way to demarcate science from pseudo-science.

For Further Reading

On Epistemology—Skepticism, Internal-Externalism, Foundationalism-Coherentism

Audi, Robert. *Epistemology: A Contemporary Introduction to the Theory of Knowledge*. 3rd ed. New York: Routledge, 2011.
BonJour, Laurence. *Epistemology: Classic Problems and Contemporary Responses*. 2nd ed. Lanham, MD: Rowman &Littlefield, 2010.
BonJour, Laurence, and Ernest Sosa. *Epistemic Justification: Internalism vs. Externalism, Foundations vs. Virtues*. Malden, MA: Blackwell, 2003.
Lehrer, Keith. *Theory of Knowledge*. 2nd ed. New York: Routledge, 2000.
Sosa, Ernest, Jaegwon Kim, and Matthew McGrath, eds. *Epistemology: An Anthology*. 2nd ed. Malden, MA: Blackwell, 2008.

On Religious Knowledge

Alston, William P. *Perceiving God: The Epistemology of Religious Experience*. Ithaca, NY: Cornell University Press, 1993.
Geivett, R. Douglas, and Brendan Sweetman, eds. *Contemporary Perspectives on Religious Epistemology*. Oxford: Oxford University Press, 1993.
Plantinga, Alvin. *Warranted Christian Belief*. Oxford: Oxford University Press, 2000.

On Philosophy of Science—Realism-Nonrealism, Methodological Naturalism

Barker, Gillian, and Philip Kitcher. *Philosophy of Science: A New Introduction*. Oxford: Oxford University Press, 2014.
Dicken, Paul. *A Critical Introduction to Scientific Realism*. New York: Bloomsbury, 2016.
McGrew, Timothy, Marc Alspector-Kelly, and Fritz Allhoff, eds. *Philosophy of Science: An Historical Introduction*. Malden, MA: Wiley-Blackwell, 2009.
Plantinga, Alvin. *Where the Conflict Really Lies: Science, Religion, and Naturalism*. Oxford: Oxford University Press, 2011.

PART TWO

Problems in Metaphysics

Introduction to Part Two

Steven B. Cowan

Does God exist? What about angels? Do human beings have souls, some immaterial part of us that can live on after our bodies die? Do we have free will? What are physical things made of?—atoms? Okay, but what are atoms made of? What is time? Does time really move or flow as it seems to, and is it the same for everybody? These are some of the questions addressed in *metaphysics*. This branch of philosophy is broadly concerned with the question, "What is real?" Metaphysics studies the nature of being or reality, and so it confronts the most fundamental problems in philosophy.

Though the topics covered in metaphysics tend to be very abstract, its importance is partly seen in that many of the solutions offered to problems in other areas of philosophy (epistemology, ethics, etc.) presuppose or depend on particular answers to metaphysical questions. For example, Rene Descartes's solution to skepticism (see chapters 1 and 8), depends upon the mind being an immaterial substance (or "soul") distinct from the human brain. Also, some versions of moral objectivism (see *Problems in Value Theory*, chapter 1) presuppose the existence of nonnatural moral properties, and the existence of such properties is a metaphysical issue.

There are many problems addressed by metaphysicians, but only four are included in this volume: the problem of universals, the mind-body problem, the problem of the compatibility (or not) of free will and determinism, and the question of the existence of God.

The Problem of Universals

Consider two dogs, Fido and Rover, and consider the following statements that might be said about them:

Fido is brown.

Rover is brown.

There are two questions a philosopher might ask about Fido and Rover and about these two statements. First, notice that the two statements assert a similarity or resemblance between Fido and Rover, namely that they are both brown. But what accounts for their resemblance? Well, you might say, it's in virtue of their both *being brown*, of course! But by putting it this way it seems that you are claiming that there is something—some *thing*—that Fido and Rover share. What thing?

Second, take just one of the statements, "Fido is brown." This is a simple subject-predicate sentence, yet have you considered exactly what we are *doing* when we make such statements? The subject of the sentence refers to a particular thing, Fido, an individual dog in this case. But what does the predicate refer to? The color brown, you might say. But the color brown is not an individual thing like Fido. It seems to be something more general. But what?

According to the metaphysical theory known as *realism*, the answer to both questions is that Fido and Rover share the property of *brownness*. And what we are doing when we predicate "Fido is brown," is attributing to Fido the property of *brownness*. In other words, the realist believes that the "thing" the two dogs share, and the "thing" that is the predicate in subject-predicate discourse is a *property*. And properties, for the realist, are kinds of *universals*. Universals areis an *abstract entities* characterized by at least three features: (1) they are multiply exemplifiable—which means they can exist in more than one thing at the same time (or at different times), (2) they exist outside of time and space—they are not spatio-temporal things like dogs, and (3) they exist necessarily—which means that they cannot not exist (or, put differently, they exist in every possible world).

Nominalism is the view that denies the existence of universals. The nominalist thinks that the idea that anything exists with such characteristics is incredible, and attempts to account for resemblance and predication in ways that do not commit us to believing in universals. For example, the nominalist might rephrase the sentence "Fido is brown" to read "Fido belongs to the set of brown things." And he might account for the resemblance between Fido and Rover by saying that they both belong to the set of brown things. In both cases, the nominalist thinks he has eliminated the need for properties understood as universals.

The *problem of universals* is the problem of giving an account, among other things, of resemblance and predication. Chapter 7 addresses this problem beginning with a defense of realism by Paul Gould (Southwestern Baptist Theological Seminary). He maintains that the major nominalist theories of properties do not adequately explain the phenomena of resemblance and predication. They either leave out of the explanation precisely what needs to be explained or they are logically incoherent. What's more, applying the familiar principle of Ockham's Razor, he contends that realism is simpler than nominalism both ideologically and ontologically. The upshot of Gould's argument is that universals exist.

Guido Imaguire (Federal University of Rio de Janeiro) thinks that the realists' belief in universals involves an unnecessary "double counting" when it comes to enumerating the things that exist. He counters that nominalism can give adequate accounts of resemblance and predication without postulating universals. On his preferred version of nominalism—so-called *ostrich nominalism*—resemblance facts (e.g., Fido and Rover are both brown) are taken as grounded in the conjuctive fact "Fido is brown and Rover is brown." And predicative facts (e.g., "Fido is brown") are simply taken as fundamental facts in need of no further explanation. Imaguire supports the latter point by presenting Bradley's Regress Argument, which purports to show that other accounts of predication lead to an infinite regress.

The Mind-Body Problem

If I were to ask you where dreams occur or where your thoughts are located, I suspect that many would reply, "In my mind." And if I asked you where your blood circulates or where you get scratches when you do yard work, you would likely say, "In (or on) my body." And if I asked you whether or not your body and your mind are different sorts of things, I'm pretty sure that a large number of you would say "yes." The question asked in chapter 8 is: What is this thing we call the mind? A related question is: What is the relation between the mind and the body? These questions form the basis for the *mind-body problem*—it's the problem of explaining the nature of the mind and its relation to the body.

There are three major positions on the mind-body problem. Most people, and most philosophers before the contemporary era, hold some form of *substance dualism*. This is the view that the mind and the body are distinct kinds of substances. The body is a physical or material substance with properties like size, weight, and spatial location. The mind, however, is an immaterial substance that has very different, nonphysical properties. Despite these differences, most substance dualists believe that the mind and body are causally interactive—the mind causes the body to move (say, raise an arm), and the body causes the mind to perceive or feel things (like pain, for instance).

Why hold this view? Many people are motivated to embrace mind-body dualism because they believe in life after death. If human beings can survive death, then it seems very difficult to explain that possibility unless there is some part of us that lives on while our bodies decay in the ground. That part of us the substance dualist calls the "soul" or "mind." Additionally, dualist philosophers argue that the nature of human consciousness and certain mental states like beliefs, desires, and intentions are best explained on the view that the mind is an immaterial substance.

The second position on the mind-body problem is called *physicalism* or *materialism*. For the physicalist, the mind is just as material as the body. The mind and body are not two different kinds of things. Rather, the mind is either (1) nothing over and above the brain; it just *is* the brain (a view called *type-identity theory*); or (2) it is a function of the brain (a view called *functionalism*). Physicalists tend to be moved by what they consider to be a scientific view of the world in which everything that exists, including human beings, is understood in purely naturalistic terms: what exists is the natural, physical world (a view called *naturalism*), and a physicalist view of the mind best fits with this worldview. Moreover, physicalists point to the strong correlation that exists between brain events and mental events (e.g., have you ever noticed that brain damage almost always means *mind* damage?) as evidence for physicalism.

Property dualism (or *epiphenomenalism*) is the third major view of the mind-body problem. This view is often seen as a middle position between substance dualism and physicalism. The property dualists do not believe that the mind can be reduced to the brain or its functions. But neither do they think that the mind is a distinct substance independent of the brain. Property dualism holds that the mind is an emergent *property* of the brain. Thus, while not identical to brain events, mental events like beliefs and desires emerge from, and depend causally upon, electrochemical events in the brain. It should be obvious that property dualism has closer affinities with physicalism than with substance dualism. For the property dualist, the physical is more fundamental than the mental; the mental is causally dependent on the physical for its existence. This view would seem to rule out (as does physicalism) any life after death, and it has a distinct problem of explaining mental causation—that is, the mind's causing things to occur—both of which are crucial for substance dualism.

Andrew Melnyk (University of Missouri) defends a version of functionalism in chapter 8. In his view, the mind is a "mental system," analogous to the human circulatory system or digestive system, that functions to gather information about the world and use it to produce behavior that succeeds in accomplishing one's goals. Melnyk responds to typical dualist objections by explaining how mental states can be understood in physical terms. And he argues that a materialist view of the mind accounts for the dependence of mental states on brain states better than substance dualism.

The case for substance dualism is taken up by Charles Taliaferro (St. Olaf College). He begins by arguing, contrary to what is commonly supposed, that we have a much clearer understanding of the mind and of mental causation than we have of any material reality. Further, our grasp of the mental state includes a knowledge of ourselves as self-aware, enduring subjects of experience. Taliaferro then defends what is called the "Knowledge Argument" to show that our minds are immaterial. This gist of the argument is that we would know our thoughts, emotions, intentions, and so on by knowing our bodies (or brain states) if our minds were material things. But, of course, knowledge of our bodies does not give us access to our mental life. So, it seems to follow that our minds are not identical to our material bodies.

Free Will and Determinism

Suppose there is a person we will call Rob who is a career criminal. And suppose that Rob has been arrested while committing an armed robbery. Normally, we would expect that the jury at Rob's trial, based on the evidence, would find Rob guilty of the crime and rightly expect that he would receive a harsh punishment for what he has done. We would expect, that is, that the justice system would hold Rob *morally accountable* for what he did. But suppose that during his trial, Rob's lawyer argued that Rob was *not* morally responsible for the crime because Rob's actions were causally determined by factors outside of his control. In other words, Rob's actions were simply the result of a long chain of causes extending far back into the past, all the way back to the beginning of the universe, in fact. And these causes culminated in building into Rob's mind the character and motives that he has, including the motive to commit armed robbery.

Now many of us would be inclined to reject this deterministic account of Rob's actions and maintain that Rob has *free will*—that is, human actions are *not* determined by all these external causes; we (including Rob) freely make our own choices. Thus, Rob is blameworthy for the crime. Of course, this response presupposes that Rob has a kind of freedom that is outside of, or independent of, the causal determinism that we think governs the physical world, and that this freedom is necessary for moral responsibility. But what if Rob's actions were determined after all? Is it necessarily the case that he would lack moral responsibility as his lawyer alleges? Does moral responsibility require that particular kind of freedom?

Such questions underscore *the problem of reconciling (or at least understanding) the relationship between determinism and free will*. There have been two basic approaches to solving this problem. The first is *incompatibilism*, the view that free will and determinism are not compatible. According to incompatibilists, if our actions are determined by factors outside of our control, then we are not free and, therefore, not morally responsible.

This is the view of Rob's lawyer as well as those who react to the lawyer's argument by insisting that Rob *is* responsible for his crime because his actions are *not* determined.

Incompatibilism, as this example shows, comes in two versions. One, represented by Rob's lawyer, is called *hard determinism*. According to this view, determinism is actually *true*. Therefore, we do not have the free will required for moral responsibility. It follows, for the hard determinist, that we lack moral responsibility for our actions. The other version of incompatibilism is represented by those who hold Rob morally accountable by rejecting the lawyer's deterministic story. This view, called *libertarianism*, agrees that free will is incompatible with determinism, but insists that determinism is *false*, and that we do have the kind of freedom required for moral responsibility.

The second approach to the free will/determinism problem is *compatibilism*. As the name suggests, compatibilists believe that the kind of freedom required for moral responsibility is consistent with determinism. The compatibilist has agreements and disagreements with each of the two versions of incompatibilism. With the hard determinists, the compatibilist agrees that determinism is true or at least very likely. But he disagrees with the hard determinist by claiming that determinism does not rule out our being free and morally responsible. With the libertarian, the compatibilist agrees that human beings are free and morally responsible for their actions, but he disagrees that this freedom and responsibility requires the falsity of determinism.

Disagreements between compatibilism and incompatibilism often boil down to a fundamental disagreement about the kind of freedom that is necessary for moral responsibility. Usually (but not always), incompatibilists understand free will in terms of the *principle of alternative possibilities*, which asserts that a person's action at a certain time is free only if he or she could have done otherwise than he or she did in the same circumstances (which is another way of saying that his or her action was not determined). Many compatibilists, however, would reject this principle and claim that a person's action is free if he or she has the ability to act in accordance with his or her desires and values. Understood this way, free will could be compatible with determinism because what desires and values a person has may not strictly be up to him or her.

Christopher Franklin (Grove City College) makes the contemporary case for incompatibilism in chapter 9. Through a series of thought experiments he seeks to motivate the belief that no person can be blameworthy for his misdeeds unless he has the freedom to do otherwise. In other words, if an agent is morally required to do A but cannot do A, then the agent cannot be accountable for failing to do A. Franklin then presents and defends an important argument called the *Consequence Argument,* which leads to the conclusion that no person has free will if his or her actions are causally determined.

The compatibilist view is defended by yours truly, the editor of this book, Steven Cowan. I first explain what I think is *not* required for moral responsibility, namely, neither (1) the ability to do otherwise (thus I reject the principle of alternative possibilities), nor (2) the requirement that agents be the ultimate source of their actions. Second, I argue that what *is* required for moral responsibility is that agents have the ability to respond to reasons that they think are sufficiently good to outweigh reasons to do otherwise, and that these reasons are derived from value systems that the agents acquire through ordinary character development. This view of freedom and responsibility, I claim, is compatible with at least some types of determinism.

The Existence of God

Chapter 10 deals with the question, "Does God exist?" It is hard to imagine a metaphysical question more important than this one. For, if God *does not* exist, then (according to many philosophers at least) it becomes difficult to explain why we should be moral, or how human beings can have meaningful lives (since, for example, the world and we come into existence for no rhyme or reason and we are all destined to die and be forgotten). And, as just noted, without God, we may have little or no hope for life after death—something many of us would find very troubling. Also troubling is the thought that, without God, we are "on our own," so to speak, with no divine help to see us through the difficult times of life. On the other hand, if God *does* exist, while the above problems might vanish, others might arise. For example, how can we reconcile the existence of evil and suffering with the existence of God (who is supposed to be all-powerful, all-knowing, and all-loving)? And is it possible for us to have free will if God exists and knows exactly what we are going to do tomorrow? Moreover, if God exists, then there is someone who knows our every thought and deed to whom we have to answer for our actions, and to whom we owe absolute allegiance—this thought, too, can be very troubling.

So, the question of whether or not God exists has serious implications either way. It is worthwhile, then, to inquire into the possible evidence that may be had both for and against God's existence. Throughout much of the history of philosophy, philosophers have defended influential arguments (often called *theistic arguments*) for the existence of God. Such arguments included the *ontological argument,* which claimed that the very idea of God proved God; various versions of the *cosmological argument* that began with the existence of the world (or some feature of it), and argued that the only way to explain why the world exists is because it was created by God; and the *teleological argument*, which contends that a purposeful, intelligent being (God) best explains our observations of things in the natural world that appear purposeful or designed.

Of course, the soundness of these arguments was challenged by Enlightenment thinkers such as David Hume (1711–1776) and Immanuel Kant (1724–1804).[1] Nevertheless, newer and stronger versions of these theistic arguments (and others) have continued to be developed—and debated—right up to the present day. Joshua Rasmussen (Azusa Pacific University) develops some of these arguments in presenting the contemporary case for God's existence. Rasmussen focuses primarily on a version of the cosmological argument that he calls the "Argument from Existence." The argument proceeds in two stages. In the first, he argues that the only possible explanation for the existence of anything is that there exists something that is *self-existent*, that is, something that exists in and of itself and does not depend upon anything else for its existence. In the second stage, Rasmussen seeks to prove that the best account of the nature of this self-existence being is provided by *theism* (the view that a perfect supreme Person—God—exists). Rasmussen concludes by suggesting other lines of evidence for the existence of God found in logic: the fine-tuning of the physical universe for life, biological evolution, objective morality, and human consciousness.

Bruce Russell (Wayne State University) defends atheism. His case rests on a particularly difficult version of the problem of evil. Russell grants that God's existence is compatible with the existence of some suffering in the world. He even grants that God's existence may be consistent with some *unnecessary* suffering. But he insists that God's existence is not compatible with the reality of *excessive and unnecessary* suffering. And the problem, as Russell sees it, is that the world does contain examples of such excessive and unnecessary suffering. He provides three putative examples of this kind of suffering and defends their reality as such from various strategies that theists use to rebut their evidential force against theism.

Note

1 David Hume criticizes both the cosmological and teleological arguments in his 1779 work, *Dialogues Concerning Natural Religion* (portions of which are reprinted in chapter 10 of this book). Kant delivered what many thought (no doubt falsely) to be the death-knell to all theistic arguments in his *Critique of Pure Reason* (1781).

7

Are There Universals?

There Are Universals

Paul M. Gould

Study Questions

1. What is the problem of universals? What is Gould's solution to the problem?
2. What are the two kinds of facts in need of explanation? What, according to Gould, is required for an adequate explanation?
3. What is Ostrich Nominalism? How does it handle the problem of universals according to Gould?
4. Why does Gould find Ostrich Nominalism explanatorily inadequate?
5. According to Gould, why is realism economically superior to Ostrich Nominalism?
6. How does Resemblance Nominalism solve the problem of universals? What are the three problems that Gould raises for Resemblance Nominalism?
7. What is Trope Nominalism? How does it compare and contrast with Platonic Realism?
8. What are the two versions of Trope Nominalism that Garcia distinguishes? What are the problems that each version has?
9. What other kinds of universals likely exist if properties do?

Consider my son's chicken, Rosie. Rosie is one thing, a particular object. Rosie also has many characteristics: she is red, weighs five pounds, has two wings, lays eggs, and likes to eat worms. When considering charactered objects such as Rosie, a key question for the ontologist is this: In addition to charactered objects are there characteristics? That is, in addition to particulars (objects such as chickens, dogs, and humans) are there *properties*? Additional questions surface when we notice that Rosie shares certain features with other chickens. Rosie is a specific *kind* of chicken, a Buff Orpington. She is a member of a natural class—the class of chickens—in which all members share certain characteristics in common. This raises another important question. What grounds the *similarities* of characteristics among various natural classes of particulars?

The question of explaining how different objects share similar characteristics (as well as the related question of how the same object can have multiple characteristics) has come to be called the *problem of universals*.[1] In this chapter I argue that the problem of universals is best solved by postulating the existence of universals—shareable properties that can be wholly possessed by distinct particulars at the same time. Thus, I am endorsing *realism* regarding universals. My positive claim entails that *nominalism*, the view that universals do not exist, is false. In the dialectic to follow, I focus primarily on the nature of properties given their centrality to virtually any ontological issue. At the end, however, I briefly consider the possibility of other kinds of universals as well.

The Problem of Universals

Keith Campbell nicely introduces the problem of universals:

> Now we can pose two very different questions about, say, red things. We can take one single red object and ask of it: what is it about this thing in virtue of which it is red? We shall call this the A question. Secondly, we can ask of any two red things: what is it about these two things in virtue of which they are both red? Let that be the B question.[2]

Following Campbell then, there are two facts in need of explanation, qualitative facts (identified in the A question) and resemblance facts (identified in the B question). These facts can be expressed by the following sentences, where the variables "a" and "b" represent the subject and the variable "F" represents the predicate:

(1) *a* is F.

(2) *a* and *b* are both F.

It is important to note that qualitative and resemblance facts are *different in kind*. Qualitative facts point to a particular's *distinctiveness*—for example, the fact that Rosie is red, five pounds, has two wings, lays eggs, and likes worms. Each of these facts is a distinct qualitative fact about one and the same object, Rosie. Resemblance facts, on the other hand, point to the *unity* of a class of objects—the chickenness or Buff Orpington-ness shared by Rosie and other chickens or Buff Orpingtons.

What constitutes an adequate solution to the problem of universals? My proposal is this. An adequate solution would explain these real-world qualitative and resemblance facts. Moreover, as I've argued elsewhere, such a solution requires a *theory of properties* and not merely the postulation of properties per se.[3] Properties per se don't explain anything. What is needed is a theory of properties that provides, at a sufficient level of detail, an account of what properties are like and what roles they play as well as the ontological commitments and grounding (or explanatory) relations among the entities postulated by the theory. I argue that a realist theory of properties provides the best explanation of the facts captured in (1) and (2). While space prohibits a detailed discussion of all versions of nominalism, I shall consider what are, in my opinion, three of the most prominent and plausible versions of nominalism, arguing that none explain qualitative and resemblance facts as well as realism. If realism is a better theory than the most plausible versions of nominalism, it is reasonable to think that realism is a better theory than any version of nominalism, or so I argue in this essay.

Ostrich Nominalism

Philosophers who deny that properties exist are often called *Ostrich Nominalists*. Since properties don't exist, the ostrich holds that *shareable* properties—universals—don't exist either. Moreover, the ostrich thinks the problem of universals is not a real problem and resemblance facts do not require any special explanation or grounding.[4] Since the ostrich does not believe in properties, there is no theory of properties on offer. Rather, the ostrich offers a theory of ontological commitment with respect to charactered objects as follows:

> ON: There are charactered objects but not characteristics. There are ontological commitments to fundamental *sorts* of things (and not just fundamental things simpliciter).

To say the ostrich is ontologically committed to fundamental *sorts* of things should not be understood as committing her to both fundamental things and some other entity—sorts—that are distinct from fundamental things. Rather, fundamental *sorts* of things—red things, sweet things, rounds things—are to be understood as objects that are fundamental and primitively charactered as they are.

Given *ON*, according to Ostrich Nominalism, all that is required to explain (2) is the following:

(3)   *a* is F and *b* is F.

As long as (3) is explanatorily equivalent to (2), then the truth of (2) does not require the postulation of resemblance facts in addition to qualitative facts and conjunctions of qualitative facts. Resemblance facts, by a clever sleight of hand, have magically disappeared. The only ontological commitments are to particulars of a certain sort: red things, green things, round things, tree things, dog things, human things, and so on. In other words, qualitative facts are metaphysically fundamental and it is these metaphysically fundamental facts that help account for similarity. For example, a red chicken and a red truck are similar in color because the chicken is red and the truck is red. All that is required for (3) to be true is the existence of objects *a* and *b* that are F. There is no appeal to a property F-ness to ground the truth of these sentences. As Michael Devitt puts it, "We have nothing to say about what makes *a* F, it just *is* F; that is a basic and inexplicable fact about the universe."[5]

My reply is simplicity itself. First, the fact that explanation can go further if we postulate a universal as the ground of qualitative facts provides reason to think that qualitative facts are not fundamental and brute, as I will show below. Second, and more importantly, contrary to the claim of the ostrich, (2) is not explanatorily equivalent to (3).[6] Rather, (2) is explanatorily equivalent to

(4)   *a* is F and *b* is F and the Fs of *a* and *b* resemble each other.

If correct, then (3) leaves out precisely what it says need not be explained—the third conjunct and the fact that there are real-world resemblances. I suspect that if the ostrich were to allow genuine resemblance facts in addition to qualitative facts, they too would be brute. As Quine puts it, "That the house and roses and sunsets are all of them red may be taken as ultimate and irreducible."[7] This is a fair reply. It also helps us to see the cost of adopting the ostrich program.

In comparing philosophical theories, it is helpful to weigh each theory's costs and benefits in terms of the virtue of economy. Ideological economy has to do with the number of brute or unexplained predicates allowed by a theory. In general, the theory with the greater number of brute predicates is costlier, and therefore worse off, than its competitor. Ideological economy, however, must be balanced with ontological economy. Regarding ontological economy, in general, theories that postulate more objects are costlier, and therefore worse off, than theories that can get by with less. Given this brief gloss, it should be obvious that Ostrich Nominalism is costlier than realism with respect to ideological economy, postulating brute facts for every charactered object and for every dimension of similarity among charactered objects. Given its relative lack of parsimony with respect to ideological economy, Ostrich Nominalism is explanatorily inferior to realism.

I now argue that Ostrich Nominalism is less ontologically economic than its realist competitor and therefore worse off with respect to ontological economy as well. This claim may come as a surprise to lovers of Quinean deserts, such as ostriches, who pride themselves on keeping ontological commitments to a minimum. As Devitt reasons, "In ontology, the less the better. Therefore [the] Realist makes us ontologically worse off without explanatory gain."[8] The opposite is actually true, however. Ostrich Nominalism commits us to more kinds of entities than the realist and thus is less ontologically parsimonious than realism without any explanatory gain. Let me explain.

In theory assessment, philosophers and scientists distinguish between *qualitative* and *quantitative* parsimony.[9] Qualitative parsimony has to do with the measure of a theory's fundamental *sorts of things*, whereas quantitative parsimony has to do with the measure of a theory's fundamental things. Qualitative economy is typically regarded as more important than quantitative economy.[10] If so, then since realism is more qualitatively parsimonious than Ostrich Nominalism, it is the better theory overall, even if both are explanatorily on par (and even though realism is less quantitatively parsimonious). Recall, the ostrich is committed ontologically to fundamental sorts of things; the use of predicates carries ontological commitments for the ostrich to charactered objects: red things, sweet things, colored things, human things, and so on. While the realist is committed to three (according to one version of realism discussed later) fundamental sorts of things, the Ostrich Nominalist is committed to far more. For the realist, red things are not fundamental sorts of things, rather red things are further explained in terms of a particular exemplifying the universal *redness*. The fundamental sorts of things for the realist are the particular, the universal, and the exemplification relation. For the Ostrich Nominalists, however, red things are fundamental sorts of things, and so too for any charactered object that shares a similarity with other charactered objects along some dimension. But then it follows that realism, and not Ostrich Nominalism, is qualitatively more parsimonious and a better overall theory.[11]

Taking stock then, realism is explanatorily superior and ontologically more parsimonious (along one important metric of ontological parsimony) than Ostrich Nominalism. A realist theory of properties does a better job explaining the real-world qualitative and resemblance facts than the ostrich. Thus, Ostrich Nominalism should be rejected.

Resemblance Nominalism

Resemblance Nominalism, like Ostrich Nominalism, allows only charactered objects and not characteristics into its ontology. The metaphysically fundamental facts are not qualitative facts, however, but resemblance facts. Red things are red in virtue of resembling other red things. Sentence (2) is not reducible to sentence (3) as it is for the ostrich; rather, sentence (3) is explained in virtue of sentence (2). Resemblance Nominalism is a version of Reductive Nominalism, reducing properties to classes of resembling charactered objects via a reductive analysis: "*a* is F" is analyzed as "*a* is a member of a class of resembling F things."[12]

Not every class of objects is a resemblance class. Some classes, such as the class consisting of my left pinky finger, the Alamo, Saturn, and my copy of Quine's *From a Logical Point of View*, are nonnatural object classes. Other classes are privileged classes, resemblances classes, such that the members of the class resemble each other more or differently than they resemble anything not in the class. According to the Resemblance Nominalist, every natural property just is a resemblance class: the property *being human* just is the class of human things, the property *being sweet* just is the class of sweet things, and the property of *being round* just is the class of round things. The theory of properties offered by Resemblance Nominalism can be summarized as follows:

> RN: There are *resembling* charactered objects but not characteristics. There are ontological commitments to fundamental *resemblances* of things (and not just fundamental things simpliciter).

While we do speak of properties, given RN, it is important to remember that properties are not fundamental; they are not part of the furniture of the world. Rather, the word "property" functions as a kind of stand-in for the resembling class of objects it denotes. Thus, the ontological commitments are to charactered objects, not properties. The "fundamental *resemblances* of things" should not be understood as committing the Resemblance Nominalist to both fundamental things and a kind of relation—resemblance—that exists as a distinct reality. Rather, the fundamental *resemblances* of things commit the believer ontologically to fundamental things that are brutely charactered resembling objects.

RN faces at least three major problems. The first worry, developed by Nelson Goodman, is called the *Companionship Problem*.[13] Notice that some pairs of properties are coextensive: every time one property is possessed by a charactered object so, too, is the other. For example, the class of things with a heart is coextensive with the class of things with a kidney, the class of featherless bipeds is coextensive with the class of things having a sense of humor, and the class of triangular things is coextensive with the class of trilateral things. The reality of coextensive properties entails a rather unfortunate result for the RN: it requires the postulation of an identity where there isn't one. Since, for the Resemblance Nominalist, properties are identified with classes and classes are identical if they have the same members, it follows that the property of *being a heart* is identical with the property of *being a kidney*, and so on for each coextensive property.

The Resemblance Nominalist can respond to the Companionship Problem by construing properties as classes of actual and *possible* objects.[14] It is possible that there are creatures with hearts but not kidneys. If so, then the property *being a heart* is not coextensive with the property of *being a kidney* since there are possible worlds, and thus possible creatures, and classes of actual and possible objects, with hearts but not kidneys. This response is problematic, however, even if we set aside the contentious issue of taking possible worlds and possible creatures as equally real with each other and the actual world. For there are coextensive properties that are *necessarily* coextensive and thus range over all possible worlds (including the actual world) such as the properties *being triangular* and *being trilateral*.

A second worry, also raised by Goodman, is called the *Imperfect Community Problem*.[15] Consider a class of three objects, called Mishmash, of the following kinds: a blue round thing, a blue soft thing, and a soft round thing. Since each of these objects resembles every other to a certain degree (all sharing either a color or a shape or a texture), Mishmash is a resemblance class. Yet, Mishmash does not have any significant degree of naturalness, since the only candidate property that all and only the members of Mishmash share is a "cooked" property, the property *mishmash* (or alternatively, the disjunctive property *being the same color or shape or texture*). So, there are resemblance classes that can't serve as natural properties. This result is unwelcome because one of the putative virtues of Resemblance Nominalism is its ability to explain how reality is carved at the joints in virtue of natural and nonnatural classes of things: only resemblance classes are natural classes that denote natural properties. Classes such as Mishmash are nonnatural, but according to Resemblance Nominalism, they too—contrary to appearance—denote a natural property. The most plausible solution to this worry is to abandon RN in favor of a view we will consider later, so-called trope theory, and admit there are, after all, properties (even if they are not shareable) that stand in resemblance relations to each other rather than multiply charactered particulars.

Finally, Resemblance Nominalism, like Ostrich Nominalism, is less ontologically parsimonious than realism, and this provides further reason to think the view false. Recall that RN is ontologically committed to fundamental things that brutely resemble (and not just fundamental things simpliciter). Resembling red things, resembling sweet things, and resembling round things are fundamental sorts of things, and so too for any charactered objects that resemble along some dimension. But then it follows that realism, and not Resemblance Nominalism, is qualitatively more parsimonious (committed to only three fundamental sorts of things) and a better overall theory. Resemblance Nominalism, like Ostrich Nominalism, ought to be rejected (and to the extent that similar and additional problems infect all versions of Reductive Nominalism, a claim I accept but cannot defend in the confines of this essay, Reductive Nominalism ought to be rejected as well).

Trope Nominalism

The problems associated with Resemblance Nominalism stem from the complexity of resembling particulars. The various resemblance classes of multiply or thickly charactered objects are just not fine-grained enough to sidestep the kinds of paradoxes the Companionship and Imperfect Community Problems, for example, surface. The Trope Nominalist attempts to avoid these problems by postulating the existence of *tropes*: nonshareable properties that ground one dimension of character only. According to *Trope Nominalism*, the red ball is red in virtue of exemplifying a red trope and round in virtue of exemplifying a round trope. Moreover, the similarity that obtains between, for example, the red ball and a red bird is grounded in the sharing of resembling red tropes. Thus, Trope Nominalism offers a theory of properties along the following lines:

> TN: In addition to thickly charactered objects there are tropes. Tropes are nonshareable properties that can stand in various degrees of resemblance to other nonshareable properties (and correspondingly belong to various resemblance classes) and are exemplified or co-instantiated by the thickly charactered objects that have them.

As unshareable properties wholly and only located wherever the thickly charactered objects that have them are located, it is argued that tropes are properly behaving objects, better qualified than universals to serve as the relata in causal relations and as the objects of sensory perception. In order to better show the comparative strengths of realism over Trope Nominalism, I offer a sketch of one version of realism, Platonic Realism (PR), as follows:

> PR: In addition to thickly characterized objects there are universals. Universals are shareable properties, abstract objects, that are exemplified by the thickly characterized objects that have them.

The version of realism highlighted here is ontologically committed to three fundamental sorts of things: particulars, universals, and the exemplification relation that connects the two.[16]

There is, unfortunately, an ambiguity over the nature of tropes that calls into question the viability of Trope Nominalism. As Robert Garcia has pointed out, trope theory can be understood in two ways, depending on how tropes ground character.[17] If, for example, a red trope is red, then it is a modular trope; if not, then it is a modifier trope. On *Modular Trope Theory* a red ball is red and round in virtue of its red and round tropes, which are themselves red and round, respectively. On *Modifier Trope Theory* a red ball is red and round in virtue of its red and round tropes, which are themselves neither red nor round, respectively.

As Garcia has argued, each version of Trope Theory has advantages over the other but, importantly, both are unstable: Modular Trope Theory threatens to collapse into Ostrich Nominalism and Modifier Trope Theory threatens to collapse into realism. I think the situation is much worse: Modular Trope Theory either collapses into Ostrich Nominalism or is saddled with all the problems of Ostrich Nominalism without any explanatory gain; Modifier Trope Theory either collapses into realism or is implausible in its own right. Moreover, both varieties of Trope Nominalism are explanatorily worse off than realism with respect to resemblance facts. Thus, either way, since I've already argued that Ostrich Nominalism is a worse theory than realism, it follows that Trope Nominalism is a worse theory too.

On Modular Trope Theory, tropes are singly characterized objects, just like regular thick particulars except that they have only one dimension of character. This conception of tropes is problematic, however, for some thin—that is, singly characterized—particulars seem to require thickening. For example, every colored object is also shaped and every shaped object is also extended. If so, then a red trope is not singly characterized after all. It has a shape and extension as well. This state of affairs presents the Modular Trope Theorists with a dilemma: either give up on very plausible principles, what Garcia calls "Thickening Principles," or the view threatens to collapse into Ostrich Nominalism.[18] The reason Modular Trope Theory may collapse into Ostrich Nominalism, according to Garcia, is because both employ the same strategy of appealing to primitive multiply characterized objects to account for qualitative facts. Actually, as Garcia points out, the situation is much worse for the Modular Trope Theorist since fully characterized objects are explained in terms of less than fully characterized tropes that are primitively charactered.[19] The Modular Trope Theorist, it seems, would be better off to dispense with tropes altogether and follow the ostrich in taking thickly charactered objects as primitive. If so, then Modular Trope Theory collapses. If not, Modular Trope Theory is saddled with all the problems of Ostrich Nominalism and more besides, with little explanatory gain. Either way, the theory should be given up.

To see how Modifier Trope Theory threatens to collapse into realism, we might begin by asking: What guarantees the unshareability of modifier tropes? Because modifier tropes are non-self-exemplifying, the only intrinsic character they have are *formal* characteristics, properties such as *being a trope*, *being self-identical*, *being a particular*, and the like.[20] There is nothing, it seems, intrinsic to the nature of modifier tropes that prevents them from being shareable. A typical answer to our question is that tropes are individuated by their location: a modifier trope is wholly located at a place in space and time. However, as Koons and Pickavance argue, the fact that modifier tropes only have a formal character, coupled with the claim that they are individuated by location, is incompatible with a plausible "Thickening Principle" such that "spatially located objects have a definite size and shape."[21] The Modifier Trope Theorist must either give up a very plausible Thickening Principle or abandon a very natural view of how tropes are individuated (by their location). If the Modifier Trope Theorist goes for the second option, it could be maintained that *being nonshareable* is part of the formal character of modifier tropes: that is, it is a primitive fact that modifier tropes are numerically distinct and unshareable.[22] This is a fair move. If taken, however, Modifier Trope Theory threatens to collapse into realism for at least two reasons.

First, tropes are no longer properly behaving concrete objects. Since modifier tropes lack an intrinsic nature—round tropes are not themselves round, for example—it seems that they lack shape, size, mass, and so on. But then modifier tropes are not, after all, the immediate objects of sense perception nor the sorts of entities that play a direct causal role.[23] Worse, it is difficult to see how modifier tropes can be located in space and time. After all, they lack a definite size and shape. Thus, it seems that modifier tropes are non-spatiotemporal[24] and it is for this reason, it seems to me, they are no longer respectable. Second, modifier tropes ground the character of a located object without being wholly located where that object is located. Modifier tropes behave like universals (at least according to PR) and it is in this sense that Modifier Trope Theory threatens collapse into realism.

Threat of collapse or not, Modifier Trope Theory is quantitatively worse off ontologically with respect to qualitative facts, and both versions of Trope Nominalism are worse off explanatorily with respect to resemblance facts. Where realism postulates a distinct universal, *redness*, had by every member of the class of red things, Modifier Trope Nominalism postulates a distinct property redness$_1$-redness$_n$ for each red thing, and so on for every distinct characteristic had by thickly charactered objects. This is a cost in terms of quantitative economy relative to realism with respect to qualitative facts. Regarding resemblance facts, Trope Nominalism (of either variety) is explanatorily inferior to realism. Realism explains why the Fs of *a* and *b* resemble (a shared universal) whereas nominalism must settle for primitive resemblances among tropes.

In sum, Trope Nominalism is an unstable theory threatening to collapse into either Ostrich Nominalism or realism. Either way, Trope Nominalist attempts to explain (or explain away) quantitative or resemblance facts fail. Realism provides a better explanation for qualitative and resemblance facts than three of the most prominent and promising versions of Nominalism. Therefore, I conclude that it is rationally preferable to believe in universals than to not believe in universals.

Other Kinds of Universals

Are there kinds of universals other than properties? Plausible candidates include numbers and propositions if they exist and belong to their own ontological category. Arguments for the reality of numbers, for example, such as the so-called *Indispensability Argument*, provide reason to think there are entities capable of multiple application that are not properties. If so, then numbers exist and are a distinct kind of universal. The basic idea of the Indispensability Argument is this. Since our best scientific theories require quantification over numbers, then there are good reasons to think numbers exist.[25] Other arguments focus on the nature of propositions noting that they are shareable intentional objects. Properties, however, are intentionally inert.[26] If so, then propositions exist and are a distinct kind of universal. Similar reasoning could establish the existence of further kinds of universals perhaps with respect to concepts, relations, shapes, states of affairs, and more besides.[27] The upshot is this: property universals exist, and perhaps other kinds as well.[28]

Notes

1. It is also called the *one over many problem*. While the problem is typically understood in terms of how to best account for resemblance facts, a related question is how to best account for qualitative facts. I shall consider both kinds of facts when exploring potential solutions to the problem of universals.
2. Keith Campbell, *Abstract Particulars* (Oxford: Basil Blackwell, 1990), 29.
3. Paul Gould, "The Problem of Universals, Realism, and God," *Metaphysica* 13 (2): 183–94.

4   The realist David Armstrong coined the term *Ostrich Nominalism*, the idea being that the nominalist in question sticks her head in the sand with respect to resemblance facts. See Armstrong, *Universals and Scientific Realism, Volume 1: Nominalism and Realism* (Cambridge: Cambridge University Press, 1978), 16; and Armstrong, "Against 'Ostrich' Nominalism: A Reply to Michael Devitt," *Pacific Philosophical Quarterly* 61 (1980): 440–49.

5   Michael Devitt, "'Ostrich Nominalism' or 'Mirage Realism,'" *Pacific Philosophical Quarterly* 61 (1980): 436.

6   I argue for this in greater detail in "The Problem of Universals, Realism, and God," 88–90.

7   Willard Van Orman Quine, *From a Logical Point of View* (Cambridge, MA: Harvard University Press, 1953), 10.

8   Devitt, "'Ostrich Nominalism' or 'Mirage Realism,'" 437.

9   The argument developed in this paragraph is from Bryan Pickel and Nicholas Mantegani, "A Quinean Critique of Ostrich Nominalism," *Philosophers' Imprint* 12, no. 6 (2012): 1–21.

10 For arguments justifying this claim see Pickel and Mantegani, "A Quinean Critique of Ostrich Nominalism," 13–15.

11 Robert Koons and Timothy Pickavance explicate this claim as follows. Assume there are m particulars and n sorts of things. Realism requires $m+n$ things whereas the ostrich requires only m things. Ostrich Nominalism is more parsimonious in terms of the quantity of fundamental things that exist in its theory. With respect to qualitative parsimony, however, whereas the realist posits three fundamental sorts of things, the ostrich posits n fundamental sorts of things, one for each dimension of similarity among particulars. Assuming reasonably n is greater than three, then realism is the more parsimonious in the way that matters. See Robert Koons and Timothy Pickavance, *Metaphysics: The Fundamentals* (Malden, MA: Wiley-Blackwell, 2015), 86–87.

12 The distinction between Ostrich and Reductive Nominalism is from Koons and Pickavance, *Metaphysics*, 86. Reductive Nominalists think there is a general explanation for similarity, whereas the ostrich does not. Other versions of Reductive Nominalism (not considered in this essay) include Predicate Nominalism, Concept Nominalism, Mereological Nominalism, and Class Nominalism. For a nice overview of each of these Nominalisms, see Douglas Edwards, *Properties* (Malden, MA: Polity, 2014), 85–111.

13 Nelson Goodman, *The Structure of Appearances* (Cambridge, MA: Harvard University Press, 1951), 160–61.

14 As does David Lewis in his *On the Plurality of Worlds* (Oxford: Blackwell, 1986), 50–69.

15 Goodman, *The Structure of Appearances*, 162–64.

16 Not all versions of realism are Platonic. There is also Immanent Realism which admits similar fundamental sorts of things but understands the nature of these fundamental sorts of things differently. For example, universals are not abstract objects—existing outside of space and time—for the Immanent Realist. Rather, universals are concrete, capable of being wholly present at multiple locations in space and time. While these differences are important,

they will not figure prominently into what follows since the issue at hand is whether or not universals exist, and all versions of realism affirm the existence of universals. There are other differences between realisms that will be ignored as well, including the question of how thickly characterized objects have their properties. For a nice canvass of the issues and options related to the debate between so-called Constituent and Relational ontologies, see Koons and Pickavance, *Metaphysics*, 102–25.

17 Robert Garcia, "Two Ways to Particularize a Property," *Journal of the American Philosophical Association* 1, no. 4 (2015): 635–52.
18 From Robert Garcia, "Moderate Nominalism: Tropes vs. Tropers," Unpublished manuscript; cited in Koons and Pickavance, *Metaphysics*, 99.
19 Garcia, "Two Ways to Particularize a Property," 649.
20 Garcia, "Two Ways to Particularize a Property," 637.
21 Koons and Pickavance, *Metaphysics*, 108.
22 In "Two Ways to Particularize a Property," Garcia only considers this option, stipulating that *being nonshareable* is a formal characteristic of modifier tropes.
23 Garcia, "Two Ways to Particularize a Property," 647.
24 Garcia, "Two Ways to Particularize a Property," 646.
25 For a nice overview of the Indispensability Argument, see Matti Eklund, "Metaontology," *Philosophy Compass* 1, no. 3 (2006): 317–34; and Mark Colyvan, *The Indispensability of Mathematics* (Oxford: Oxford University Press, 2003).
26 As argued by Paul M. Gould and Richard Brian Davis, "Modified Theistic Activism," in *Beyond the Control of God? Six Views on the Problem of God and Abstract Objects*, ed. Paul M. Gould (New York: Bloomsbury, 2014), 55.
27 For a discussion of shapes as universals, see Peter van Inwagen, "Did God Create Shapes?," *Philosophia Christi* 17, no. 2 (2015): 285–90; for a discussion of states of affairs as universals, see Charles Taliaferro, "Abstract Objects and Causation: Bringing Causation Back into Contemporary Platonism," *Revista Portuguesa de Filosofia* 71, no. 4 (2015): 769–80.
28 Many thanks to Robert K. Garcia and Ross D. Inman for helpful comments on an earlier draft of this paper.

There Are No Universals

Guido Imaguire

Study Questions

1. How does Imaguire characterize the difference between particulars and universals?

2. In Imaguire's hypothetical two-sphere world, how many things, respectively, would the nominalist and the realist count there? How might realists differ over "where" universals are located?

3. Why, according to Imaguire, does saying that "x is of kind K" *not* imply that there are K's? What are those who think otherwise guilty of doing?

4. What is the "One over Many" Argument? Why does Imaguire think that the expression "there is" should not be taken seriously ontologically?

5. How does the nominalist handle sentences that have apparent universals as subjects (e.g., "Red and blue are both colors")?

6. What is the realist argument from semantics? Why does Imaguire reject the realist view of predicates?

7. Why does Imaguire find Armstrong's type of Predicate Nominalism implausible? What is his preferred nominalist view of predicates?

8. What is "ontological grounding"? What is Bradley's Regress Argument? According to Imaguire, what is this argument supposed to show?

This apple and that rose are both red. Metaphysicians often explain this fact by saying that this apple and that rose are concrete particulars or objects that instantiate the universal property *redness*. While particulars are unrepeatable entities, universals are typically repeatable: they may be wholly present in different places at the same time. There is redness in this apple, in that rose, and in many other places in space. Although the distinction between particulars and universals is quite intuitive, it is not easy to offer a criterion for distinguishing them.[1] Anyway, this may be enough for our purpose in this chapter: universals are qualitative; they characterize the objects and are usually expressed by predicates. If we assume the relation of instantiation as primitive, we may say that universals are entities that can be instantiated, while particulars can instantiate but cannot be instantiated. Usually, particulars instantiate universals, but universals (like *redness*) may also instantiate other higher-order universals (e.g., *being a color*). According to an old metaphysical tradition, particulars and universals are the two most fundamental ontological categories: everything that is, is arguably a particular or a universal.

The debate on the status of universals, whether they do really exist or not, is usually bound to the label "The Problem of Universals," and has been intensely discussed at least since the Middle Ages. Metaphysicians who accept their existence are called *realists*, while those who deny them are called *nominalists*.[2]

This is the main question of this essay: Do universals exist or not? As the title reveals, my answer will be negative. Thus, nominalism will be defended against realism. As simple as the question about the existence of universals may sound, it is far from being a simple question. There is no agreement, even about what is really at stake in this debate. In any case, we will examine the most common arguments for universals and show why they are not convincing.

How Many Things Are There?

We live in a huge universe with numerous galaxies with all their stars and planets. On our planet there are continents and seas, mountains and stones, trees and animals of many different kinds. But suppose for a moment there were only two spheres, similar to common billiard balls, a red and a blue one in an otherwise empty universe. No planets, no stars, no trees or animals, just these two spheres. If you were to take an inventory of this meager universe, how many entities would you say there were?

Let us ignore here all compositional aspects of our imaginary universe, that is, the fact that the spheres are composed of many particles. In this case, the most natural answer is that there are only two entities, namely, the two spheres. The controversy between realists and nominalists starts at this point. The typical realist is willing to accept the qualitative aspects in the inventory of reality: beyond the two spheres, there is also roundness, redness, blueness, similarity (the relation that holds between the two balls in virtue of both being round), difference (the relation that hold between the two balls in virtue of one being red and the other blue), and so on.[3] I said "the typical" realist would assume this because there are different brands of realism, and each one will differ in their catalog of entities according to some additional requirements: some realists will only accept properties but reject relations, others will accept properties and relations but only those that "cut reality at the joints," for example, that ground causal powers, or that occur in basic laws of nature, and so on.

Realists also disagree about "where" these universals are located: the immanent realist (or *in re* realist) claims that they are inside space and time ("redness is wherever there is a red thing") while the transcendent realist (or *ante rem* realist) claims that universals are habitants of a realm of abstract entities, sometimes called "Third Realm" or "Platonic Heaven." Thus, the transcendent realist may agree with the nominalist that, strictly speaking, "in" the space-time realm there are only two concrete spheres, but he will insist that "there are" entities beyond this realm. And not rarely the transcendent realist will even claim that that realm of abstract entities is more robust and fundamental than the space-time realm—this is at least one traditional reading of Plato's own theory. The nominalist will refuse to accept universals "inside" or "outside" the world: after all, universals are not strictly *things*, but merely *ways* things are.

Classification and Existence

The realist can argue for the existence of universals asking whether the two balls are similar or different. The nominalist will probably answer: "They are similar in one aspect—they are both round—but different in another aspect—one is red and the other blue." "Do you see?" the realist will reply, "What are these entities you call 'aspects'? Aren't they as real as the two balls? Roundness, redness and blueness are objective entities just as their bearers. Thus, there are universals."

Indeed, one of the most important tasks of metaphysics is to offer a system of the most general categories of reality. Some believe that there are only objects, like the two spheres. Others believe that there are only universals and that a concrete particular is nothing over and above a bundle of co-present universals (this is the so-called Bundle Theory). Others believe that the world is composed basically of facts, like the facts that *this ball is red* and *that ball is blue*. Yet others believe in entities called "tropes," the particular (not universal!) properties of each concrete particular like the-redness-of-this-sphere and the-blueness-of-that-sphere. In any case, there are different ways to "cut" reality into kinds that yield different systems of ontological categories. And it is always possible to ask "What is x?"—a question whose answer will present an instance of a particular category. This sphere is a particular, redness is a universal property, that the sphere is red is a fact, the-redness-of-this-sphere is a trope, and so on. But should we then conclude that there are objects, properties, facts, and tropes all together?

Certainly not! And the reason is simple: in ontology, by saying that a given x is of the kind K, we are not implying that "there are K's." In ontology, contrary to empirical sciences, classification does not imply existence. You may say that Pegasus is a fiction, without implying that it exists.[4] You may say that the round square is an impossible entity without implying that it exists. In metaphysics, we are not looking for superficial, but for *fundamental*, existence. Further, if we list in our inventory the concrete red sphere, the universal redness, the universal roundness, the fact that this sphere is red, and the trope the-redness-of-this-sphere as different items, we are simply "double counting." When the nominalist counts this one concrete red sphere as one thing, he automatically rejects counting redness, the fact that this sphere is red, and the-redness-of-this-sphere as additional entities. As Lewis[5] wonderfully formulated (somewhat adapted): the way the sphere is makes "the sphere is red" true, but ways that objects are, are not additional entities alongside the objects that are those ways.

With the thesis that everything that exists is a particular, the nominalist does not mean that redness was wrongly classified, that is, that redness is a particular instead of a universal. What she denies is the fact that this universal must be counted as an additional entity. We may be used to distinguishing between the object, the sphere, and its properties like redness, roundness, and so on. But this distinction is arguably only the result of an act of intellectual abstraction: we are separating entities that are inseparable like the two faces of a coin. For what is the pure object beyond its properties? This mysterious entity is often called a "bare" or "thin" particular, in opposition to the "thick" particular with all its properties. But an entity with no properties, with no determination, like the bare particular, is a metaphysical monster, an unintelligible "blob." For this reason, the nominalist can claim that, by counting the entities of our imaginary universe, we are better off not separating the inseparable: to count the properties as additional entities alongside the objects would be like counting the coin twice because of its two faces.

One over Many

But the realist has more arguments. In fact, probably the most famous argument is the so-called *One over Many argument*. It is based on the possibility of different particulars sharing the same nature: "How is it possible that different particulars have something in common?" asks the realist. For some realists[6] this question is the most adequate formulation of the problem of universals, and its most plausible answer appeals to the existence of universals. For take our simplified universe again: both objects are spheres. Thus, "they have something" in common or, in other words, "there is" something that both objects have, namely, the universal roundness. Therefore, there is roundness and, more generally, there are universals.[7]

This is a remarkable argument because it "proves" the existence of universals from a very simple and uncontroversial fact in an unexpectedly direct way. Of course, the nominalist cannot plausibly deny that both spheres are round. She can also hardly deny that both things "have something in common." What she can do is to deny that the expression "there is" in the conclusion "there is something that both objects have in common" is to be taken ontologically seriously. It is similar to the "there is" in "There is something you believe exists that I do not believe exists, namely Pegasus."

Another slogan used to express the insight that a universal is *one* thing that is present in *different* objects is "identity in the difference." How can two spheres, which are different insofar as they are two, be identical in one respect (e.g., both are round)? Things are identical and different at the same time—how is this possible? This formulation is supposed to be puzzling for, of course, identity and difference are contradictory qualifications. The most obvious reaction to this puzzle is the appeal to the distinction between numerical and qualitative identity: the two spheres are not identical and different in the same respect. They are *numerically* distinct, but *qualitatively* similar in one respect. But the realist may insist that this explanation just sweeps the problem under the rug, for it is based on the very distinction at stake here, viz., the distinction between objects (which grounds the numerical aspect) and universals (which grounds the qualitative aspect). And still, as Peacock[8] argued, there is the problem that both spheres are qualitatively identical (both are round) and qualitatively different (one is red, the other blue) at the same time.

Be that as it may, the important question is how the nominalist can block the conclusion of the existence of universals from this line of reasoning. Why is she allowed not to take the "there is" in the conclusion seriously? That not taking the "there is" here seriously is a reasonable attitude was suggested by Quine in his highly influential paper *On What There Is*: "One may admit that there are red houses, roses, and sunsets, but deny, except as a popular and misleading manner of speaking, that they have anything in common."[9] Quine does not explicitly explain why this is a merely "misleading" manner of speaking. But he proposed a universal criterion for deciding virtually all questions of existence or, more exactly, for deciding what are the "ontological commitments" of a given theory: we should formalize the sentences we consider true in our theories according to the canonical first-order logic with quantification and then check which are the values of our variables. This cannot be accurately explained without appealing to some technicalities of classical logic. For our purpose here, however, it may suffice to give a superficial explanation of our two-spheres world. Call the red sphere "*a*" and the blue sphere "*b*." A correct and complete description of that world could be given in terms of the following four sentences:

(1)   *a* is round

(2)   *a* is red

(3)   *b* is round

(4)   *b* is blue

From this description, we may conclude in first-order logic that there is something (namely *a*) that is round and red, and there is something (namely *b*) that is round and blue, but *not* that there is roundness, redness, and blueness. The realist's argument seems to be that from (1) and (3) we must conclude that

(5) There is something that *a* and *b* have in common, namely, roundness.

But the nominalist can claim correctly that (5) is not really required in the full description of the world. It simply states, in a misleading way, what is expressed by the conjunction of (1) with (3). If we accepted the realist's ontological commitments from any one of such redundant descriptions, we would be forced to accept extravagant new entities. Notice that this is not to say that (5) is false—in fact, it is true. But we should not take it ontologically seriously. For (5) is of the same kind as the true sentence "The average woman has 1.5 children." No one would suppose that that this poor woman really exists and gave birth to one and half babies. Similarly, since (5) is a non-fundamental redundant description of reality, it does not have to be taken seriously.

Anyway, the only two things we "quantify over" in sentences (1)–(4) are the two spheres. There is nothing over and above them. The realist's claim that "there is something that both entities are" is based on second-order logic, a logic that quantifies over properties—something that we should avoid (Quine has some technical reasons for rejecting second-order logic, but this does not have to worry us now[10]).

However, the realist can press his point even conceding Quine's principle of ontological commitment. For how can the nominalist explain the commitment of the following sentences?

(6) Orange is more similar to red than to blue.

(7) Wisdom is a virtue.

(8) Red and blue are both colors.

In all these sentences, we quantify over properties: there is something that is more similar to red than to blue, viz. orange; there is something that is a virtue, viz. wisdom. And if the truth of "*a* and *b* are both round" commits us to *a* and *b*, by parity of reasoning, the truth "red and blue are both colors" commits us to redness and blueness. Sentence (8) is quite interesting because it makes clear that the One over Many phenomenon is not restricted to the basic level of objects. First-order universals (i.e., properties of objects) also have something in common, viz. second-order universals (i.e., properties of properties): so red and blue have something in common, they are both colors;

round and square also have something in common, they are both geometrical shapes, and so on.

The typical move of the nominalist at this point is to offer a first-order paraphrase of the sentence in order to eliminate the apparent commitment to universals. A possible paraphrase of sentence (6) would be "Anything orange is more similar to anything red than to anything blue." Indeed, in this sentence our variable "anything" ranges only over concrete particulars. The obvious objection is that this sentence does not capture the original meaning of (6). Worse, the original sentence is true, while this paraphrase is false: this orange billiard ball is more similar to that blue billiard ball than to that red car. Thus, the nominalist must appeal to modal notions (possibility and necessity) and offer the paraphrase:

An orange particular must resemble a red particular more closely than an orange particular can resemble a blue particular.[11]

Alternatively, the nominalist may keep far from possible worlds and appeal to the logic of grounding[12] (which introduces a new "in virtue of" operator) and offer the paraphrase:

For any three objects a, b, and c, whenever a is orange, b is red, and c is blue, then, when a is more similar to b than to c, then a is more similar to b than to c partly in virtue of a being orange, b red, and c blue, and when a is not more similar to b than to c, then a is more similar to c than to b despite a being orange, b red, and c blue.

In all these paraphrases, we quantify only over concrete particulars and the commitment to universals is rigorously avoided. Admittedly, the debate between realists and nominalists concerning what counts as an acceptable paraphrase of this kind of sentences is still open[13].

Semantics

When we say that "Socrates is mortal" we are saying something true, for this sentence expresses the fact that Socrates is mortal. More exactly, the name "Socrates" stands for Socrates and the predicate "is mortal" stands for the property of *being mortal*, and according to our usual syntactical rules, both expressions are combined for expressing the fact that Socrates is mortal. More generally, in a usual subject-predicate sentence, the subject term stands for the object and the predicate stands for the universal instantiated by the object. If there were no universals, the predicate would stand for nothing, which sounds like nonsense. This is a realist argument from semantics: we need universals as semantic values of predicates.[14]

The relation between predicates and universals is a highly debated topic in the philosophy of language. On the one side, some realists believe that to any, or almost any, predicate, there is a corresponding universal. On the other side, some nominalists claim that we do not need universals as ontological counterparts of predicates. For the fact that Socrates is mortal is to be explained in just terms of the predicate "is mortal" being correctly applied to Socrates. At least, this is the way Armstrong[15] characterizes *Predicate Nominalism*. Both positions are extreme and hardly plausible.

The adoption of the first position yields a radical form of realism: to any well-formed predicate of language there is a corresponding property. So, "is red," "is red and round," "was bought yesterday in a supermarket" are all predicates that express universals. If we accept this position, there are as many universals as there are predicates in our language—indefinitely many, in fact. Most realists reject this position today, for there are many predicates that cannot express universals since they are paradoxical. Take the predicate "heterological" which means "it does not instantiate itself." The property *abstractness, for example,* is not heterological for abstractness is itself abstract. Yet the property *roundness* is heterological, since as an abstract entity it has no shape and, in particular, is not round. But what about the property *heterological* itself? If it is heterological, then by definition it does not instantiate itself. Thus, it is not heterological. But if it is not heterological, it *does* instantiate itself, for it satisfies its definition. Therefore it is heterological. In other words, the universal heterological is heterological if and only if it is not heterological—which is a contradiction. The necessary conclusion, therefore, is that "heterological" may be a predicate, but it cannot correspond to any universal (unless you accept that reality may be inconsistent).[16]

On the other hand, the nominalist strategy to simply denigrate the instantiation of properties to merely satisfaction of predicates is also highly implausible. It seems quite implausible, for instance, that Socrates is mortal because he satisfies the predicate "is mortal." However, I do not think that Armstrong's characterization of Predicate Nominalism is fair. To be sure, if nominalism is understood as the rejection of the existence of universals, it is clear that anyone who is a nominalist must reject the existence of universals beyond predicates. But this does not imply that she must deny that there is something predicates stand for. It only implies that this something is not a universal. Indeed, standard semantics take these entities to be sets, which are quite acceptable entities for the nominalist, for sets are particulars. Thus, the predicate "round" stands for the set of all round things, the predicate "red" stands for the set of all red things, and so forth. The domain of the elements of these sets may be conceived as simply particulars of our world or, better, the sets of all particulars of all possible worlds.[17]

Class Nominalism is usually defined as the kind of nominalism that takes sets as the adequate substitute for properties. In the case of n-ary relations, instead of sets of particulars, we must take sets of n-tuples. But a nominalist may not be a class nominalist and still defend the idea that what the predicate "F" stands for is not the universal F-ness, but an adequate set. In fact, this is not an ad hoc solution, but the standard conception in our usual logical semantics.

Bradley's Regress

Another way metaphysicians formulate the problem of universals is in terms of grounding for predication. Ontological grounding is a relation of metaphysical determination that explains why something is the case in virtue of some other thing being the case.[18] So, take our red sphere. In virtue of what is this sphere red? The question of predication seems to require an answer of the following form

a is F in virtue of P

where P is more fundamental than, and explains or determines why, *a* is *F*. The fact P itself may be absolutely fundamental or grounded in further more fundamental facts that necessarily do not entail the fact that *a* is *F* (otherwise, the explanation would be circular).

As we saw earlier, the transcendent realist defends the following explanation:

a is F in virtue of *a* participating in F-ness.

Thus, this apple is red because it participates in redness, that sphere is round because it participates in roundness, and so on. The immanent realist offers a similar explanation:

a is F in virtue of *a* instantiating the property F.

Almost all kinds of nominalism offer alterative explanations, all of them, of course, without appealing to universals:[19]

Predicate nominalism: *a* is *F* in virtue of the predicate "F" being true of *a*.

Concept nominalism: *a* is *F* in virtue of *a* falling under the concept F.

Class nominalism: *a* is *F* in virtue of *a* being a member of the class F.

Resemblance nominalism: *a* is *F* in virtue of *a* being similar to *b* (and all other F particulars).

Now, do we really have to offer an explanation for the fact that *a* is *F*? What is the reason for supposing that there will be such an explanation at all? *Ostrich Nominalism* is so called because, like the ostrich, he "puts his head into the sand" and rejects the need or even the possibility of giving an explanation for predication. According to Armstrong,[20] because of this dismissive attitude, Ostrich Nominalism should not be considered a solution to the problem at all, but rather a position of rejecting it as a pseudo-problem. Indeed, if the problem of universal is just the problem of giving a ground for simple predicative facts, Ostrich Nominalism would not be a solution. But if the problem is, instead, more impartially, the task of determining the fundamental status of predication, Ostrich Nominalism offers a solution just as any other position. Why is the answer "*a* is *F* in virtue of X and X is fundamental" acceptable, but the simpler answer "*a* is *F* is a fundamental fact" not?

As a matter of fact, I think Ostrich Nominalism is supported by a very strong argument: the so-called *Bradley's Regress Argument*. For ease of exposition, let's take only the explanation of transcendent realism. According to it, *a* is *F* in virtue of *a* participating in F-ness. Thus, the realist explains that the particular *a* is in a certain way, *F*, in virtue of participating in F-ness. But, with this explanation the realist is only appealing to a new property the particular *a* has: instead of having the property *being F*, *a* is now characterized by means of the property *participating in F-ness*. And so, at the end, we are left with a new mysterious fact (or, at least, with a fact that is as mysterious as the original fact). If we felt compelled to explain the fact that *a is F* because it was considered mysterious, we should feel compelled to ask again: in virtue of what does the particular *a* participate in F-ness? By parity of reasoning, the answer should be: *a* participates in F-ness in virtue of *participating in the participation in F-ness*. However, this is just a new and no less mysterious fact. Thus, it calls for a new explanation, which can only be: *a participates in the participation in F-ness* in virtue of *a participating in the participation in the participation in F-ness*, and so on. The conclusion: the explanation offered by the realist is not a genuine explanation at all.

Only when we accept simple predicative facts as fundamental, as the ostrich nominalist does, do we avoid this problem.[21] Of course, some explanations seem to be better prepared to face the challenge of the regress than others. Class Nominalism, for instance, may claim that *a* is *F* in virtue of *a* being a member of *F*, and since the set-theoretical membership relation is just a formal internal relation, the fact that *a* is a member of *F* is a fundamental fact that does not need additional grounding. Indeed, if the class *F* exists, the relation that holds between *a* and *F* simply emerges from the existence of *a* and *F*. Such a strategy is not open to the realist (neither the transcendent nor the immanent). For neither the mere existence of the particular *a* nor the existence of *F* (or F-ness) explains by itself the fact that *a* is *F*: since *a* and *F* can exist without *a* being *F* (at least when *F* is not an essential property of *a*, and this case must be considered since the explanation is supposed to hold for any kind of predication, not only of essential ones).

Conclusion

The problem of universals is a highly controversial topic in metaphysics.[22] There is not even general agreement about the formulation of the problem. Anyway, at the core of the problem is the debate about the ontological status of universals. Realists claim that universals are needed for some theoretical purposes. Nominalists deny this.

The main purpose of this essay was to examine some of the most common arguments for realism and show why they are not compelling. I suppose that some realists will contend that I simply overlooked or ignored *one* or even *the* most compelling argument. The dialectic of the realism versus nominalism debate is still open for new arguments, and we must not underestimate the creativity of realists for establishing new reasons for assuming universals. The nominalist must be able to face each new challenge. Of course, she does not have to present a unified answer: she may appeal to sets, *possibilia*, mental tokens, and so on, for facing these challenges—insofar as she does not appeal to universals, everything goes well.

Notes

1. For a criticism of the distinction, see F. M. Ramsey, "Universals," *Mind* 34 (1925): 401–17; and F. MacBride, "The Particular-Universal Distinction: A Dogma of Metaphysics?" *Mind* 114, no. 455 (2005): 565–614.
2. However, one should be cautious with the labels "realism" and "nominalism" for since N. Goodman and W. v. O. Quine ("Steps Toward a Constructive Nominalism," *Journal of Symbolic Logic* 12 (1947): 105–22) these terms have been used to designate not the positive and negative attitude toward universals, but toward abstract entities in general (whatever is not in space and time). The rejection of universals and the rejection of abstracts are different claims, for some particulars like numbers and sets may be abstract, and according to some theories, properties are located in space and time. Therefore, it may be useful to distinguish the *traditional*

nominalism—the rejection of universals—from the *Harvard nominalism*—the rejection of abstracts.

3   For a defense of immanent realism, see D. M. Armstrong, *Universals and Scientific Realism. Vol. II: A Theory of Universals* (Cambridge: Cambridge University Press, 1978); and E. J. Lowe, *Four Category Ontology: A Metaphysical Foundation for Natural Science* (Oxford: Oxford University Press, 2006). For a defense of transcendent realism, see M. Jubien, *Contemporary Metaphysics: An Introduction* (Cambridge, MA: Blackwell, 1997).

4   See W. v. O. Quine, "On What There Is," *Review of Metaphysics* 2 (1948). Reprinted in W. V. Quine, *From a Logical Point of View* (Cambridge, MA: Harvard University Press, 1980), 1–19.

5   D. Lewis, "Things qua Truthmakers," in *Real Metaphysics: Essays in Honour of D. H. Mellor*, eds. H. Lillehammer and G. Rodriguez-Pereyra (London: Routledge, 2003), 25–33.

6   See, for example, D. M. Armstrong, *Nominalism and Realism, Vol. I. A Theory of Universals*, (Cambridge: Cambridge University Press, 1978), 11.

7   For a contemporary formulation of the argument, see W. Sellars, "Grammar and Existence: A Preface to Ontology," *Mind* 69, no. 276 (1960): 499–533; B. Aune, *Metaphysics: The Elements, Minneapolis* (London: University of Minnesota Press, 1985); and M. Balaguer, "Platonism in Metaphysics," *The Stanford Encyclopedia of Philosophy* (2014), E. Zalta (ed.) http://plato.stanford.edu/archives/spr2014/ entries/platonism.

8   H. Peacock, "What's Wrong with Ostrich Nominalism?" *Philosophical Papers* 38, no. 2 (2009): 183–217.

9   Quine, "On What There Is," 81.

10 In particular, the absence of a complete proof procedure in second-order logic is a very serious inadequacy. Thus, first-order logic is more familiar and convenient (see W. V. O. Quine, "Logic and the Reification of Universals," in *From a Logical Point of View*, 102–29).

11 G. Rodriguez-Pereyra, "Resemblance Nominalism and Abstract Nouns," *Analysis* 75, no. 2 (2015): 223–31.

12 For a presentation of the logic of ground, see K. Fine, "The Pure Logic of Ground," *Review of Symbolic Logic* 5, no. 1 (2012): 1–25.

13 For the debate on the paraphrase, see M. Loux, *Metaphysics: A Contemporary Introduction* (New York, London: Routledge, 1998); D. Lewis, "New Work for a Theory of Universals," in *Properties*, eds. D. H. Mellor and A. Oliver (Oxford: Oxford University Press, 1997); F. Jackson, "Statements about Universals," *Mind* 86 (1977); and G. Rodriguez-Pereyra, "Resemblance Nominalism and Abstract Nouns."

14 See this argument in Loux, *Metaphysics*, 25–30.

15 Armstrong, *Nominalism and Realism*, 13.

16 For more restrictions of predicates, see Lewis, "New Work for a Theory of Universals"; Loux, *Metaphysics*, 34–35; Armstrong, *Universals and Scientific Realism. Vol. II: A Theory of Universals*; and S. Shoemaker, "Causality and

Properties," in *Time and Cause*, ed. P. van Inwagen (Dordrecht: D. Reidel, 1980), 109–36.

17 If you identify the predicates "unicorn" and "flying elephants" with the corresponding sets of instances, both predicates will be identical to the empty set, for none of them have instances. But then, by transitivity of identity, you should conclude that both predicates are identical, which is sheer nonsense. Thus, we usually appeal to the universe of *possibilia*: there are possible unicorns that are not flying elephants and vice versa.

18 The notion of *grounding*, its definition and its formal properties, has become a hotly debated topic in contemporary analytic metaphysics that we cannot discuss here. For more on grounding, see F. Correia and B. Schnieder, "Grounding: An Opinionated Introduction," in *Metaphysical Grounding: Understanding the Structure of Reality*, eds. F. Correia and B. Schneider (Cambridge: Cambridge University Press, 2014).

19 For a detailed presentation of these forms of nominalism, see Armstrong, *Nominalism and Realism, Vol. I. A Theory of Universals*, part 2; for resemblance nominalism, see G. Rodriguez-Pereyra, *Resemblance Nominalism. A Solution to the Problem of Universals* (Oxford: Clarendon Press, 2002).

20 Armstrong, *Resemblance Nominalism. A Solution to the Problem of Universals*, 16.

21 For a defense of Ostrich Nominalism, see J. Van Cleve, "Predication Without Universals? A Fling with Ostrich Nominalism," *Philosophy and Phenomenological Research* 54, no. 3 (1994): 577–90; M. Devitt, "'Ostrich Nominalism' or 'Mirage Realism?'" *Pacific Philosophical Quarterly* 61 (1980): 433–49; J. Melia, "Truthmaking Without Truthmakers," in *Truthmakers: The Contemporary Debate,* eds. H. Beebee and J. Dood (Oxford: Clarendon Press, 2005), 67–84; G. Imaguire, "In Defence of Quine's Ostrich Nominalism," *Grazer Philosophische Studien* 89 (2014): 185–203.

22 For the meta-metaphysical aspects of the debate, see G. Imaguire, "The Platonism vs. Nominalism Debate from a Meta-metaphysical Perspective," *Revista Portuguesa de Filosofia* 71, nos. 2–3 (2015): 375–98.

RESPONSES

Response to Gould

Guido Imaguire

Study Questions

1. What are the three ways to formulate the problem of universals? How does Imaguire argue that Ostrich Nominalism is not dismissive toward the first two of these?

2. How does Imaguire respond to Gould's charge that Ostrich Nominalism fails to ground resemblance facts?

3. Why does Imaguire think that Gould is mistaken in claiming that Ostrich Nominalism is less ontologically economic than realism?

Gould's essay presents an interesting defense of realism and a forceful criticism of nominalism. The article explains and criticizes three of the main nominalistic solutions to the problem of universals, and I am glad to see that he considers, among them, Ostrich Nominalism, whose explanation I consider adequate in most, but not all, aspects, as I want to argue in this short reply. Also, Resemblance Nominalism and trope theory, the other two nominalistic solutions, could be defended against Gould's criticism, but for reasons of space, I will restrict myself to the defense of the ostrich version.

There are some more general background issues that could be discussed, as for instance Gould's proposal that an adequate solution to the problem of universals requires a theory of properties. As I see the problem of universals, the existence or nonexistence of universal properties, the grounding of predication, and the fact of resemblance are at the very core of the problem, but this does not necessarily require a full theory of properties.

Not a Real Problem?

One first misconception concerning Ostrich Nominalism is the idea that the "ostrich" thinks the problem of universals is not a real problem and resemblance facts do not require any special explanation or grounding. Indeed, this is a quite ubiquitous opinion about the ostrich, but I think it is rather unfair. In order to decide if the ostrich is dismissive or not, we should first of all be clear about what exactly is the nature and the suitable formulation of the problem of universals. The three most common formulations are:

(i) Are there universals?
(ii) Given the fact that a is F, in virtue of what is a F?
(iii) How is it possible that different particulars share the same property?

Now, is the ostrich really dismissive concerning any one of these questions? Certainly not! The ostrich offers a criterion for ontological commitment according to which we decide which entities exist and which entities do not. This criterion is based on our use of the quantifier in the sentences we consider true: "To be is to be the value of a bound variable," to use Quine's slogan. This criterion is much more substantial than those other solutions offer—in fact, it has become the standard criterion for deciding virtually all questions of existence in ontology, including numbers, mereological sums, and so on. Anyway, applied to the problem of universals, the solution is quite straightforward: since we do not have to quantify over properties in our fundamental facts, we may conclude that "no" is the right answer to question (i), there are no universals—and to answer "no" is not dismissive. Dismissive would be the attitude of rejecting the question as meaningless or unimportant, and this is not the claim of the ostrich at all. The ostrich is widely interested in what exists and in what is fundamental.

Fundamentality is the core of question (ii). It is perhaps the most delicate question, for the ostrich thinks, indeed, that a simple predicative fact like a is F has no ground. If you suppose that a is F must be a derivative fact, there must be a ground for it. However, all solutions of the problem of universals ground this fact in a more fundamental fact which is considered absolutely fundamental, that is, a fact without ground. At this point, the ostrich complains: if every theory has the right to propose its own fundamental facts, so does the ostrich. And for him, this fact is simply the simple predicative fact that a is F. If the status of predication is at stake here, that is, its grounding relations to other facts, the more neutral and general formulation should not be "which is the ground for the derivative fact that a is F," but simply "which are the fundamental facts?" The ostrich is just proposing a theory of fundamental facts like any other solution. And, as argued in the main article, her theory is the only one that does not fall into a regress.

How Is Resemblance Possible?

Question (iii) is, as I see it, the core formulation of the problem. Question (iii) asks for an explanation of resemblance facts. And the ostrich is not dismissive here, either, but explicitly offers a ground for resemblance facts. I think this is the point Gould misses in his explanation of Ostrich Nominalism. According to him, the ostrich takes the sentence

(1) *a* and *b* are both F

as explanatorily equivalent to

(2) *a* is F and *b* is F.

However, according to Gould, this is wrong because (1) is rather equivalent to

(3) *a* is F and *b* is F and the Fs of *a* and *b* resemble each other,

and by explaining (1) in terms of (2) the ostrich "leaves out precisely what it says need not be explained—the third conjunct and the fact that there are real-world resemblances" (p. 250). As he puts it: "Resemblance facts, by a clever sleight of hand, have magically disappeared. . . . I suspect that if the ostrich were to allow genuine resemblance facts in addition to qualitative facts, they too would be brute."

Far from the truth! The ostrich offers a grounding analysis, according to which resemblance facts neither are brute or primitive nor do they magically disappear. They are ontologically grounded: the resemblance fact that *a* resembles *b* is fully grounded in the conjunctive fact (2), which is, on its turn, partially grounded in the fact that *a* is F and also partially grounded in the fact that *b* is F. We may express this in the logic of grounding (with "x > y" meaning "x grounds y"):

   a is F, *b* is F   >   *a* is F and *b* is F   >   *a* resembles *b*

This is not equivalent to simply saying that (1) "does not require the postulation of resemblance facts in addition to qualitative facts and conjuncts of qualitative facts" (p. xx). In a sense, the opposite is the case: whenever we say that the fact F1 grounds fact F2, we are requiring F2, for grounding is a kind of determination. Further, even if one rejects this grounding analysis and accepts (3) as a fundamental fact, this would not damage the nominalistic stance, for this sentence only entails quantification over particulars: "There are two particulars, *a* and *b*, such that *a* is F and *b* is F, and they are similar to each other" is the standard logical reading of the sentence.

How Many Entities?

Ostrich Nominalism is a quite radical form of nominalism. It sounds, therefore, surprising when Gould claims that it is less ontologically economic than realism. Gould's claim is based on his view according to which the realist is committed to three sorts of things (particulars, universals, and the exemplification relation) while the ostrich is committed ontologically to many sorts of things (since for her the use of predicates carries ontological commitments to charactered objects: red things, sweet things, colored things, human things, and so on). For the realist, red things are not fundamental sorts of things; rather, red things are further explained in terms of a particular exemplifying the universal *redness*.

This is probably the most controversial and difficult point of disagreement—a typical instance of a crossroad where philosophers part ways over basic intuitions. The idea seems to be this: since the ostrich takes thick or charactered objects as fundamental, she is committed to many "sorts" of things. I think the problem lies in the expression "sorts." Of course, the ostrich accepts many particulars of different sorts: red things, sweet things, colored things and so on. But these are only particulars—and these are all that exist. The ostrich accepts no other ontological category than particulars: no universal properties, no instantiation relation, no tropes, no bare particulars, no states of affairs, and so on. To accept red things, sweet things, colored things is not to accept additional ontological categories. For the ostrich, the question of classification precedes the question of existence: first of all, the ostrich—like the realist—accepts the classification according to which this ball is a particular and its redness is a universal property. Both also agree that neither this ball nor redness is an ontological category—these are just instances of the general categories of particular and universal. After that, the ostrich accepts the challenge of the problem of universals, that is, question (i), whether universals do really exist or not. Finally, applying his theory of fundamentality and ontological commitment, the ostrich concludes that only charactered particulars exist: red, blue, sweet, and any such sort of particulars.

Response to Imaguire

Paul M. Gould

Study Questions

1. Why is Gould unpersuaded by Imaguire's charge of "double counting" in the two-sphere world?

2. Why does Gould think that in the two-sphere world the Ostrich Nominalist has to be committed to the existence of multiple sorts of things?

3. According to Gould, why is the resemblance captured in sentence (5)—"There is something that *a* and *b* have in common, viz. roundness"—not redundant?

4. Why does Gould think that Imaguire's worry over Russell's Paradox is a red herring?

5. How does Gould respond to the Bradley Regress Argument?

Guido Imaguire's excellent essay highlights the central issues involved in the debate over universals. It does not, unfortunately, provide good reasons to think its central thesis, the thesis that there are no universals, is true.

Classification and Existence

Imaguire asks us to imagine a universe containing a red round sphere and a blue round sphere. How many fundamental entities are there in this meager universe? "The most natural answer," according to Imaguire is that "there are only two entities, namely, the two spheres" (p. 261). To admit into our inventory of the world the universals redness, blueness, and roundness, the tropes the-redness-of-this-sphere, the-blueness-of-this-sphere, and the roundness-of-this-sphere, and the facts that this sphere is red, blue, and round, is to engage in "double counting" (p. 263). Only particulars exist, "ways that objects are, are not additional entities alongside the objects that are those ways" (Ibid.).

What exactly is the argument here? As far as I can tell, Imaguire relies on an innocuous principle of classification and an appeal to theoretical simplicity (no "double counting" allowed) in order to establish the nominalist thesis. Imaguire stipulates, "In ontology, by saying that a given x is of the kind K, we are not implying that 'there are K's' .... Classification does not imply existence" (p. 262).[1] In reply, it may be true that classification does not "imply" existence, but so what? Very little in metaphysics amounts to one thing "implying" another. Rather, costs and benefits are weighed along a number of metrics including explanatory power and theoretical simplicity. As a realist, I agree that there is some double counting in the list of possible entities provided by Imaguire: no tropes are needed in addition to universals, and I'm happy to treat facts as derivative entities that need not be counted when classifying *fundamental* entities. The issue, then, boils down to whether realism or nominalism is simpler in terms of ontological and ideological economy. I've argued, perhaps surprisingly, that in addition to being more ideologically economic (less primitives) than nominalism, realism is more ontologically economic along one metric (less fundamental *sorts* of things) than nominalism.

One over Many

A full and correct description of our two-sphere world can be given, according to Imaguire, in terms of four sentences (where the variable *a* denotes the red sphere and the variable *b* the blue sphere):

(1) *a* is round

(2) *a* is red

(3) *b* is round

(4) *b* is blue

Quine's criterion of ontological commitment leads us, then, to conclude that two objects, *a* which is red and round, and *b* which is blue and round, exist. This is not quite right, as I've argued, however. Imaguire follows the ostrich nominalist in taking "simple predicative facts as fundamental" (p. 269). This means that in addition to our two fundamental particulars, Imaguire is committed to at least three fundamental *sorts* of things: round things, red things, and blue things. On my preferred gloss of realism, there are three fundamental *sorts* of things too: particular, universal, and the exemplification relation. So, in our two-sphered world, the ostrich and realist come out equal in terms of qualitative economy. Of course, the actual world is much more diverse than our two-sphere world, and thus, Ostrich Nominalism is ultimately worse off than realism in terms of qualitative ontological economy.

Moving on, Imaguire correctly notes, the realist claims our two-sphere world is not yet fully described. In addition to sentences (1)–(4) we need:

(5) There is something that *a* and *b* have in common, viz. roundness.

But, argues Imaguire, (5) is redundant, merely restating facts already expressed by the conjunction of (1) and (3). Sentence (5), while true, provides no new ontological commitments, "for (5) is of the same kind as the true sentence 'The average woman has 1.5 children'" (p. 7). But is the resemblance captured in (5) a derivative predicative fact, akin to the predicates "the average woman" and "1.5 children"? I claim that the two are not alike. Resemblance facts are what D. M. Armstrong calls "Moorean."[2] They are *fundamental* facts in need of philosophical explanation. Putting my point in set-theoretic terms, we might say, along with the nominalist, that (1) and (3) pick out two different objects that belong to the same class, the class of round things. Fair enough. What is left out if resemblance is not treated with ontological seriousness, however, is *why* the class of round things is a natural class, a unity of exactly resembling charactered objects. It is reasonable to think that members of the class of round things share something in common, viz. the universal *roundness*. The postulation of a universal explains the unity of the class of round things in our two-sphere world, and the unity of the many natural classes found within the actual world, whereas appeal to qualitative facts (and class membership) alone does not.[3]

Russell's Paradox and Bradley's Regress

The second half of Imaguire's essay raises well-known problems that are not typically thought to be devastating to realism and thus elicit brief commentary. If endorsing an abundant theory of properties such that all predicates refer to properties, setting aside those predicates that lead to Russellian paradox, is to endorse a "radical form of realism" (p. 267), I plead guilty. Importantly, however, my case for universals does not rely on endorsing an abundant theory of properties. Any sparser base of predicates will do, as long as those predicates are best understood, as I've argued, as referring to universals. Worry over Russell's paradox is a bit of a red herring, especially since Imaguire appeals to sets in order to explicate his nominalistically friendly account of subject-predicate discourse. For, as is well known, sets fare no better than properties when it comes to Russell's paradox.[4]

The assumption that generates Bradley's regress is that relations are entities that themselves need to be related. If so, then the participation, instantiation (or exemplification—my preferred designation) relation must itself be further related by another relation ad infinitum, and genuine explanation of predicative facts remains elusive. The Bradley regress argument need not detain the realist, however, for it can be argued either that there is no regress or the regress, if it exists, is not vicious.[5] My preferred way out of the worry, following Reinhardt Grossmann, is the former: relations relate without being related to the things they relate.[6] The exemplification relation, on my preferred version of realism, is a fundamental sort of thing, the glue that joins together a particular and its properties to form a whole without itself needing to be glued to the things it joins together.

Notes

1. A better principle: classification provides prima facie evidence of existence. Or, a more permissive principle: classification provides prima facie evidence of fundamental or derivative existence. Of course, reasons can be supplied that overrule the prima facie evidence. On the latter neo-Aristotelian conception of metaphysics, the trick is not to decide *that* Kind K exists, but in determining *how* it exists. For more on a neo-Aristotelian conception of metaphysics, see Jonathan Shaffer, "On What Grounds What," in *Metametaphysics: New Essays on the Foundations of Ontology*, eds. David J. Chalmers, David Manley, and Ryan Wasserman (Oxford: Oxford University Press, 2009), 347–83. For an ontologist who does, contra Imaguire, think classification entails existence, see Reinhardt Grossmann, *The Existence of the World* (New York: Routledge, 1992).
2. D. M. Armstrong, "Against 'Ostrich' Nominalism: A Reply to Michael Devitt," *Pacific Philosophical Quarterly* 61 (1980): 441.
3. While space prohibits a detailed discussion of Imaguire's treatment of abstract singular terms and the sentences that contain them, even if an appeal to modal notions or the "in virtue of" relation can be employed without loss of meaning, I doubt nominalistically acceptable paraphrases result. "Ways things can resemble" or "ways things can be more similar" or the "in virtue of" relation seem to be objects themselves best understood as universals. For more on the difficulty of finding nominalistically acceptable paraphrases of sentences containing abstract singular terms, see Peter van Inwagen, "A Theory of Properties," in *Oxford Studies in Metaphysics*, vol. 1, ed. Dean W. Zimmerman (Oxford: Clarendon Press, 2004), 113–24.
4. As Bertrand Russell showed in 1902, so-called naïve set theory cannot be true, since the set of all sets that are not members of themselves leads to paradox. See Russell's 1902 "Letter to Frege," where he reports the discovery of the paradox in Jean van Heijenoort, ed., *From Frege to Gödel* (Cambridge, MA: Harvard University Press, 1967), 124–25. For an accessible explanation of Russell's paradox applied to sets, see David Papineau, *Philosophical Devices* (Oxford: Oxford University Press, 2012), chap. 1.
5. For a nice discussion of the options open to the realist in response to the worries raised by Bradley, see Robert C. Koons and Timothy H. Pickavance, *Metaphysics: The Fundamentals* (Malden, MA: Wiley-Blackwell, 2015), 81–83; and Michael J. Loux and Thomas M. Crisp, *Metaphysics: A Contemporary Introduction*, 4th ed. (New York: Routledge, 2017), 29–35.
6. Grossmann, *The Existence of the World*, 55. See also Anna-Sofia Maurin, "Trope Theory and the Bradley Regress," *Synthese* 175, no. 3 (2010): 311–26, where the "relations relate without needing to be further related" reply is developed in defense of trope theory. While Maurin thinks nontransferable compresence tropes provide the only viable solution to Bradley's regress, I see no reason why her general strategy could not be applied by the realist as a solution too, whether exemplification is considered a universal or a particular. Thanks to Robert K. Garcia for pointing me to Maurin's essay.

Questions for Reflection

1. If Platonic Realism is true, then there are likely an infinite number of universals such as properties and relations. Nominalists claim that this makes for an implausibly bloated ontology. Is it too bloated, or is this just the necessary price to be paid to solve the problem of universals? Why?

2. Imaguire denies Gould's charge that Ostrich Nominalism is ontologically less economic than realism. Has Imaguire adequately addressed that charge or has he missed Gould's point? Why?

3. Which view, nominalism or realism, gives the most satisfying account of resemblance facts? Why?

4. Nominalism denies that universals like "humanness" or "humanity" exist. What implications, if any, would this have for ethics? For example, can there be human rights if there is no such thing as humanity? Why?

8

What Is the Mind?

The Mind Is Material

Andrew Melnyk

Study Questions

1. What, according to Melnyk, are the two things you can almost certainly believe about your goldfish?

2. What is materialism?

3. How does Melnyk respond to the charge that materialism reduces people to being like "rocks and tables"? Does his response imply that ordinary material objects have minds? Why?

4. What two features of human behavior have people noticed that lead them to think that humans can't be machines? How does Melnyk address these points?

5. What are the different kinds of mental states that humans have? How, according to Melnyk, can these be understood in physical terms?

6. What is the most common materialist view of the mind? What view does Melnyk prefer instead?

7. What are the five components of the human "mental system"? What overarching goal do they work to achieve?

8. What evidence does Melnyk present in favor of materialism?

9. Why wouldn't we expect the dependence of the mental on the brain if interactionist substance dualism were true?

10. How does property dualism fare better than interactionist dualism? Why does Melnyk reject property dualism anyway?

What Is Materialism?

Materialism (or *physicalism*; the terms are interchangeable in philosophy) is the view that something you almost certainly believe to be true of your goldfish is also true of you and me, and of all human beings. The thing you almost certainly believe about your goldfish can be broken down into two claims: (i) a claim about your goldfish's *parts* and (ii) a claim about its *properties* (i.e., its attributes or characteristics) and the properties of its parts.

The *first* claim is that your goldfish is made up of certain bodily systems—its digestive system, its circulatory system, its muscular system, its nervous system, its immune system, and so on. Each of these systems is in turn made up of organs; for example, your goldfish's circulatory system is made up of its heart, gills, and blood vessels. Each of these organs is made up of specialized cells of about two hundred kinds, and each of these cells is made up of organelles and various molecules. The organelles are made up of molecules too, and all molecules are made up of atoms, which are made up of fundamental physical particles such as electrons and quarks. This first claim is not just that your goldfish has all these parts, but that it has no others; parts of the kinds mentioned are the only kinds of parts it has.

The *second* claim is that all the properties of your goldfish and of its parts (bodily systems, etc.) fall into one of two groups. In the first group are properties (e.g., the properties of electrons and atoms) that *physics* talks about—such properties as mass, charge, or spin. We may call such properties *physical properties*. In the second group are properties (e.g., the properties of cells and organs) that I'll call *functional properties*. For our purposes, let us say that a property of something (e.g., an organ) is a *functional* property if having the property is just a matter of its having parts that are *organized* in a certain way, for example, organized so as to produce a particular *effect*. Your goldfish has the property of metabolizing glucose; but its having this property is just its having parts (e.g., insulin molecules, glucose transporters, insulin receptors) whose interaction has the net effect of converting glucose into energy that cells can use. Your goldfish's heart has the property of being a heart (obviously!); but its having this property is just its (cardiac) cells' being organized—related to one another—in such a way as to form an organ capable of drawing in and then pushing out blood.

Materialism is the view that what these two claims say about your goldfish is also true of every human being. So materialism is the view that

(i) every human being can ultimately be broken down into parts all of which are physical,

and

(ii) every property possessed by a human being, or by its parts, is either a physical property or a functional property in the sense already explained.

For the sake of a handy abbreviation, we can say that materialism is the view that every human being is *purely physical*.

Confusingly, the term "materialism" is also used in everyday life to refer to the view that the most important thing in life is acquiring wealth. But materialism in the sense of this essay doesn't make any claim about how people *ought* to live their lives; it only makes a claim about how the world, in fact, *is*. So materialism in the sense of this essay is a different view from materialism in the everyday sense. Materialism in the sense of this essay might still lead *indirectly* to materialism in the everyday sense; but if it does, that would need to be shown by an argument.[1]

The truth of materialism isn't at all obvious; on the contrary, it initially strikes most people as crazy. Nevertheless, a case can be made for it. Making a case for materialism just means providing evidence for it—providing reasons to believe it. It doesn't mean proving it, either in the mathematical sense in which Pythagoras's Theorem can be proved by deducing it from self-evident axioms or in the weaker sense of providing so much evidence for a claim that there's no room for reasonable doubt. Neither materialism nor its rivals can be proved in the mathematical sense. And if either materialism or its rivals could be supported by evidence that left no room for reasonable doubt, there wouldn't be very smart people who accept materialism *and* very smart people who reject it; but, of course, there are both.

My case for materialism will be as follows. In the next section, I clarify what does and doesn't follow from the claim that we humans are purely physical. In the following two sections, I tackle the obvious objection that we cannot be purely physical because we have *minds*. These sections spell out in a little detail what a materialist view of the mind would look like, and offer some positive evidence for thinking that our minds are purely physical.

Two Common Reactions

One common reaction to materialism is to think, "But if materialism is true, we're all just *material objects*, like rocks or tables."

The trouble with this reaction is that rocks and tables aren't typical of all material objects. They have rather simple physical constitutions, and, of course, they don't really *do* anything. But not all material objects are like that. Your digestive system is a material object, but it can break down and process a huge variety of different foods and turn them all into energy and molecules that your body can use. A plane's autopilot is a material object, but it can fly and land an airliner. The arrangement of computers and servers that stands behind Apple's "Siri" virtual assistant is a material object, but it can do jobs that until recently would have required a human assistant. Unlike rocks or tables, these material objects have highly complex physical constitutions, which enable them to react to their respective environments (e.g., different foods, different altitudes, different commands) with elaborate and appropriate behavior. If humans *are* material objects, they're material objects with a unique physical nature of immense complexity and a unique suite of abilities.

On the internet, I've seen a similar argument: if humans were material objects, then material objects like bottles of soda would have minds, just as humans do. But this argument misunderstands what materialism is committed to. Materialism says that all humans are material objects, not that all material objects are humans. And the claim that all humans are material objects doesn't *entail* that all material objects are humans—just as the claim that all cats are mammals doesn't entail that all mammals are cats. So materialists aren't forced to say that all material objects are humans—so they aren't committed to the crazy claim that bottles of soda have minds.

A second common reaction to materialism is to think, "But if materialism is true, we're just *machines*." But why couldn't we be machines? People feel sure that humans couldn't be machines because they've noticed two significant features of human behavior.

The first is that, when a human receives the *same* stimulus on two *different* occasions, he or she doesn't necessarily respond with the same behavior on both occasions. For example, on one occasion you might respond to, "Would you like a cookie?," by saying, "Yes, please," and taking a cookie, and then, five minutes later, respond to, "Would you like a cookie?," by saying, "No, thanks; I just had one" and not taking a cookie. Or on one occasion you might respond to, "Who is the current prime minister of the UK?" by saying, "Sorry, I don't remember," and then respond to the very same question five minutes later, having just read a newspaper, by saying, "Theresa May." Machines, it seems, don't act like this: they respond to the same stimulus with the same behavior. For example, whenever a doorbell's button is pressed, it rings.

The second feature of human behavior is that a human can receive *different* stimuli on two occasions and yet on both occasions respond in the *same* way. For example, you could learn that you'd won a scholarship either by reading an email or by hearing a voice on the phone. The physical characteristics of the two messages would be very different, the first being a pattern of light on a screen, the second a (different) pattern of vibrations in the air. But you would react in the same way, by calling your parents, say. A machine, it seems, couldn't appreciate that the two stimuli were in some sense the same and merited the same behavioral response.

So, do these two features of human behavior show that humans couldn't be machines? They don't. The two features of human behavior are perfectly genuine, but the assumption that the behavior of machines couldn't possibly have those features is false. Let us consider each feature in turn.

Feature #1. It's not true that machines always respond to the same stimulus with the same behavior. Many machines do, of course, like the doorbell, but many don't. An example of one that doesn't is your laptop, when it's running *Word*, and connected to a printer. On different occasions when you click on "Print," the laptop behaves differently, sending different signals to the printer. The signal it sends depends both on earlier stimuli—what keys were pressed when the document was typed—but also on the current internal state of the machine—what application it's running. Another example of a machine that can respond to the same stimulus with different behavior is a one-armed bandit at a casino. Nearly always, when you put in the money and pull the handle, you win nothing; but occasionally, when you put in the money and pull the handle, you win the jackpot.

In general, what behavior a machine produces depends on two things: (i) the stimulus the machine is currently receiving and (ii) the internal state of the machine. And the internal state of the machine is itself determined by two factors: (1) all the *past* stimuli the machine has received and (2) the internal state of the machine before it received its first stimulus.

We can now see why the doorbell can only respond with a single behavior when its button is pressed. The doorbell is sensitive to just *one* stimulus: the pressing of its button. And its internal state never changes. True, you change its internal state when you press its button, but only for as long as you hold down the button. You don't make a *lasting* change to the internal state of the doorbell that would make a difference to what behavior the doorbell produced the *next* time its button was pressed.

If humans are machines, then our behavior at a particular time depends on (i) the multiple influences that our environments have on our eyes and ears (and other sense organs) at that time and (ii) the internal state of our brains at that time (since human behavior depends in the first instance on what happens in our brains). And the internal state of our brains at a particular time depends on (1) the history of environmental influences on our brains up to that time, interacting with (2) the gene-guided development of our brains from before birth up to that time. One consequence is that even if humans are machines, no two people's brains are exactly the same in both these respects, so we shouldn't expect that two people will always, or even often, react in exactly the same way to the same stimulus. Another consequence is that even if humans are machines, we shouldn't expect to be able to *predict* a human's behavior in detail. To do so, we would need to know the exact state of every neuron in his or her brain, plus how the brain will be affected by every feature of his or her current environment. Obviously we have no way of knowing such things.

Feature #2. Let's now turn to the assumption that a machine couldn't react with the same behavior to two different stimuli—for example, to good news communicated in speech and the same good news communicated in writing. Again, many machines are not like that. One example is an Android phone on which the Google search function can be controlled either by speaking words or by typing them; Google will perform the same search whether the instruction takes the form of sounds or of screen touches. (It doesn't matter whether the phone *understands* the spoken or typed words. The point is that the phone can respond to dramatically different stimuli with the same appropriate behavior.) Consider also the capacity of a dog to learn that its owner has come home by hearing a key in the front door or by seeing the owner walk toward the house or perhaps by catching the owner's scent from a distance; these are three very different stimuli eliciting the same behavior. If you think that dogs are purely physical (like goldfish), then dogs are also examples of machines that can react with the same behavior to very different stimuli.

What about Our Minds?

We have minds. That is, we *believe* that boarding starts in ten minutes, we *hope* that we have packed the right clothes, we *fear* that the pipes might leak while we are away, we *want* to have a safe flight, we *expect* that the flight will be uneventful. These mental states are called by philosophers *propositional attitudes*, because they consist of an *attitude* (e.g., belief, hope, fear, wanting, expectation) toward a *proposition* (e.g., that boarding starts in ten minutes, that we have packed the right clothes, or that the flight will be uneventful). But there is more to having a mind than propositional attitudes. We also dream and hallucinate; we have yellow afterimages after looking at a bright light; we feel pain, nausea, tingling, dizziness; we smell the smell of gasoline, taste the taste of mustard, see the redness of ketchup, feel the smoothness of glass. These mental states are called by philosophers *sensations*, because they seem to be episodes of sensing or feeling. And, of course, we also *reason*, that is, go through thought processes. We can think to ourselves that no one at all is in the classroom at 11:05 a.m., that the professor said something at the start of semester about canceling a class, and that therefore class is probably canceled today. In this example, we are reasoning to a *factual* conclusion, about what *is* the case. We can also think to ourselves that the needle of the gas gauge is in the red zone, and that therefore we should buy some gas at the next exit. In this example, we are reasoning to a *normative* conclusion, about what *should* be the case.

Now if materialism is true, human minds and human mental states must be purely physical. How could that possibly be? I will try to explain, starting with *mental states*, and then turning to *minds*.

Let me start with *believing*, by which philosophers just mean *thinking that something is the case* (e.g., thinking that it's sunny). Our behavior (e.g., going to the store) can be explained in part by what we believe to be the case about our environments (e.g., that we're out of milk). So it's natural to think of *believing* something as having inside one's head "a map . . . by which we steer."[2] Think of how having a map of the campus helps you get around the campus. Beliefs are *map-like* in the sense that they represent the world (our bodies as well as our environments) as being a certain way, whether accurately or inaccurately. And we *steer* by beliefs because they play a part in guiding our behavior. But it looks like a purely physical state of the brain—the activation of a particular neural circuit, say—could play these two roles. A brain state could count as representing a certain state of affairs because, under the right conditions, it is caused by that state of affairs. And obviously, brain states guide our behavior, by sending electrical signals along motor neurons to the right muscles at the right times.

Desiring can be viewed as a different kind of map by which we steer. The difference is that desires represent not a currently actual state of affairs but the state of affairs *desired*. For example, your desire for a soda represents your having a soda. And a desire guides behavior by having the job of helping to bring about the state of affairs represented. For example, your desire for a soda has the job of helping to bring it about that you have a soda.

Sensations, too, can be thought of as a kind of mental representation. A perceptual sensation (e.g., a visual sensation of red) can be regarded as a representation of our immediate environment—of things *outside* our bodies *right now* (e.g., a red object). A bodily sensation (e.g., a pain in the left foot) can be regarded as a representation of things *inside* our bodies right now (e.g., potential or actual tissue damage in the left foot).

Finally, *thought processes* can be thought of as *computations*—or at least as analogous to computations. What computers do is to take a string of complex symbols as input, perform operations on the symbols in accordance with a set of rules (a program), and then emit a different string of complex symbols as output. We're used to thinking of the symbols as 1's and 0's printed on a tape, or as magnetized and non-magnetized particles in a hard drive; but the symbols could equally well be different levels of electrical activity in neural circuits, and they will be if thought processes are computations.

Now for minds. The commonest materialist view of minds is that, strictly speaking, there are no such things—whether physical *or* nonphysical! The idea is that we talk in everyday life about the human mind, and there's nothing wrong with that, but when we do, we're just talking about the *mental capacities* that we have—capacities to believe, to hope, to feel pain, and so on—rather than about an object. Aristotle, in his *De Anima*, was the first to suggest such a view: he recommended replacing talk of humans "having a soul" with talk of our "being ensouled," thus avoiding commitment to souls as objects. Two analogies may make the view more plausible. We may talk about Ruth's *personality*, but no one thinks that Ruth's personality is an *object* inside her, not even an *immaterial* object. We all understand that talk about Ruth's personality is just talk about her *personality traits*—traits like being friendly or cheerful or reserved or difficult. We may also talk about Ruth's *gait*, but we all know that a surgeon shouldn't expect to find Ruth's gait by opening up her body and looking inside. We know we're just talking about how Ruth walks—about the features that her walking has. Likewise for our talk of Ruth's mind: her mind is not an object inside her.

That's the commonest materialist view of minds. But I prefer a different view. On my view, people's minds are just as real as their circulations, or digestions, or immune systems. Indeed, we could call minds "*mental systems*," on the model of "circulatory systems," "digestive systems," "immune systems," and so on. And, just as your digestive system, say, is made up of an interconnected series of organs—your stomach, liver, small intestine, and so forth—so also your mental system is (mainly) made up of your *brain*, itself an immensely complex network of subnetworks of brain cells constantly getting signals from our sense organs and sending signals to the body's muscles and to one another.

The digestive system has the function of converting food into usable energy and ingredients for bodily growth, and the immune system has the function of destroying harmful microbes. So what is the function of the mental system? The defining function of the human mental system, I suggest, has five components:

1. *To use sensors to form descriptive representations of both the current external environment and the current internal states of the containing organism.*

Examples of *sensors* would be the familiar five senses. *Descriptive representations* represent something as in fact being a certain way, that is, as actually having a certain property. An example of a descriptive representation of the organism's current *external environment* would be a sensation representing—a sensation *of*—a red, round thing in front of you, or a belief that a tomato is in front of you. An example of a descriptive representation of the organism's current *internal states* would be an itch (which represents histamine in a part of your body) or a hunger pang (which represents that your stomach is contracting).

2. *To undergo internal processes in which these sensory descriptive representations give rise to further descriptive representations of the organism's external environment and its internal states.*

Examples of *internal processes* would be the rule-governed manipulation of descriptive representations to accomplish deductive or inductive reasoning. The *further descriptive representations* would be the conclusions of such reasoning, for example, the belief that all tomatoes are red, or the belief that if a tomato is red, then something is red, or the belief that I need food.

3. *To store some of these descriptive representations for later use.*

The *storage* of representations would be something like *memory*.

4. *To undergo internal processes in which these descriptive representations interact with one another and with representations of goal-states so as to produce organismic behavior, which behavior, often enough, achieves the organism's goals.*

Examples of *internal processes* in this case would be the rule-governed manipulation of representations to accomplish *practical* reasoning, the kind of reasoning that supports a conclusion about what *ought* to be done. Examples of *representations of goal-states* would be desires; a desire for lunch, for example, would be a representation of your goal: having lunch. The representations manipulated in practical reasoning include both descriptive representations *and* representations of goal-states, reflecting the fact that, for example, we decide to walk to the freezer because we both *desire* ice cream and *believe* that there is ice cream in the freezer. The desire *alone* wouldn't make us decide to walk to the freezer; we might, instead, decide to drive to the store. And the belief *alone* wouldn't make us decide to walk to the freezer; we might be so full of pizza that we have no desire for ice cream.

5. *To monitor the sensing and internal processing we engage in, and the descriptive representations and goal-state representations that we form, so as to form descriptive representations of these activities and states.*

The idea here is that part of the defining function of a human mental system is to keep tabs on itself—on its own activities and states. Examples of "descriptive representations of these activities and states" would therefore be beliefs *about* one's own sensations and beliefs and desires and thought processes.

The five subfunctions I have just distinguished can be thought of as working together to achieve a single overarching goal: that of gathering information about our world as it changes on timescales both short and long, and then using that information to generate behavior that succeeds in getting us what we want, whatever our world is like.

Evidence That the Mind Is Material

I promised some positive evidence that our minds are purely physical. One kind of such evidence is the remarkable way in which mental states of every kind are *dependent* on purely physical states of the brain, namely, patterns of electrical activity in particular neural circuits. I don't just mean the obvious point that, if our brains stopped working, our minds would stop working too. After all, if our *hearts* stopped working, our minds would stop working too, but that's no evidence that mental states are nothing over and above *cardiac* states! I mean, instead, that, as far as we know, being in a particular mental state (whatever the mental state) requires—never occurs without—being in a particular brain state. We have learned this from a huge number of imaging studies. In such studies, the brains of experimental subjects are monitored with an imaging device (e.g., an fMRI machine) while the subjects are in certain mental states; the subjects are typically asked to perform a particular mental task, such as mentally rehearsing a learned motor skill, doing mental arithmetic, attending to an unstimulated body part, and visualizing a scene. What is found in these imaging studies is that, whenever someone is in a particular mental state, there is always a particular brain state that the person is in at the same time. This sort of highly detailed dependence of mental states on neural states is exactly what we would expect to find if the mind is purely physical.

But it's *not* what we would expect to find if the most intuitively appealing non-materialist view—*interactionist substance dualism*—were true. It'll take a while to explain why. First, what is interactionist substance dualism? It's the view that your mental states are states of an *immaterial* entity—your mind—assumed to be distinct from your brain. So, for instance, when you're recalling childhood memories of your sister, that's because your immaterial mind is in a certain immaterial state; but if you start recalling childhood memories of your brother instead, that's because your immaterial mind has shifted into a different immaterial state. On this view, however, your mind still interacts causally with your brain, rather as an airline pilot causally interacts with the cockpit's instruments and controls, though distinct from them. So, for instance, when you notice an orange, the orange causes a change in the state of your visual cortex, which then causes a change in the state of your immaterial mind, and you have an experience of orange. Similarly, but in the opposite direction, when you decide to grasp a cup, that change in the state of your immaterial mind causes a change in the state of your motor cortex, which in turn causes muscles in your arm to contract.

Here's what's crucial: on this dualist view, our brains serve *merely* to pass signals between our bodies and our immaterial minds. When we feel the heat of a fire, our brains relay signals *to* our immaterial minds *from* sensory neurons originating in our fingers. When we decide to step back from the fire, our brains relay signals *from* our immaterial minds *to* the motor neurons that run to muscles in our legs. According to this dualist view, then, our brains *merely* play these mediating roles: in perception and in deciding to act. Our brains aren't where the *thinking* happens; our *immaterial minds* are. So, if you're daydreaming, and you stop recalling childhood memories of your sister, and start recalling childhood memories of your brother instead, there's every reason on this dualist view to expect a simultaneous change in the state of your *immaterial mind*, but no particular reason to expect any simultaneous change in the state of your *brain*—because daydreaming is neither perceiving nor deciding to act. The same goes for mentally rehearsing a learned motor skill, or doing mental arithmetic, or attending to an unstimulated body part, or visualizing a scene. Interactionist substance dualism doesn't predict that these mental activities will be accompanied by a distinctive kind of brain activity.

Interactionist substance dualism isn't the only kind of dualism. There is another kind—*property dualism*—and it *does* lead us to expect that mental states depend on neural states in the detailed ways we observe. Property dualism doesn't say that our mental states are states of an immaterial entity distinct from the brain; it says that mental states are states of the brain itself, but *immaterial* states of the brain—in other words, that the brain has certain *immaterial* properties in addition to its physical properties, these immaterial properties being our mental properties. Property dualism also says that the brain's immaterial mental properties march in lockstep with its physical properties; it posits laws of nature that bind each of the brain's immaterial mental properties to one of its neural properties in such a way that you can be in a particular immaterial mental state if, but only if, you're in a certain neural state; for example, you can feel cheerful if, but only if, a certain neural circuit in your brain is active. Because it posits laws of this kind, property dualism leads us to expect that mental states depend on neural states in the detailed ways we observe.

So property dualism (unlike interactionist substance dualism) at least predicts the detailed ways in which mental states depend on neural states. But it's still *less plausible* than materialism in light of this dependence, because it can't explain the dependence as *economically* as materialism can—and the more economical of two theories that can explain the same facts is preferable. Property dualism can't explain the dependence as economically as materialism because property dualism must say that (1) immaterial properties of brains exist *in addition to* the physical properties of brains that everyone agrees exist, and that (2) laws of nature hold (binding the brain's immaterial to its physical properties) *in addition to* the laws of nature that everyone agrees hold.

There is other evidence that our minds are purely physical, which I can't go into here, but it also takes the form of facts that can be explained more economically by materialism than by any kind of dualism.

Notes

1 Even more confusingly, the term "materialism" is sometimes used in philosophy for the broader view that absolutely everything in the world, not just every human being, is purely physical. Some philosophers think that human beings are purely physical, but also that God exists, and isn't purely physical. These philosophers accept materialism in the sense of this essay, but reject it in the broader sense.

2 As the philosopher and mathematician Frank Ramsey put it in his 1929 paper, "General Propositions and Causality," reprinted in *F. P. Ramsey: Philosophical Papers*, ed. D. H. Mellor (New York: Cambridge University Press, 1990).

The Mind Is Immaterial

Charles Taliaferro

Study Questions

1. What is the precise thesis that Taliaferro defends?
2. What are the different characterizations of the physical that Taliaferro discusses? Why, in each case, does he think that we know the mental better than the physical?
3. What evidence does Taliaferro offer for mental causation?
4. Who and what are we, according to Taliaferro? Why does he think this?

5. What are the reasons that philosophers have given for thinking that self-reference is an illusion? How does Taliaferro respond to these arguments?

6. Why does Dennett think that there really is no first-person self-awareness? What problems does Taliaferro find with his view?

7. What is the principle of the "indiscernibility of identicals"? How is it relevant to the question of whether or not the mind is material?

8. What is the Knowledge Argument? What is its key claim?

9. How does Taliaferro respond to the objection that all the Knowledge Argument shows is that the concept of the mind is distinct from the concept of the body?

10. What three further objections does Taliaferro consider? How does he respond to them?

The title of this chapter is appropriately negative, namely that the mind is *not* material. I shall be advancing a positive position, namely that you and I are persons with experiences, intentions, desires, memories, beliefs, sensations, and more. Indeed, I shall maintain we are *embodied agents* not floating, ghostly immaterial stuff. But I shall also be advancing a negative position: that we ourselves with all our experiences, intentions, and so on, are not (strictly speaking) identical with our material or physical bodies or some part of our bodies such as our brains. Even more negatively, I propose that we currently lack a clear, problem-free understanding of what philosophers today think of as a mind-independent realm of material or physical things or events. We have, instead, a clearer understanding of mind or the mental. So, while I defend the view that you and I function as an embodied unity of person and body, I also hope to convince you that we are not the very same thing as our brains or physical bodies. Moreover, I contend that none of the findings in neuroscience gives us reason to believe the mind is material.

A minor point of terminology: I will use the term "mind" to stand for what may variously be referred to as the person, self, or subject (namely, you and me), and the term "mental" to refer to our psychological or subjective states or properties such as thinking, experiencing, sensing, desiring, intending, and so on.

What Is Material or Physical?

I shall treat the terms "material" and "physical" as synonymous, thus putting to one side the question of whether "material" only refers to "matter" (as distinct from energy).

An initial suggestion about what counts as physical is to give examples: our brains and central state nervous systems, apples, mountains, atomic and subatomic particles, water, the sun. From a common sense perspective, this seems proper, though philosophers (and some scientists) have raised questions about whether all the properties that we attribute to such objects are fully properties of the objects or, rather (in some cases), are mental properties in the minds of perceivers. Consider an apple: Isn't its taste, color, smell or the sound it makes when you bite into it, more a matter of what persons taste, see, smell or hear? Philosophers have sometimes thought of these as *secondary properties* which refer to how material objects stimulate sensations in a person and not to mind-independent phenomena. Primary physical properties might be limited to size and magnitude (and perhaps weight), but we should note that while such properties are good candidates for being mind-independent, we only know of such properties by way of our mental properties: we see, feel, observe and think about size and magnitude. I suggest that we only know of that which is mind-independent by using our minds, and we have a clearer grasp of our minds and the mental than we do of that which is independent of mind. To bring out the difficulty of maintaining the opposite view (that we have a clearer understanding of mind-independent physical things than the mental), consider the following, often-cited characterization of materialism by Daniel Dennett:

> The prevailing wisdom, variously expressed and argued for, is materialism: there is only one sort of stuff, namely matter—the physical stuff of physics, chemistry, and physiology—and the mind is nothing but a physical phenomenon. In short, the mind is the brain. According to the materialists, we can (in principle!) account for every mental phenomenon using the same physical principles, laws, and raw materials that suffice to explain radioactivity, continental drift, photosynthesis, reproduction, nutrition, and growth.[1]

Note that Dennett's appeal to the natural sciences does not include the social sciences such as psychology, and his examples of "physical principles, laws, and raw materials" presumably contain no references to ideas, concepts, reasons, desires, intentions, plans, and so on. Continents do not drift out of desires or intentions! There are no evident minds or mental phenomena involved in accounting for radioactivity, nutrition, and so on. Is there a problem with advancing this materialist claim, implying that we can explain *everything* without appealing to factors other than the ones we employ in accounting for radioactivity and so on?

I propose that Dennett's depiction of materialism makes no sense whatever *unless we have a more confident grasp of the mind and the mental than we have of any of the material phenomenon he references*. That is because we cannot even understand Dennett's claims unless we have the *ideas* and *concepts* involved in physics, the *idea* of the brain, the *concept* of physical principles and laws, the *idea* of radioactivity, and so on. The claim that "the mind is the brain" would not be understandable unless *we had the ideas involved, and a grasp of entailment relations* (his claim only makes sense if we can reason that *if the mind is the brain*, then it follows that *the brain is the mind*). We cannot have a clearer grasp of continental drift than we have of *the idea of continental drift*, *the concept* of causation, an *understanding* of what is an explanation, and an *understanding* of how one explanation relates to the *understanding* of another explanation. What we refer to as "explanations" (which involve an understanding of causal and noncausal relations) is intrinsically mental as opposed to referring to some mind-independent pheonomena. All this is not to provide good reasons for thinking Dennett must be mistaken, but it is to make the point that his very presentation of "prevailing wisdom" is saturated with what is intrinsically mental (presumably wisdom itself involves the mind). We have, I submit, a clearer understanding of what may be called *mental causation* (my *belief* that photosynthesis involves transferring light energy into chemical energy *causes me to think* it is false to deny the truth of that belief), than we do of mind-independent causal relations.

The difficulty of claiming that we have a clearer understanding of mind-independent physical reality than the mental (or mental causation) emerges in another, closely related account of what counts as physical. Consider this commonplace depiction of what is physical implied in Dennett's account: *something is physical if it is (or can be) described and explained in an ideal form of the natural sciences*. Apart from noting that this depiction or analysis is committed to a controversial prediction (can we guarantee that the natural sciences will never posit that which is nonphysical, mathematical propositions, or God, for example?), it also rests on our having a clear *understanding* of the natural sciences and coming to terms with the fact that *it is impossible to have science without scientists*. We can form no idea of science without being able to grasp *the idea that there are persons who are scientists who think, reason, advance theories, make observations, predictions, offer explanations and descriptions*, and so on. *All these involve intrinsically mental phenomena.* The definition does not offer us a clear understanding of mind-independent things; rather, it presupposes a clear understanding of the mental. Again, we cannot claim to have a clearer grasp of physics or the findings of physics than we have of *the concept of physics and all the ideas, reasons, theories, observations involved in physics*.

Consider one more characterization of what is physical: *X is physical if and only if it occurs in space and time*. This also presupposes the mental, our grasping *the idea of space* and *the idea of time,* and so does not offer a clear, mental or mind-independent notion of what is physical. We are still left with a situation in which the mental is more apparent or evident than that which is independent of the mental. Moreover, this spatio-temporal characterization of the physical is also controversial insofar as many philosophers have and do claim that sensations are not physical and yet are spatial. For example, dream images, the color sensations we have in our visual field, and so on, have spatial extension (shape and size) but are not the same as physical things or processes.[2] We will consider reasons for thinking this is true later.

At this stage, I have not yet argued that the mind is immaterial. All that has been advanced is that we have a clearer grasp of what is customarily considered the mental than we have of any mind-independent physical realities, though I have proposed that the evident existence of scientists who reason and draw conclusions based on observations and entailments is evidence of mental causation (whether it turns out that such mental causation is wholly physical or it involves that which is nonphysical). We may not need to appeal to what scientists do, however, in order to reach the conclusion of this section: if it is evident to you that you are reading this chapter and the claims I am making are causing you to think about them, then you have evidence of mental causation: something mental (claims about materialism) are causing something mental (imagine they cause you to raise questions) no matter how this is filled out in a fuller account of brain processes, visual stimulation, writing, and reading.[3]

So, Who and What Are You?

If you are reading this, it is a fair inference that you are a thinking, feeling, sensing, experiencing subject who endures over time as a person. You have to endure over time and to realize this in order to read a single sentence. In the language used in the philosophy of mind, you have your own experiences of the world, and this involves *a first-person point of view*. Mature, self-aware beings are aware of themselves in virtually all reflective experiences: if I am feeling cold right now (writing this in Minnesota in the winter) *I am aware of myself feeling a certain way*. I do not (as it were) experience *coldness* and then conclude it is me who is experiencing the coldness (e.g., by seeing someone who looks like me in a mirror shivering in the snow). These observations may seem too obvious to be worth noting, but unfortunately they require some defense today. I will strengthen the earlier observations about who and what we are by considering two objections.

Objection One: Self-Reference

According to the first objection, when you or I use the first-person indexical "I," this is not a matter of referring to a person or self. Descartes famously claimed, "I think, therefore I am." This was foundational in his case against skepticism. If he is thinking, he must exist. Doubting involves thinking, and it would be incoherent to acknowledge that he is doubting and at the same time to deny his existence. There is a great deal of scholarship on how to interpret Descartes, and I have contributed to this elsewhere.[4] For now, I simply note the apparent sensibility of Descartes's position. Doubting, thinking, worrying, reading, and so on, all seem to make sense only if there is some person (individual or self or mind) that is doing the doubting, thinking, and so on. that we customarily see as activities of persons. Nonetheless, this common sense approach has been challenged.

Peter Geach claims that the "I" is redundant. "I am very puzzled at this problem" says no more than "This problem is puzzling."[5] Bertrand Russell claims that, instead of "I think," Descartes should have stopped with "There is thinking."[6] John Campbell (following Elizabeth Anscombe and David Hume) asks, "How do you know which person that use of 'I' refers to? In introspection, as Hume put it, 'I always stumble on some particular perception or other, of heat or cold, light or shade, love or hatred, pain or pleasure. I never can observe any thing but the perception.'"[7]

None of the above should dissuade us from believing that things are as they seem: when I claim, "I will die some day," I am saying something about me.[8] To render such a claim in a way that avoids the first-person is to lose the meaning involved. Let me return to this point after commenting on Geach, et al.

Contra Geach, claiming "I am very puzzled at this problem" says more than "This problem is puzzling." This is because a problem may be puzzling (it should cause perplexity), but I feel no perplexity at all. On the proposal by Russell, it is profoundly implausible to suppose (let alone imagine) that there can be thinking without a thinker. It might be claimed that this is a linguistic matter and not a matter of reality, but this is a case when linguistic necessity reflects a necessary feature of reality—for example, it is not just a linguistic fact *that there cannot be more red balls than there are balls*; such a claim is a matter of necessity. Moreover, *thinking* is by its very nature an activity carried out by some *thing* or *subject*. I know of no thought experiment in which we can successfully imagine that there is thinking but no thinker (e.g., in the room, there was the activity of thinking *that the murderer was the butler*, but the thinking was not the thinking of any thinker).

As for John Campbell's invocation of Hume and Anscombe, it seems (in ordinary experience) that we observe ourselves in virtually all our perceptions and observations. How can you feel heat, without you feeling that you yourself are warm or hot? To take Hume's other examples, when you feel cold, see light or shade, are loving or hating, in pain or pleasure, it certainly appears that *you yourself are feeling cold*, *you* are seeing light or shade, *you* love, *you* hate, and so on. Think of you reporting, "I do not think I feel pain, but *it* . . ." you say, pointing to your body, "is having a painful headache." This way of thinking and acting would be highly eccentric.

Campbell seems to think that *it should puzzle us* if we try to establish whether a person's use of "I" refers to the person using the term. He writes:

> Consider now your own use of the first person. Suppose, for example, that you say, "I am tired and sleepy." How do you know that this is true? If we employ the model of a perceptual demonstrative, we should say that the first thing you have to establish is which person is being talked about. How do you know which person that use of "I" refers to? On the model of the perceptual demonstrative, perception, or something like it, should provide you with your knowledge of which thing is in question . . . . Remarks like, "I am tired and sleepy," self-ascriptions of psychological states, are typically not made on the basis of observation of oneself. It can happen that you catch sight of your exhausted face in a mirror and say, "I am tired and sleepy," but that is a somewhat unusual case. Ordinarily, you do not need to observe yourself at all to know that you are tired and sleepy. So it does not seem that your knowledge of which person you are talking about is provided by, for example, visual observation of yourself.[9]

In response, I counter-claim that there is almost no clearer experience of self-reference than the use of "I" in "I am tired and sleepy." Campbell is using the term "observation" in a peculiar third-person fashion, rather than allowing that a person's self-awareness counts as an observation. Campbell seems to think that your observing yourself would involve inferences as when you observe an image of yourself in a mirror and then draw a conclusion about your state of mind. But I propose *you cannot observe an image of yourself without observing (or being self aware) of you making that observation*. When Campbell writes: "If we employ the model of a perceptual demonstrative, we should say that the first thing you have to establish is which person is being talked about," I suggest he misidentifies what comes first. "I" is not like "it" or "that" as used of external objects. "I" is more foundational than such perceptual demonstratives, and we would not know how to begin to interpret the use of "it" or "that" without prior, more foundational self-awareness. My saying "I think that person"—pointing—"looks sleepy and tired" only makes sense if the use of "that" means that thing (or person) I (a person or subject) am drawing your attention to. The stubborn, evident referential use of "I" or "you" comes to the fore in Campbell's setting up of his example, as when he writes about "how do *you* know" and "the first thing *you* have to establish" (emphasis mine). Unless you have a grasp of yourself (in self-awareness), how would you even know whether Campbell is addressing you or someone else?

So far, then, I hope to have convinced you that you have mental states and an awareness of you, yourself as a person who thinks, feels, and so on.

Objection Two: First-Person Self-Awareness

According to the second objection, we do not have a robust first-person awareness of ourselves; our so-called first-person point of view is only reasonable if supported by a third-person, scientific point of view. The objection comes from Daniel Dennett. In the following passage, Dennett proposes that his third-person methodology can accommodate the first-person point of view. Dennett characterizes the natural sciences as essentially taking up a third-person point of view:

> The third-person methodology, dubbed heterophenomenology (phenomenology of another not oneself), is, I have claimed, the sound way to take the first-person point of view as seriously as it can be taken . . . . Most of the method is so obvious and inconsequential that some scientists are baffled that I would even call it a method: basically you have to take the vocal sounds emanating from the subjects' mouths (and your own mouth) and interpret them! Well of course. What else could you do? Those sounds aren't just belches and moans: they're speech acts, reporting, questioning, correcting requiring, and so forth. Using such standard speech acts, other events such as button-presses can be set up to be interpreted as speech acts as well, and highly specific meanings and fine-tuned resolutions.[10]

This passage reveals multiple problems. First, one can have no conception of a third-person point of view without having a more fundamental first-person point of view. A third-person point of view involves more than one person having a view, or more than one person being able to view or observe the same thing. But *there cannot be more than one person having a point of view unless each person has a point of view, and this involves first-person awareness.* The problem with proposing that you and I can take self-awareness seriously only by studying noises that people make and making inferences is that you and I would not know how even to record, let alone hear, noises unless you and I each have first-person self-awareness. I can't know that Jones is uttering sentences rather than belching unless I am aware of myself hearing and interpreting what Jones is (or might be) doing. The data that needs to be explained is the first-person awareness that is essential for there to be any science or any observations in which you knowingly record what you see, hear, and observe. Dennett mistakenly thinks you do not get to have access to the authority of first-person awareness unless this is earned through the third-person study, but such a study cannot be conducted without presupposing that each of the parties has first-person points of view.

So far, I hope to have convinced you that we have a clearer grasp of ourselves and the mental than we have of mind-independent physical things and processes, and that we have good reason to think that we are self-aware persons who have experiences, act, feel, think, and so on. I now turn to the further matter of considering whether we are the very same thing as our bodies or a part of our body (such as the brain), or whether we might be not material, yet materially embodied.

The Mind Is Immaterial

When considering whether what appear to be different things truly are different or not, we consider whether what we know or observe about the one is the same as what we know or observe about the other. So, for example, at one time it was thought that *The Evening Star* is different from *The Morning Star*. But then we realized that they were actually the same thing, the planet Venus. We learned this once we came to see that what we know about each so-called star was actually true of a single planet. Conversely, we come to believe that we have two different things or processes when we realize that what we know of one thing differs from what we know of another. So we have some reason to distinguish the sensation of heat from mean kinetic energy when we are (or seem to be) in a position to know all about mean kinetic energy without feeling heat. This is an instance of what philosophers call the *indiscernibility of identicals*: if A is B, then whatever is true of A, is true of B. If the mind is the brain, then whatever is true of the mind is true of the brain.

In this section, we will consider one major argument supporting the position that the mental is immaterial and then consider some objections.

A Knowledge Argument

If you are the same thing as your body, then to know your body and bodily states would be to know your thoughts, emotions, intentions, desires, and so on. But it is possible for me or any number of scientists to know all about your body without knowing these mental states. Therefore, your mental life is not identical to your body or bodily states. It is, of course, possible for us to draw reasonable inferences about your mental states based on observing your physical states, but (according to the knowledge argument) this is because we draw inferences from the correlation between physical states and reports about our subjective experiences. Such inferences, however, underscore a key claim of the knowledge argument: examining the brain and nervous system involves examining what may be the cause of acute pain (for example), but it is not to directly observe the subjective experience of painfulness.

Knowledge arguments like this have a long history, going back at least to Goethe, but in recent times it is principally associated with T. L. S. Sprigge, Thomas Nagel, and Frank Jackson. Here is Sprigge's succinct development of the position:

> The main reason for holding [that there is a distinction between the mental and the physical] is that it seems entirely possible that a scientist should have complete knowledge of a human organism as a physical system and yet be ignorant of the special character of that individual's consciousness.[11]

Sprigge presses his point further in terms of our experience of other persons:

> For that matter, there is nothing physical about another person, which absolutely proves that he is conscious. His consciousness is not something which could be located in his brain for everything about the brain could be as it is without the individual being conscious.[12]

To fill out this version of the knowledge argument, consider an example that Paul Churchland deploys in *Matter and Consciousness*.[13] He asks us to imagine a neuroscientist who has mapped out an exacting account of the brain, but has not observed any mental phenomena such as thinking. Churchland introduces the example to prompt us to be skeptical about the phenomena of thinking, but surely the last thing a neuroscientist should doubt is the phenomena of thinking. For her to doubt there is thinking would be to doubt that there is neuroscience and to doubt her own ideas and concepts of the brain and her work. I suggest that cases like Churchland's can be turned on their head: if you remain convinced that thinking is real, and you are convinced that you cannot find any place for thinking in your purely physical account of the brain, then you have reason to believe that thinking is not identical with your brain as a physical reality.

However, consider the following *objection*: maybe knowledge arguments only establish that *our concept of the person* (mind or the mental) is distinct from *our concept of the body*. And yet the person and the body are still one and the same thing known in two different ways, just as the planet Venus was experienced or known from two different points of view. I may think the Evening Star is different from the Morning Star, and indeed *the concept of the evening star* is different from *the concept of the morning star*, and yet both concepts pick out the same thing.

Reply: How things appear is the very essence of what is mental. When we refer to thinking, feeling, experiencing, or being myself, these terms refer to modes of awareness; when I am thinking about an idea, the thinking and the idea are themselves apparent to me in the process of thinking about an idea. If knowing the physical properties of the brain is not knowing the modes of subjective experiences, then that is a reason (according to the indiscernibility of identicals) to conclude that the brain is not identical with the mental. The example of the Evening Star and the Morning Star actually does involve nonidentical properties: *seeing a luminous object in the morning* is distinct from *seeing a luminous object in the evening*. But there is nothing about this distinction that entails that the same object (in this case a physical object) cannot appear to persons from different visual angles. I should not doubt, for instance, that you and I both see the same penny because it looks round from my angle of vision and oval from yours. All we need to do is rotate the penny to see its shape from either angle. But there is no such parallel exercise that would allow us to see that the mental and physical are one and the same thing seen from different angles. Moreover, we can see in the cases of the penny and planet how it is that to know all about the penny and planet from each of the different perspectives is actually to know the same things. But, as Sprigge and others have argued, this is not the case with the mental and physical. To know all about what Churchland, Dennett, and other materialists identify as physical is *not* to know what we know in our own conscious, mental experiences. I can know of myself—the sensations, thinking, feeling, intending, and so on—in my first-person self-awareness, but this is not available from third-person, scientific accounts of my brain and anatomy.

Other Arguments

There are other arguments for believing that the mental is not material. Elsewhere I have argued that there are truths about persons that are not true about their (our) bodies. I have defended the view that it is reasonable to believe that persons can exist without their bodies, or switch bodies, while these possible states of affairs are not possible with physical bodies. Indeed, as some philosophers argue, the difference between person and body may be evident in the fact that while persons endure over time, physical bodies do not; my present body is not identical to the body I had when I was in Kindergarten, but I am the self-same person who went to Kindergarten.[14] Due to lack of space, in this chapter I will stick with the knowledge argument and refer you to other sources to further back up my claim.[15]

Three Further Objections

Consider in closing three objections.

> *Objection I*: This chapter has not made a case for the non-identity of the mind or the mental and physical by engaging in neuroscience. Don't the brain sciences strongly support the idea that whatever is mental must be physical?
>
> *Reply*: I suggest that no findings of the brain sciences establish the identity of a single mental experience with anything physical. What we discover in the brain sciences is the *correlation and causal interaction between the mental and physical, but this is not the same thing as identity*. It is agreed by everyone that brain damage impairs consciousness, and (most would agree) that your intentions (for example, your intention to read this chapter) impacts your bodily movements (your reading) and all the physical circuitry involved in seeing, thinking, and so on. In keeping with the knowledge argument, it might be added that the only way we can link brain and other bodily activity with experiences is by inference. To exhaustively analyze your brain as only a physical thing (as envisaged by materialists such as Dennett, Churchland, and others) is not the same as analyzing a person's consciousness.[16]
>
> *Objection II*: But what is the mental (or the person) made out of? In exploring the physical world, we can form highly sophisticated models involving particles and subatomic particles. Compared to what we categorize as physical, the mental seems utterly mysterious.
>
> *Reply*: The mystery is the other way around. If what I argued in the first section is correct, we cannot have any idea of what is physical unless we can grasp ideas (concepts, models, categories, etc.). There is nothing mysterious in the sense of being suspect (as in superstitions) about the existence and nature of the mental (we could not do science unless thinking, reasoning, observing are deemed evident, reliable mental operations). What inspires us is how to identify and account for the interaction of the mental and the physical; the "mystery to be solved" is not how to dissolve the mental (explaining away a superstition) but to robustly understand the mental in causal interaction with the brain, body, and so on.

Objection III: The view that the mental is immaterial is at odds with a secular view of the world. If there is a God, perhaps a distinction or dualism between the mental and physical might make sense. But if we leave God out of the equation, isn't the simpler theory the materialist one—that everything in the cosmos is made up of the same stuff, namely matter and energy?

Reply: We should not confuse simplicity with philosophical adequacy. If there was more space, I could provide independent reasons for thinking that there is more to the cosmos than matter and energy (logical truths and propositions exist, in fact necessarily exist, but are not identical with matter or energy). For now, I propose that the form of dualism defended here (insofar as I have argued that the mental is not identical to, and is thus more than, what is material or physical) is neutral with respect to theism or atheism. Perhaps the cosmos itself has a disposition to bring about conscious, mental beings that emerge from and are distinct from the material world. But if readers are interested, I have argued elsewhere that evident facts about our conscious lives (along with other facts) do make theism more reasonable than its secular alternatives.[17]

Notes

1 Daniel Dennett, *Consciousness Explained* (Cambridge, MA: MIT Press, 2001), 33.
2 See chapter one of my *Consciousness and the Mind of God* (Cambridge: Cambridge University Press, 1994).
3 My proposal in this chapter goes beyond Bertrand Russell in his book, *The Analysis of Matter*. Russell writes: "As regards the world in general, both physical and mental, everything we know of its intrinsic character is derived from the mental side, and almost everything we know of its causal laws is derived from the physical side" ([London: Kegan Paul, 1927], 402). I suggest all we know of both the intrinsic character of the world and our knowledge of causal laws is from the mental side.
4 Charles Taliaferro, *Evidence and Faith* (Cambridge: Cambridge University Press, 2005).
5 Peter Geach, *Mental Acts* (London: Routlege and Kegan Paul, 1957), 120.
6 Bertrand Russell, *A History of Western Philosophy* (New York: Simon & Schuster, 1945), 567.
7 John Campbell, "The Self," *The Routledge Companion to Metaphysics*, eds. Robin LePoidevin, et al. (London: Routledge, 2009), 576.

8 On this point, I am following Lynne Baker in her *Naturalism and the First-Person Perspective.*
9 Campbell, "The Self," 576.
10 Daniel Dennett, "Who's On First?" in *Trusting the Subject?* eds. A. Jack and A. Roepstorff (Exeter: Academic Impact, 2003), 19.
11 Sprigge, *The Importance of Subjectivity* (Oxford: Clarendon Press, 2011), 9.
12 Sprigge, *The Importance of Subjectivity*, 9.
13 Paul Churchland, *Matter and Consciousness* (Cambridge, MA: MIT Press, 1988).
14 See Charles Taliaferro and Jil Evans, *The Image in Mind* (London: Continuum, 2011).
15 See such works as *The Waning of Materialism*, eds. R. Koons and G. Bealer (London: Routledge, 2010) and *Beyond Physicalism*, eds. E. Kelly, A. Crabtree, and P. Marshall (New York: Rowman and Littlefield, 2015).
16 See Richard Swinburne on the work of B. Libet for reasons why his work does not provide evidence against mind-body interaction, *Mind, Brain, and Free Will* (Oxford: Oxford University Press), 2013.
17 See *The Image in Mind*. Some of the material in this chapter was presented as the Dunbar Lecture at Millsaps College, Mississippi (thanks to Kristen Golden), and as a presentation, "Philosophy can help you keep your head, when all about you are losing theirs" as part of the Oxford Brookes Public Philosophy Lecture Series, with support from the Royal Institute of Philosophy (thanks to Daniel O'Brien), both in the Spring of 2017. Thanks also to Steven Cowan, Dempsey Olsen, and Wassim Askool.

RESPONSES

Response to Melnyk

Charles Taliaferro

Study Questions

1. What is the central point of the Knowledge Argument? How, according to Taliaferro, does Melnyk's description of what goes on in an fMRI support this point?

2. How does Melnyk's goldfish example support Taliaferro's Knowledge Argument? What about Nagel's bat?

3. What does Taliaferro think is missing from Melnyk's account of the versatility of machines? What does he think we should conclude if a machine *were* to become conscious?

4. In what way does Melnyk misunderstand substance dualism, according to Taliaferro?

5. How does Taliaferro respond to Melnyk's claim that materialism is the more economical view?

Like Professor Melnyk, I do not think debate over dualism and materialism can be settled by proofs; rather than proofs (as in mathematics and logic), we must, instead, develop, critically evaluate, and compare arguments. I appreciate his identifying interactionist substance dualism (a view I accept) as "the most intuitively appealing nonmaterialist view." In what follows, I indicate why I think the case for substance dualism is stronger than the case for materialism.

The Knowledge Argument Again

I begin by reminding readers that my defense of substance dualism begins with proposing that we may be confident that you and I are subjects, individual persons who endure over time, thinking, reasoning, feeling, sensing, and so on. While we function as united, embodied beings, I developed a knowledge argument that advances (what I believe to be) a good reason to deny that persons and our thinking (and so on) are identical with our brains or our bodies as a whole. *If we were the same thing as our bodies or parts of our bodies, then we would observe or know about persons and their thinking and sensing by observing or knowing their bodies or parts of their bodies.* But we can know all about a person's brain, body, behavior, and so on, without knowing their consciousness. In order to know about a person's consciousness, we must infer from what persons (or we ourselves) experience and report about the correlation of consciousness and bodily life.

I believe that the central point of the knowledge argument is supported in Professor Melnyk's description of what goes on in monitoring someone's brain with an fMRI machine: "Whenever someone is in a particular mental state, there is always a particular brain state that the person is in at the same time" (p. 291). Question: How do you know what mental state a person is in? "The subjects are asked to perform a particular mental task, such as . . . doing mental arithmetic." You find out the correlation of the mental and physical *not by observing that the physical is the very same thing as the mental* (or observing the arithmetic calculations themselves), but by inquiring into what persons are thinking, doing, feeling, and so on, and then *correlating* them with brain states. The knowledge argument is also supportable by looking more closely at Melnyk's goldfish. Why are scientists undecided about whether goldfish feel pain? A plausible reason is that no external, physical description can definitely conclude that goldfish have sensations. Yes, we can observe their nerve cells and we can observe how they respond to being jabbed and prodded (which we may label "pain stimuli") and observe their "pain avoidance" behavior, but this is still not enough to observe that they are consciously feeling pain. The philosopher Thomas Nagel developed such a point in an important essay, "What Is It Like to Be a Bat?" He argued that it is plausible for us to believe that bats do have feelings and sensations, but we cannot know what these are like from observing their anatomy and behavior. That is because there is a difference between these.[1] Richard Swinburne rightly summarizes the point at hand: "However much we know about a bat's brain, we can get from it very little understanding of how (if at all) the bat perceives (i.e. has a sensory picture of and beliefs about) its surrounding."[2]

The Weakness of Materialism

Melnyk seems to think we have a problem-free concept of what it is to be physical by appealing to what "physics talks about." I believe that we cannot have a conception of what physics talks about without having a conception of physicists who talk, experience, observe, have ideas, theories, reason, explain things, and so on, and it is highly controversial to claim that all that is physical. What would the claim that materialism is true mean when it comes to describing and explaining experiences such as those? I have no idea. As Melnyk rightly observes: "The truth of materialism is not obvious" (p.xx). It is because of the nonobvious concept of materialism and what is physical, that I advance dualism as a negative thesis. We do know about ourselves as persons who are subjects who think, experience, and so on. This is not similar to making a conceptual mistake of treating *personality* or *the way a person walks* as a substance or thing. Presumably, someone's personality refers to *the way the person (as an individual, enduring subject) tends to act, express emotions, and so on*, and walking is clearly *a way that an individual, substantial person acts*. These are modes, not substances. I claim that we may know that we are substantial individuals, not modes of (for example) our bodies. Modes cannot think or act or feel or argue or walk, but persons as individuals can think, act, feel, argue, and walk, even at the same time!

Melnyk rightly points out the versatility of machines. There is, however, something unclear in his account: Does he (or do you) believe that the machines he describes actually undergo the same sensory experiences and reasoning that we do when we have sensations and when we reason? For example, does an autopilot mechanism fly an airplane with conscious, intentional desires the way human pilots do? I suggest they do not, not any more than the computer you use actually has a memory or has conscious intentions. These are devices that assist persons in remembering and doing things. If we actually thought such mechanisms were conscious, we would presumably have to regard them with moral sensitivity. I do not take a dogmatic view on such matters. Perhaps it is possible that one day we can construct machines that are conscious, but in such a case the knowledge argument would come into play. I propose that no matter how sophisticated a machine, we will never directly observe the machine's conscious states; these will have to be inferred because conscious states are more than the physical states we observe.

Melnyk's description of substance dualism near the end of his essay seems awkward to me. On his view, substance dualists construe the brain as "merely" playing a process role:

> When we feel the heat of a fire, our brains relay signals to our immaterial minds from sensory neurons originating in our fingers. When we decide to step back from the first, our brains relay signals from our immaterial minds to the moter neruons that run to muscles in our legs. According to this dualist view, then, our brains merely play these mediating roles in perception and in deciding to act. Our brains aren't where the thinking happens. (p. xx)

I suggest that the dualist account would begin, rather, with what we know to be the case: when your hand is burned by fire and you feel a searing pain, you either automatically or deliberately move your hand out of the fire. Dualists support *a holistic account* in which scientists highlight the role of your central state nervous system, nerve endings, muscle movements, brain activity along with the role of your sensations, thinking, and so on. Presumably, a medical doctor working with burn victims will treat persons identically, whether she is a dualist or a materialist. The only difference would be when the doctor contemplates her philosophy of mind. The medical doctor who is a dualist will (rightly, in my view) conclude that the reason why she must rely on reports (and not direct observations of the wound) to know the victim's level of pain is related to the truth of dualism. I suggest Melnyk does not appreciate the dualist recognition of the functional unity of person and body.

Melnyk's case for materialism rests on its being a more economical view. In this line of reasoning, dualism posits two kinds of things, while materialism only posits one kind of thing. I have sought to make clear that dualism (despite its name) is not so much claiming that there are two things; we rather claim that there is more than one kind of thing. For all we know, there may be indefinitely many kinds of things, not limited to the physical world (propositions, logical laws, abstractions, numbers, etc.). Melnyk's appeal to economy does not seem to count as a strict principle, for he does not side with the extremely economic form of materialism that denies the reality of minds. "The commonest materialist view of minds is that, strictly speaking, there are no such things—whether physical or non-physical!" (p. 289). I believe Melnyk rightly wants to recognize the reality of thinking, reasoning, sensing, and more. My point in reply is that once you recognize this robust domain of feeling, thinking, and more, and acknowledge that we do not merely grasp these activities (or functions), but we experience ourselves as being self-aware subjects undergoing all these activities and experiences, it becomes very hard to square this evident, real awareness with materialism.

Notes

1 Thomas Nagel, "What Is It Like to Be a Bat?" *Philosophical Review* 83, no. 4 (October 1974): 435–50.
2 Richard Swinburne, *The Evolution of the Soul* (Oxford: Clarendon Press, 1997), x.

Response to Taliaferro

Andrew Melnyk

Study Questions

1. What claim of Taliaferro does Melnyk agree with? Why does he think that a materialist is entitled to accept this claim?
2. In what way are mental states utterly unique on the materialist view?
3. According to Melnyk, how are materialist mental-to-physical identity claims discovered? What example does he use to show how this works in practice?
4. What premise of the Knowledge Argument does Melnyk believe to be false? Why? How does he illustrate his point?

I have space to discuss just two of the claims that Charles Taliaferro makes in his essay. I will start with a claim that, happily, we both accept, before moving on to a claim that I reject.

We Know Our Own Mental States

Taliaferro claims that "we are self-aware persons who have experiences, act, feel, think, and so on" (p. 301). Very few materialists deny this claim, but I'm not one of them. I quite agree that not only do we think and feel things but we also *know* that we think and feel things. And the *way* we know that *we* think and feel things is quite different from the way we know that *others* think and feel things. We know our *own* thoughts and feelings "from the inside," as they say. We don't know anyone *else's* thoughts and feelings "from the inside." To know what *others* are thinking and feeling, we need to look at their outward behavior—their bodily movements, their posture, their facial expressions, their speech—and the circumstances they're in. For example, if *we* stub a toe and then feel pain in it, we know directly that we're in pain: we have no *evidence* from which we *infer* that we're in pain. But if *others* stub a toe and then feel pain in it, we *do* have evidence from which we infer that they're in pain: the fact that their toe struck a door frame, and that they're now wincing, groaning, and hopping about.

Am I *entitled*, as a materialist, to accept this first claim of Taliaferro's? Is it consistent with materialism? I think so. Our knowledge of the shapes and colors of objects around us arises from *vision*, a process by which we gain information about the outside world. Somewhat similarly, our knowledge of our own mental states "from the inside" is often said to arise from *introspection*, a process by which we learn directly about what's going on inside our minds. According to materialism, of course, human vision is a purely physical process: our capacity for vision is simply a matter of innumerable neurons of the right kinds in certain parts of our brains being organized into networks and subnetworks and feedback loops and so forth that can take patterns of light falling on our retinas as inputs and yield visual beliefs—representations of the scene before our eyes—as outputs. Materialism can say that introspection is purely physical too: our capacity for introspection is simply a matter of innumerable neurons of the right kinds in certain parts of our brains being organized into networks that can take mental activity (= appropriately organized neuronal activity in one part of the brain) as input and yield beliefs about that mental activity (= differently organized neuronal activity in another part of the brain) as output. In effect, introspection is one part of your brain monitoring another part of your brain, in something like the way that your laptop computer keeps track of everything (else) that it does.

However, the materialist view of introspection entails that our mental states are purely physical states[1] that are utterly unique in a certain way. *Your* mental states are the only purely physical states in the universe that *you* can learn about in two quite different ways: first, in the same way anyone else can, using microscopes or CT scanners or MRI machines; but also, second, in a way unique to you that requires neither fancy scientific instruments nor even your five senses, using introspection. Indeed, *each* of us has a special route to knowledge of certain purely physical states: those that are our *own* mental states. But our mental states are still just purely physical states.

Why the Knowledge Argument Fails

Taliaferro claims that "we ourselves with all our experiences, intentions, and so on, are not (strictly speaking) identical with our material or physical bodies or some part of our bodies such as our brains" (p. 294). This is the claim of Taliaferro that makes him *not* a materialist. A materialist must say that anything mental is *identical* with—is one and the same thing as—something purely physical. For example, a materialist must say that you, a thinking, feeling person, are *one and the same thing as* a certain animal with a properly functioning brain—that you are *nothing over and above* a certain member of the species, *Homo sapiens*, whose brain is working as it should.[2] In the quoted claim, Taliaferro is denying this mental-to-physical identity claim. A materialist must make other mental-to-physical identity claims, too, such as the claim that *being in pain* is one and the same thing as *being a system composed of parts so organized as* to form a subsystem that (i) has the job of detecting damage to the containing system, and of getting it to respond appropriately, and that (ii) is currently activated. I'm sure that Taliaferro would deny these other mental-to-physical identity claims too.

Do note that the word "identical" in English has two different meanings. We can say that twin sisters are identical, or that two peas in a pod or two electrons are identical; but in these cases we are saying, of *two* things, that *one* of them is *exactly similar* to the *other*. But we use "identical" in a different sense when we say that Superman is identical with Clark Kent. We mean that Superman is *the very same man as* Clark Kent. In these cases, we are talking about just *one* thing, namely, Superman (or Clark Kent). Each thing has two *names*, of course; but we must not confuse a name with the thing it names. The name "Boston" consists of six letters, but the city it names doesn't consist of letters at all. When materialists make a mental-to-physical identity claim, they mean to be talking about *one* thing with *two* names.

The mental-to-physical identity claims that materialists make are modeled on identity claims made in the sciences, such as the claims that alcohol is identical with C_2H_6O, that water is identical with H_2O, that genes are identical with segments of the DNA molecule, or that having consumption (the disease) is identical with being infected with *Mycobacterium tuberculosis*. But these scientific identity claims weren't discovered by abstract logical reasoning or by reflecting on the meanings of words; they were discovered *empirically*, inferred from observational evidence. It's the same with materialists' mental-to-physical identity claims. They shouldn't be expected to be discoverable *a priori* (i.e., independently of sensory experience) by performing logical deductions or by reflecting on the meanings of words like "pain" or "belief" or "think." Rather, mental-to-physical identity claims must be inferred from what we observe. Suppose we find that people are introspectively aware of being in a particular mental state, say, pain, when, but only when, their brains are in a particular purely physical state; we *never* find one without the other. Suppose, moreover, that this purely physical state plays the sort of causal role that we know that pain plays; toe stubbing causes it, for example, and in turn it causes wincing and groaning. Then the most reasonable conclusion to draw is the economical one that pain simply *is* that purely physical state.

We're now ready to examine Taliaferro's "knowledge argument" for the nonidentity of mentality with anything purely physical. I quote:

> If you are the same thing as your body, then to know your body and bodily states would be to know your thoughts, emotions, intentions, desires, and so on. But it is possible for me or any number of scientists to know all about your body without knowing these mental states. Therefore, your mental life is not identical to your body or bodily states. (pp. 301–02)

But Taliaferro's knowledge argument fails to establish its conclusion, because its first premise is not true. Even if having a mind is, in actual fact, one and the same thing as having a properly functioning brain, to know (i.e., to know all about) someone's properly functioning brain is *not* automatically to know (i.e., to know all about) someone's mind. To see why not, consider an analogous case. Alcohol is the very same substance as C_2H_6O. But perhaps I first heard of alcohol and first heard of C_2H_6O in very different settings; perhaps I first heard of C_2H_6O in a chemistry class, and first heard of alcohol in a sermon condemning the demon drink. But it's not *a priori* that alcohol and C_2H_6O are the very same thing, as we noted earlier; and I could easily fail to discover the identity claim empirically. In that case, I could then know that the bottle on the shelf contains C_2H_6O (I chemically analyze its contents, or perhaps the label just says "C_2H_6O") *without* my knowing, or even suspecting, that the bottle contains alcohol.[3]

There's a similar explanation for how we can know all about a person's properly functioning brain without automatically knowing all about the person's mind. Presumably, it's through introspection of our own mental states that we become aware of mental states in the first place; and we renew our acquaintance with them in the same way daily. Only much later, if we take a class in cognitive neuroscience, say, do we first hear of brain states and the functional organization of neurons into networks capable of various cognitive tasks. But even if a mind just is a (properly functioning) brain, we can't discover this identity claim *a priori*. And we may well not, in fact, discover it empirically. So, if a reliable authority gives us an accurate and complete description of Dr. Taliaferro in the specialist vocabulary of cognitive neuroscience, we won't know that he is wondering where the aspirin is — even if the description says that he's in a purely physical state that is, in fact, identical with wondering where the aspirin is.

I noted that the mental-to-physical identity claims that materialists make are modeled on identity claims made in the sciences. But there's also a major difference between the mental-to-physical identity claims that materialists make and identity claims familiar from the sciences. When we learn *any* (nontrivial) identity claim, we come to realize that we have *two* (or more) perspectives on—two ways of thinking about and finding out about—*one thing*. For identity claims familiar from the sciences, *both* these perspectives are perceptual or inferential (or both). For example, when we learn that having consumption (the disease) is identical with being infected with *M. tuberculosis*, both our perspective on consumption (e.g., seeing patients breathless and coughing up blood) and our perspective on *M. tuberculosis* (e.g., seeing the bacteria under a microscope) are perceptual-cum-inferential. But with mental-to-physical identity claims, while our perspective on the purely physical states of our brains is perceptual-cum-inferential (e.g., seeing an fMRI scan or reading a textbook in cognitive neuroscience), our prior perspective on our mental states is not. When we're aware of our own mental states through introspection, we neither *infer* them nor *perceive* (i.e., see, hear, touch, taste, smell) them. We are aware of them in an entirely different way unique to (those purely physical states of ourselves that are identical with) mental states.

Notes

1. In the special sense of "purely physical" explained in my first essay.
2. Your brain must be functioning properly because to the extent that it isn't, you won't be thinking and feeling. Materialists should identify thinking and feeling people not with human *bodies*, which can be dead, but with living animals.
3. Sometimes "know" means "be acquainted with." And, arguably, if X is identical with Y and you're *acquainted with* X, then you *must* be acquainted with Y too (even if you don't *know* that you are). On this construal of "know," Taliaferro's first premise may therefore be true. But his argument still fails. Now it begs the question against materialism—with its premise that scientists who know all about your body are *not* acquainted with your mind. If materialism is true, they *are* acquainted with your mind; they just don't *know* that they are.

Questions for Reflection

1. Melnyk's view would entail that a robot or computer that perfectly reproduced the structure and functioning of the human brain would necessarily be conscious. Do you think that's right? Why?
2. Both Melnyk and Taliaferro reject the most common materialist view that denies that minds are real things. Why do you think they reject this view? Can this view be defended?
3. Is Melnyk correct that the best explanation for the correlation between mental states and brain states is that the mental states just are brain states? Why?
4. What is your assessment of the Knowledge Argument? Does it show that the mind is distinct from the body, as Taliaferro claims? Why?

9

Is Free Will Compatible with Determinism?

Freedom Is Not Compatible with Determinism

Christopher Evan Franklin

Study Questions

1. How does Franklin understand moral responsibility? What kinds of conditions need to be met for an agent to be morally responsible?
2. What "freedom condition" does Franklin derive from his discussion of the three cases involving Sam? What related principles does he derive?
3. How does Franklin define determinism? What does he mean by "conditional necessity"?
4. What is the Consequence Argument? What does Franklin think it shows?
5. In what sense does David Lewis think that humans have the ability to break a law of nature? How is this ability supposed to rebut the Consequence Argument?
6. Why does Franklin think that Lewis's "weak ability" is too weak?

I aim to convince you in this essay of the truth of *incompatibilism*: the thesis that freedom is not compatible with determinism. By "freedom" I mean, roughly, the kind of control required for it to be fair or just to blame others when they do something immoral. By "determinism" I mean, roughly, the idea that "everything that happens is the *inevitable* result of the distant past and laws of nature." While it might seem obvious that freedom is incompatible with determinism, the majority of philosophers are *compatibilists*, contending that freedom and determinism are compatible. I will argue that these philosophers are wrong, and that freedom is, indeed, incompatible with determinism.

Moral Responsibility

Let's begin by thinking about moral responsibility. When a person is morally responsible for an action, she *deserves* blame if the action was morally wrong. By "blame," I have in mind a wide range of activities beginning with emotions (e.g., anger and indignation), moving to linguistic activities (e.g., verbal rebukes), and to more robust kinds of sanctions (e.g., breaking off a friendship). Note that it is sometimes appropriate to blame people even when they don't deserve it. When my one-year-old son attempts to put his fork in the light socket, I verbally rebuke ("Don't do that!") and mildly punish him (flick his finger). I don't do these things because he *deserves* them. He isn't morally responsible for his foolish behavior. Rather, I punish him because I want to protect him from harm. So also when I punish my three-year-old daughter for disobeying me: I don't punish her because she deserves it, but because I want her to learn obedience. Thus, when parents blame in order to protect their children or cultivate good character, they aren't necessarily holding their children *morally responsible*. The difference has to do with desert. When a person deserves blame, it is fitting or right to blame him not because it will bring about some good consequence (e.g., cultivation of character), but simply because of the wrong he did. While we might hope that punishing a murderer will reform him or deter others, we also punish him simply because of his horrific action, simply because of what he did. Likewise, when we feel anger toward a racist, while such an emotional reaction might have good consequences, it seems that anger is justified because the racist deserves it—it is appropriate simply because of how the racist treats others.

A central philosophical question is: under what conditions are agents blameworthy for their actions? Historically, philosophers have argued that agents are morally responsible only if they meet epistemic conditions and freedom conditions. The *epistemic conditions* concern agents' understanding or awareness. My daughter doesn't deserve blame for disobeying me since she doesn't have a good enough understanding of morality. The *freedom conditions* concern agents' control over their actions. My son doesn't deserve blame for trying to stick a fork in the socket because he doesn't have enough control over his actions (of course, he too lacks understanding). In what follows, I will argue that the kind of freedom required for moral responsibility is incompatible with determinism. So putting aside the epistemic dimension of responsibility, let's focus a bit more on the freedom condition.

Freedom and Responsibility

Suppose it is Sunday afternoon and you have an important exam Monday morning that you need to study for. Suppose that yesterday you lent a book to a recent acquaintance who promised to return the book to you by Sunday afternoon and that you need the book to prepare for tomorrow's exam. This person, let's call him Sam, lives in a dorm across campus from you. Finally, to simplify the case, let's suppose it is the year 1900. This means your dorm room isn't equipped with a telephone, there is no internet, and there are certainly no smartphones. The only way for Sam to return the book to you is to do it in person (or ask someone else to do it in person). Suppose the afternoon has gone by and Sam hasn't shown up. As the clock strikes 5:00 p.m. you begin to worry, and by 6:00 p.m. you are frustrated. You head across campus and find Sam deeply engrossed in a novel. Sam sees you and quickly says, "Sorry, I forgot!" In such a case, you would seem perfectly justified in feeling some mild anger toward Sam. He made a promise to you that he easily could have fulfilled, but instead he decided to read a novel. Sam is morally responsible for failing to keep his promise, and, more specifically, he is *blameworthy*—he deserves blame for what he has failed to do.

Now consider a slight variation of this case. Everything is the same as before, but when you enter Sam's room you discover him lying down with his ankle bandaged. When he sees you, he explains that he sprained his ankle and so couldn't return the book. You ask him why he didn't ask someone else to do it for him and he explains that nobody has been around. You ask why he didn't use his crutches and he says: "Well, I suppose I could have, but they cause me some mild discomfort."

What would your reaction be in this case? It seems that mild anger would again be justified. Given your kindness in lending him the book, your absolute need of having the book to prepare properly for the exam, and the fact that Sam was able to return the book, Sam should have returned the book, mild pain notwithstanding. However, it also seems to me that Sam is less blameworthy in this case than in the first. There is a mitigating factor: namely, the pain involved in fulfilling his promise. Rather than simply flouting his obligation to you in order to read a novel, he flouted his obligations so as not to cause himself more pain. While this is understandable, it doesn't completely get him off the hook. After all, mild discomfort is merely mild discomfort. Therefore, as in the first case, Sam is blameworthy, but he is, I submit, less blameworthy than in the first case.

What explains why Sam is less blameworthy in the second case? The following seems to me to be a plausible answer: it was, through no fault of his own, more difficult for him to keep his promise in the second case than in the first case.

Consider another slight variation of the original case. When you arrive at Sam's room, you find it in disarray and Sam tied tightly to a chair with his mouth gagged. As you untie Sam, he explains that he was robbed earlier that morning and that the robbers tied him up to ensure their escape. He is sorry about the inconvenience this caused you.

What is your reaction in this case? It seems to me that Sam is *completely* excused from responsibility. It wouldn't be fair to blame Sam, not even a little. But why? Why does mild discomfort only mitigate Sam's blameworthiness, whereas the robbers and ropes expunge his blameworthiness entirely? The difference is that in the second case, even though it was more difficult for Sam to fulfill his promise than it was in the first case, he was still able to fulfill his promise. In the third case, however, Sam lacked this ability. Given that he was tied up (and let's assume the robbers did a good job at this), he was unable to fulfill his promise. There were factors outside of his control that made it impossible for him to do so.

These three cases illustrate that responsibility is partly a function of what you are able to do. If you are less able than others to do what you are morally required to do, then your blameworthiness is mitigated. If you aren't able at all to do what you are morally required to do, then you aren't blameworthy at all. It would seem, then, that if a person is, through no fault of her own, unable to do something, then she cannot be blameworthy for failing to do it. The qualification "through no fault of her own" is important. If you lend me $20 and I promise to pay you back after I get my paycheck on Friday, but instead blow my whole paycheck over a weekend in Vegas, then I can hardly excuse myself from responsibility by pointing to my inability to pay you back. This is because my lack of ability is my fault. Notice also that we sometimes say, "I couldn't do it" when really we mean, "I could do it, but it was hard for me." In the second case described earlier, it would have been natural for Sam to say, "I sprained my ankle, and so couldn't return the book," when, in fact, he was able to return the book. The sprained ankle didn't eliminate that ability, but simply made it more difficult for him to exercise that ability. Thus, often when people say, "I couldn't have helped it," we still (justifiably) blame them. However, it seems that if it is, strictly speaking, true that someone was unable to fulfill her promise, and if her lacking this ability wasn't her fault, then she isn't blameworthy for failing to fulfill her promise.

To put this point slightly differently, there is a freedom condition on blameworthiness: *a person is blameworthy for what he does only if he was free to do otherwise.* In the third case, Sam isn't blameworthy for failing to fulfill his promise, because he was unable to do otherwise (i.e., he wasn't able to *fulfill* the promise). Let's call this principle *No Freedom, No Blameworthiness*. I believe that this principle is well supported by general moral reflection on the earlier described cases. It is this principle that explains why Sam isn't blameworthy in the final case. A related principle would be: *Less Freedom, Less Blameworthiness*. It is this principle that explains why Sam is blameworthy in the second case, but less so than in the first case.

Determinism

The final idea we need to get a handle on before I give my argument for incompatibilism is *determinism*. Determinism is a slippery idea, one easily confused with other ideas. I will define it as "the thesis that every event that occurs (including choices and actions and their consequences) is the inevitable result of the distant past and laws of nature." Determinism is a kind of *conditional* necessity. It does not state that everything that does happen *must* happen. Rather, it states that everything that does happen must happen *given* the past and laws of nature. If our universe is deterministic, then, it does not follow that every event that occurs is inevitable. After all, the past could have been different than it, in fact, was, or the laws of nature could have been different than they, in fact, are. And had either been different, then the unfolding of our universe also would have been different. But if our universe is deterministic, then it *does* follow that every event is inevitable, *given* how the past was and how the laws of nature actually were/are. So, if determinism is true, then my writing this essay is the inevitable consequence of the past and laws of nature. But had the past been different or had the laws of nature been different, then perhaps I would not have written this essay. Indeed, perhaps I would not have existed at all.

Just what a law of nature is, is a rich philosophical question. But I will assume that laws of nature are descriptions of how objects must causally interact with each other. For example, the law of gravity (as stated by Newton) is that every particle attracts every other particle in the universe with a force that is directly proportional to the product of their masses and inversely proportional to the square of the distance between them. This is why objects we drop fall to the ground (assuming there is no equal or greater contrary force). Importantly, this law does not simply tell us how things have acted so far: it tells us how things *must* act. If the law of gravity is, indeed, a law of nature, then natural objects—barring divine interference—must behave this way. Determinism is the idea that if you take all the laws of nature there are (not just the law of gravity), and combine them with how things began in the past (say, at the moment of the Big Bang), then every event that happens throughout all history *must* happen—no exceptions.

In summary, determinism is the idea that if the past and laws are the same, then the future must be the same. In slogan form we could say: No difference in the future without a difference in the past or a difference in the laws of nature.

Incompatibilism

Suppose Sam's universe is deterministic and suppose he decided not to return the book but, rather, to read his novel. It seems, then, that Sam is not blameworthy since he was not free to do otherwise. Sam is not free to do otherwise because he was determined to refrain from returning the book by factors outside of his control, namely the distant past and the laws of nature. Therefore, it seems that determinism is incompatible with Sam's being free.

Let's state this argument more carefully:

(1) If determinism is true, then Sam's refraining from returning the book is the inevitable consequence of the past and the laws of nature.

(2) If Sam was able to return the book, then (given determinism) he was able to either change the past or change the laws of nature.

(3) Sam was not able to change the past or the laws of nature.

(4) Therefore, if determinism is true, Sam was not able to return the book.

Of course, there is nothing unique about Sam. This argument applies to all agents in all deterministic universes, and thus implies that no agent in a deterministic world has the freedom to do otherwise. Peter van Inwagen, who was one of the first to rigorously formulate this kind of argument—known as the *Consequence Argument*—summarizes the argument thus:

> If determinism is true, then our acts are the consequences of the laws of nature and events in the remote past. But it is not up to us what went on before we were born, and neither is it up to us what the laws of nature are. Therefore, the consequences of these things (including our present acts) are not up to us.[1]

When evaluating an argument, we always want to ask two questions: "Do the premises support the conclusion?" and "Are the premises true?" Careful thought should reveal that premises (1)–(3) do support (4). Indeed, it is not possible for the premises to be true and the conclusion false. Thus, in order for a compatibilist to show that this argument fails, she must give us a reason to deny one of the premises. So let us consider each premise in turn.

Premise (1) is true by definition. Given our supposition that Sam's world is deterministic, it follows that his refraining from returning the book is inevitable given the past and the laws of nature.

Premise (2) seems plausible. Suppose you have the ability to ask your professor a question. And suppose (somewhat implausibly) that *the only possible* way to ask her a question is to raise your hand. It would seem that if you didn't have the ability to raise your hand, you wouldn't have the ability to ask a question. After all, raising your hand is a necessary condition for asking a question. Thus, if you have the ability to ask a question, then you have the ability to raise your hand. Likewise, suppose you have the ability to score a goal and suppose (again somewhat implausibly) that *the only way* to score a goal is to kick the ball. In this case, if you have the ability to score the goal, then you have the ability to kick the ball. Returning to Sam, remember our determinism slogan: no difference in the future without a difference in the past. This means that *the only way* for Sam to return the book (which is a change in the future) is if there were either a change in the past or the laws of nature. So, by the above logic, it would seem that Sam has the ability to return the book only if he has the ability to change either the past or the laws of nature.

Premise (3) also seems plausible. No one, at least no human, has the ability to change the past or the laws of nature. The past is over and done with, outside of our control, sometimes painfully so. I am not able to stop Hitler, I am not able to abolish American slavery, and I am not able to prevent the Archduke of Austria from being assassinated. Had I existed earlier in time, then perhaps I would have been able to do something about these tragic events. But given that I only came to exist long after they occurred, they are outside of my control. When I deliberate about what to do, I exclusively deliberate about the future. What should I do this weekend? What college major should I choose (philosophy, of course!)? How should I spend my summer vacation? I never ask what I should do yesterday. Of course, I might wonder how I should have acted. I might try to determine whether my past actions were morally right or wise. But if I come to discover that I have made a mistake, there is nothing I can do to change this.

The same goes for the laws of nature. Perhaps the laws could have been different. But it is not up to me to decide. If it is, indeed, a law of nature that nothing can travel faster than the speed of light, then there is no point in trying to create a machine that travels faster than the speed of light. For the laws of nature tell us how things *must* go, and we have no choice about this.

So, it seems that freedom is incompatible with determinism. If I have the freedom to do otherwise in a deterministic universe, then I am free to change either the past or the laws of nature. But I am not free to change the past, and I am not free to change the laws of nature, and thus I am not free to do otherwise. Given *No Freedom, No Blameworthiness*, if our universe is deterministic, then a truly startling conclusion follows: no one is morally responsible for anything they do.

An Objection

While I find the argument from the previous section compelling, important questions and objections remain. One of the most important objections is due to David Lewis.[2] He contends that the Consequence Argument turns on an equivocation of "is able." That is, he contends that there are two importantly different understandings of the statement "Sam is able to change either the past or the laws of nature." On the first understanding, (3) is true but (2) is false; and on the second understanding, (2) is true but (3) is false. Hence, Lewis claimed that there is no way to interpret the statement "Sam is able to change either the past or the laws of nature" on which both (2) and (3) come out true. Let's flesh out this objection.

Are we able to break the laws of nature? Lewis thinks that in one sense of "is able" the answer is "Yes," but in another sense of "is able" the answer is "No." He distinguishes these two senses of "is able" as follows:

(Weak Thesis) I am able to do something such that, if I did it, a law of nature would be broken.

(Strong Thesis) I am able to do something such that, if I did, it would constitute a law of nature's being broken or would cause a law of nature to be broken.

Suppose I am able to throw a rock in a certain direction such that, if I throw the rock in that direction, it would cause a window to break. In this case, I am able to do something such that, if I did it, a window would be broken. Moreover, I am able to do something such that, if I did it, it would cause the window to break. In such a case, I have both the weak and the strong ability to break a window. Suppose I am able to throw a rock and yet, for whatever reason, have promised a friend never to throw a rock. In this case, I am able to do something such that, if I did it, a promise would have been broken. Moreover, I am able to do something such that, if I did it, it would constitute a promise being broken. In such a case, I have both the weak and the strong ability to break a promise.

"I am able to break a law of nature" can be understood according to the weak thesis or the strong thesis. According to the strong thesis, if I am able to break a law of nature, then I am able to do something such that, if I did it, it would either constitute or cause a law of nature's being broken. Lewis contends that it is "incredible" to think humans have such an ability. However, compatibilists need not claim, so Lewis argued, that humans who are free have this incredible ability. Rather, they need only claim that humans who are free have the weak ability to break the laws of nature. That is, free human beings are able to do things such that, if they so acted, a law of nature would be broken. But humans are not able to do something that *is* a violation of a law of nature or would *cause* a law of nature to be broken.

Recall that determinism says that any universe with the same past and laws of nature will have the same future. Suppose that Sam is in a deterministic world and refrains from returning the book to read his novel instead. Since Sam's world is deterministic, any world that has a different future, such as Sam's returning the book, will be a world with a different past or different laws of nature (or both). Let's focus on a difference in laws. Any universe in which Sam acts otherwise—that is, any universe in which Sam returns the book—must have different laws of nature. Does it follow that if Sam is able to return the book, then he is able to cause the laws of nature to be different than they, in fact, are? Lewis thinks not. All that follows is that if Sam had returned the book, then some law (or laws) of nature would be different.

Consider again the second two premises of the Consequence Argument:

(2) If Sam was able to return the book, then he was able to either change the past or change the laws of nature.

(3) Sam was not able to change the past or the laws of nature.

Lewis's objection is as follows. On the one hand, if "is able" refers to the strong ability to break the laws of nature, then (3) is true, but (2) is false. It is, indeed, incredible to think that Sam is able to break the laws of nature in the strong sense and so (3) is true, but on this reading (2) is false since compatibilists are only committed to Sam's having the ability to break the laws of nature in the weak sense. On the other hand, if "is able" refers to the weak ability to break the laws, then (2) is true, but (3) is false. It is, indeed, the case that if Sam is able to return the book, then he is able to break a law of nature in the weak sense and so (2) is true, but, so Lewis contends, there is nothing incredible about Sam's being able to break a law of nature in the weak sense, and so (3) is false.

Does this objection succeed? I don't think it ultimately does, though I do think it succeeds in showing that incompatibilists have some more work to do. Many incompatibilists have responded to Lewis by contending that even the weak ability is incredible.[3] That is, they have argued that even the weak ability is too strong. I think that the real problem is that the weak ability is *too weak*. Let me explain.

Lewis maintains that the following three propositions are consistent:

(i) Sam has the ability to return the book.

(ii) A necessary condition for Sam's retuning the book fails to obtain (i.e., that the laws of nature be different than they actually are).

(iii) Sam is unable to bring about this necessary condition (i.e., he is unable to cause a change in the laws of nature).

It seems to me, however, that (ii) and (iii) are incompatible with (i). Consider again the third case about Sam—in which he fails to return the book because he is tied up by robbers. Suppose that, given the strength of the ropes, Sam is unable to free himself from the ropes. In this case, a necessary condition for Sam's standing up is that he is free from the ropes. Moreover, Sam is unable to do anything to free himself from the ropes. Intuitively, this would seem to imply that Sam *lacks* the ability to stand up. But this implication does not follow for Lewis. From the facts that Sam can stand up only if the ropes are removed, and the fact that Sam cannot do anything to remove the ropes, it does not follow, on Lewis's account, that Sam lacks the ability to stand up. This is because Sam's having the weak ability is consistent with (ii) and (iii). Consequently, if the weak ability is *enough* freedom to ground moral responsibility, then, contrary to our intuitive verdict about the third version of Sam's case, Sam is blameworthy for failing to return the book. After all, he was able (in the weak sense) to stand up, and he was able (in the weak sense) to walk across campus. And thus it seems that Sam is blameworthy.

But this is the wrong verdict. While it might be true that had Sam stood up, the ropes would have been removed, he is not able to stand up *in the sense relevant to freedom*, because he is not able to remove the ropes himself or cause someone else to remove the ropes. Likewise, while it is true that if Sam had returned the book, then a law of nature would have been broken, and thus Sam is able to return the book in the weak sense, he is, nonetheless, not blameworthy because this ability is too weak. For him to be blameworthy, he would also need to be able to change the laws of nature himself, and, as Lewis concedes, it is incredible to think he could do this.

Lewis is committed to saying that Sam has all the freedom required for being blameworthy for failing to return the book, even though a necessary condition for his returning the book (i.e., the laws of nature being different) was not fulfilled and there was nothing Sam was able to do that would have caused this necessary condition to obtain. This strikes me as incoherent. Suppose I promise to pay back the money you loaned me by this Friday. Suppose that in order to pay you back I need to refrain from spending my whole paycheck on other things. It seems like I am able to pay you back because I am able to make it the case that I refrain from spending the money. In contrast, in the case in which Sam is tied up, he is not able to return the book. This is because in order to return the book, the ropes must be removed from him—and he is not able to make it the case that the ropes are removed. Likewise, in the case in which Sam is not tied up but exists, instead, in a deterministic universe, he is not able, in the sense relevant to freedom, to return the book. This is because, in order for Sam to the return the book, the laws of nature must have been different, and he is not, by Lewis's own concession, able to make the laws of nature different. There is more to freedom than the weak ability to do otherwise. While the weak ability may be compatible with determinism, this is not enough to show that freedom is compatible with determinism, for there is more to freedom than the weak ability to do otherwise.

Conclusion

I believe that compatibilism about freedom and determinism is a powerful but, nevertheless, false philosophical thesis. I don't take myself to have decisively established that. There are other interesting objections that we don't have space to consider. But I hope to have shown that incompatibilism is both incredibly intuitive and well supported by philosophical reflection, and thus that compatibilists owe us a powerful reason to accept compatibilism. The ball is, as it were, squarely in the compatibilists' court.[4]

Notes

1. Peter van Inwagen, *An Essay on Free Will* (Oxford: Oxford University Press, 1983). Other influential formulations of the Consequence Argument can be found in Carl Ginet, *On Action* (New York: Cambridge University Press, 1990); and John Martin Fischer, *The Metaphysics of Free Will* (Malden, MA: Blackwell Publishing, 1994).
2. David Lewis, "Are We Free to Break the Laws?" *Theoria* 3 (1981): 113–21.

3 Peter van Inwagen, "Freedom to Break the Laws," *Midwest Studies in Philosophy* 28 (2004): 334–50.
4 Thanks to Micah Quigley for helpful comments on an earlier draft.

Freedom Is Compatible with Determinism

Steven B. Cowan

Study Questions

1. How does Cowan define "determinism"? Why might someone hold this view?

2. How do most incompatibilists understand free will? How does the compatibilist understand it? What neutral definition of free will does Cowan suggest?

3. What is a Frankfurt-type Counterexample? What is it supposed to show? What objection is the second version of the counterexample designed to address and how does it do so?

4. What is Derk Pereboom's Four-Case Manipulation Argument in defense of ultimate sourcehood? What is the hardline reply to the argument? What is the softline reply?

5. What, according to Cowan, are the conditions of moral responsibility?

6. What does it mean for an agent to be reasons-responsive? Why is this condition important?

7. According to Cowan, what do people always choose? What does this reveal about our desires and about what we consider "sufficiently good"?

8. What, according to Cowan, does it mean for an agent to own his system of values? What objection may be raised to this view of values ownership? How does Cowan respond to the objection?

If everything is determined, then is human freedom or free will possible? That is the central question of this essay. It is a question that has been discussed by philosophers for centuries. As with almost all important philosophical questions, various answers have been given by different philosophers. Those philosophers who answer "no" to this question are called *incompatibilists*; those who answer "yes" are called *compatibilists*. My sympathies lie with compatibilism. In this essay, I will explain how it can be the case that human freedom is compatible with determinism.

What Do We Mean by Free Will and Determinism?

As with many problems in philosophy, a proper understanding of the problem, as well as finding an adequate solution, requires getting clear on the meanings of the key terms involved. So, we will start by defining our two key terms.

Determinism

First, what do we mean by "determinism"? Roughly, *determinism* is the idea that every event is determined (caused, dictated, or in some way necessitated) by some prior event or state of affairs. Put another way, determinism is the thesis that, at any given time, only one future is possible. According to the opposite view, *indeterminism*, the future is a "garden of forking paths." But on determinism, the path never forks.

There are several reasons why someone might believe in determinism. Some have thought that the physical universe is a closed system governed by invariable natural laws. From the first moment of the Big Bang, everything that has happened and will happen, including human choices, is the inevitable causal result of the initial state of matter and the laws of nature.[1] Another reason to be a determinist is that you believe that God exercises meticulous providence over his creation. For example, Christians in the Augustinian–Calvinist tradition believe, as stated in the *Westminster Confession*, that God "ordains whatsoever comes to pass." There are no accidents in God's universe. Everything that happens, including human choices, is in accordance with God's sovereign will.[2]

So, let's define determinism more precisely as follows:

(D) For any event E, facts about God's will and/or facts about the past together with the laws of nature, entail E.

Free Will

When most ordinary people think about free will, they tend to think about it in terms of having options or being able to do otherwise. This is why many people, when they first hear about compatibilism, immediately balk. The compatibilist, insofar as he embraces determinism, holds that the path does not fork. Which means that when a person does some action, say, eats toast and jam for breakfast, there is a real sense in which he could not have done anything else. If your immediate reaction to this scenario is to say that such a person is not free with respect to what he has for breakfast, then you are most likely sympathetic to what philosophers call the *principle of alternative possibilities* (or PAP, for short):

> (PAP) An agent S is morally responsible for some action A only if, when choosing to do A, he could have done something other than A.

The most common form of incompatibilism understands free will in terms of PAP. On this view, free will is, primarily, *having the ability to do otherwise*. So, when a person has toast and jam for breakfast, his action was a free action only if he could have had eggs and grits (or something else) instead. Other incompatibilists believe that what matters in human freedom is that an agent's actions have no causes that are outside of or prior to the agent. They understand free will in terms of an agent *being the ultimate source of his actions*, whether or not he has alternative possibilities.

The compatibilist, of course, has yet another understanding of what free will is all about. For him, free will is not about having alternative possibilities, nor is it about being the ultimate source of one's actions. Rather, free will is, very roughly (but this will be expanded upon later), *being able to act in accordance with one's desires and values*. When I have toast and jam for breakfast, that choice was a free choice if, all things considered, I was doing what I wanted to do—even if I could not have done anything else.

So, we see that there are different ways in which philosophers have defined free will. This makes things somewhat complicated when we are trying to figure out whether free will is compatible with determinism. On the first two definitions above, it would seem that free will is not compatible with determinism, while on the third (compatibilist) definition they clearly are compatible. The upshot of this observation is that the question of whether or not free will is compatible with determinism comes down to the question of which definition of free will is the right one.

Having said that, however, there is another important observation to make about these various views of human freedom: What they all have in common is a concern for *moral responsibility*. Why is it that the incompatibilist thinks that alternative possibilities or ultimate sourcehood is crucial to understanding free will? Likewise, why is the compatiblilist concerned about an agent being able to act in accordance with his desires and values? It's because they (we) think that those are the conditions that must be met in order for an agent to be morally responsible for his actions. Many of the actions that we do are not like the mundane choice between having toast and jam or eggs and grits for breakfast. Many of our actions have *moral* significance. The choice between whether or not to cheat on your taxes, or to break a promise to a friend, or to kill another person—these are actions for which we hold people morally accountable. And in cases like these the definition of free will matters because it matters what it means to be morally responsible. So, what really lies at the heart of the debate over the compatibility between freedom and determinism is the question of what it takes for an agent to be morally responsible for his actions.

This observation about moral responsibility allows us to provide a working definition of free will without having to first decide which of the above definitions is correct. Let's define free will this way:

> (FW) An agent S exercises free will in performing some action A if and only if, when doing A, S meets the conditions required for moral responsibility.[3]

This definition is neutral between all of the other ones outlined above. What's more, this definition lets us see all of those earlier definitions as different ways of understanding moral responsibility. Free will simply is that which makes it possible for us to be morally responsible for our actions. The questions for the rest of this essay, then, are: (1) What is required for an agent to be morally responsible? and (2) Is determinism compatible with whatever is required to be morally responsible?

What Is *Not* Required for Moral Responsibility

Before explaining what is required for moral responsibility, I will rule out the two major conditions proposed by incompatibilists, namely, alternative possibilities and ultimate sourcehood.

Not *Alternative Possibilities*

Many incompatibilitsts, as we have seen, hold that moral responsibility (and free will) requires having the ability to do otherwise. That is, they endorse PAP as a necessary condition for moral responsibility. In recent decades, however, PAP has been shown to be doubtful if not false. Philosopher Harry Frankfurt initiated the challenge, offering what has come to be called *Frankfurt-type*

Counterexamples to PAP.[4] Here's a modified version of Frankfurt's original counterexample:

> Let's imagine that we are back in the fall of 2016 shortly prior to the last US presidential election. And suppose there's a mad scientist named Black who wants another person, Jones, to vote for Hillary Clinton. So he secretly plants a computer device in Jones's brain that can monitor Jones's thoughts. The device can also manipulate Jones's thoughts so as to force him to decide to vote for Hillary. But Black prefers to avoid showing his hand unnecessarily. So, he waits until Jones is about to make up his mind what to do, and he does nothing unless it is clear to him that Jones is going to decide to vote for Trump instead. If it does become clear that Jones is going to decide to vote for Trump, Black will take effective steps to ensure that Jones decides to do what he wants him to do, namely, vote for Hillary. Now suppose that Black never has to show his hand because Jones, for reasons of his own, decides to perform the very action Black wants him to perform. Jones votes for Hillary.

The moral of the story is that it seems that Jones could not have done anything other than vote for Hillary. Yet, it also seems clear that Jones is morally responsible for his action.

In light of Frankfurt-type Counterexamples, most philosophers have come to believe that PAP is false. However, there have been attempts to respond to this challenge and show that, despite appearances, agents in situations like Jones's do have alternative possibilities after all. For example, let's suppose that Jones's decision as to whether to vote for Hillary or Trump is undetermined right up to the point of the choice. In that case Black cannot know beforehand which choice Jones will make. If he waits until Jones makes his choice before deciding to intervene, it will be too late. And in that case, Jones *will* be responsible for his choice, but he will also have had *alternative possibilities* since he could have chosen either way. On the other hand, if Black wants to ensure that Jones chooses Hillary, he will have to intervene before Jones chooses, and in that case, Jones would not be morally responsible because his choice will be the result of Black's manipulation.[5]

But we can construct other Frankfurt-type Counterexamples to get around this problem. Consider this modification of the Black–Jones scenario:

> Jones, in the fall of 2016, is strongly leaning toward voting for Hillary Clinton in the US Presidential election. However, because of the high standards of conduct he expects of elected officials, if he were to learn all the details being reported about Clinton's email scandal, there is a good possibility that he would choose to vote for Trump instead. Indeed, this is the only thing

that would lead him to not vote for Hillary. Jones knows this and typically avoids watching *Fox News* and any other news outlet that discusses Clinton's use of government emails in a bad light. Suppose, though, that the mad scientist, Black, wants to guarantee that Jones votes for Hillary. So he secretly plants a computer device in Jones's brain that can monitor Jones's thoughts and determine if Jones is thinking about the Clinton email scandal or about watching or reading any news item concerning it. And, if the device detects that he is, it will force him to think about something else. Now suppose that Black's device never has to intervene and manipulate Jones's thoughts because Jones, on his own, keeps avoiding thoughts of the email scandal. And when election day comes, he votes for Hillary.[6]

In this scenario, Black does not have to be able to predict what Jones will do beforehand. Yet, it seems clear that Jones is morally responsible for voting for Hillary. And it also seems clear that Jones could not do other than vote for Hillary.

The debate over PAP is ongoing in philosophical circles. The least we can say, though, is that it is plausible to think that alternative possibilities are *not* required for moral responsibility.

Not *Ultimate Sourcehood*

Many incompatibilists are willing to grant that the lack of alternative possibilities does not by itself pose a threat to moral responsibility. What *does* pose a threat, they say, is the specter of determinism itself. Whether or not an agent has alternative possibilities, if his actions are determined as specified by (D) above, he lacks moral responsibility for those actions. What matters for moral responsibility, then, is that an agent's actions are not causally determined by factors outside himself. In other words, moral responsibility requires that an agent be *the ultimate source of his actions*. Thus, instead of PAP, these incompatibilists endorse something like the following principle:

(US) An agent is morally responsible for an action A only if A is not determined by causal factors outside the agent's control.

Many arguments might be given for (US), but perhaps the most persuasive is Derk Pereboom's *Four-Case Manipulation Argument*.[7] Pereboom asks us to consider these four cases involving Professor Plum:

Case 1: Professor Plum was created by a team of neuroscientists, who can manipulate him directly through radio-like technology, but he is as much like an ordinary human being as possible, given his history. The neuroscientists manipulate him to undertake a process of reasoning, directly producing every state of his mind, which leads to his forming the intention to kill Ms. White, which he does.

Case 2: Plum is like an ordinary human being, except that a team of neuroscientists programmed him at the beginning of his life to weigh reasons for action so that he usually (but not always) acts out of self-interest, with the result that in his current circumstances, he is causally determined to act out of self-interest and kill Ms. White.

Case 3: Plum is an ordinary human being, except that he was determined by the rigorous training practices of his home and community to weigh reasons for action so that he usually (but not always) acts out of self-interest, with the result that in his current circumstances, he is causally determined to act out of self-interest and kill Ms. White.

Case 4: Physical determinism is true, and Plum is an ordinary human being, born and raised under normal circumstances, who has grown up to weigh reasons for action so that he usually (but not always) acts out of self-interest, with the result that in his current circumstances, he is causally determined to act out of self-interest and kill Ms. White.

According to Pereboom, our intuitions in the first three cases—despite the fact that the degree of manipulation decreases in each case—is that the agent in question is not morally responsible for his action. The fourth case, however, does not differ in any relevant way from the first three cases. If our judgment in the former is that the agent is not responsible, our judgment in the latter should be the same. But the fourth case involves the kind of determinism assumed in most arguments for compatibilism. The upshot of Pereboom's argument, then, is that (US) is true and compatibilism (which denies (US)) is false.

The first response to make to Pereboom's argument is that he seems to beg the question against compatibilism right from the start. He simply assumes, without argument, that Professor Plum is not morally responsible for his action in the first three cases. But why not? Many compatibilists would take what is called the "hardline" reply and claim that there is no reason to grant that Plum is not responsible in the first three cases so long as we assume that Plum "had a rich history of moral development just like any psychologically healthy person who emerges from childhood into adulthood."[8] There is certainly no reason to deny that Plum could experience such development in case 3, and possibly not even in cases 1 and 2.

A second, more "softline" reply, grants that Plum is not morally responsible in the first three cases, but argues that case 4 is different from them in a way that allows us to maintain that Plum *is* (or may be) responsible in that case. Consider the following four cases developed by Alfred Mele:[9]

Case A: Scarlet's car was struck by a falling large, wet, lead pipe.

Case B: Scarlet's car was struck by a falling large, wet wrench.

Case C: Scarlet's car was struck by a falling large, wet, metal candlestick.

Case D: Scarlet's car was struck by a falling large, wet sponge.

Suppose that someone claimed that in cases A–C, Scarlet's car was damaged. Plausible enough, right? But suppose that the same someone claimed that Scarlet's car was also damaged in case D because, after all, the sponge was *wet* just as the falling objects in the first three cases were. Of course, that conclusion would be absurd. Although the property of wetness is present in all four cases, it is not the wetness of the objects that is relevant to assessing whether or not the car is damaged.

Now back to Pereboom's four cases involving Professor Plum. Granted, causal determinism is present in all four cases. But, is causal determinism the relevant property that leads many people to have the intuition that, in the first three cases, Plum is not morally responsible? That's very unlikely. Mele asks us to consider, for example, a variation on case 2:

> In case 2a, the program the scientists install in Plum is indeterministic. It works just like the program in case 2 except that there is a tiny chance every few seconds that the program will incapacitate Plum. As it happens, Plum is not incapacitated. If Plum is not morally responsible for killing White in case 2, he is not morally responsible for killing her in case 2a either . . . . That the causation in Pereboom's case is deterministic is not essential to Plum's lacking moral responsibility for the killing.[10]

The point is that our intuition that Plum is not responsible in Pereboom's first three cases is not due to the presence of determinism, but to some other factor present in those cases. Plausibly, the relevant factor is the presence of human manipulators with nefarious motives. But notice that such manipulators are *absent* in case 4 (just as hard metal objects are absent in Scarlet's case D). So, if it is the case that nefarious manipulators are what makes Plum not responsible in cases 1–3, then we cannot judge that Plum is not responsible in case 4.

The upshot of these responses to Pereboom is that we have no good reason to think that determinism poses a threat to moral responsibility; and thus no good reason to accept (US).

What *Is* Required for Moral Responsibility

So, what are the conditions that an agent must meet for moral responsibility? Earlier, when discussing the nature of free will, I said that a compatibilist would define free will roughly as "being able to act in accordance with one's desires and values." Relying on this definition, a compatibilist might say that a morally responsible action was simply an action done in accordance with one's desire and values. I think this is basically right, but it is vague and imprecise. Here, more exactly, is what I believe to be an adequate account of moral responsibility:

> (MR) An agent S is morally responsible for an action A if (i) S does A for reasons that (ii) S considers sufficiently good to outweigh any reasons to do not-A, and (iii) the "value system" S uses to make this judgment is his own.

In the rest of this section I will explain in more detail what the conditions stated in MR mean and defend it against objections.

Reasons Responsiveness

According to MR, moral responsibility requires that agents act "for reasons." For example, when Professor Plum kills Ms. White, he does so *for the reason that* she poses some threat to him and he wants to remove that threat. Likewise, when you contribute money to, say, *The Samaritan's Purse*, you do so *for the reason that* you want to help needy people in third world countries.

Acting for reasons in this way presupposes, of course, the condition that agents be *aware of* reasons for acting and are able to appropriately *respond* or *react* to those reasons.[11] Being aware of reasons just means that one recognizes or knows (at least some of) the reasons why he might (or might not) perform some action. An agent's being able to respond to reasons is a bit more complicated. An incompatibilist who accepts PAP would likely insist that a responsible agent must be able to respond to any reason presented to him by being able to choose that reason and act upon it in the actual situation in which he finds himself. But given the falsity of PAP, all we need claim is that an agent, *in some possible world*, be able to act upon some reason presented to him in that world that issues in a different action. Suppose, for example, that Jones voted for Trump in the last election because of the candidate's strong stance against illegal immigration. And let us suppose also that Jones was causally determined to vote for Trump for this reason. Jones is appropriately responsive to reasons so long as there is a hypothetical scenario in which

Jones would have voted differently—for example, if Jones was less concerned about illegal immigration than he actually is.

It is important to recognize the importance of this condition. We intuitively understand that actions done irrationally are often (if not always) excusable. Agents who are insane, who make decisions on no basis or on very strange bases are not held responsible (or as responsible) as someone who acts on well-founded reasons, even if those reasons lead to immoral acts. So, ascriptions of moral responsibility require that an agent know what he is doing, and knows why he is doing it.

Two important qualifications need to be made at this point, however. First, when an agent does some morally significant action, for him to be adequately responsive to reasons, some of the reasons that he is aware of must be *moral* reasons, and he must recognize them as such. Agents who do not know the difference between right and wrong (e.g., young children, the mentally retarded, or psychopathic persons) are often not held morally responsible for their actions. We believe that their responsibility is at least mitigated because they are incapable (or less capable) of recognizing the moral significance and/or consequences of their actions. So, let's stipulate that an agent does not meet the condition of reasons responsiveness unless, when his action is morally significant, some of the reasons he is aware of are moral reasons.

Second, in order to avoid an obvious objection, we also need to stipulate that meeting the reasons-responsiveness condition requires that an agent's reasons *fit into a coherent structure of values*. Someone might object to our discussion of reasons responsiveness so far by citing a case of a person who is responsive to reasons but those reasons happen to be bizarre or incoherent. Imagine, for example, a person who goes on a killing spree in a fast-food restaurant. And let us say that he is reasons-responsive in this sense: if he were to see a chimpanzee smoking a pipe in the restaurant, he would cancel his killing spree.[12] Obviously, if this kind of bizarre reason is all that being responsive to reasons comes to, then MR fails as an account of moral responsibility. The restaurant killer's "responsiveness" is too erratic for us to be able to make sense of his action. Thus, we can hardly think that he is morally responsible. For an agent, then, to be adequately responsive to reasons, his reasons for action must fit into a system of values that is recognizably coherent. By this I mean that if we know a person's values and the reasons for his action, we could understand his motivation.

Acting for the "Good"

Condition (ii) of MR states that a morally responsible agent does what he considers sufficiently good enough to outweigh reasons against what he does. To understand this point, we need to take note of what seems to be a psychological fact about human action. The fact is that whenever a mentally healthy person makes a choice to perform some action, *that person always chooses what he desires most at that precise moment*. Take a mundane example. When I am presented with the option of having for dessert either a lemon meringue pie or a hot fudge sundae, I will choose the sundae every time—because I very much like (desire) hot fudge sundaes, but don't care all that much for lemon meringue. This is how it is with *all* of our choices; we choose whatever we most desire.

Some people have denied this, of course. Consider what we may call the "mugging case." Suppose you are confronted on a dark street by a mugger who demands, "Your money or your life!" When you hand over your wallet (as most of us would do), aren't you doing what you *do not* want to do? Not at all. Of course, all things being equal, you would prefer to keep your money. But all things are not equal. In the mugging case, you are facing a situation in which you have two *competing* desires: the desire to keep your money and the desire to preserve your life. When you hand over your wallet, you are acting on the desire to preserve your life, which is stronger than your desire to keep your money.

This analysis of action reveals something important for our account of moral responsibility. The examples given above show that our desires are ranked hierarchically. By this I do not mean simply that some desires are stronger or more intense than others (though that is often true). What I mean is that a person often chooses to fulfill certain desires based on how important fulfilling that desire (as opposed to some other desire) is to him. This brings us back to the notion of *values*. People value things. And they value some things more than others. Some of the things people value are the fulfilling of their desires, and they value fulfilling some desires more than other desires. Let's call the hierarchical "scale" of values that a person has his "system of values" or "value system."

Again, MR states that a morally responsible agent does whatever he considers sufficiently good at the moment of choice. And our discussion of desires and values suggests that what a person considers sufficiently good is dictated by his value system. So, when an agent is deliberating on what to do in a given situation, he does that action that he considers (perhaps together with its consequences) higher on his scale of values than any alternative actions that are open to him.

We must be careful to note, however, that an agent's value system has some flexibility. Agents acquire new values and lose old ones. Some values may become more (or less) valuable through moral education, changes in personality, and so on. Also, values can change locations on the scale from situation to situation. If I've had a particularly frustrating day at work, for example, I might do something I ordinarily wouldn't do, say, yell at my son, because the value I place on his feelings is not as important to me at the time as letting off steam. This flexibility in one's value system is important for explaining why people who care about morality often do what is morally wrong as well as accounting for the phenomenon of weakness of the will. Of course, the flexibility of one's value system must be limited. Otherwise, the structure of the system will be useless. So some values will be *core* values, which will seldom if ever be moved from their places in the hierarchy.

So, then, the morally responsible agent is one who has a value system in which he chooses what seems to him at the time to be the good thing to do (either morally good or good *for him*, or practically useful, or some such notion of good).

Values Ownership

What makes MR a version of compatibilism is the deterministic connection (discussed in the previous subsection) between a person's value system and his actions. Since the agent does whatever he considers sufficiently good at the time, and what he considers good is fixed by the present state of his value system, the agent is thus determined to act in accordance with his value system.

What makes it possible for an agent whose actions are determined this way to be morally responsible is that (as MR (iii) stipulates) his value system *is his own*. Values ownership has both a subjective and an objective component. Subjectively, for a person to own his values means that he recognizes that his actions make a difference in the world. Objectively, it means that his values are acquired through a natural and normal process. The phrase "natural and normal process" is admittedly vague, but it has to do with the everyday kind of social upbringing and "character development" that almost all of us experience as we grow up interacting with our environment and other people. "Natural and normal" excludes "sci-fi" scenarios in which our values are directly implanted in our minds by malevolent scientists, as well as extreme cases of brainwashing.

It must be noted, of course, that MR's account of values ownership presupposes that, ultimately, agents are *determined* to have the value systems they have. Even when "natural and normal," no human has a choice about when and where they are born, or what people will bring them up, or the precise content of their moral and practical education (or, for that matter, what genetic and biological factors may impact their character development).

This fact may generate an *objection*: since an agent's values are ultimately determined, how can we say that he is morally responsible for the actions that issue from those values? Shouldn't we conclude, rather, that he is *not* responsible? However, this objection assumes that moral responsibility requires either alternative possibilities or ultimate sourcehood (or both). Yet we have already seen that neither of these is required for moral responsibility. And once we lay these aside, the answer to the question of whether or not an agent is morally responsible whose values are acquired naturally and normally is: *Why not?*

Conclusion

Is free will compatible with determinism? In this essay, I have endeavored to show that there is no good reason to think not, so long as we are clear on what we mean by "determinism" and "free will." As we have seen, the real issue in this debate is what it takes for an agent to be morally responsible. I have argued that, even though an agent lacks alternative possibilities and ultimate sourcehood, if he meets the conditions laid out in MR, he is morally responsible for his actions.

Notes

1 Those who hold such physical determinism have to qualify it in light of contemporary quantum physics according to which the behavior of some subatomic particles is indeterministic. Physical determinists thus claim that while indeterminism may exist at the quantum level, the behavior of objects at the macro-level is nonetheless deterministic.

2 Some biblical texts that suggest this doctrine include Prov. 16:4, 9, 33; Dan. 4:34-35; Acts 4:27-28; Rom. 9:14-24; Eph. 1:11.

3 This definition is adapted and modified from the libertarian philosopher Kevin Timpe. See his *Free Will in Philosophical Theology* (New York: Bloomsbury, 2014), 7.

4 Harry G. Frankfurt, "Alternate Possibilities and Moral Responsibility," *Journal of Philosophy* 66 (1969): 829–39.

5 This response to Frankfurt-style Counterexamples is owing to Robert Kane, *A Contemporary Introduction to Free Will* (Oxford University Press, 2005), 87–88.

6 The counterexample is a variation on one developed by Derk Pereboom, "Hard Incompatibilism," in *Four Views on Free Will*, eds. John Martin Fischer, et al. (Malden, MA: Blackwell, 2007), 90–91.

7 Derk Pereboom, *Living Without Free Will* (Cambridge: Cambridge University Press, 2001), 112–15.

8   Michael McKenna and Derk Pereboom, *Free Will: A Contemporary Introduction* (New York: Routledge, 2016), 168.
9   Alfred R. Mele, *Free Will and Luck* (Oxford University Press, 2006), 143–44.
10 Mele, *Free Will and Luck*, 140.
11 Here I adopt the account of moderate reasons responsiveness defended by John Martin Fischer and Mark Ravizza, *Responsibility and Control: A Theory of Moral Responsibility* (Cambridge University Press, 1998), 62–91.
12 This example is a variation on Fischer and Ravizza's "Saber Killer" case in Ravizza, *Responsibility and Control*, 65.

RESPONSES

Response to Franklin

Steven B. Cowan

Study Questions

1. What is Cowan's stance on the soundness of the Consequence Argument? Why?
2. What does the Consequence Argument prove? What, according to Cowan, does it not prove?
3. What is Cowan's assessment of the PAP? Why does Cowan think that Franklin's defense of his version of PAP (No Freedom, No Blameworthiness) is inadequate?
4. What are the two varieties of incompatiblism? How do they compare and contrast with each other and with compatibilism?
5. What is the Libertarian's Dilemma? What is it supposed to show? How does Cowan illustrate the problem?

Christopher Franklin provides a clear and challenging defense of incompatiblism. The centerpiece of his defense is the famous *Consequence Argument*, which purports to show that freedom (and thus moral responsibility) necessitates that agents have the ability to do otherwise. In my response, I will argue that the Consequence Argument fails to show that moral responsibility requires the ability to do otherwise. I will also argue that the most popular form of incompatiblism—libertarianism—is actually inconsistent with moral responsibility.

The Failure of the Consequence Argument

As Franklin presents it (using the example of Sam and the loaned book), the Consequence Argument goes like this:

(1) If determinism[1] is true, then Sam's refraining from returning the book is the inevitable consequence of the past and the laws of nature.

(2) If Sam was able to return the book, then (given determinism) he was able to either change the past or change the laws of nature.

(3) Sam was not able to change the past or the laws of nature.

(4) Therefore, if determinism is true, Sam was not able to return the book.

On the basis of this argument, and combining it with the principle he calls *No Freedom, No Blameworthiness*, Franklin concludes that, if determinism is true, "no one is morally responsible for anything they do" (p. xx).

The only objection to the Consequence Argument that Franklin considers is that by David Lewis. According to Lewis, the Consequence Argument is guilty of the *fallacy of equivocation*, requiring two different senses of the phrase "is able" in order to make premises (2) and (3) true. Moreover, compatibilists need only accept the weak sense of "is able"—"I am able to do something such that, if I did it, a law of nature would be broken"—which allows them to reject premise (3). Franklin argues that the weak sense of "is able" turns out to be *too* weak since it would require us to say that Sam has the ability to return the book even in the third case in which he is bound by ropes. I agree with Franklin about this. So, I agree that Lewis fails to undermine the Consequence Argument.

There are other strategies for responding to the Consequence Argument, however.[2] Space does not allow me to elaborate on other possible and (perhaps) more promising responses. All I will say is that the jury may still be out on the soundness of the Consequence Argument. Either way, though, it doesn't matter. I am willing to concede the soundness of the Consequence Argument. But what does this prove? Does it prove that Sam is not morally responsible for not returning the book? No. All the Consequence Argument establishes is that Sam lacks the ability to do otherwise. And many compatibilists, myself included, are more than comfortable granting that Sam (and the rest of us) lack the ability to do otherwise.

The careful reader will notice that Franklin's defense of the Consequence Argument simply does not undermine moral responsibility, at least not by itself. In order to get to the conclusion that determinism rules out moral responsibility, Franklin has to combine the conclusion of the Consequence Argument to his *No Freedom, No Blameworthiness Principle*, which he states as follows: *"A person is blameworthy for what he does only if he was free to do otherwise"* (p. 320). This principle, of course, is Franklin's version of the principle of alternative possibilities (PAP), which reads:

> (PAP) An agent S is morally responsible for some action A only if, when choosing to do A, he could have done something other than A.

In my main essay, I argued that PAP is false by appealing to what are called *Frankfurt-type Counterexamples*—examples in which an agent lacks alternative possibilities but, intuitively, is morally responsible for his actions. I won't rehearse that discussion here but simply refer the reader to my main essay in this chapter.

Here I want to point out that Franklin motivates his version of PAP—the No Freedom, No Blameworthiness principle—primarily by appealing to the *third* Sam case in which he is unable to return the book because he has been tied up and gagged by robbers. In that case, Franklin claims, Sam is not morally responsible for failing to return the book because he simply could not return the book. Of course. Who could disagree with that? Sam was prevented from returning the book because of external constraints. All parties to the debate agree that in such cases agents are not morally responsible. The problem is that Franklin extends his reasoning (via the Consequence Argument) to *all* cases of determined action. Compatibilists believe that not all cases of determinism are created equal. Let us consider a variation on the *first* Sam case in which Sam fails to return the book because he wanted to stay home and read a novel. And let us suppose in this case that determinism is true, but that Sam's desires and values have been acquired as I detailed in my main essay—through a "natural and normal" process of character development. I contend that in this case, even though he could not do otherwise (his actions are determined), it is at least arguable that Sam is morally responsible for failing to return the book, and not nearly so obvious as in the third Sam case that he's not morally responsible.

Libertarianism and Moral Responsibility

Incompatibilism actually comes in two varieties: (1) hard determinism, and (2) libertarianism. What unites both versions is their commitment to the incompatibility of free will and determinism. But they differ over their stance toward determinism. The hard determinist accepts that determinism is true and thus denies that we are free and morally responsible. The libertarian maintains that we are free and morally responsible by denying determinism. The compatibilist, of course, denies the claim that free will and determinism are incompatible and argues that we can be free and responsible even if determinism is true.

Due to space limitations, I will not address the merits and demerits of hard determinism.[3] Most incompatibilists are libertarians and Franklin falls into this camp. I want to conclude my response by showing that, whether or not compatibilism is plausible, the kind of freedom that incompatibilists believe is necessary for moral responsibility—the kind that libertarians believe we actually have—cannot ground moral responsibility. That is, if we have the kind of freedom espoused by libertarianism, *we cannot be morally responsible for our actions*. My argument is not new. David Hume wrote long ago that "liberty [freedom], when opposed to necessity [determinism] . . . is the same thing with chance, which is universally allowed to have no existence."[4] He went on to argue: "Actions . . . where they proceed not from some cause in the character and disposition of the person who performed them, they can neither redound to his honor if good, nor infamy if evil."[5]

To see what Hume means, imagine that Jane must choose between two job offers—Job_A and Job_B. And let's suppose that she freely accepts the offer for Job_A. Now the question is, *why* did she choose Job_A and, more importantly, why did she choose it *rather than* Job_B? The libertarian has to say that there is nothing that determined that Jane accept Job_A—nothing about her character or her desires, nothing about her environment, nothing about the job offer, or anything else, that made her accept that job offer. Since it was a free act, she could have done otherwise in exactly the same circumstances. To be sure, Jane might very well have reasons that favor Job_A—maybe Job_A pays more than Job_B and is located closer to home, and those reasons outweigh any reasons for accepting Job_B. But those reasons cannot really explain why she chose as she did. Why not? Because even with these reasons, Jane's choice is undetermined. The reasons she has for accepting Job_A do not determine that she accept it. There is, as it were, a causal gap between her reasons for the job and her choosing to accept the job. It seems, then, that Jane's choice was *an uncaused event*, something that "just happened." But, if her choice was something that happened by chance, it is hard to see how it was under her control in any sense. How then can it be something that she is responsible for? Let us call the problem we are raising, the *Libertarian's Dilemma* and state it formally as follows:[6]

(1) If a person's actions are *determined*, then her actions are not under her control (because she lacks the ability to do otherwise).

(2) If a person's actions are *undetermined*, then her actions are not under her control (because they happen by chance).

(3) Hence, whether a person's actions are determined or undetermined, they are not under her control.

Of course, if an agent's actions are not under her control, she cannot be morally responsible for them. So, this dilemma seems to show that if we have the kind of freedom that libertarians say we have, then we are not morally responsible for our actions.

Notes

1. It is worth noting that Franklin understands determinism strictly in terms of physical or causal determinism. But there are other forms of determinism as I noted in my main essay. There is, for example, *theological* determinism, which sees all events as determined by God's sovereign or preordaining will rather than by the laws of nature. Of course, Franklin could simply recast the Consequence Argument in terms of God's preordination, so that the first premise would read: "If theological determinism is true, then Sam's refraining from returning the book is the inevitable consequence of God's sovereign will." Similar adjustments could be made in the remainder of the argument.
2. For discussion of all the major responses to the Consequence Argument, see Michael McKenna and Derk Pereboom, *Free Will: A Contemporary Introduction* (New York, Routledge, 2016), 72–101.
3. For arguments for and against hard determinism, see John Martin Fisher, Robert Kane, Derk Pereboom, and Manuel Vargas, *Four Views on Free Will* (Malden, MA: Blackwell, 2007), 85–125, 185–88; and Michael McKenna and Derk Pereboom, *Free Will: A Contemporary Introduction*, 262–85.
4. David Hume, *An Inquiry Concerning Human Understanding*, VIII.1.
5. Hume, *An Inquiry Concerning Human Understanding*, VIII.2.
6. This dilemma is discussed in more detail, along with possible responses in Robert Kane, *A Contemporary Introduction to Free Will* (Oxford University Press, 2005), Chaps. 4–6.

Response to Cowan

Christopher Evan Franklin

Study Questions

1. What is the distinction Franklin makes between free action and free will?

2. Why does Franklin disagree with Cowan's view that we always choose what we desire most? How does this pose a challenge to Cowan's second condition on free action?

3. What worry does Franklin have with Cowan's account of values ownership? How does he illustrate his concerns?

4. What is the only way, according to Franklin, that our values can be our own?

Cowan's defense of compatibilism shows that while at first glance compatibilism may seem unintuitive, this position has considerable plausibility and resources to respond to key objections. I concede much of what Cowan claims. For example, I agree that free will should be understood as the kind of control that would make us morally responsible for our actions, that free will requires reasons responsiveness, and that free will is intimately connected to our values. Nevertheless, I believe that compatibilism should be rejected. Rather than responding directly to the important objections Cowan raises against incompatibilists' contention that the ability to do otherwise and ultimate sourcehood are necessary for free will and moral responsibility, I will, instead, focus on what I take to be the heart of the deficiency in Cowan's positive defense of compatibilism: his accounts of free action and free will.

Morally Responsible Action

Consider first Cowan's account of morally responsible action:

> (MR) An agent S is morally responsible for an action A if (i) S does A for reasons that (ii) S considers sufficiently good to outweigh any reasons to do not-A, and (iii) the "value system" S uses to make this judgment his own. (p. 335)

(i) and (ii) state conditions on free action and (iii) states a condition on free will. To see the difference between free action and free will, compare my having a significant commitment to being in excellent physical shape to my going running one morning. My running is an *action* that expresses my *will*. Will has to do with aims, purposes, commitments, and choices, whereas action has to do with the ways we carry out or fail to carry out our aims, purposes, commitments, and choices. For your will to be free it must be *up to you* what your will is, and for your action to be free it must be *up to you* what you do. Let's now consider some worries for Cowan's analyses of free action and free will.

I think Cowan is right that (i) is a necessary condition of free action, but I reject (ii). Cowan explains (ii) in this way: "To understand this point, we need to take note of what seems to be a psychological fact about human action. The fact is: whenever a mentally healthy person makes a choice to perform some action, *that person always chooses what he desires most at that precise moment*" (p. 337). To appreciate Cowan's mistake, think first about the idea of strength of will. This seems to be a desirable character-trait. All of us have faced situations in which we wished we had more strength of will. Why?

The answer seems straightforward: we often find ourselves in situations in which our strongest desires go against our ideals, goals, and commitments. Strength of will is desirable because it would enable us to hold fast to our commitments in the face of our competing desires. That is, we desire to have the strength to act against our strongest desires. Consider a simple example. I decided last night to go running this morning. But upon waking, I don't desire to go running anymore: my bed feels much too comfortable and there is always tomorrow. In such situations, we often succumb to temptation, and succumbing to temptation is often followed by regret. We regret that we did not live up to our decision or that we have such strong desires that contradict our aims. But doesn't it also make sense to regret that we did not exercise more strength of will—that we did not act against our strongest desire and live up to our aims?

If, like me, you think it does, then (ii) must be false. For (ii) implies that it is impossible (at least for normal people) to act against their strongest desires. But the idea of strength of will is precisely the idea of a power to act against our strongest desires. Cowan is surely right that values have an important role to play in our acting freely. My contention is that free will requires the *ability* to translate our values into action. It seems to me that my decision to stay in bed is free even though it contradicts my values of being healthy and my specific commitment to go running that morning. My decision is free because I was able at that time to act in a way that accorded with my values, and I had this ability because I had the power to resist my strongest desire and, instead, to get up and go running. After all, I do often go running when I do not feel like it. I do it not because I feel like it but because I know it is good for me.

I take the upshot of these reflections to be that, contra Cowan, the ability to do otherwise is necessary for free will and moral responsibility. Free action does not require that our actions express our values, but rather that we had the ability to act in a way that expressed our values.

Free Will

Turn now to Cowan's analysis of free will. Cowan contends that your will is free only if your will is your *own*. But what does this mean? Cowan explains: "Values ownership has both a subjective and an objective component. Subjectively, for a person to own his values means that he recognizes that his actions make a difference in the world. Objectively, it means that his values are acquired through a natural and normal process" (p. 9). This seems right to me as far as it goes, but what does it mean to say that your values are acquired through "a natural and normal process"? Cowan notes: "'Natural and normal' excludes 'sci-fi' scenarios in which our values are directly implanted in our minds by malevolent scientists, as well as extreme cases of brainwashing" (p. 9). This too seems right. My worry is that Cowan, given his commitment to compatibilism, can offer us no *principled* reason for why values produced in "sci-fi" scenarios are not our own in the sense relevant to free will and moral responsibility. Imagine a case in which a powerful scientist, Jeff, has created a zygote in his laboratory in such a way that the person who is or develops from the zygote, Ernie, is causally determined to have a value structure that, in turn, causally determines him to murder Diana, the scientist's archenemy, thirty years from now.[1] Does Ernie seem either morally responsible for his decision to murder Diana or free in having the values that causally determined him to decide to murder Diana? Surely not. How can an agent have free will if he is completely controlled by some other agent? If you were a judge in the trial of Ernie, and you discovered that Jeff determined Ernie to have certain values that, in turn, determined him to murder Diana, wouldn't this discovery lead you to exculpate Ernie and conclude that it is really Jeff who is responsible? It would for me and Cowan seems to agree. Here's the rub: What is the relevant difference with respect to free will and moral responsibility between a scenario in which Ernie's values are brought about in a causally deterministic way by a manipulator like Jeff, and one in which Ernie's values are brought about in a causally deterministic way by normal processes, such as genes and parenting? In both cases, Ernie's values are causally determined by processes over which he has no control, and in both cases Ernie's values causally determine him to murder Diana. Thus, it seems Ernie is either free and morally responsible in both cases or in neither case. As we have just seen that Ernie is not free and responsible in the case where Jeff manipulated him, it follows that he is also not free when his values are produced in the natural and normal process.

Compatibilism is the view that the mere fact that your values, decisions, and actions are causally determined by factors outside of your control is no threat to freedom. But, then, it seems compatibilists must accept that our values, decisions, and actions being entirely controlled by other agents via a deterministic causal process is, in and of itself, no threat to free will. This seems to reveal the inadequacy of compatibilism.

In addition to being reasons-responsive and having the ability to translate our values into action, we must also be the ultimate source of our values in such a way that is incompatible with causal determinism. Only then will our values be our own in the sense relevant to free will and moral responsibility, and only then will we be responsible for translating these values into action. In the end, incompatibilism seems to be the right account of free will and moral responsibility.

Note

1 This example is adapted from Alfred R. Mele, *Free Will and Luck* (New York: Oxford University Press, 2006), 188–95.

Questions for Reflection

1. Do you see any problems with the Consequence Argument? If so, what?

2. Can you defend PAP against the Frankfurt-type Counterexample? How?

3. How might Cowan respond to Franklin's claim that we do sometimes act contrary to our strongest desire? Who is closer to the truth on this issue, Cowan or Franklin? Why?

4. What response, if any, could Franklin make to the Libertarian's Dilemma?

10

Does God Exist?

God Exists

Joshua Rasmussen

Study Questions

1. What led Rasmussen to become a truth-seeker? Where did his commitment eventually lead him?
2. What tool of reasoning does Rasmussen introduce? What are its "action steps"? What disclaimers for this tool does he invoke?
3. What is the Argument from Existence that Rasmussen presents? What support does he offer for the third premise?
4. What two reasons does Rasmussen give in support of the fourth premise of the Argument from Existence?
5. What five objections to the Argument from Existence does Rasmussen consider? How does he respond to them?
6. What is the probability argument schema that Rasmussen uses? How does he illustrate its use?
7. Based on the use of the probability schema, what five other things does Rasmussen believe are best explained by theism? Why?
8. What asymmetry does Rasmussen note between his arguments for theism and what he calls "arguments from harm"? What conclusion does he draw from this asymmetry?

I felt worried when I lost belief in God. My religious beliefs had given me security, a sense of purpose, hope for the future, and a feeling of significance as a person. I realized, though, that I could not simply hold on to a belief in God because *I wanted to*. In fact, my desire to believe fueled my doubts. I wondered: Had my desire for God blinded me from honestly facing reality? As I looked out beyond my local culture (family, church, friends), I saw that different cultures had different beliefs. I also saw that a group's most sacred beliefs tended to bring its members great security, just as belief in God had brought me security. How could I go on believing in *my* God among the many? I could not.

My doubts about God led me to become a truth-seeker. A noble root of atheism, I discovered, is the courage to face reality *as it is*, rather than as you may want it to be. In a moment, I made a commitment to follow reason and evidence wherever they might lead me. Thus, I began to investigate things for myself—to test everything. I exchanged blind faith for the light of reason. Later, however, I found that reason led me to faith.

This chapter considers how reason can lead to God. Although rational arguments carve away certain limited, arbitrary conceptions of God, I will present classic reasons that point to a culturally transcendent, Supreme Foundation of all things. I have two objectives: (i) to mark out some of the reasons (about existence, life, and reason itself) one can have for thinking that God exists, and (ii) to display a method of inquiry that readers may use to explore these issues further.

A Truth-Seeker's Tool: The Best Explanation

In order to investigate a subject as deep as the existence of God, it will help to start with a basic tool of reasoning. Much of what we reasonably believe in science and everyday life is based upon *explaining* things. For example, suppose you become aware of water covering streets, signs, cars, and houses. This experience gives you a basis to infer that it *probably* rained last night. That is because rain, in this context, *best explains* what you see. This method of reasoning is called "inference to the best explanation" (IBE).

It is useful to divide IBE into three basic action steps:

> Step 1. Start with what you know or observe.
>
> Step 2. Search for possible explanations of what you know or observe.
>
> Step 3. Select the best—most adequate and reasonable—explanation.

Before we continue, a few disclaimers are in order. First, IBE is not the *only* method to know things; philosophers investigate others. Second, the best explanation can be false, even if it is the *most probable* explanation. Third, there can be reasonable disagreement about which explanation is actually the best.

With IBE in hand, let us return to the investigation at hand: Does God exist? IBE gives us a procedure for investigating this question. We can gather up various things we take ourselves to know already, and then we can ask whether any of them are best explained by God's existence or nonexistence.

Explaining Existence

In this section, I will give a reason to think that the existence of God best explains why there is anything at all. I will begin by presenting the main premises of a two-part argument (based upon the history of *cosmological* arguments about reality as a whole). We will consider support for the premises and then turn to some common objections.

Here is the *Argument from Existence*:

Part I: Foundation

1. You exist.

2. Therefore, something exists.

3. The best explanation of the existence of something is in terms of a self-existent foundation.

Part II: Identification

4. The best explanation of the nature of a self-existent foundation is in terms of a *supreme* foundation—something maximal in every positive respect.

5. Therefore, the best explanation of the existence of something is in terms of something whose nature is best explained in terms of a supreme foundation (God).

Let us look more closely at each of the premises. I trust you will accept the first premise: that you exist. If you do not, then there is no "you" for me to convince.

Assuming you exist, you may now wonder: Why does anything exist? Why not, instead, *nothing*? Things would be far simpler if there had never been anything at all. As strange as it is, however, there is something rather than nothing. Why might that be?

The classic answer is the simplest: there is something because there *must be*. We can further explain why *there must be something* in terms of a self-existent, necessary foundation of all things. The foundation exists *on its own*, without any help from anything. It exists just because it *cannot not exist*. On this theory, reality divides into two sections. There is the bottom section, which is fundamental, uncaused, and self-existent. It exists because of its *necessarily existent* nature. The upper section of reality, by contrast, is dependent, caused, and explained by a prior or more fundamental state of reality. Let's call this theory "Foundation."

Reason repels the alternative. Suppose for a moment that there are *only* dependent things: each dependent thing depends upon another in an infinite, bottomless stack. The problem is that nothing within the stack could make the stack itself *independent*. By merely stacking together *dependent* things, you cannot produce an *independent* thing or stack: from dependence comes only more dependence. How then can the dependent stack stand in existence without any foundation? It seems it cannot.

We may summarize the above reasoning—as support for (3)—as follows:

3.1. Every stack of dependent things is itself dependent.

3.2. Therefore, the stack of all dependent things is dependent.

3.3. The stack of all dependent things cannot depend upon a dependent thing.

3.4. Therefore, the stack of dependent things depends upon an independent foundation.

This argument implies that the Foundation theory not only provides the *best* explanation of existence but also provides the *only* genuinely possible explanation.

The next part of the Argument from Existence is the "identification" part. Its main premise, (4), is about the nature of the foundation. It says that the best explanation of its nature is in terms of a Supreme Foundation.

We shall examine two reasons in support of (4). The first is that *theism* (the thesis that God exists) gives us the *simplest possible*—and thus least contrived, least arbitrary, and most intrinsically probable—theory of the foundation's nature. The theistic account of the foundation allows us to grasp the nature of the foundation with a single basic concept: *perfection*. From perfection, we deduce the classical attributes of God: perfect in power, knowledge, and goodness. These attributes, unlike the attributes of a Flying Spaghetti Monster, are far from arbitrary. The theistic attributes are all positive—*great*-making—to the maximal conceivable degree.[1] To illustrate what I mean by "great-making," suppose someone begins to praise you saying, "you are so great: you are stronger than everyone I know, you have much wisdom, and you tend to be rather cruel." If the third attribute just mentioned strikes you as out of step with the others, then you probably grasp the relevant concept of greatness. A "great-making" attribute contributes to something's overall greatness, excellence, or praiseworthiness. A *perfect* reality, then, is something that merits the highest degree of admiration and praise. It is maximally great: it has the most greatness that anything could have. Anything less than perfect, by contrast, has specific boundaries and parameters, such as the power to produce up to 9,102,231,231,232,132,151,453,642,999,823,122,873,122 electrons. Such non-maximal specifications require far greater complexity to express. One reason, then, to anticipate that the foundation is perfect is that this hypothesis is the simplest and least arbitrary.

Of course, there is other data to consider, and sometimes the simplest theory is not the correct one. The suggestion so far is just that we have some weight on the side of theism. If that is correct, then until counterweights are identified, we have reason to at least *lean* toward the theistic explanation by default.

Here is a second, related reason in support of the theistic explanation. Suppose the foundation has some *limit*, such as with respect to its total power. Then that limit would be arbitrary. Why *that* limit? The problem here is that nothing "underneath" the foundation could explain its basic features. Unlike you and me, the foundation is capable of existing and having features without any help from anything. That means that there cannot be a deeper, more fundamental explanation of its basic features. Yet any limits would require an explanation. Therefore, the foundation cannot have limits. We may summarize this argument from limits—as further support for (4)—as follows:

4.1. Only a perfect Being can be unlimited in every respect.[2]

    4.1.1. Whatever is unlimited in every respect is unlimited in greatness.

    4.1.2. Whatever is unlimited in greatness is perfect.

    4.1.3. Therefore, whatever is unlimited in every respect is perfect.

4.2. The foundation of all things cannot have any limit in any respect.

4.3. Therefore, the foundation of all things is a perfect Being.

In summary, theism explains existence in the least arbitrary manner. With God at the foundation, we have a self-existent, necessary foundation upon which all other things ultimately depend. Since this theory is the simplest conceivable account of the foundation (if not the only possible account via the argument from limits), we have some reason, then, to think the theistic theory is true.

As a way of further examining this argument, we will now consider several objections.

Objection 1. Who created God? If the universe must be created, why mustn't God?

Reply. This objection invites a clearer understanding of the concept of "God." The classical definition of "God" (the God of Abraham, Isaac, and the philosopher Anselm) is in terms of a *maximally supreme* being. Such a being would exist in the greatest way possible. Thus, it would enjoy *necessary existence* and would not depend on a creator for its existence. The very concept of God—as supreme—precludes the possibility of God having a creator. Things are different for limited beings. Anything less than supreme has certain arbitrary limits, such as a limit in power or goodness or greatness. Although limited things may require a cause, it does not follow that an *unlimited* Thing should, or even could, have a cause.

Objection 2. Maybe the universe is eternal. Perhaps for each physical state of the universe, some prior physical state explains it. Wouldn't an explanation of each *part* of history constitute an explanation of the entire infinite show?

Reply. This objection actually brings to light a strength of the Argument from Existence, which is that the argument *leaves open* the age of the universe. Even if the universe is eternal, we may still wonder why there is this eternal universe at all, rather than no universe or a different one. As Richard Taylor has suggested, the age of a thing does not by itself explain the existence of that thing. Suppose there were an infinitely old blue ball, for example.[3] We could still wonder why there is that blue ball at all. Similarly, we can wonder why there is any universe at all, no matter its age. The proposed answer is that the foundation of the universe has a special nature, which allows it to exist *independently* and *necessarily*. Readers are encouraged to consider whether there could be any better answer than that.

Objection 3. Maybe there simply is no explanation of the universe. As the philosopher David Hume has argued, even if each part of the universe has an explanation, it would be a fallacy (of "composition") to infer that the whole thereby also has an explanation.[4]

Reply. I offer two replies. First, according to IBE, the best explanation is preferable to *no* explanation. If, instead, you allow for no explanation, then you face the problem of chaos: random universes or parts of universes might snap into—and out of?—existence anywhere at any time without any explanation. This is too implausible to believe. Moreover, giving up IBE threatens the value of reason itself. Why follow reason if your thinking (and memories) might exist without any explanation whatsoever? Reason itself pressures us to think there is an explanation.

Second, it is not fallacious to infer that dependent things stacked together form a dependent whole. Although it is a fallacy to assume that a whole has *all* the properties of its parts, it is far from fallacious to infer that a whole inherits *some* properties of its parts. For example, the intrinsic nature of Play-Doh does not change merely by lumping together more and more Play-Doh. Similarly, the intrinsic nature of dependent things does not change by stacking more and more dependent things. It is a basic principle of reason (and confirmed by all experience) that from dependence comes only dependence.

Objection 4. Adding a supernatural being to our world adds unnecessary complexity. Therefore, the best explanation of natural reality is a *natural* foundation, not a supernatural one.

Reply. There is wisdom in this objection. In fact, although people sometimes imagine "God" as referring to something spooky and wholly beyond our world, the classical view has allowed a more immanent conception of God. What is at issue is not whether the foundation is wholly "other," but whether it is supreme. If we have a natural order with a natural foundation, still, we can consider how great the foundation is on the scale of conceivable greatness. The simplest theory of any foundation is that it is *perfect*, since any imperfections require a more complex theory about the details of its limits. In a sense, then, theism allows for the most natural account of the foundation. Pure naturalism *without* a supreme foundation, by contrast, is unnecessarily complex.

Objection 5. Maybe the foundation is "perfect" in some sense, but why think it is an omniscient, omnipotent, morally perfect personal being (i.e., God)?

Reply. I offer two considerations. First, absolute perfection is the highest level of greatness and so implies *no limits* with respect to any great-making attribute. A foundation that has some, but not all, great-making features would be less perfect—and so less simple and more arbitrary—than a foundation that is unlimited in greatness.

Here is a second consideration. The foundation has some *ability* to cause or sustain the existence of things, for it is the foundation of all things. Now the simplest, least arbitrary theory of how much ability it has is this: *the greatest conceivable ability*. Conceptual analysis reveals that the greatest conceivable ability includes cognitive and moral abilities. Therefore, the simplest, least arbitrary theory of the foundation's abilities *implies* that the foundation has maximal cognitive and moral abilities, just as a perfect Person would.

All these considerations invite further inquiry. To advance that inquiry, it is useful to separate the Argument from Existence into its two parts: foundation and identification. Maybe the foundation part appeals more to your mind, while the identification part inspires additional questions. Even so, the foundation part can provide a backbone for other arguments. The foundation argument gives us a self-existent foundation of all things (putting aside whether that foundation is supreme in other ways). One may then look at other data points to identify its nature further, as we shall do in the next section.

Explaining Much More

In this section, we will examine how theism best explains a wide range of data points. Toward that end, I will consider a sample of relevant data: the existence of logic, fine-tuning, biological evolution, morality, and minds. I will first present an argument structure designed to help determine the best explanation of data more generally, and then I will fill in the structure in terms of the above examples. My goal is to present an introductory survey of a family of important arguments.

To find the best explanation, it helps to see whether relevant data increases or decreases the probability of candidate explanations. Suppose we have some data D and a candidate hypothesis H. We may consider whether D makes H more likely by considering the following probability argument:

Probability Premise 1: D is expected (likely) if H is true.

Probability Premise 2: D is unexpected (unlikely) if H is not true.

Conclusion: D supports—makes more likely—H.

To illustrate the reasoning in play, let *H* be the hypothesis that it rained last night, and *D* be your observation that everything you see outside is wet. Then, assuming your observation of wetness is more likely if *H* is true than if *H* is not true, your observation of wetness *supports* the hypothesis that it rained last night. This argument underwrites ordinary and scientific reasoning.

We can use this probability argument structure when considering data with respect to the God hypothesis. Let *H* be the hypothesis that God exists, and let *D* stand for various data points. If *D* is more expected on theism than on atheism, then *D supports* the theistic explanation. I will briefly survey five examples as a way of illustrating this general method of investigation.

Reason (Logic)

Logic is the study of *rules of reason*, such as the rule that a statement cannot be both true and false simultaneously. Why, however, do such rules exist? Moreover, how do mere molecules and chemical reactions discover and follow these rules?

The *"mind-first"* hypothesis predicts good answers. Let's suppose the foundation of all things is a self-existent, perfect mind. The foundational mind includes all rules of reason, since it reasons perfectly. Therefore, it follows (from the rules of reason themselves) that theism *predicts* the existence of rules of reason. Moreover, with a mind at the foundation, there is literally a "reason" within the Foundation of reality for that Foundation to intend the existence of other minds capable of apprehending rules of reason.

Imagine, by contrast, that a bunch of material stuff springs into existence from nothing, with no mind behind it. In that case, it is far from clear that there would even *be* logic. If there are no minds, why would there be rules telling minds how to think rationally? Moreover, if there are no minds, why would any force within reality be inclined to produce a mind? Imagine the material stuff breaks apart into particles that eventually evolve to form molecules and chemical reactions. Even if natural selection leads to an array of complex machines, there is no reason within the fabric of reality for any pattern of particles to become "aware" of logical principles. Thus, even if we grant that mind from non-mind is somehow possible (not a trivial assumption), the suggestion here is that without a foundational mind, the existence of reason and other minds is far from *expected*.

Reason gives this result, therefore: the existence of minds that apprehend rules of reason is more likely—expected—with a mind at the foundation than without any such mind. Therefore, one may infer that rules of reason themselves support the mind-first hypothesis.

Fine-Tuning

You may have heard that the universe is finely tuned for the existence of life. The idea is that many things have to be *just right* for there to be life-forms. Physicist Alan Lightman recounts a bunch of examples of "right for life" features of our universe in his book, *The Accidental Universe*. Elsewhere he writes in summary: "If these fundamental parameters were much different from what they are, it is not only human beings who would not exist. No life of any kind would exist."[5]

Fine-tuning expert Robin Collins estimates that the degree of fine-tuning is analogous to hitting a target an inch in diameter with a dart launched across the Milky Way.[6] It would be easier to do that by chance, he calculates, than to get a universe suitable for life by chance.

What best explains the existence of a universe suited for life? Some theorists have proposed we can explain the fine-tuning of our universe in terms of many, many random universes. Given enough universes, perhaps it is probable that *some* universe would happen to be fit for life just by chance.

A problem with the "many-universe" explanation, however, is that it pushes back the question as to why there are the "right" many universes. Consider that an infinite number of car factories will never produce a turtle. Similarly, an infinite number of universes does not automatically guarantee life. We need a many-universe theory that explains how the probability of getting life in some universe is not so low. Interestingly, Collins argues that the best many-universe theory is a *theistic* one: the foundation of all universes is a mind. The thinking here is that minds are known to be inclined to create complex, interesting things, and a multiverse that includes a life-suitable universe counts as complex and interesting. By contrast, a purely material, non-mental universe-generator requires a high degree of fine-tuning and specification of its own. Therefore, it is unclear how a many-universe theory could explain fine-tuning unless there is a mind at the foundation of the many universes.[7]

Biological Evolution

We live on a planet where complex life-forms have evolved. Why has that happened? Part of the answer is *natural selection*: the more fit organisms are more likely to pass on their genes. But natural selection cannot be the whole story. A few years ago I wrote a grant-funded computer program that simulated randomized evolution (for the Randomness and Divine Providence group), and I discovered that randomized natural selection in a randomized environment tends to select *simpler* organisms, not more complex ones. In order to get complex structures, I had to fine-tune the environment in which the evolution would take place. The complexity research at the Santa Fe Research Institute further confirms this result.[8] The data, then, is this: evolution has produced complex life-forms. Computer simulations show—decisively to my mind—that evolution of complex life-forms is far *less likely* to happen without a design plan than with one. Therefore, the existence of biological evolution further supports a theistic explanation of the fine-tuning of the universe itself.

Morality

In addition to rules of right thinking (reason), we also recognize rules of *right living*. For example, inflicting pain on someone in order to feel powerful falls off the rails of right living. We may debate where all the moral lines are, and even whether our moral sense actually reveals an objective moral order outside our heads. Nevertheless, at least this much is clear: we have concepts of good and bad.

Why are there beings with moral concepts in the first place? Unguided evolution is not a complete explanation. The computer-based simulations of evolution to date have never produced creatures with a genuine moral sense—not even close to anything like them. That is not surprising: without a moral foundation and a design plan, there is no reason to *expect* the existence of morally sensitive beings to emerge ever. On the contrary, we may expect nonmoral states to continue producing nonmoral states indefinitely. The theistic foundation, by contrast, predicts the existence of a moral order at the foundation because it predicts that the foundation is morally perfect. Moreover, on theism there is a reason at the foundation of reality to intend there to be other moral beings who can apprehend that order. Therefore, by the probability argument, we have reason to infer that moral debates themselves point—at least to some extent—to a transcendent moral order rooted in a Supreme Foundation.

Minds

Your thoughts are not merely patterns of particles organized into brain states. Here is how you can know that

> M1. You are currently aware of your thoughts but not aware of any of your brain states.
>
> M2. For any A and B, if A = B, then you cannot be aware of A without being aware of B.
>
> M3. Therefore, your thoughts are not brain states.

The first premise is justified by your immediate experience of your own thoughts and *lack of experience* of the neurons inside your brain. The second premise is justified by the logic of identity: if A is identical to B, then whatever is true of A is true of B. The conclusion follows: your thoughts are not brain states.[9]

To be clear, brain science tells us that thoughts *affect* brain states, and vice versa. However, it would be a mistake to infer that thoughts *are* brain states. No science shows that.

It is sometimes suggested in response that perhaps awareness of our thoughts is nothing more than a subjective way of being aware of our brain. Consider that Lois Lane can be aware of Clark Kent without realizing he is actually Superman. Similarly, perhaps you can be aware of your thoughts without realizing that those thoughts are actually brain states.

This response fails, however, to account for the different *states* of the one person. Consider that the only way Lois can get confused about Clark Kent in the first place is that there is a *difference* between the "Clark Kent" states (such as sitting in an office, wearing glasses, etc.) and the "Superman" states (flying around, no glasses, etc.). Although there is one person who has both kinds of states, the states are not the same. In the same way, in order for you to be aware of your thoughts without being aware of your brain states, there must be a *difference* between your mental and material states.

Here, then, is our data: there are mental states in addition to material states. The existence of these mental states is precisely what we expect if the foundation is a mind that precedes the existence of all matter. By contrast, there is no reason to expect the existence of mental states from a purely non-mental foundation.

Summing Up

Many books have been devoted to exploring, debating, and unpacking each of the arguments we have considered. This brief introduction sows the seeds for further thought.

I will close this section by offering a summary assessment of the explanatory power of theism. Theism—understood in terms of a Supreme Foundation—provides a simple, nonarbitrary explanation of a wide range of data. No competing explanation of all the relevant data is simpler and less arbitrary. To be clear, there are challenging data points, such as the existence of pointless suffering, harms from religion, and God's hiddenness. One must weigh all these considerations in the balance. Even here, however, there is an important asymmetry. Arguments from harm typically require an inference from what we *don't see*. For example, we *don't see* God's reasons for allowing every case of harm. Interestingly, our lack of sight may be expected—at least to some extent—if God *exists*: for if there is an unlimited mind, you might expect there to be events that occur for reasons that are currently beyond what we see. Developing an argument against God from harm is tricky because harm itself requires many of the conditions—life, consciousness, moral sense—that are expected on *theism*. In any case, the arguments we considered in support of theism depend upon an inference from what we *see* immediately within ourselves: rules of reason, the existence of complex life, moral sense, and our own thoughts. In conclusion, one could reasonably think that theism provides the best explanation of what is seen.

Faith That Sees

The biggest threat to the discovery of God, and to productive truth-seeking more broadly, is *blind faith*. I join my nontheist friends, therefore, in proclaiming the great value of following reason and evidence wherever they lead. Be a free thinker. Seek truth. Follow the evidence. Align with reason. It is the only way to be free from the traps of groupthink and the errors of religion. There is a cost to count: if you follow reason and evidence wherever they lead, you risk finding truth you do not like. On the other hand, you may come to discover that the foundation of reality is greater than you had imagined.

Notes

1 The advanced reader may wonder whether some *conceivable* perfections may be *impossible*. Consider, for example, the power to convert a prime number into a prime minister. That power is conceivable (in some sense). Yet no *possible* being has that power. Should we say, then, that some perfections are impossible? My answer is that impossible features cannot actually be perfections because they *mar* a being by precluding these perfections: *coherence* and *necessary existence*. Alternatively, we may also proceed with the more modest account of perfection in terms of features that a greatest possible something would have.
2 Note that any being that is unlimited in a negative attribute—like moral evil—would not be unlimited in *every* respect. For it would be limited in its total *greatness*.
3 Richard Taylor, *Metaphysics* (Englewood Cliffs: Prentice-Hall, 1992), 84–94.
4 David Hume, *Dialogues Concerning Natural Religion* (London. Reprinted Indianapolis: Hackett, 1980), 58–59.

5 Alan Lightman, "The Accidental Universe," *Harper's Magazine* (December 2011), 3.
6 Robin Collins, "God, Design, and Fine-Tuning," in *God Matters: Readings in the Philosophy of Religion*, eds. Raymond Martin and Christopher Bernard (New York: Longman Publications, 2003).
7 There is Tegmark's multiverse theory that all possible geometries are real. This theory faces the problem of *incoherence*, however: the possible geometry consisting of a single dot surrounded by endless nothing in every dimension cannot coherently exist in the same reality as any other possible geometry.
8 For more on this subject, see, for example, Andreas Wagner's *Arrival of the Fittest: Solving Evolution's Greatest* Puzzle (New York: Penguin Group, 2014).
9 I give a more advanced, mathematical argument for this same conclusion in "Building Thoughts from Dust: A Cantorian Puzzle," *Synthese* 192 (2015): 393–404. I argue, in brief, that there can be a conceivable thought about any given brain states, while there cannot be a conceivable *brain* state for any given brain *states* (plural)—else there would be more conceivable brain states than conceivable brain states, which is contradictory.

God Does Not Exist

Bruce Russell

Study Questions

1. How does Russell define "evil"? What three examples does he give of such evil?
2. What is the first version of the Argument from Evil? What objections have been raised against it?
3. What is the second version of the Argument from Evil? What is the difference between necessary and unnecessary suffering?
4. What are van Inwagen's two objections to the second version of the Argument from Evil? How does Russell respond to these objections?
5. What is the third version of the Argument from Evil? What is the skeptical theist's objection to this argument?
6. Why does Russell reject the strategy of skeptical theism?
7. How might theists attempt to turn the Argument from Evil on its head? What does Russell say about this strategy?
8. What objections does Russell have to the idea of a "lesser God"?

Background

I will assume that God is an all-powerful, all-knowing, wholly good being. God may have other attributes, too, such as being perfectly free and the creator of the universe, but the problem of evil concerns how a being with even just these three attributes could allow all the evil we see in the world. By "evil" I will mean "what is intrinsically bad," that is, bad in itself apart from its consequences. The suffering of innocent beings is that sort of "bad thing," and so the focus is on the question of how God, if he exists, could allow all the suffering of innocents that we see in the world, and especially the terrible suffering of children. To help understand the sort of suffering I have in mind, I will cite three examples of such suffering.

Between 2:00 a.m. and 3:45 a.m. on New Year's Day in 1986, a little girl in Flint, Michigan, was brutally raped, beaten, and then strangled to death. The prime suspect was her mother's boyfriend who was kicked out of a bar where he, the mother, and someone who had rented a room in their house were drinking. When the mother came home, she got into a fight with her boyfriend, knocked him out, and then went to bed. It was thought that the boyfriend raped, beat, and then killed the little girl when she came downstairs to go to the bathroom in the middle of the night. However, the boyfriend's lawyer argued that there was not enough evidence to show that the boyfriend, rather than the roomer, committed the heinous crime, so the boyfriend got off scot-free.

On January 31, 2000, Edward Swinson and Linda Paling killed their daughter, Ariana, first throwing her to the floor for not eating properly and then drowning her by pouring water down her throat while she was unconscious. There were many bruises on Ariana's body. She had a broken elbow and a four-inch skull fracture, brain hemorrhaging, ears that showed signs of tearing, and the piece of skin that connects the upper lip to the gums was torn, probably from sharp blows to her mouth. Ariana was malnourished, dehydrated, and had lost more than half her blood on the day of her death. Before calling the police, Swinson and Paling coached their two younger children to take the blame for killing Ariana.

On August 30, 2012, Mitchelle Blair killed her nine-year-old son, Stephen, by placing a plastic bag over his head after punching and kicking him, lifting him with a belt around his neck until he became unconscious, forcing him to drink Windex, and throwing scalding water on his genitals. She considered all these acts as fitting punishment for what Stephen had done to his six-year-old brother. On March 25, 2013, Mitchelle punched her daughter, Stoni, beat her in the head with a wooden stick, and threw scalding water on her before killing her by placing a plastic bag over her head. She killed her two children because her younger son, who was six in 2012, told her that Stephen and Stoni had raped and sexually abused him. After killing Stephen, she placed his body in a freezer, and after killing Stoni, she had her older daughter, then fifteen, put Stoni in the freezer on top of Stephen. Both of the surviving children knew that their siblings were in the freezer. The bodies were discovered on March 24, 2015, when a crew came to evict Mitchelle from the Martin Luther King Apartments in Detroit where she lived. In her confession to the court, she said she had no remorse and saw the abuse and killing of her two children as just punishment for what they had done to her young son. Ironically, it was reported in the *Detroit Free Press* (March 27, 2015, 6A) that her now eight-year-old son had, "25 scars and injuries on his back 'both old and new,' as a result of physical abuse by Mitchelle Blair" herself.

Following other philosophers, I will call such acts and such outcomes "horrors." My argument is not that if God exists, he would have prevented all of these heinous acts, for maybe certain virtues like empathy and compassion could only exist if some horrors like these have occurred, and it is better to have some horrors like these and the virtues that they make possible than no horrors and none of the relevant virtues. But I will argue that there are *way too many* horrors for it to be reasonable to believe that God exists. These three examples are but the tip of the iceberg. Similar acts occur every day all over the world. And we should not forget the Armenian genocide in Turkey in the early twentieth century when 1.5 to 2 million Armenians were killed, the Jewish Holocaust in Nazi Germany where six million Jews were killed, the Tutsi genocide in Rwanda in 1994 in which around 800,000 Tutsi were killed, and the killing fields in Cambodia where the Khmer Rouge led by Pol Pot killed around 1.7 million people between 1975 and 1979. Of course, over the years millions of innocent people have suffered agonizing deaths due to earthquakes, tsunamis, volcanic eruptions, fires, floods, starvation, and disease. How could a perfectly good God who knows about all this suffering and could prevent it allow it to occur?

Versions of the Argument from Evil

There are various versions of the argument from evil, some better than others. The first version goes as follows:

1a. If God exists, there would be no suffering.

2a. But there is suffering.

3a. So God does not exist.

This argument has the following form:

1a. If P, then Q.

2a. Not-Q.

3a. Therefore, not-P.

Arguments of that form are valid, which means that, necessarily, IF the premises are true, THEN the conclusion is true. So any objection to the argument must show that at least one of the premises is false.

There are two standard objections to the first premise. One says that God could allow *some* suffering because it is needed if people are to develop virtues like empathy, compassion, forgiveness, courage, and perseverance, and it's better to have those virtues and some suffering than no suffering but also none of those virtues. The other objection has come to be called "the free will defense." It says that a good God would want people to have free will and the freedom to act on that will in ways that can make a significant difference in the world, either good or bad. People could not have that sort of will if God always intervened to prevent the exercise of their will whenever they intended to do something bad, and it's better for people to have free will and the bad consequences that sometimes ensue than to have no bad consequences but also no free will.

In light of these objections, philosophers have modified the first version of the argument from evil, and it goes as follows:

1b. If God exists, there would be no *unnecessary* suffering (suffering that is *not itself* needed to bring about a greater good or prevent a greater evil, nor is *allowing it* needed to do that).

2b. But there is such *unnecessary* suffering.

3b. So God does not exist.

Sometimes there is no way to bring about a good without imposing suffering. This happens when a dentist first injects a child's gums to numb the area around the tooth he is going to fill. This is *necessary* suffering because the good that results from having the tooth filled cannot be achieved without the dentist causing some suffering by injecting the anesthetic. However, if the dentist drilled the child's tooth without first injecting a local anesthetic when one is readily available, the suffering caused by that drilling would be *unnecessary*. If a parent could stop the dentist from proceeding without first administering the anesthetic but does not, she would be *allowing* unnecessary suffering.

If a good parent allows her child to exercise his free will which she knows will result in *unnecessary suffering* to her child, then the suffering itself would be unnecessary but *allowing* her child to exercise his free will (which will result in his suffering) *is necessary* for the child to have the good of exercising his free will. A good parent might allow her teenage son to go out with his friends the night before an important test, thereby allowing him to exercise his free will, but knowing that he will probably suffer the consequences of a bad grade on the test as a result. In the case of the tooth that needs filling, the good that results from a repaired tooth cannot be realized without the suffering that comes from injecting the child's gums with a local anesthetic. However, the good that comes from the child's exercise of his free will does not require the bad consequences of doing poorly on his test; he could have freely chosen to stay home and study. So the bad consequences are not needed to realize the good. But the parent's *allowing* her child to make a choice *is needed* for the intrinsic good that exercising that choice represents. Premise (2b) says that sometimes neither *suffering itself* nor *allowing the act which leads to it*, is needed to bring about a greater good or prevent a greater bad.

Peter van Inwagen is a philosopher at Notre Dame University. He has criticized (1b) on two grounds. First, he argues that a good person (a good ship's captain) could allow unnecessary suffering, which shows that a good being could allow such suffering. He imagines that Atlantis is sinking and 1,000 people will drown if the captain does not put them aboard and sail to a safe port. However, for each person he puts aboard, the chance that the ship will sink increases by 0.1 percent. So if the captain puts all 1,000 aboard, the ship will sink and all will drown. If he puts none aboard, all will drown when Atlantis goes under. Van Inwagen says that a good captain would not take all but a handful (say, would not take 990 people) and would take at least a handful (say, at least 10). Van Inwagen thinks that a good captain could take any number between those extremes and not do anything wrong. But we can imagine that he could have taken, say, twenty on board and the ship would have made it safely to port. So if the good captain took only ten aboard, he would allow at least ten to suffer and die *unnecessarily* as Atlantis went under. The point of this story is that being good is compatible with allowing *unnecessary* suffering. So a good God could allow *unnecessary* suffering. So premise (1b) is false.

The problem with van Inwagen's example is that the captain is finite and so does not know exactly how many he can take aboard and still make it safely to port. But a good God is omniscient, all-knowing, so he would know exactly how many to take aboard. The captain has ignorance as an excuse for allowing some to drown unnecessarily, but God, if he exists, would not have that excuse. So it seems that God would not allow *unnecessary* suffering, which is what (1b) asserts.

The second objection that van Inwagen offers is more subtle. Assume that a good dentist must leave the needle in the child's gums more than 10 seconds in order to inject enough local anesthetic to numb the area around the tooth. If the dentist leaves it in there for 11 seconds, the desired effect will occur, but so also if he leaves it there for 10.5 seconds, and 10.25 seconds, and 10.125 seconds, and so on. There is no least amount of time greater than 10 seconds that will achieve the desired level of anesthetic, but every extra millisecond means slightly more pain for the child. So the dentist could always cause less suffering by pulling the needle out a millisecond earlier and still achieve the end of numbing the tooth. Yet, even if he pulls the needle out just a fraction of a second beyond 10 seconds, he does nothing wrong even though he could have pulled it out a millisecond earlier and achieved the same result.

A good God may be in a similar position. It may be that there is a limit to the amount of suffering God can prevent. At some point, if he prevents more suffering, a greater good cannot be achieved or a greater bad prevented. But that point can be approached nearer and nearer without ever being reached. So whatever amount of suffering God allows, he could have allowed less and still achieved the desirable end of bringing about a greater good or preventing a greater bad. But it would not be wrong of him to allow an amount of suffering very near the limit even though that amount of suffering *is not necessary* to achieve the desirable end since he could always have allowed slightly less suffering and still achieved that end. So a good God, like a good dentist, could allow *unnecessary* suffering to occur. So premise (1b) is false.

Perhaps a response can be made to this subtle objection of van Inwagen, but I am going to sidestep the issue by offering a third version of the argument from evil that starts with a different premise. It goes as follows:

1c. If God exists, there would be no *excessive and unnecessary* suffering (that is, there would not be *way more* suffering than need be allowed, or that itself is needed, to bring about a greater good or prevent a greater evil).

2c. But there is such suffering (recall the suffering of little children that occurs every day and all the genocide and mass killings that have occurred).

3c. Therefore, God does not exist.

I do not think that the first premise of this version of the argument from evil is open to objection. Even if there is the kind of limit to the amount of suffering God could allow that van Inwagen imagines, it would be wrong of God to allow *way more* suffering than is needed to bring about the relevant desirable end. It would be permissible for God to allow an amount of suffering very near that limit, but not an amount far greater than that limit. If the limit were, say, 100 units of suffering, it may be permissible for God to allow 100.01 units of suffering but not 200, and certainly not 10 million units.

So I think premise (1c) is not open to objection. But some have argued that the second premise in this version of the argument from evil is false, or at least that we have no reason to think that it is true.

Skeptical Theism

I think it is pretty hard to show that the second premise in the last version of the argument from evil is false, that is, to show that there is *not excessive, unnecessary* suffering. *Some* of the suffering in the world might be needed to develop some virtues, and God might have to allow *some* suffering that results from the exercise of free will if we are to have significant freedom. But there would seem to be ample opportunity to develop the virtues with a lot less suffering, and a good being would more often curb the exercise of free will when its exercise results in the terrible suffering of innocent children.

The more typical response to (2c) is that of *skeptical theism*. Skeptical theists do not argue that (2c) is false. They argue that we are in no position to judge whether it is true or false. They appeal to analogies in which some person lacks the intelligence, experience, or training of someone else, and thus is in no position to judge what the other person does or believes. For example, a novice chess player is in no position to judge that a master in chess has made a blunder; a beginner in physics or math is in no position to judge that the views of a Nobel Prize winner in physics or math are mistaken, and so on. Similarly, we are in no position to judge that God would not allow all the terrible suffering of innocents that we observe in the world. God may know of goods and bads of which we are unaware, know how to weight these goods and bads (and the ones of which we are aware) against each other, and know how what happens in the world helps to bring about the goods and minimize the bads. We are no more in a position to judge that there is excessive, unnecessary suffering than a novice chess player is in a position to judge that Kasparov has made a bad move in chess. God may allow all the suffering we see for reasons beyond our ken, just as a chess master might make moves that are beyond the ken of a novice.

The problem with this move by the skeptical theists is that a similar move can be made by Young Earthers to defend their view that the world was created recently (6,000 or 100 years ago, or even just five minutes ago with all its signs of age). The critics argue against Young Earthism as follows:

I. If Young Earthism is true, then the earth was created recently.

II. But the earth was not created recently.

III. So Young Earthism is false.

The defenders of this argument point to deep river valleys such as the Grand Canyon, fossils, even cave paintings to argue that the earth is older than 6,000 years and so obviously more than 100 years or five minutes old. So it was not created recently. So premise II is true.

The Young Earthers are Skeptical Theists of sorts. They say that we are in no position to judge that the earth was not created recently, that is, in no position to judge that II is true. We think that the earth is millions of years old, but God could have created the world very recently with all the observable evidence the critics of Young Earthism cite, with the books and documents that back up the critics, and even with people who have seeming, but not real, memories of the past. He might have done that so the people he ultimately creates will have a good idea of what the natural world is like and how best we can live together. If that knowledge had been gained through a long and actual history, many animals and innocent people would have suffered terribly throughout the course of that history. Better to learn the lessons of history without, rather than with, actual suffering. Better for people to begin to exist with more rather than less knowledge and wisdom.

The Young Earthers agree with standard theists that freedom of the will and the ability to make a significant difference in the world by acting on it are great goods. So God would want creatures with that sort of freedom to exist. But he would want them to come into existence better prepared to use that freedom well than if they lacked the justification for their beliefs that history provides. But he also would not want that justification bought at the price of the suffering of their ancestors. So the best way to satisfy all these desiderata is for God to make the world look old and plant false memories in some people while creating the world only recently.

Of course, some of God's reasons for creating the world only recently, and with people that have just the amount of knowledge and wisdom gained from "history" that they do, are beyond our ken. We don't know why he didn't provide the people he ultimately created with more, or maybe even less, knowledge and wisdom than they have, and why he didn't create the world a little earlier or later than he did. But Skeptical Theists resort to the same sort of move when they say that God allows all the suffering of innocents that we observe for reasons beyond our ken. At certain points, both the Young Earthers and the Skeptical Theists resort to appeal to God's having reasons beyond our ken to defend their views.

On the story the Young Earthers tell, God is a deceiver because he has given us evidence that the earth is much older than it really is, but deception is not always wrong. If people could have deceived the Nazis by telling them that the Jews had already fled while actually hiding them in a large underground city, that is what they should have done as a means of saving thousands of Jews. Deception may always be prima facie wrong, but it is not always wrong all things considered. Contra what some philosophers say, a good God could deceive if that is the only way he could achieve some very good end.

It's true that the Skeptical Theists do not reject established science while the Young Earthers do. But that is irrelevant since the nature of their defenses is the same and that is what matters. Someone who accepts science but consults a crystal to defend his belief that there are ghosts is no better off when it comes to his belief in ghosts than someone who consults a crystal ball to defend Young Earthism and rejects science. The first is not an adequate defense of belief in ghosts; the second, not an adequate defense of belief in Young Earthism. Similarly, the defense of belief in God by the Skeptical Theists against the argument from evil is no more an adequate defense of that belief than is the similar defense of Young Earthers against the evidence from science despite the fact that Skeptical Theists do not reject science while Young Earthers do reject the part of science that says, or implies, that the earth is billions of years old (though they accept the rest of science in the same way as Skeptical Theists). The defenses are alike in that both suggest what some of God's reasons might be for causing, or allowing, relevant phenomena and answer challenges where it is not obvious what God's reasons might be by reference to his having reasons beyond our ken.

Can Theists Turn the Argument on Its Head?

Theists might accept the first premise of the third version of the argument from evil that I have offered. But instead of denying its consequent by arguing that there is excessive, unnecessary suffering, and then concluding that God does not exist (as the atheist does), theists might argue that God exists and conclude that there is *not* excessive, unnecessary suffering, despite appearances to the contrary. That is, theists might try to turn the argument from evil on its head like this:

1d. If God exists, there would be no *excessive and unnecessary* suffering.

2d. God exists.

3d. Therefore, there is no such suffering.

There are many arguments *for* the existence of God, and all of them have been severely criticized. The Design Argument and the Cosmological Argument at most conclude that there is, or was, a Designer or Creator of the universe, or certain things in the universe (for example, the human eye), or certain properties of the universe (say, fundamental regularities described by laws of nature like the Law of Gravity, or certain fundamental constants that would not allow for the emergence of life if they were only very, very slightly different). They do not conclude that the Designer or Creator is wholly good. So their conclusions do not contradict the conclusion of the argument from evil which says that a God that is all-knowing, all-powerful, *and* wholly good does not exist.

The Ontological Argument starts from the concept of a perfect being or the greatest possible being and concludes on the basis of that concept and a few other supposedly obvious principles that such a being exists. If we were justified in believing the premises of that argument, and that its conclusion follows from those premises, we would be justified in believing that an all-knowing, all-powerful, *and* wholly good being exists. I cannot discuss various versions of this argument here, but I think very few philosophers now believe that there is some version that meets the test of our being justified in believing its premises and justified in believing they support its conclusion.

Arguments for a Lesser God?

Suppose someone concedes that there is no good argument for the existence of God understood as a being who is all-knowing, all-powerful, and wholly good, and that the argument from evil is a good argument against the existence of such a being. They might still contend that the Design Argument or the Cosmological Argument or what is called the Fine-Tuning Argument are good arguments for the existence of a lesser God, one who is very knowledgeable and very powerful, even if not wholly good, nor all-powerful and all-knowing.

There may be good arguments for the existence of such a lesser God. We'd have to look at each of them one by one to see. But all of the plausible versions will face the problem of explaining how an immaterial being can interact with the physical world. It's similar to what has been called the mind-body problem which concerns how an immaterial soul could interact with our material bodies. And they will have to compete with hypotheses that say that some material universe has always existed and that matter necessarily has certain properties in the same way that water necessarily has the property of being composed of H_2O. Maybe there is some argument for a lesser God that will overcome the obstacles and beat the competition. Let's see, but let's not forget that there is a version of the argument from evil which is a good argument against the existence of the God of Judaism, Christianity, and Islam, a God that is all-knowing, all-powerful, and wholly good.

RESPONSES

Response to Rasmussen

Bruce Russell

Study Questions

1. What three reasons does Russell give for why God is not the best explanation for the existence and nature of the universe?
2. How does Russell reply to the objection that the God hypothesis, despite its flaws, is still better than its rivals due to its simplicity?
3. What is Russell's "gremlin analogy"? What is it supposed to show?
4. How does Russell respond to Rasmussen's arguments that God best explains the existence of logic and morality?
5. How does Russell respond to Rasmussen's argument that God best explains biological evolution?
6. What, according to Russell, is the flaw in Rasmussen's Fine-Tuning Argument?
7. What is the premise that Rasmussen's argument against mind-brain identity relies on? Why does Russell think this premise is false? What additional response does Russell make to the argument?

The two most fundamental metaphysical questions are the following: (1) Why is there something rather than nothing, and (2) Why is the world (the universe) the way it is rather than some other way? Joshua Rasmussen thinks that the existence of God provides the best answer to these two questions. He arrives at this conclusion by relying on IBE, which he calls a basic tool of reasoning.

I accept IBE as a basic tool of reasoning and will even point out how I rely on it in my version of the argument from evil. But before applying that tool, we must properly understand it so we do not misapply it and reach unjustified conclusions. When we do that, the theist's answer to questions (1) and (2) will not look so good.

Is the God Hypothesis the Best Explanation of the Existence and Nature of Our Universe?

To the first question of why there is something rather than nothing, Rasumussen says the answer must be in terms of something that *must* exist, something that exists *necessarily*; otherwise, something will remain unexplained. But why should we think that it's possible for there to be a *necessary* agent or person, as God must be if he creates or sustains the universe through his will? We are agents and persons, but we do not exist necessarily. We can cease to exist. Perhaps numbers (say, the number 2) and mathematical propositions (say, that 2 +2 = 4) exist necessarily, but they are not agents or persons. We have no examples from experience that indicate that an agent or person can exist necessarily. One criterion of whether an explanation is a good one is how well it fits with our background knowledge, and the God explanation fits poorly with our background knowledge of agents and persons, all of which are contingent, not necessary, beings.

Second, a good *causal* explanation provides some detailed causal story of how the thing that does the explaining brings about what it explains. The explanation that opium causes sleep in virtue of its dormative powers is not a good one because it lacks any detailed account of how opium brings about sleep. An explanation in terms of what the chemicals in opium do to the neurons in our brains is a better explanation because it does contain such a story. God is supposed to be an immaterial being, a being that does not occupy space (though he may exist in time). But the explanation that God causes the universe to exist (and perhaps sometimes intervenes in the events of the universe), lacks any detailed causal story of how God brings about these results. It is like the explanation that opium causes sleep in virtue of its dormative powers, but even worse. Further investigation can reveal the details of the causal story of how opium causes sleep, but it is *in principle impossible* to figure out how God brings the universe into existence or intervenes in its history. One version of the so-called mind-body problem is the problem of explaining how an immaterial soul can interact with the material brain. The problem of how an immaterial God can create, or interact with, the material world is the mind-body problem writ large. Positing an immaterial soul to explain why our neurons fire the way they do is not a good explanation of how they do. Similarly, positing an immaterial God to explain why the universe exists is not a good explanation of its existence. It is an explanation that invokes an insoluble mystery.

Even if these objections could be overcome, the God hypothesis does not really explain why we have *this* universe rather than some other. One might claim that we have this universe because God chose to create it and not some different one. But the question remains as to why he chose to create it instead of some other equally good universe. If the answer is that there is no reason, he just did, the atheist can give a similar answer by saying of our universe that there is no reason why it exists; it just does. Both explanations leave something unexplained.

Rasmussen might reply that even if these objections show that there are weaknesses in the God explanation, they do not show that it is not *the best* answer to the two fundamental metaphysical questions he addresses. That hypothesis can be *better than* all its rivals despite its flaws. His argument that it is better ultimately turns on his claim that it is a *simpler* hypothesis than its rivals because it posits the existence of a *perfect* being. Perfection does not require further explanation because it implies maximal greatness, which does not require further explanation. Rival hypotheses that try to answer the two fundamental metaphysical questions leave unexplained why the cause they posit has just the amount of power, knowledge, goodness, and so on, that it has rather than some other amount. So they are less complete; Rasmussen says that they are more complex. Other things being equal, simpler hypotheses are better than more complex ones. So, *other things being equal*, the God hypothesis is simpler, and hence better, than any of its rivals.

But *are* other things equal? If my argument from evil is sound, it is reasonable to believe that a perfect God does not exist because it is not reasonable to believe that a good God would allow all the suffering that we see. So no good explanation can posit the existence of a perfect God. At best, Rasmussen could hold that a being perfect only in knowledge and power is responsible for the existence of the universe. Of course, that sort of being could be Satan, not God as we traditionally understand him.

I should point out that I rely on IBE myself at the stage in my argument where I claim that it is more reasonable to believe that much of the suffering of innocents that we observe has no point, is unnecessary, than to believe that God allows it for reasons beyond our ken. Because this God hypothesis posits an extra being who is immaterial and has mysterious reasons and powers that are beyond our grasp, this hypothesis is not as good as the one that says there is no such being and there is pointless suffering in the world. The latter is a much simpler hypothesis to explain what we observe.

Finally, consider the following analogy that counts against nearly any God hypothesis, even one that does not posit a perfect God. Suppose I hear noises in the attic and that my view is that they are caused by squirrels, or tree branches, or something material even though I have no evidence that they are, and even though I have made great efforts to gather such evidence. You, on the other hand, believe that they are caused by invisible, untouchable, unsmellable, unhearable gremlins who, for reasons beyond our ken, have chosen to reside in my attic. Even if I have no good explanation for the noises in the attic, intuitively, we should all reject your gremlin hypothesis. So, by analogy, even if atheists have no good explanation of why there is something rather than nothing and why we have the universe we do rather than some other one (which I believe is the case), we should reject the God hypothesis. The problem of evil is grounds for rejecting the hypothesis that there is a perfect God (perfect in knowledge, power, *and goodness*); the gremlin analogy is grounds for rejecting the hypothesis that there is a less than perfect God.

What More Can the God Hypothesis Explain?

If I am right, a God hypothesis cannot be the best explanation of anything. But I also want to say a few things about Rasmussen's claim that the God hypothesis does much more than answer the two fundamental metaphysical questions.

Rasmussen characterizes logic as the study of the rules of reason and then argues that it is more likely that there would be rules of reason if God exists than if he does not. But logic is not the study of rules of reason; it's the study of what follows from what or what forms of argument guarantee that a conclusion is true if its premises are. These rules of logic are like mathematical propositions, such as $2 + 2 = 4$, which are necessarily true, that is, true in all possible worlds, including a world where God does not exist. I would say the same about fundamental moral principles. It is necessarily true that happiness that is not achieved at the expense of others is intrinsically good and that torturing babies for the fun of it is wrong. Those evaluative and moral claims, like certain mathematical claims, are true in all possible worlds, including ones where neither God nor humans exist.

We have beings who *recognize* mathematical and moral truths because *recognizing* them provided people with an evolutionary advantage. As Derek Parfit has said,[1] our ancestors who could do subtraction had an advantage over others who could not when they saw three tigers go into a cave and only two come out. The same could be said of people who cooperated on the basis of rules of justice and morality. That computer simulations have not yet produced such creatures is not sufficient reason to think that actual unguided evolution did not. Computers probably have also not produced creatures that can do advanced mathematics. There is no reason to think that "non-moral states will continue to produce non-moral states indefinitely." After all, non-intelligent states did produce more and more intelligent states. There is no reason to think things are different when it comes to moral states.

Rasmussen argues further that computer simulations of randomized evolution tend to produce simpler, not more complex, organisms, which suggests that actual evolution unguided by a Designer could not produce complex organisms like ourselves. This reminds me of earlier arguments of the same sort. People back in Darwin's day claimed that evolution could not explain what has come to be called "irreducible complexity"—for example, a complex structure like a wing that has "parts" all of which are needed for it to fly, but which could not have evolved all at once. Evolutionary theorists answered the challenge by invoking the idea of "function switching." For instance, some insects originally have "wing buds" that serve to regulate their temperature but do not allow for flight. Gradually these "wing buds" in some members of the population evolved into wings that did allow for flight. So even if a wing is an "irreducibly complex" feature of an insect, evolution can explain its gradual emergence through the idea of "function switching." The point is that what seemed in the past to be unanswerable challenges to the theory of unguided evolution were later answered. So there is inductive evidence to support the belief that current challenges will be answered in the future.

Rasmussen defends what is called the Fine-Tuning Argument. This is the argument that there are fundamental constants in the universe that allow for the emergence of life and intelligent life and, if these constants were only very slightly different, the emergence of life and intelligent life would be impossible. The argument is that it is very likely that we would have such a universe friendly to life if God exists, but very unlikely that we would if he did not. The assumption is that the more likely hypothesis is the best explanation; so we should accept the God hypothesis as the best explanation of why the universe is friendly to life.

The flaw in this argument starts with Rasmussen's assumption that if some data, D, is likely on a hypothesis, H, and not-likely on not-H, we have reason to accept H (his argument requires this assumption even if what he explicitly states to be the basis of his reasoning is slightly different). To return to the undetectable gremlins, it might be likely that gremlins would make the very peculiar scratching noises we hear in my attic, and unlikely that those noises would exist if there were no such gremlins. Still, we should reject the gremlins hypothesis because of its intrinsic improbability. Ignoring the intrinsic probability of a hypothesis is an instance of what is called the "base rate fallacy."[2] We need to consider the likelihood of the hypothesis itself, not just the likelihood, given that hypothesis, of what is to be explained before we can assess the likelihood of the hypothesis on the evidence or data. Given the low intrinsic probability of the God hypothesis, we should not accept it on the basis of the fine-tuning phenomena even if it's true that, given that God exists, it's very likely that the universe would be fine-tuned.

Lastly, Rasmussen argues that we are not identical to our brains. I believe his argument for this claim is flawed because it rests on the following false premise: For any A and B, if A = B, then you cannot be aware of A without being aware of B. But lightning is identical to electricity in the clouds, and I can be aware of the lightning without being aware of the electrical particles that comprise it. They are too small for me to be aware of them.

In any case, an atheist can accept that we are not identical to our brains. Atheists can hold that our mental lives (which consist of our thoughts, desires, aims, goals, emotions, what we value, etc.) *depend* on our brains. So, if our brains cease to exist, then so do our mental lives and so do we.

In conclusion, let me note that Rasmussen and I share a commitment to seeking the truth and to following reason wherever it may lead. Of course, we think it leads in quite different directions. I think it leads to a truth that many will dislike and find uncomfortable. Given Rasmussen's condemnation of blind faith and believing something just because you want to, I hope that he, and others, will follow me to where I think reason leads us.

Notes

1. Derek Parfit, *On What Matters*, vol. 2 (New York: Oxford University Press, 2011), 496. All of Chapter 32, "Epistemology" (pp. 488–510) is relevant to answering the question of how evolutionary theory can account for the reproductive and survival advantages of being able to recognize and respond to nonempirical truths (mathematical, logical, and normative).
2. The base-rate fallacy is committed by people when they just consider how likely it is that some disease causes some symptom (say, an irregular heart rate) and ignore how rare that disease is in the relevant population. Maybe it's less likely that an electrolyte imbalance will cause the irregular heart beat than the disease, but such an imbalance is much more prevalent in the population than the disease. So a doctor should think an electrolyte imbalance, not the rare disease, is the cause of the arrhythmia.

Response to Russell

Joshua Rasmussen

Study Questions

1. Why does Rasmussen think that a moral standard would be expected to exist if God exists? Why would a moral standard be unexpected if atheism is true? What's the relevance of this to the problem of evil?

2. What is Bayesian probability? How does Rasmussen use it to show that the existence of mysterious evils is more likely if God exists?

3. What is the distinction Rasmussen makes between fierce and soft skeptical theism? How is it supposed to help in his response to Russell?

4. What is a theodicy? What is Rasmussen's "Love Story Theodicy"? How does it address the problem of evil?

Russell provides an excellent summary of an important challenge to the proposition that God is wholly good. In this brief piece, I will lay some groundwork for further analysis of that challenge. First, I will suggest how the very challenge from evil can actually flip into a reason for believing in God. Second, I will offer three tools for thinking further about the implications of various kinds of evil: (i) Bayesian analysis, (ii) soft Skeptical Theism, and (iii) Theodicy.

How Can There Be Bad?

Russell draws our attention to horrible aspects of reality, where kids suffer unspeakable tragedies. When we face these horrors, everything within us says, "That ought not to be." They are *bad*.

Before we even consider why a perfect Being might allow very bad events, let us consider how there even could be genuine (intrinsic) bad in the first place. How can one motion of molecules be "bad" while another is "good"? Part of the problem here is that we cannot even say which events a wholly *good* Being should prevent unless there is some *moral standard* by which we can say that some events are actually not good.

As hinted in my opening statement, one way to unpack the puzzle of morality is in terms of what is *expected* on theistic versus atheistic perspectives. Suppose, first, that the foundation of reality is a perfect Being. Then it follows (just by definition and logic) that a morally perfect standard exists as part of the nature of the perfect Foundation. The thought here is *not* that you must believe in God to discern right from wrong. Rather, it is that the very existence of a moral order with agents who can apprehend that order is precisely what you would expect if there were a supreme Foundation, whose nature sets a moral standard.

Suppose, by contrast, there is no supreme nature at the ground of reality. What is expected *then*? Is it expected that there would be a moral standard *and* that molecules would produce intrinsically valuable beings *and* that those beings could apprehend aspects of that standard? Some philosophers (I, too, among them) think that getting moral agents from purely nonmoral matter is impossible, in the way that it is impossible to make an iPhone out of liquid nitrogen or to produce a prime minister out of prime numbers. In such cases, the nature of the effect is incompatible with the nature of the cause. In any case, even if responsible moral agents *could* spring from nonmoral patterns of motion, it still would not follow that moral communities are exactly what you would *expect* from a mindless, nonmoral foundation. The challenge, then, is to see how a moral order could be nearly as expected, if even possible, unless the ground level of reality has a wholly good nature that defines the moral standard. In view of this challenge, a number of philosophers have thought that while the horrors of life invite important questions, their *intrinsic badness* is actually delegitimized on a purely naturalistic framework.[1]

How Skeptical Can We Be?

We have many samples of evidence against God's goodness. I will focus on the most perplexing class of them: these are bad events for which we fail to see any good reason a perfect Being could have for allowing them. Call these cases "mysterious evils." We bring the mysterious evils to the stand.

I would like to acknowledge that suffering and tragedies pose legitimate questions and concerns. My aim here is not to "justify" evils. Rather, I will offer some tools to help you continue in your own analysis of their evidential weight.

The first tool is *Bayesian probability*. Recall that for any given data D and hypothesis H, we can investigate whether D supports H by asking two questions:

Q1. How likely (expected) is D given H?

Q2. How likely (expected) is D without H?

If D is more likely given H than without H, then D supports H. In this case, D = the existence of mysterious evil, and H = the hypothesis that a perfect Being exists. The two questions, then, are these:

Q1. How likely (expected) are mysterious evils if a perfect Being exists?

Q2. How likely (expected) are mysterious evils if a perfect Being does not exist?

These are not easy questions to answer. What I wish to point out here is merely that it is not trivial to show that the existence of mysterious evil is more likely without a perfect Being than with a perfect Being. Consider that a perfect Being would include a perfect mind. Such a mind would grasp values far beyond what any limited mind could grasp. For that reason, we may expect, just by logic, that if God were to exist, God would allow some events for "God-size" reasons that moral agents would not grasp.

Meanwhile, in the absence of a perfect Being, expectations are different. Part of the problem is that there is no purely logic-based reason for there to be *any* moral agents without God. Another part of the problem is that there is no purely logic-based reason to expect there to be the highly specific situation in which moral agents *contemplate why God may allow evil*. As a result, you could infer that a theistic framework actually *better predicts* the existence of some mysterious evil.

So far, I have suggested that the existence of mysterious evils is not by itself clear evidence against God. I have not thereby shown that no event can in principle count as evidence against God. In fact, I am sympathetic with Russell's argument that extreme Skeptical Theism is *too* skeptical. Russell's piece is helpful because it exposes a problem with an overly skeptical stance toward potential evidence against God. It also invites a fruitful distinction: we may distinguish *fierce* skepticism from *soft* skepticism (with a spectrum in between). Fierce skepticism insists that no event in principle could be evidence against God, while soft skepticism merely invites further inquiry.

A second tool, then, for probing the problem of evil carves a distinction between *different levels* of skepticism. Fierce skepticism leads to overly skeptical results where you cannot even be confident that the world is older than five minutes. Even so, the Bayesian analysis above inspires a more modest result. There is also a practical benefit: anyone who steers between fierce skepticism and dogmatism is in a good position to seek deeper insights into potential "God-sized" reasons a perfect Being may actually have.

Theodicy

The final tool I offer is *theodicy*. A theodicy is an account of the good reasons a perfect Being may have for allowing various evils. Theodicies do not answer all our questions, but they can help put some of our questions into a larger perspective.

To illustrate, I will sketch a theodicy that is inspired by both theory and testimony. I call it the *Love Story Theodicy*. Various people have reported meeting a Being of Light upon cardiac arrest.[2] Before they experience "returning to their body," in some cases they experience asking the Being of Light questions, including questions about evil and suffering. I have heard many such cases, and in all the cases of which I am aware, there is a core theme: they feel a sense that this life is part of a far greater eternal story and that love is central to their purposes. Whether or not you believe any of these reports, my observation here is just that this theme of love and a greater story interweaves the world's spiritual traditions, and it enters all the major theodicies.

The Love Story Theodicy connects love and a greater story to the following question: *what are the elements of a great story*? Here are some: adventure, exploration, progress, tensions and releases, heroism, comic relief, courage in the face of uncertainty, layers of truth, layers of discovery, sacrifice, cleverness, good and evil, elements of horror, victory, interwoven stories that build toward something greater, consistent rules that cannot be broken willy-nilly, unpredictable surprises, a variety of dynamic characters, episodes that contribute to a larger plot, romance, hints of the future, trials, and displays of love. A truly great story would involve a great sacrifice of love by the Greatest Being in that story, and it would involve layers of mystery to be uncovered. There would be tragedy, yet all tragedies for all souls would be transformable into something beautiful and unexpected, perhaps in later scenes. The Love Story Theodicy gives a basis for real hope to anyone facing real horror.

Interestingly, the Love Story Theodicy is consistent with the canons of both logic and history. Furthermore, something like the Love Story Theodicy is predicted by the "Maximal Being" theism I argued for in my opening essay. Whether Love Story is a framework for a *true* story or merely a fantasy ultimately produced by mindless motions is a question for every moral agent to consider.[3]

Notes

1 See, for example, J. L. Mackie's *Ethics: Inventing Right and Wrong* (Harmondsworth: Penguin Books). See also the exchange in this volume by Matthew Flannagan and Graham Oppy.

2 For recent scientific investigation into the veridicality of such experiences, see Sam Parnia, et al., "Awareness During Resuscitation: A Prospective Study," *Resuscitation* 85, no. 12 (2014): 1799–1805 (online at: http://www.horizonresearch.org/publications).

3 Thanks to Haigen Messerian for thoughtful feedback on an earlier draft.

Questions for Reflection

1. What explanation might the atheist offer for the origin and nature of the universe? Would these explanations be better than the theist's? Why?

2. What do you think of Russell's gremlin analogy? Does it treat the God hypothesis fairly? Why?

3. What responses, if any, could Rasmussen make to Russell's objections to his "much more" arguments?

4. Should we or should we not expect there to be "mysterious evils" if God exists? Why?

5. Does Rasmussen's Love Story Theodicy adequately address the problem of evil? Why?

Essay Suggestions

A. In light of the debate over universals, do you think that universals exist? Write an essay in which you present an argument (or arguments) defending your answer to this question. Be sure to consider and respond to any arguments from the other side.

B. An issue related to the mind-body problem involves personal identity over time. Given that our bodies and brains are constantly changing, what is it that makes me the same individual person from moment to moment? Write a paper in which you explore ways in which a physicalist could answer this question and then argue either for or against some or all of these answers.

C. The term "strong artificial intelligence" (AI) refers to a computer that is able to think and reason at a level equivalent to humans, including being self-conscious. Write a paper in which you argue either for or against the possibility of a strong AI based on what you think is the correct view of the mind-body problem.

D. Hard determinists believe that we are not morally responsible for our actions, and yet they believe that criminal punishment is justifiable on the grounds that it can restrain and/or modify criminals' behavior. Write an essay in which you either defend or criticize this hard determinist case for criminal punishment.

E. Write a paper in which you defend libertarianism in response to the Libertarian's Dilemma, or defend compatibilism in response to Franklin's "Jeff and Ernie" case.

F. Write an essay in which you either defend Rasmussen's cosmological argument against Russell's "gremlin" analogy, or defend Russell's argument from evil by raising objections to Rasmussen's "Love Story" theodicy.

G. Write an essay in which you construct an argument either for or against the existence of God that's different from the arguments presented by Rasmussen and Russell.

For Further Reading

On Metaphysics—Universals

Allen, Sophie R. *A Critical Introduction to Properties*. New York: Bloomsbury, 2016.
Kim, Jaegwan, Daniel Z. Korman, and Ernest Sosa, eds. *Metaphysics: An Anthology*. Malden, MA: Wiley-Blackwell, 2011.
Loux, Michael J., and Thomas M. Crisp. *Metaphysics: A Contemporary Introduction*. 4th ed. New York: Routledge, 2017.
Moreland, J. P. *Universals*. Montreal: McGill-Queen's University Press, 2001.

On the Mind-Body Problem

Goetz, Stewart, and Charles Taliaferro. *A Brief History of the Soul*. Malden, MA: Wiley-Blackwell, 2011.
Heil, John. *The Philosophy of Mind: A Contemporary Introduction*. New York: Routledge, 2012.
Warner, Richard, and Tadeusz Szubka. *The Mind-Body Problem: A Guide to the Current Debate*. Malden, MA: Wiley-Blackwell, 1994.

On Free Will and Determism

Fischer, John Martin, Robert Kane, Derk Pereboom, and Manuel Vargas. *Four Views on Free Will*. Malden, MA: Wiley-Blackwell, 2007.
Kane, Robert. *A Contemporary Introduction to Free Will*. Oxford: Oxford University Press, 2005.
McKenna, Michael, and Derk Pereboom. *Free Will: A Contemporary Introduction*. New York: Routledge, 2016.

On the Existence of God

Gale, Richard M. *On the Nature and Existence of God*. Cambridge: Cambridge University Press, 2016.

Meister, Chad, and Paul K. Moser. *The Cambridge Companion to the Problem of Evil*. Cambridge: Cambridge University Press, 2017.
Moser, Paul K., and Paul Copan, eds. *The Rationality of Theism*. London: Routledge, 2003.
Plantinga, Alvin, and Michael Tooley. *Knowledge of God*. Malden, MA: Wiley-Blackwell, 2008.
Sennett, James F., and Douglas Groothuis. *In Defense of Natural Theology: A Post-Humean Assessment*. Downers Grove, IL: InterVarsity Press, 2005.

Index

ability 244, 245, 316, 319, 322, 342, 347, 348, 357, 370
  strong 323–4
  weak 323–4, 325, 326
abortion 12
abstract entities 240, 261, 262, 270 n.2
access (epistemic) 21–2, 95, 97–8, 99, 100, 101–2, 103, 105, 106 n.2, 110, 114, 119, 121–2, 123, 124, 243, 301
The Accidental Universe 359
acting for the good 336–8
aesthetics 4
Albertus Magnus 191
Anscombe, Elizabeth 298
appearances 28–9, 31, 34, 37, 100, 125, 159, 171
Aquinas, Thomas 191
argument from evil, *see* problem of evil
argument from existence, *see* cosmological argument
arguments 5, 6–8, 11, 12, 29, 138, 147, 156, 234, 366, 385
  deductive 6–8, 11, 146, 202, 290
  inductive 6, 8, 146, 163, 166, 187, 290, 378
  soundness 7, 8, 11, 147, 156, 168, 246, 341, 342, 376
  validity 7, 8, 11, 40, 41, 52, 68, 147, 155, 156, 187, 366
arguments from harm 350, 361–2
Aristotle 1, 78, 79, 134, 159, 186, 194, 210, 230, 289
Armstrong, D. M. 258, 260, 267, 269, 279
atheism 135, 149, 199, 200, 204, 246, 305, 351, 358, 379

attributabulism 118 n.9
Austin, J. L. 45

base rate fallacy 163, 378, 379
basic beliefs 20–1, 23, 61–3, 65, 67, 86–7, 90, 91
Bayesian probability 380, 381, 382
Berlinski, David 205
Big Bang 213, 321, 328
biological evolution, *see* evolution, biological
Blanshard, Brand 76
Bohr, Niels 171
Boltzmann, Ludwig 164, 166, 213
BonJour, Laurence 76, 81, 107, 110, 114
Boyle, Robert 191, 209–10, 228, 229
Bradley's regress argument 241, 260, 268–70, 277, 279, 280 n.6
brain-in-a-vat argument 26, 33–6, 37, 40, 52, 54, 55, 57, 60
Brownian motion 163–4
bundle theory 262

caloric 172
Campbell, John 298–300
Campbell, Keith 248
Cartesian circle 83 n.3
cause, causation 25, 66, 97, 128, 133, 134–5, 160, 164, 186, 190–231, 232, 241, 242, 243, 288, 292, 296–7, 305 n.3, 313, 320, 329, 332, 334, 344, 355, 357, 375, 376, 381
character development 245, 317, 338–9, 343, 347
Christianity 22, 143, 195, 230, 373
Churchland, Paul 302–3, 304
Clifford, W. K. 140

closure principle   41, 46, 47, 49, 53, 55, 233
coherentism   20, 21, 65, 72–85, 86–7, 88, 94
   explanatory   21, 77, 91, 92, 93–4
Collins, Robin   359
companionship problem   253, 254
compatibilism   244, 326, 327–40, 341, 343, 346, 348, 385
Comte, Auguste   199
consciousness   108, 242, 246, 302, 304, 308, 362
consequence argument   244, 316, 321–6, 341–3, 345 nn.1, 2, 349
contextual negations   190, 197
Copernicus, Nicholas   24, 159–60
cosmological argument   245, 246, 246 n.1, 352–7, 372, 385
cosmology   205, 213, 231
Course of Positive Philosophy   199
creation   25, 193–5, 198, 226 n.1, 228, 229, 230, 328

Darwin, Charles   211, 230, 378
Davidson, Donald   61, 65–7
De Anima   289
definitions (analytic)   8–11, 12, 56, 57–8, 60
demarcation problem   205, 229, 234
Democritus   173, 180 n.5
Dennett, Daniel   209, 294, 295–6, 300–1, 303, 304
Denton, Michael   205
Descartes, Rene   19, 32–3, 38, 39–40, 41, 72, 73, 83, 96, 97, 99, 119–20, 239, 298
design argument, *see* teleological argument
desires   242, 244, 288, 290, 291, 294, 295, 301, 309, 313, 327, 329–30, 335, 337, 343, 346–7, 379
determinism   9, 239, 243–5, 316–17, 318, 320–1, 322, 323, 324, 326, 327, 328, 329–30, 332, 333–4, 339, 339 n.1, 341–2, 345 n.1, 348
   theological   328, 345 n.1
Devitt, Michael   250, 251

divine providence, *see* providence, divine
dogmatism   38, 48–9, 52, 56, 382
doxastic attitudes   50 n.2, 132, 152
Dretske, Fred   55
dual systems theory   139, 145–7
Duhem, Pierre   161, 177

economy   250, 310
   ideological   250–1, 277–8
   ontological   251, 277–8, 278
   quantitative   251, 257
electrons   165, 172, 180 n.2, 182, 186, 283, 313, 354
Encyclopedia of DNA Elements Project (ENCODE)   207
Enquiry Concerning Human Understanding   48
epiphenomenalism, *see* property dualism
epistemology   4, 17, 18, 41, 53, 72, 149, 239, 379 n.1
evidence   18, 22, 23, 25, 28, 30, 33–4, 35, 37, 41–2, 44, 45, 46–9, 55, 57, 62, 97, 98–9, 107, 108–9, 111, 112, 113–17, 118 n.9, 119, 120, 121–2, 123–6, 127, 128–32, 134, 135–6, 137–8, 139–49, 150, 151, 152–3, 154–6, 157, 159, 163, 165, 166, 167–8, 172–3, 175, 176, 180 n.4, 181, 184, 186, 187–8, 190, 196–7, 198, 200, 205, 206, 223, 227, 233–4, 280 n.1, 284, 313, 351, 362, 378
   experiential   23, 82, 132, 141, 155
   sources of   2, 3, 23, 127, 132–3, 136, 138, 139, 141, 156
evidentialism   22–3, 41, 127, 128–33, 134–6, 137–8, 139, 140–3, 150–6, 157
evolution, biological   207, 212, 216 n.8, 246, 357, 359–60, 374, 377–8, 379 n.1
Ewing, A. C.   76
Exclusivism   61–2, 65
exemplification relation   251, 255, 276, 278, 279, 280 n.6
experience   20, 21, 24, 28, 33–6, 41, 54, 57, 61, 62–3, 64–70, 76, 79,

80–2, 86–90, 91–4, 100–1, 105, 105 n.2, 120–1, 125, 129–30, 131, 134–5, 140, 141, 142, 146, 147, 152, 153, 156, 159, 173, 179, 184, 185, 186, 188, 196, 233, 243, 294, 298, 301–13, 356, 361, 369, 375
explanations, scientific   18, 24–5, 178, 190–231, 296
externalism   18, 21–2, 95, 99–100, 105, 107–17, 121–2, 123, 126

Factionalism   161
faith   137, 139, 143–4, 171, 351, 362, 379
fallacies   227, 228–9, 232
  ad hominem   39, 228
  appealing to consequences   170–1, 177, 185, 187
  begging the question   32, 198, 205, 206, 222, 229, 315 n.3
  composition   356
  equivocation   323, 342
  privileged cynicism   228
  red herring   217 n.8, 229, 277, 279
  straw man   221, 223–4, 228
fallibilism   19, 38, 42–5, 46, 47, 53, 55, 60
Faraday, Michael   200
fine-tuning (of cosmos)   210, 213, 246, 257, 259, 360, 372, 374, 378
first-person point of view   97, 103, 294, 297, 300–1, 303, see also self–awareness
foundationalism   19–21, 61–71, 72, 79, 82, 86, 87–90, 94
  experiential   20–1, 62, 63, 64, 65–71
four-case manipulation argument   327, 332–4
Frankfurt, Harry   330–1
Frankfurt-type counterexamples   327, 330–2, 342, 349
freedom conditions   317
free will, freedom   2, 9, 239, 243–4, 245, 316–18, 320, 323, 325, 326, 327–30, 335, 339, 341, 343–8, 366–7, 369, 370

free will defense   366
Fuller, Steve   205
Functional Annotation of Mammalian Genome (FANTOM)   207–8
functionalism   342
function switching   378

Geach, Peter   298
Gettier, Edmund   43, 97, 107, 108
Gettier problem   4, 43–4, 95, 97–8, 233
God   3, 25, 32, 134, 138, 156, 175, 190, 193, 195, 197, 198–200, 203, 222, 223, 225, 228, 245, 296, 305, 328, 350–1, 356, 362, 374, see also theistic arguments
  action   191, 198–9, 223, 225, 228, 229
  attributes   22, 227, 246, 353–5, 364, 372–3, 375
  belief in   23, 50 n.2, 62, 134–5, 139–40, 142–9, 153, 155, 200, 204, 222, 228, 350–1, 371, 380
  existence   2, 5, 22, 23, 143, 144, 149, 150, 155, 232, 239, 245–6, 293 n.1, 350–84, 385
  freedom   194, 375–6
  goodness   364, 365, 367, 368, 371, 372–3, 376–7, 380, 381
  hiddenness   361
  omnipotence   364, 372–3
  omniscience   364, 367, 372–3
God hypothesis   34, 191, 358, 374, 375–9
god-of-the-gaps   205
Goethe   302
Goodman, Nelson   253
gravity, law of, theory of   162, 167, 168, 210, 320–1, 372
Great Pumpkin Objection   18, 233
Gregory, Brad   190, 199–200, 221–2
gremlin analogy   374, 376–7, 378, 384, 385
Grice, Paul   48
Grossmann, Reinhardt   279
grounds   6, 8, 21–2, 44, 95–126, 166, 179, 193, see also reasons

INDEX

Hanks, Tom   3
hard determinism   244, 343, 385
historical pessimism   24, 158, 165–8
The Hobbit   92–3
horrors   365, 380–1, 383
Hume, David   9, 48–9, 246, 246 n.1, 298–9, 344, 356

imperfect community problem   253–4
incarnation   25, 193–5, 225
incompatibilism   243–4, 316, 320, 321–6, 327, 329, 343–4, 348
indiscernibility of identity   294, 301, 303
indispensability argument   257
infallibilism   41, 42–3, 44, 45, 46, 47, 52–3, 60, 98
inference to the best explanation (IBE)   53–4, 162, 164, 351–2, 356, 374, 376
instrumentalism   24, 160
intelligent design theory (ID) 25, 203, 204–11, 214, 215 n.5, 216 nn.6, 8, 221, 222–4, 228–9, 231 n.3, 232
internalism   18, 21–2, 41–2, 52–3, 95–106, 107–9, 110–17, 120, 122, 123–6, 233
internalism's dilemma   22, 107, 112–13, 115, 117 n.5, 123–6
irreducible complexity   378
Islam   22, 373

Jackson, Frank   302
Jefferson, Thomas   17, 134
Jesus   144, 156
Jewett, J. W.   182
JTB account of knowledge   17–18, 43, 97, 106 n.4, 108, 151
Judaism   22, 373
junk DNA   207–8, 226 n.5
justification   17, 18, 19–22, 26, 27–9, 31, 37, 44, 45, 53–5, 56, 58, 61–94, 95–126, 127, 129–31, 134–9, 143, 146–9, 150–1, 153, 154, 156, 162, 233, 370
  doxastic   95, 99, 130–1, 138

propositional   53, 99, 129–31, 137
responsibility   90, 92, 93–4, 104, 114, 120
truth-conducive   90, 92–3, 105

Kant, Immanuel   230, 246, 246 n.1
Kelvin, William T. (Lord)   171
Kierkegaard, Soren   144–5, 157
Kitcher, Philip   167
Klein, Peter   55, 82, 90, 91
knowledge   1, 2, 4, 11, 17, 18–19, 21, 22, 23, 26–60, 76, 96–8, 100, 105, 106 nn.4, 5, 108, 113–14, 116, 125, 127, 131, 135, 138, 140, 159, 165, 185–6, 193, 198, 370–1
  definition of   9, 18, 26, 27–8, 43, 97, 98, 100, 105, 107, 108, 118 n.9, 126, 131, 151, 233
knowledge argument   243, 294, 301–3, 304, 307–8, 309, 311, 312–15
Koonin, Eugene   212, 230–1

Laplace, Pierre-Simon   172, 230
Laudan, Larry   166
laws of nature   34, 191, 192, 199, 210, 213, 261, 292, 293, 316–17, 320–6, 328, 341–2, 345 n.1, 372
Lewis, C. I.   75–6
Lewis, David   43, 45, 263, 316, 323–6, 342
Lewontin, Richard   212, 214
libertarianism   244, 341, 343–4, 385
libertarian's dilemma   341, 344, 345 n.6, 349, 385
Lightman, Alan   359
Lindberg, David   191
Linnaeus, Carl   211
logical negations   190, 197–8
lottery problem   44–5
love story theodicy   380, 382–3, 384, 385

Mach, Ernst   177
Makalowski, Wojciech   207
materialism   212, 242, 282, 283–93, 293 n.1, 295–6, 307, 308–10, 311–12, 315 n.3

INDEX

material objects 282, 284–5, 295
Mather, Cotton 192
The Matrix 19, 33, 172
Matter and Consciousness 302
meaning of life 3
measure problem 213
mechanical philosophy 210
Mediations on First Philosophy 38 n.5, 39, 40, 72, 96, 97, 99, 119
Mele, Alfred 334
memory 21, 132, 147, 155, 290
Mendel, Gregor 211
The Meno 107–8
mental causation 241, 242–3, 292, 293, 296–7
mentalism 105 n.2, 109, 113
mental states 70, 86, 89–90, 105 n.2, 128, 130, 136, 138, 242–3, 282, 287–8, 291–3, 300, 301–2, 308, 311–12, 313–5, 361
metaphysical naturalism 190, 198, 199–200, 203, 204, 222, 228, 230–1, *see* also naturalism
metaphysics 4, 132, 200, 203, 209, 210, 222, 223, 229, 239, 251, 252, 262, 270, 272 n.18, 274, 277, 280 n.1, 281
methodological naturalism 25, 190, 192–8, 199–200, 203, 204–11, 221–3, 224–5, 227–31, 234
mind, minds 40, 128, 209, 239, 241–3, 282, 284, 287–93, 294–7, 301–5, 310, 314, 315, 357, 358–9, 360–1, 362, 374, 382
mind-body problem 4, 239, 241–3, 282–315, 373, 375, 385
minimalism 61, 62
moderate fideism 137–8
molecular hypothesis 163
Monton, Bradley 205
morality 2, 136, 140, 246, 317, 338, 357, 360, 374, 377, 380
moral responsibility 243–5, 316, 317–18, 325, 327, 329–39, 341, 342, 343–4, 346, 347, 348
multiverse theory 212–14, 231, 259, 263 n.7

Nagel, Thomas 205, 302, 307, 308
naturalism 195, 222, 242, 356, *see* also metaphysical naturalism
naturalism-of-the-gaps 25, 203, 211–14, 227, 230–1
necessary conditions 10–11
Neurath, Otto 74
New Atheists 209
Newcomb, Simon 162
Newton, Isaac 168, 191, 209–10, 228, 229–30, 320
Newton-Smith, W. H. 166
nihilism (epistemic) 65, 91
noetic structure 20–21
no freedom, no blameworthiness principle 320, 323, 341, 342, 343
nominalism 240–1, 248, 249, 257, 261, 267, 268, 270, 270 n.2, 273, 277–8, 281
 class 258 n.12, 268, 269–70
 concept 258 n.12, 268
 mereological 258 n.12
 ostrich 247, 249–52, 258 n.4, 11, 12, 269, 273–6, 281
 predicate 258 n.12, 260, 267–8
 reductive 254, 258 n.12
 resemblance 247, 252–4, 269, 273
 trope 247, 254–7
no miracles argument 158, 161–3, 181, 183
nonbasic beliefs 61, 62
Numbers, Ronald L. 195

Ockham's razor 241
oculi contemplationis 135
one over many problem 257 n.1, 260, 263–6, 278–9, *see* also problem of universals
On the Revolutions of the Heavenly Spheres 159
ontological argument 245, 372
ontological commitment 249–51, 252, 264, 265, 274, 276, 278
ontological grounding 260, 266, 268–9, 275, 272 n.18
ontology, *see* metaphysics
On What There Is 264

Optiks 230
Origin of Species 211, 230
Osiander, Andreas 158, 160

panpsychism 206
panspermia hypothesis 216 n.7
parable of the alien artifact 170, 173–9
Parfit, Derek 377, 379 n.1
parsimony 251, 258 n.11
Peacock, Howard J. J. 264
Pereboom, Derk 327, 332–4
perfect being 354, 372, 376, 380, 381–2
perfection 353–4, 357, 362 n.1, 376
Perrin, Jean 163–2, 164–5
phenomenal conservatism 26, 28–9, 53
philosophy 1–4, 6, 9, 23, 30, 41, 69, 191, 239, 283, 293 n.1, 322, 328
philosophy of language 267
philosophy of mind 297, 310
philosophy of science 23–4, 166
physicalism 242, 283, *see also* materialism
physics 36, 137, 167, 170, 182, 213–14, 231, 283, 296, 308, 339 n.1, 369
Plantinga, Alvin 22–3, 190, 200, 221–2
Plato 17, 39, 107, 108, 262
Poincare, Henri 164, 166–7, 177
political philosophy 4
predication 240–1, 268–70, 273, 274
Principia 210, 230
principle of alternative possibilities (PAP) 244, 245, 329, 330–2, 335, 341, 342–3, 349
principle of avoiding arbitrariness 82
probability 35, 44, 125, 132, 163, 188, 350, 357–8, 360, 380, 381–2
problem of arbitrariness 68, 82–3, 86, 88–9
problem of articulability 68–70
problem of evil 149, 246, 363, 364, 365–9, 371–3, 374, 376, 377, 379, 380–3, 384

problem of experience 81–2, 88, 89–90
problem of the person in the pew 154–6
problem of universals 239–41, 247, 248–9, 257 n.1, 260, 263, 268, 270, 273–4, 276, 281
properties 57, 182, 184, 240, 241, 247, 248–9, 252–7, 259 n.16, 261, 262–3, 265–6, 268, 270 n.2, 272 n.18, 273, 274, 276, 279, 281, 283, 292, 295, 356–7
  functional 283
  great-making 354
  mental 292, 294, 295
  moral 239
  physical, material 192, 199–200, 283, 293, 303
  theory of 249, 251–2, 254, 273, 279
property dualism 242, 282, 292–3
propositional attitudes 287
propositional content 66–7, 68–70, 92, 130
providence, divine 199, 328, 359
Pyrrho of Elis 18

quantum theory, physics 182, 213, 339
Quine, W. V. O. 250, 252, 264–5, 270 n.2, 274, 278

rational intuition 11–13, 28, 42, 44, 101, 103, 104, 119, 132, 136, 138, 226 n.8, 276, 333–4
Ray, John 211
realism (about universals) 240–1, 247, 248, 249, 251, 254, 255–7, 258 nn.11, 16, 261, 269, 270, 270 n.2, 273, 276, 277–8, 279, 281
  Platonic (Platonism) 247, 255, 258 n.16
The Reality of Molecules 163
reasons 6, 27–8, 29–37, 41, 69, 72, 73, 75, 78–83, 97–105, 105 n.2, 114, 119, 120, 132, 134, 140, 144, 151, 245, 295, 333, 335–6,

344, 346, 361–2, 370–1, 376, 382, see also grounds
reasons commonsensism 23, 132–3, 138, 153–4
reasons responsiveness 335–6, 340 n.11, 346
reformed epistemology 138
regress problem, see skeptical regress argument
relations 20, 21, 61, 76, 81, 86, 105 n.2, 125, 161, 167, 249, 254, 257, 261, 268, 274, 279, 280 n.6, 281, 296
reliabilism 95, 99–100, 102, 105, 109, 148–9, see also externalism
religious beliefs 17, 18, 22–3, 127, 128, 129, 133–9, 139–41, 142, 143, 145, 148–9, 150, 152, 154–7, 190, 233, 350
representations, representational states 125–6, 128, 288, 289–91, 312
resemblance 240–1, 247, 248–57, 257 n.1, 258 n.4, 269, 273, 275, 277, 278–9, 281
revelation 191, 193
Rovelli, Carlo 188, 189
rules of reason 258, 260, 262, 377
Russell's paradox 267, 277, 279

Santa Fe Research Institute 360
science, natural 18, 23–5, 136, 158, 159, 160–1, 162, 165–9, 170, 171–80, 180 n.2, 185–6, 187–8, 189, 190–5, 198, 199–200, 202, 203–15, 221–5, 227, 228–9, 232, 234, 295, 300, 301, 304, 314, 351, 361, 371
scientific method 136, 165, 188, 192, 193–4, 195, 198–9, 206, 209, 221, 222, 228
scientific nonrealism 23–4, 170–80, 234
scientific realism 23–4, 158, 160, 161–9, 181, 188, 234
scientific revolution 158, 159, 203, 209–11, 221, 224, 230, 232

seemings 23, 28, 54, 63, 111, 123, 124–6, 129, 132–3, 134, 139, 150, 152–4
self-awareness 112, 294, 299–301, 303
Sellars, Wilfred 67, 81
sellarsian dilemma 61, 67–70, 88, 94
sensations 101, 132, 171, 186–7, 287, 288, 289, 291, 294, 295, 297, 303, 308, 309, 310
Serway, R. A. 182
Sextus Empiricus 18, 29, 37 n.3, 38–9, 49, 50 n.2, 78
skeptical regress argument 21, 26, 29–32, 64–5, 70, 78–81, 83, 88–9, 94
skeptical theism 363, 369–71, 380, 382
skepticism 5, 18–19, 26–7, 31, 32, 36–7, 38, 42, 45, 47, 48–9, 52, 56, 59–60, 78, 80, 162, 186, 189, 233, 239, 298, 382
 Academic 39, 49
 Cartesian (external world) 19, 32–4, 39–41, 42, 47, 49, 52–5, 124
 global 26–7, 30, 33, 124
 Pyrrhonian 18, 29–30
Socrates 1, 3–4, 107–8, 113–14, 266, 267
Sosa, Ernest 115
soul 2, 239, 242, 289, 373, 375
Sprigge, T. L. S. 302–3
Stanford, Kyle 167–8
strength of will 346–7
Studies in Science and Religion 191
sub-optimal design 216 n.8
substance dualism 241–3, 282, 291–3, 307, 309
sufficient conditions 9–11, 233
supreme foundation 351, 352–3, 356, 360, 361, 380
Swinburne, Richard 308

Taylor, Richard 355
Tegmark, Max 213–14, 363 n.7
teleological argument 246, 246 n.1
teleology 194
Tertullian 144
testimony 21, 97, 103–4, 106 n.11, 382

theism 134, 199, 204, 205, 209, 228, 246, 305, 350, 353, 354–5, 356, 357–8, 360, 361–2, 383
theistic arguments 22, 245–6
theodicy 216 n.8, 380, 382–3, 384, 385
theology 191, 192–3, 225
third-person point of view 299, 300–1, 303
Thomas (the Apostle) 144, 156
thought experiments 11–13, 22, 24, 107, 110, 173, 244, 299
threshold problem 45
Tolstoy, Leo 166
Torrance, Thomas 192–5, 199, 200, 222, 225, 225 n.1
traditional account of knowledge, *see* JTB account
The Truman Show 103
truth 7–8, 11, 30, 38, 42, 44, 48, 49, 64, 73, 96–8, 100, 105, 120, 125, 128–9, 132, 134, 137, 159, 163, 165, 171–3, 174, 180, 186, 187–8, 192, 350, 351, 362, 379, 383
approximate 93, 160, 163, 176, 181, 183–5, 189
type-identity theory 242

ultimate sourcehood 245, 327, 329, 330, 332–4, 339, 346, 348
underdetermination principle 41, 46–7, 159, 167–8
uniformitarianism 203, 214, 221, 224, 227 n.9
universals 240–1, 247–81, 385
unnecessary suffering 246, 363, 366–9, 371–2
unobservables 24, 165, 168–9, 186–7, 189

Vaihinger, Hans 161
values 128, 137, 244, 329, 335, 336, 337–9, 343, 345, 346–8, 382
ownership 327, 338–9
system of 327, 336
value theory 4
van Inwagen, Peter 321, 363, 367–9
Vestiges of the Natural History of Creation 199

warrant 96
Wolterstorff, Nicholas 22
Wright, George F. 191

Young Earthism 370–1

www.ingramcontent.com/pod-product-compliance
Lightning Source LLC
Chambersburg PA
CBHW071237300426
44116CB00008B/1069